A HISTORY OF WESTERN SOCIETY

Volume B: From the Renaissance to 1815

A HISTORY OF WESTERN SOCIETY

Second Edition

Volume B: From the Renaissance to 1815

John P. McKay

Bennett D. Hill

John Buckler

University of Illinois, Urbana

Houghton Mifflin Company

Boston
Dallas   Geneva, Illinois
Hopewell, New Jersey   Palo Alto
London

About the Authors

John P. McKay A native of St. Louis, Missouri, John P. McKay received his B.A. from Wesleyan University (1961), his M.A. from the Fletcher School of Law and Diplomacy (1962), and his Ph.D. from the University of California, Berkeley (1968). He began teaching history at the University of Illinois in 1966 and became a professor there in 1976. John won the Herbert Baxter Adams Prize for his book *Pioneers for Profit: Foreign Entrepreneurship and Russian Industrialization, 1885–1913* (1970). He has also written *Tramways and Trolleys: The Rise of Urban Mass Transport in Europe* (1976) and has translated Jules Michelet's *The People* (1973). His research has been supported by fellowships from the Ford Foundation, the Guggenheim Foundation, and IREX. Recently named general editor of *Industrial Development and the Social Fabric: An International Series of Historical Monographs,* John continues to serve on the editorial board of the *Journal of Economic History.*

Bennett D. Hill A native of Philadelphia, Bennett D. Hill earned an A.B. at Princeton (1956) and advanced degrees from Harvard (A.M., 1958) and Princeton (Ph.D., 1963). He is a professor of history at the University of Illinois at Urbana, where he served as chairman of the department from 1978 to 1981. He has published *English Cistercian Monasteries and Their Patrons in the Twelfth Century* (1968) and *Church and State in the Middle Ages* (1970); and articles in *Analecta Cisterciensia, The New Catholic Encyclopaedia, The American Benedictine Review,* and *The Dictionary of the Middle Ages.* His reviews have appeared in *The American Historical Review, Speculum, The Historian, The Catholic Historical Review,* and *Library Journal.* He has been a fellow of the American Council of Learned Societies, served on numerous committees for the National Endowment for the Humanities and the Woodrow Wilson Foundation, and is currently an associate editor of the *American Benedictine Review.*

John Buckler Born in Louisville, Kentucky, John Buckler received his B.A. from the University of Louis-ville in 1967. Harvard University awarded him the Ph.D. in 1973. He is currently an associate professor at the University of Illinois, and is serving on the Subcommittee on Cartography of the American Philological Association. In 1980 Harvard University Press published his *The Theban Hegemony, 371–362 BC.* His articles have appeared in American journals, like the *American Journal of Ancient History* and *Classical Philology,* and numerous European journals, including *Rheinisches Museum für Philologie, Classical Quarterly, Wiener Studien,* and *Symbolae Osloenses.*

Text Credit

Excerpts from "Richard II," Act II, Scene I, and "Hamlet," Act III, Scene I, in *The Complete Plays and Poems of William Shakespeare* (edited by William A. Neilson and C. J. Hill). Copyright © 1942 by Houghton Mifflin Company. Copyright renewed, 1969.

Cover: # 677 *The Dancing Couple* by Jan Steen (c. 1626–1679) National Gallery of Art, Washington; Widener Collection

Printed in the U.S.A.

Library of Congress Catalog Card Number: 82-81321

ISBN: 0-395-32801-2

CONTENTS

MAPS

PREFACE

A HISTORY OF WESTERN SOCIETY grew out of the authors' desire to infuse new life into the study of Western civilization. As we wrote in the preface to the first edition, "History is the study of change over time and historians have seen many changes in their own discipline in recent years. Imaginative questions and innovative research have opened up vast new areas of interest and increased historical knowledge rapidly." We noted that the pushing back of the frontiers of knowledge had been especially dramatic in European social history, but that similar advances had characterized economic and intellectual history, while new research and fresh interpretations were simultaneously revitalizing the study of the traditional mainstream of political, diplomatic, and religious development. Yet it seemed to us that although new discoveries and controversies were stimulating professional historians, both the broad public and the intelligentsia often appeared to be losing interest in the past. The distinguished mathematical economist of our acquaintance who smugly quipped "What's new in history?" – confident that the answer was nothing and that historians were as dead as the events they examine – was not alone.

It was our conviction, based on considerable experience introducing large numbers of students to the broad sweep of Western civilization, that a book reflecting current trends could excite readers and inspire a new interest in history and a heightened curiosity about our Western heritage. Our strategy was twofold. First, we made social history the core element of our work. Not only did we incorporate recent research by social historians, but also we sought to re-create the life of ordinary people in appealing human terms. At the same time we were determined to give the great economic, political, intellectual, and cultural developments the attention they unquestionably deserve. We wanted to give individual readers and instructors a balanced, integrated perspective, so that they could pursue on their own or in the classroom those themes and questions that they found particularly exciting and significant.

In preparing the second edition we have worked hard to build upon the favorable response to our efforts. Social history remains the core element of our work, and once again important recent research on such subjects as population, diet, women, and the family has been integrated into the text. At the same time we have expanded somewhat our treatment of major intellectual and cultural developments in order to realize fully the promise of the balanced approach of the first edition. Thus the discussion of such topics as Judaism, Islam, medieval philosophy, the baroque, romanticism, and nineteenth-century science has been substantially expanded, for example, while new material on ancient Egypt, medieval drama, Renaissance literature, French classicism, Descartes, Darwin, and realism has been woven into the work. Finally, every chapter of the book has been painstakingly reviewed for content and clarity, resulting in a wholly new chapter on the ancient Near East and in many small improvements, notably in the discussion of feudalism, the English Reformation, and the French Revolution. In all our endeavors the encouraging, constructive comments and suggestions of many readers have been greatly appreciated.

Other distinctive features from the first edition remain in the second. To help guide the reader toward historical understanding we have posed specific historical questions at the beginning of each chapter. These questions are then answered in the course of the chapter, each of which now concludes with a concise summary of the chapter's findings. Timelines, which students find useful, have been added in many chapters.

We have also tried to suggest how historians actually work and think. We have quoted rather extensively from a wide variety of primary sources and have demonstrated in our use of these quotations how historians sift and weigh evidence. We want the reader to realize that history is neither a list of cut-and-dried facts nor a senseless jumble of conflicting opinions. It is our further hope that the primary quotations, so carefully fitted into their historical context, will give the reader a sense that even in the earliest and most remote periods of human experience history has been shaped by individual men and women, some of them great aristocrats, others ordinary folk.

Each chapter concludes with several carefully selected suggestions for further reading. These suggestions are briefly described, in order to help readers know where to go to continue thinking and learning about the Western world. The chapter bibliographies have been expanded in order to keep them current with the vast and complex new work being done in many fields. In a number of areas each new journal or monograph may present fresh perspectives or challenge accepted views, and the best of these recent works have been singled out for citation.

The second edition has many new illustrations and all the illustrations in *A History of* *Western Society* have been carefully selected to re-enforce both the book's social theme and its balanced treatment of all aspects of Western history. Artwork is an integral part of our book, for the past can speak in pictures as well as words. Maps and line drawings are also a fundamental part of the book and, as with illustrations, they carry captions to enhance their value.

Western civilization courses differ widely in chronological structure from one campus to another. To accommodate the various divisions of historical time into intervals that fit a two-quarter, three-quarter, or two-semester period, *A History of Western Society* is being published in three versions, each set embracing the complete work:

One-volume hardcover edition, A HISTORY OF WESTERN SOCIETY; two-volume paperback, A HISTORY OF WESTERN SOCIETY *Volume I: From Antiquity to the Enlightenment* (Chapters 1–17), *Volume II: From Absolutism to the Present* (Chapters 16–31); three-volume paperback, A HISTORY OF WESTERN SOCIETY *Volume A: From Antiquity to the Reformation* (Chapters 1–13), *Volume B: From the Renaissance to 1815* (Chapters 12–21), *Volume C: From the Revolutionary Era to the Present* (Chapters 21–31).

Note that overlapping chapters in both the two- and the three-volume sets permit still wider flexibility in matching the appropriate volume with the opening and closing dates of a course term. Furthermore, for courses beginning with the Renaissance rather than antiquity or the medieval period, the reader can begin study with Volume B.

A History of Western Society also has a study guide for students, as well as an instructor's manual. Both of these excellent aids have been written primarily by Professor James Schmiechen of Central Michigan University. Professor Schmiechen read all our drafts, from the first prospectus to the final typescript of the second edition, and he gave us many valuable suggestions in addition to his enthusiastic and warmly appreciated support. His *Study Guide* contains chapter summaries, chapter outlines, study questions, self-check lists of important concepts and events, and a variety of study aids and suggestions. An innovation in this revision of the *Study Guide* – one that we feel will be extremely useful to the student – is our step-by-step Reading with Understanding exercises, which take the reader by ostensive example through reading and studying activities like underlining, summarizing, identifying main points, classifying information according to sequence, and making historical comparisons. To enable both students and instructors to use the *Study Guide* with the greatest possible flexibility, the guide is available in two volumes, with considerable overlapping of chapters. Instructors and students who use only Volumes A and B of the text have all the pertinent study materials in a single volume, *Study Guide, Volume* 1 (Chapters 1–21); likewise, those who use only Volumes B and C of the text also have all the necessary materials in one volume, *Study Guide, Volume* 2 (Chapters 12–31).

It is also a pleasure to thank Roger Schlesinger, Washington State University; Charles Rearick, University of Massachusetts at Amherst; Donald Buck, DeAnza College; James Powell, Syracuse University; John M. Riddle, North Carolina State University; Laurence Lee Howe, University of Louisville; and Archibald Lewis, University of Massachusetts at Amherst, Jack R. Harlan, University of Illinois; Marc Cooper, Southwestern Missouri State University; and Lowell L. Blaisdell, Texas Tech University; Kevin K. Carroll, Arizona State University; Robert G. Clouse, Indiana State University; Albert A. Hayden, Wittenberg University; Harry M. Hutson, University of Tennessee at Martin; Dorothy Vogel Krupnik, Indiana University of Pennsylvania; Charles A. Le Guin, Portland State Univer-

sity; Carolyn C. Lougee, Stanford University; Paul J. Pinckney, University of Tennessee-Knoxville; C. Mary Taney, Glassboro State College; William M. Welch, Jr., Troy State University; and John C. White, University of Alabama-Huntsville, who read and critiqued the manuscript through its development.

Many of our colleagues at the University of Illinois kindly provided information and stimulation for our book, often without even knowing it. N. Frederick Nash, Rare Book Librarian, gave freely of his time and made many helpful suggestions for illustrations. Barbara Bohen, Director of the World Heritage Museum at the University, allowed us complete access to the sizable holdings of the museum. James Dengate kindly supplied information on objects from the museum's collection. Caroline Buckler took many excellent photographs of the museum's objects and generously helped us at crucial moments in production. Such wide-ranging expertise was a great asset for which we are very appreciative. Bennett Hill wishes to express his sincere appreciation to the Rt. Rev. James A. Wiseman, Abbot of St. Anselm's Abbey, Washington, D.C. for his support and understanding in the preparation of this second edition; and to William McKane for help with the maps.

Each of us has benefited from the generous criticism of his co-authors, although each of us assumes responsibility for what he has written. John Buckler has written the first six chapters; Bennett Hill has continued the narrative through Chapter 16; and John McKay has written Chapters 17 through 31. Finally, we warmly welcome any comments or suggestions for improvements from our readers.

JOHN P. MCKAY
BENNETT D. HILL
JOHN BUCKLER

A History of Western Society

Volume B: From the Renaissance to 1815

Chapter 12

·

The Crisis of the

Later Middle Ages

IN THE LATER MIDDLE AGES, the last book of the New Testament, the Book of Revelation, inspired thousands of sermons and hundreds of religious tracts. The Book of Revelation deals with visions of the end of the world, with disease, war, famine, and death. It is no wonder this part of the Bible was so popular. Between 1300 and 1450, Europeans experienced a frightful series of shocks: economic dislocation, plague, war, social upheaval, and increased crime and violence. Death and preoccupation with death make the fourteenth century one of the gloomiest periods in Western civilization.

The miseries and disasters of the later Middle Ages bring to mind a number of questions. What were the social and psychological effects of repeated attacks of plague and disease? Some scholars maintain that war is often the catalyst for political, economic, and social change. Does this theory have validity for the fourteenth century? Finally, what provoked the division of the church in the fourteenth century? What other ecclesiastical difficulties was the schism a sign of, and what impact did it have on the faith of the common people? This chapter seeks to answer these questions.

PRELUDE TO DISASTER

The fourteenth century began with serious economic problems. In the first decade, the countries of northern Europe experienced a considerable price inflation. The costs of grain, livestock, and dairy products rose sharply. Bad weather made a serious situation worse. An unusual number of storms brought torrential rains. Almost everywhere, heavy rains ruined the wheat, oats, and hay crops on which people and animals depended. Since long-distance transportation of food was ex-

pensive and difficult, most urban areas depended for bread and meat on areas no more than a day's journey away. Poor harvests — and one in four was likely to be poor — led to scarcity and starvation. Almost all of northern Europe suffered a terrible famine in the years 1315–1317.

Hardly had western Europe begun to recover from this disaster when another struck. An epidemic of typhoid fever carried away thousands. In 1316, 10 percent of the population of the city of Ypres in Belgium may have died between May and October alone. Then in 1318 disease hit cattle and sheep, drastically reducing the herds and flocks. Another bad harvest in 1321 brought famine, starvation, and death.

The large province of Languedoc in southern France presents a classic example of agrarian crisis. For over 150 years, Languedoc had enjoyed continual land reclamation, steady agricultural expansion, and enormous population growth. Then the fourteenth century opened with four years of bad harvests, 1302 through 1305. Torrential rains in 1310 ruined the harvest and brought on terrible famine. Harvests failed again in 1322 and 1329. In 1332, desperate peasants survived the winter on raw herbs. In the half-century from 1302 to 1348, poor harvests occurred twenty times. The undernourished population was ripe for the Grim Reaper, who appeared in 1348 in the form of the Black Death.

These catastrophes had inevitable social consequences. Poor harvests meant that marriages had to be postponed. Later marriages and the deaths caused by famine and disease meant a further reduction in population. Thus, after the steady population growth of the twelfth and thirteenth centuries, western Europe suffered a gradual decline in the first third of the fourteenth century. Meanwhile, the international character of trade and commerce meant that a disaster in one country had serious implications elsewhere. For example, the infection that attacked English sheep in 1318 caused a sharp decline in wool exports in the following years. Without wool, Flemish weavers could not work, and thousands were laid off. Without woolen cloth, the businesses of Flemish, French, and English merchants suffered. Unemployment encouraged many men to turn to crime.

To none of these problems did governments have any solutions. In fact, they even lacked policies. After the death of Edward I in 1307, England was governed by the incompetent and weak Edward II (1307-1327), whose reign was dominated by a series of baronial conflicts. In France the three sons of Philip the Fair who followed their father to the French throne between 1314 and 1328 took no interest in the increasing economic difficulties. In the Holy Roman Empire power drifted into the hands of local rulers. The only actions the governments took tended to be in response to the demands of the upper classes. Economic and social problems were aggravated by the appearance in western Europe of a frightful disease.

THE BLACK DEATH

Around 1331, the bubonic plague broke out in China. In the course of the next fifteen years, merchants, traders, and soldiers carried the disease across the Asian caravan routes until, in 1346, it reached the Crimea in southern Russia. From there the plague had easy access to the Mediterranean lands and western Europe.

In 1291, Genoese sailors had opened the Straits of Gibraltar to Italian shipping by defeating the Moroccans. Then, shortly after 1300, important advances were made in the design of Italian merchant ships. A square rig was added to the mainmast, and ships began to carry three masts instead of just one. Additional sails better utilized wind power to propel the ship. The improved design permitted year-round shipping for the first time, and Venetian and Genoese merchant ships could sail the dangerous Atlantic coast even in the winter months. With ships continually at sea, the rats that bore the disease spread rapidly beyond the Mediterranean to Atlantic and North Sea ports.

In October 1347, Genoese ships brought the plague to Messina, from which it spread to Sicily. Venice and Genoa were hit in January 1348, and from the port of Pisa the disease spread south to Rome and north to Florence and all Tuscany. By late spring southern Germany was attacked. Frightened French authorities chased a galley bearing the disease from the port of Marseilles, but not before plague had infected the city, from which it spread to Languedoc and Spain. In June 1348, two ships entered the Bristol Channel and introduced it into England. All Europe felt the scourge of this horrible disease (See Map 12.1).

PATHOLOGY

Modern understanding of the bubonic plague rests on the research of two bacteriologists, one French and one Japanese, who in 1894 independently identified *Pasteurella pestis,* the bacillus that causes the plague (so labeled after the French scientist's teacher, Louis Pasteur). The bacillus liked to live in the bloodstream of an animal or, ideally, in the stomach of a flea. The flea in turn resided in the hair of a rodent, sometimes a squirrel but preferably the hardy, nimble, and vagabond black rat. Why the host black rat moved so much, sci-

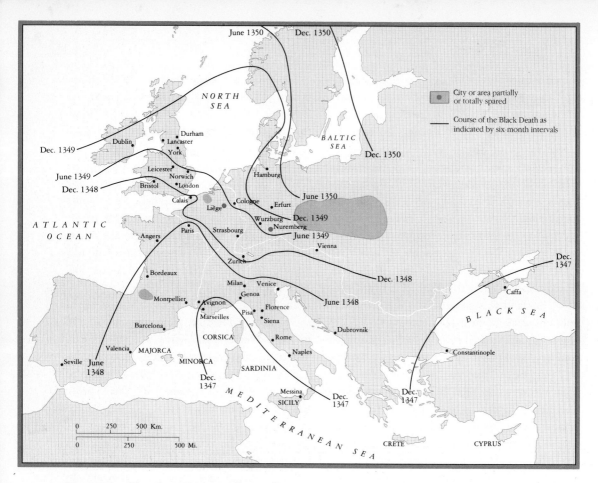

MAP 12.1   THE COURSE OF THE BLACK DEATH IN FOURTEENTH-CENTURY EUROPE   Note the routes that the bubonic plague took across Europe. How do you account for the fact that several regions were spared the "dreadful death"?

entists still do not know, but it often traveled by ship. There the black rat could feast for months on a cargo of grain or live snugly among bales of cloth. Fleas bearing the bacillus also had no trouble nesting in saddlebags.[1] Comfortable, well fed, and often having greatly multiplied, the black rats ended their ocean voyage and descended upon the great cities of Europe.

Although by the fourteenth century urban authorities from London to Paris to Rome had begun to try to achieve a primitive level of sanitation, urban conditions remained ideal for the spread of disease. Narrow streets filled

with mud, refuse, and human excrement were as much cesspools as thoroughfares. Dead animals and sore-covered beggars greeted the traveler. Houses whose upper stories projected over the lower ones eliminated light and air. And extreme overcrowding was commonplace. When all members of an aristocratic family lived and slept in one room, it should not be surprising that six or eight persons in a middle-class or poor household slept in one bed — if they had one. Closeness, after all, provided warmth. Houses were beginning to be constructed of brick, but many remained of wood, clay, and mud. A determined rat had little trouble entering such a house.

Standards of personal hygiene remained frightfully low. Since water was considered dangerous, partly for good reasons, people rarely bathed. Skin infections, consequently, were common. Lack of personal cleanliness, combined with any number of temporary ailments such as diarrhea and the common cold, naturally weakened the body's resistance to serious disease. Fleas and body lice were universal afflictions: everyone from peasants to archbishops had them. One more bite did not cause much alarm. But if that nibble came from a bacillus-bearing flea, an entire household or area was doomed.

The symptoms of the bubonic plague started with a growth the size of a nut or an apple in the armpit, the groin, or on the neck. This was the boil, or *buba,* that gave the disease its name and caused agonizing pain. If the *buba* was lanced and the pus thoroughly drained, the victim had a chance of recovery. The secondary stage was the appearance of black spots or blotches caused by bleeding under the skin. (This syndrome did not give the disease its common name; contemporaries did not call the plague the Black Death. Sometime in the fifteenth century the Latin phrase *atra mors,* meaning "dreadful death" was translated "black death," and the phrase stuck.) Finally, the victim began to cough violently and spit blood. This stage, indicating the presence of thousands of bacilli in the bloodstream, signaled the end, and death followed in two or three days. Rather than evoking compassion for the victim, a French scientist has written, everything about the bubonic plague provoked horror and disgust: "All the matter which exuded from their bodies let off an unbearable stench; sweat, excrement, spittle, breath, so fetid as to be overpowering; urine turbid, thick, black or red."[2]

THE PLAGUE-STRICKEN   *Even as the dead were wrapped in shrouds and collected in carts for mass burial, the disease struck others. The man collapsing has the symptomatic buba on his neck. As Saint Sebastian pleads for mercy (above), a winged devil, bearer of the plague, attacks an angel. (Walters Art Gallery)*

Medieval people had no rational explanation for the disease nor any effective medical treatment for it. Fourteenth-century medical literature indicates that physicians could sometimes ease the pain, but they had no cure. Most people — lay, scholarly, and medical — believed that the Black Death was caused by some "vicious property in the air" that carried the disease from place to place. All authorities assumed that some corruption of the atmosphere caused the disease.

PROCESSION OF FLAGELLANTS *The horrors of the Black Death provoked terrible excesses. People believed that the disease was God's punishment for humanity's sins, which could be atoned for only through severe penances. In this procession of robed and hooded flagellants, two of the men flog those ahead of them. (Bibliothèque Royale Albert I, Brussels)*

The Italian writer Giovanni Boccaccio (1313–1375), describing the course of the disease in Florence in the preface to his book of tales, *The Decameron,* pinpointed the cause of the spread:

Moreover, the virulence of the pest was the greater by reason that intercourse was apt to convey it from the sick to the whole, just as fire devours things dry or greasy when they are brought close to it. Nay, the evil went yet further, for not merely by speech or association with the sick was the malady communicated to the healthy with consequent peril of common death, but any that touched the clothes of the sick or aught else that had been touched or used by them, seemed thereby to contract the disease.[3]

The highly infectious nature of the plague was recognized by a few sophisticated Arabs.

When the disease struck the town of Salé in Morocco, Ibu Abu Madyan shut in his household with sufficient food and water and allowed no one to enter or leave until the plague had passed. Madyan was entirely successful. In European cities, those who could afford it fled to the countryside, which generally suffered less. Few were so wise or lucky, however, and the plague took a staggering toll.

The mortality rate cannot be specified, because population figures for the period before the arrival of the plague do not exist for most countries and cities. The largest amount of material survives for England, but it is difficult to use and, after enormous scholarly controversy, only educated guesses can be made. Of a total population of perhaps 4.2 million, probably 1.4 million died of the Black Death in its several visits.[4] Densely populated Italian cities endured incredible losses. Florence lost between half and two-thirds of its 1347 population of 85,000 when the plague visited in 1348. In general, rural areas suffered much less than urban ones. The disease recurred intermittently in the 1360s and 1370s and reappeared several times down to 1700. There have been twentieth-century outbreaks in such places as Hong Kong, Bombay, and Uganda.

SOCIAL AND PSYCHOLOGICAL CONSEQUENCES

Predictably, the poor died more rapidly than the rich, because the rich enjoyed better health to begin with; but the powerful were not unaffected. In England two archbishops of Canterbury fell victim to the plague in 1349, King Edward III's daughter Joan died, and many leading members of the London guilds followed her to the grave.

It is noteworthy that in an age of mounting criticism of clerical wealth and luxury, the behavior of the clergy during the plague was often exemplary. Priests, monks, and nuns cared for the sick and buried the dead. In places like Venice, where even physicians ran away, priests remained to give what ministrations they could. Consequently, their mortality rate was phenomenally high. The German clergy, especially, suffered a severe decline in personnel in the years after 1350. With the ablest killed off, the wealth of the German church fell into the hands of the incompetent and weak. The situation was already ripe for reform.

The plague accelerated the economic decline that had begun in the early part of the fourteenth century. In many parts of Europe there had not been enough work for the people to do. The Black Death was a grim remedy to this problem. Population decline, however, led to an increased demand for labor and to considerable mobility among the peasant and working classes. Wages rose sharply. The shortage of labor and steady requests for higher wages put landlords on the defensive. They retaliated with such measures as the English Statute of Laborers (1351), which attempted to freeze salaries and wages at pre-1347 levels. The statute could not be enforced and therefore the move was largely unsuccessful.

Even more frightening than the social effects were the psychological consequences. The knowledge that the disease meant almost certain death provoked the most profound pessimism. Imagine an entire society in the grip of the belief that it was at the mercy of a frightful affliction about which nothing could be done, a disgusting disease from which family and friends would flee, leaving one to die alone and in agony. It is not surprising that some sought release in orgies and gross sensuality while others turned to the severest forms of asceticism and frenzied religious fervor. Some extremists joined groups of flagellants, who collectively whipped and scourged themselves as penance for their and society's sins in the belief that the Black Death was God's punishment for humanity's wickedness.

The literature and art of the fourteenth century reveal a terribly morbid concern with death. One highly popular artistic motif, the Dance of Death, depicted a dancing skeleton leading away a living person. No wonder survivors experienced a sort of shell shock and a terrible crisis of faith. Lack of confidence in the leaders of society, lack of hope for the future, defeatism, and malaise wreaked enormous anguish and contributed to the decline of the Middle Ages. A long international war added further misery to the frightful disasters of the plague.

THE FRENCH AND ENGLISH SUCCESSIONS

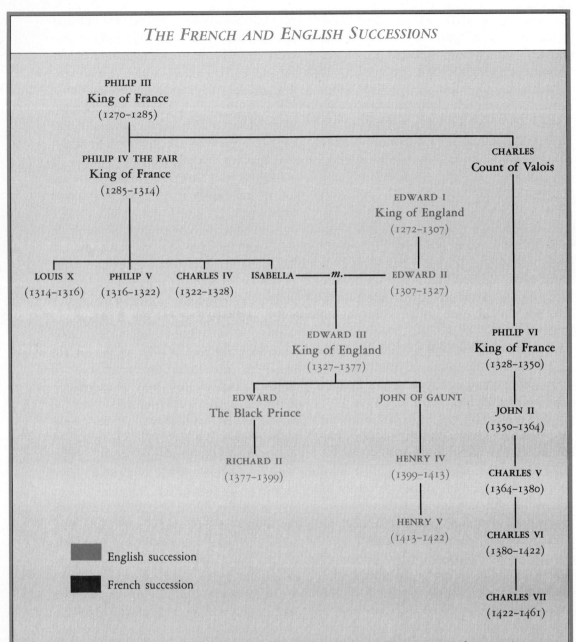

PHILIP III
King of France
(1270–1285)

PHILIP IV THE FAIR
King of France
(1285–1314)

CHARLES
Count of Valois

EDWARD I
King of England
(1272–1307)

LOUIS X   PHILIP V   CHARLES IV   ISABELLA —— *m.* —— EDWARD II
(1314–1316)   (1316–1322)   (1322–1328)   (1307–1327)

EDWARD III
King of England
(1327–1377)

PHILIP VI
King of France
(1328–1350)

EDWARD
The Black Prince

JOHN OF GAUNT

JOHN II
(1350–1364)

RICHARD II
(1377–1399)

HENRY IV
(1399–1413)

CHARLES V
(1364–1380)

HENRY V
(1413–1422)

CHARLES VI
(1380–1422)

CHARLES VII
(1422–1461)

English succession

French succession

In discussing the causes of the Hundred Years' War, modern scholars emphasize economic factors or the French-English dispute over the province of Gascony. Fourteenth-century Englishmen, however, believed they were fighting because King Edward III was denied his legal right to the French crown. He was the eldest surviving male descendant of Philip the Fair.

THE HUNDRED YEARS' WAR
(CA 1337–1453)

In January 1327, Queen Isabella of England, her lover Mortimer, and a group of barons, having deposed and murdered Isabella's incompetent husband King Edward II, proclaimed his fifteen-year-old son king as Edward III. A year later Charles IV of France, the last surviving son of the French king Philip the Fair, died childless. With him ended the Capetian dynasty. An assembly of French barons, intending to exclude Isabella – who was Charles's sister and daughter of Philip the Fair – and her son Edward III from the French throne, proclaimed that "no woman nor her son could succeed to the [French] monarchy." The barons passed the crown to Philip VI of Valois (1328–1350), a nephew of Philip the Fair. In these actions lie the origins of another phase of the centuries-old struggle between the English and the French monarchies, one that was fought intermittently from 1337 to 1453.

CAUSES

Edward III of England, as the eldest surviving direct male descendant of Philip the Fair of France, believed he was entitled to the French throne. God had given him the French kingdom, he maintained, and it was his special duty to claim it. Edward was also duke of Aquitaine, in France (see Map 12.2), and in 1329 he did homage to Philip VI for the duchy. Thus Edward was a vassal of the French ruler, though their interests were diametrically opposed. Moreover, the dynastic argument had feudal implications: in order to increase their independent power, French vassals of Philip VI used the excuse that they had to transfer their loyalty to a more legitimate overlord, Edward III. This position resulted in widespread conflicts.

Economic factors involving the wool trade, the ancient dispute over Aquitaine, control of the Flemish towns – for centuries these had served as justifications for war between France and England. The causes of the conflicts known as the Hundred Years' War were dynastic, feudal, political, and economic. Recent historians have stressed the economic factors. The wool trade between England and Flanders served as the cornerstone of the economies of both countries; they were closely interdependent. Flanders was a fief of the French crown, and the Flemish aristocracy was highly sympathetic to the monarchy in Paris. But the wealth of the Flemish merchants and cloth manufacturers depended on English wool, and the Flemish burghers strongly supported the claims of Edward III. The disruption of their commerce with England threatened their prosperity.

It is impossible to measure the precise influence of the Flemings on the cause and course of the war. Certainly, Edward could not ignore their influence, because it represented money he needed to carry on the war. Although the war's impact on commerce fluctuated, over the long run it badly hurt the wool trade and the cloth industry.

Why did the struggle last so long? One historian has written in jest that if Edward III had been locked away in a castle with a pile of toy knights and archers to play with, he would have done far less damage.[5] The same might be said of Philip VI. Both rulers glorified war and saw it as the perfect arena for the realization of their chivalric ideals. Neither king possessed any sort of policy for dealing with his kingdom's social, economic, or political ills. Both sought military adventure as a means of diverting attention from domestic problems.

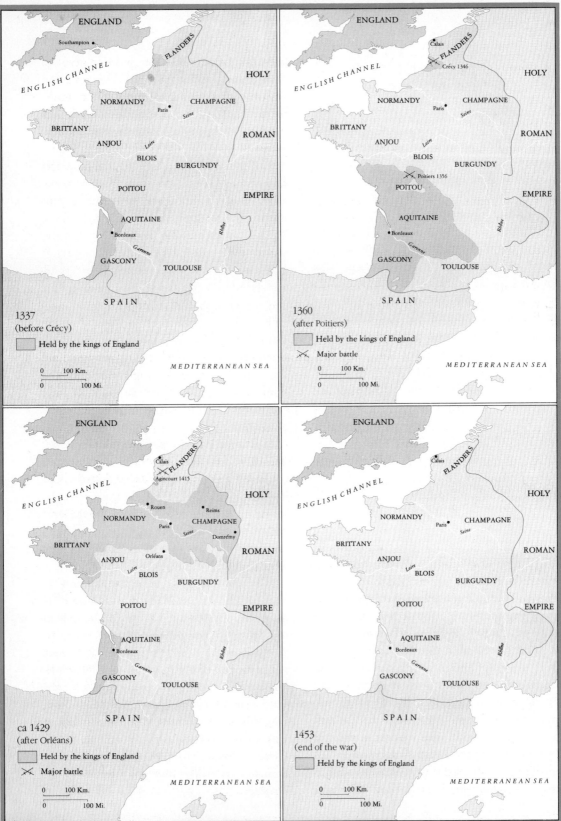

ENGLAND

Southampton •

ENGLISH CHANNEL

FLANDERS

HOLY

NORMANDY

CHAMPAGNE

Paris •

Seine

ROMAN

BRITTANY

ANJOU

Loire

BLOIS

BURGUNDY

POITOU

EMPIRE

AQUITAINE

Rhône

Bordeaux •

Garonne

GASCONY

TOULOUSE

SPAIN

1337
(before Crécy)

Held by the kings of England

MEDITERRANEAN SEA

0   100 Km.

0   100 Mi.

ENGLAND

Calais

ENGLISH CHANNEL

FLANDERS

Crécy 1346

HOLY

NORMANDY

CHAMPAGNE

Paris •

Seine

ROMAN

BRITTANY

ANJOU

Loire

BLOIS

BURGUNDY

Poitiers 1356

POITOU

EMPIRE

AQUITAINE

Rhône

Bordeaux •

Garonne

GASCONY

TOULOUSE

SPAIN

1360
(after Poitiers)

Held by the kings of England

Major battle

MEDITERRANEAN SEA

0   100 Km.

0   100 Mi.

ENGLAND

Calais

ENGLISH CHANNEL

FLANDERS

Agincourt 1415

HOLY

Rouen •

• Reims

NORMANDY

CHAMPAGNE

Paris •

Seine

Domrémy •

ROMAN

BRITTANY

ANJOU

Orléans •

Loire

BLOIS

BURGUNDY

POITOU

EMPIRE

AQUITAINE

Rhône

Bordeaux •

Garonne

GASCONY

TOULOUSE

SPAIN

ca 1429
(after Orléans)

Held by the kings of England

Major battle

MEDITERRANEAN SEA

0   100 Km.

0   100 Mi.

ENGLAND

Calais

ENGLISH CHANNEL

FLANDERS

HOLY

NORMANDY

CHAMPAGNE

Paris •

Seine

ROMAN

BRITTANY

ANJOU

Loire

BLOIS

BURGUNDY

POITOU

EMPIRE

AQUITAINE

Rhône

Bordeaux •

Garonne

GASCONY

TOULOUSE

SPAIN

1453
(end of the war)

Held by the kings of England

MEDITERRANEAN SEA

0   100 Km.

0   100 Mi.

MAP 12.2 ENGLISH HOLDINGS IN FRANCE DURING THE HUNDRED YEARS WAR *The year 1429 marked the greatest extent of English holdings in France. Why was it unlikely that England could have held these territories permanently?*

THE POPULAR RESPONSE

The governments of both England and France manipulated public opinion to support the war. Whatever significance modern students ascribe to the economic factor, public opinion in fourteenth-century England held that the war was waged for one reason: to secure for King Edward the French crown he had been denied.[6] Edward III issued letters to the sheriffs describing in graphic terms the evil deeds of the French and listing the royal needs. Royal letters instructed the clergy to deliver sermons filled with patriotic sentiment. Frequent assemblies of Parliament – which theoretically represented the entire nation – spread royal propaganda for the war. The royal courts sensationalized the wickedness of the other side and stressed the great fortunes to be made from the war. Philip VI sent agents to warn communities about the dangers of invasion and to stress the French Crown's revenue needs to meet the attack.

The royal campaign to rally public opinion was highly successful, at least in the early stage of the war. Edward III gained widespread support in the 1340s and 1350s. The English developed a deep hatred of the French and feared that King Philip intended "to have seized and slaughtered the entire realm of England." As England was successful in the field, pride in the country's military proficiency increased.

Most important of all, the war was popular because it presented unusual opportunities for wealth and advancement. Poor and unemployed knights were promised regular wages.

Criminals who enlisted were granted pardons. The great nobles expected to be rewarded with estates. Royal exhortations to the troops before battles repeatedly stressed that, if victorious, the men might keep whatever they seized. The French chronicler Jean Froissart wrote that at the time of Edward III's expedition of 1359, men of all ranks flocked to the king's banner. Some came to acquire honor, but many came in order "to loot and pillage the fair and plenteous land of France."[7]

THE INDIAN SUMMER OF MEDIEVAL CHIVALRY

The period of the Hundred Years' War witnessed the final flowering of the aristocratic code of medieval chivalry. Indeed, the enthusiastic participation of the nobility in both France and England was in response primarily to the opportunity the war provided to display chivalric behavior. Chivalry was a code of conduct originally devised by the clergy to improve the crude and brutal behavior of the knightly class. A knight was supposed to be brave, anxious to win praise, courteous, loyal to his commander, gracious, and generous. What better place to display these qualities than on the field of battle?

War was considered an ennobling experience; there was something elevating, manly, fine, and beautiful about it. When Shakespeare in the sixteenth century wrote of "the pomp and circumstance of glorious war," he was echoing the fourteenth- and fifteenth-century chroniclers who had glorified the trappings of war. Describing the French army before the battle of Poitiers (1356), a contemporary said, "Then you might see banners and pennons unfurled to the wind, whereon fine gold and azure shone, purple, gules and ermine. Trumpets, horns and clarions – you might hear sounding through the camp; the Dauphin's great battle made the earth ring."[8]

The chronicler Froissart repeatedly speaks of the beauty of an army assembled for battle. Writing of the French army before the battle of Bergues in 1383, Froissart reflected the attitudes of the aristocratic classes: it was "a great beauty to see the banners, pennons, and basinets glittering against the sun, and such a great multitude of men-at-arms that the eye of man could not take them in, and it seemed that they bore a veritable forest of lances." At Poitiers, it was marvelous and terrifying to hear the thundering of the horses' hooves, the cries of the wounded, the sound of the trumpets and clarions, and the shouting of war cries. The tumult was heard at a distance of more than three leagues. And it was a great grief to see and behold the flower of all the nobility and chivalry of the world go thus to destruction, to death, and to martyrdom on both sides.

This romantic and "marvelous" view of war holds little appeal for modern men and women, who are more conscious of the slaughter, brutality, dirt, and blood that war inevitably involves. Also, modern thinkers are usually conscious of the broad mass of people, while the chivalric code applied only to the aristocratic military elite. Chivalry had no reference to those outside the knightly class.

The knight was supposed to show courtesy, graciousness, and generosity to his social equals, but certainly not to his social inferiors. When English knights fought French ones, they were social equals fighting according to a mutually accepted code of behavior. The infantry troops were looked upon as inferior beings. When a peasant force at Longueil destroyed a contingent of English knights, their comrades mourned them because "it was too much that so many good fighters had been killed by mere peasants."[9]

Armies in the field were commanded by rulers themselves, by princes of the blood such as Edward III's son Edward, the Black Prince — so-called because of the color of his armor — or by great aristocrats. Knights formed the cavalry; the despised peasantry served as infantrymen, pikemen, and archers. Edward III set up recruiting boards in the counties to enlist the strongest peasants. Perhaps 10 percent of the adult population of England was involved in the actual fighting or in supplying and supporting the troops. The French contingents were even larger. By medieval standards, the force was astronomically large, especially considering the difficulty of transporting men, weapons, and horses across the English Channel. The costs of these armies stretched French and English resources to the breaking point.

The war was fought almost entirely in France and the Low Countries. It consisted mainly of a series of random sieges and cavalry raids. In 1335 the French began supporting Scottish incursions into northern England, ravaging the countryside in Aquitaine, and sacking and burning English coastal towns, such as Southampton. Naturally, such tactics lent weight to Edward III's propaganda campaign. In fact, royal propaganda on both sides fostered a kind of early nationalism.

In the early stages of the war, England was highly successful. At Crécy in northern France in 1346, English longbowmen scored a great victory over French knights and crossbowmen. Although the fire of the longbow was not very accurate, it allowed for rapid reloading, and the English archers could send off three arrows to the French crossbowmen's one. The result was a blinding shower of arrows that unhorsed the French knights and caused mass confusion. The firing of cannon —

THE BATTLE OF CRÉCY, 1346 *Pitched battles were unusual in the Hundred Years' War. At Crécy, however, the English (on the right with lions on their royal standard) scored a spectacular victory. The longbow proved a more effective weapon than the French crossbow, and the low-born English archers withstood a charge of the aristocratic French knights. (Photo: Larousse)*

probably the first use of artillery in the West – created further panic. Thereupon the English horsemen charged and butchered the French.

This was not war according to the chivalric rules that Edward III would have preferred. The English victory at Crécy rests on the skill and swiftness of the despised peasant archers, who had nothing at all to do with the chi-valric ideals for which the war was being fought. Ten years later Edward the Black Prince, using the same tactics as at Crécy, smashed the French at Poitiers, captured the French king, and held him for ransom. Again at Agincourt near Arras in 1415, the chivalric English soldier-king Henry V (1413–1422) gained the field over vastly superior numbers. Henry followed up his triumph at Agincourt

FIFTEENTH-CENTURY ARMOR   *This kind of expensive plate armor was worn by the aristocratic nobility in the fifteenth and sixteenth centuries. The use of gunpowder gradually made armor outmoded. (Courtesy, World Heritage Museum. Photo: Caroline Buckler)*

with the reconquest of Normandy. By 1419, the English had advanced to the walls of Paris (see Map 12.2).

But the French cause was not lost. Though England had won the initial victories, France won the war.

JOAN OF ARC AND FRANCE'S VICTORY

The ultimate French success rests heavily on the actions of an obscure French peasant girl, Joan of Arc, whose vision and work revived French fortunes and led to victory. A great deal of pious and popular legend surrounds Joan the Maid, because of her peculiar appearance on the scene, her astonishing success, her martyrdom, and her canonization by the Catholic church. The historical fact is that she saved the French monarchy, which was the embodiment of France.

Born in 1412 in the village of Domrémy in Champagne to well-to-do peasants, Joan of Arc grew up in a religious household. During adolescence she began to hear voices, which she later said belonged to Saint Michael, Saint Catherine, and Saint Margaret. In 1428, these voices spoke to her with great urgency, telling her that the dauphin (the uncrowned King Charles VII) had to be crowned and the English expelled from France. Joan went to the French court, persuaded the king to reject the rumor that he was illegitimate, and secured his support for her relief of the besieged city of Orléans.

The astonishing thing is not that Joan the Maid overcame serious obstacles to see the dauphin, not even that Charles and his advisers listened to her. What is amazing is the swiftness with which they were convinced. French fortunes had been so low for so long that the court believed only a miracle could save the country. Because Joan cut her hair short and dressed like a man, she scandalized the court. But hoping she would provide the necessary miracle, Charles allowed her to accompany the army that was preparing to raise the English siege of Orléans.

In the meantime Joan, herself illiterate, dictated the following letter calling upon the English to withdraw:

JHESUS MARIA

King of England, and you Duke of Bedford, calling yourself regent of France, you William Pole, Count of Suffolk John Talbot, and you Thomas Lord Scales, calling yourselves Lieutenants of the said Duke of Bedford, do right in the King of Heaven's sight. Surrender to The Maid *sent hither by God the King of Heaven, the keys of all the good towns you have taken and laid waste in France. She comes in God's name to establish the Blood Royal, ready to make peace if you agree to abandon France and repay what you have taken. And you, archers, comrades in arms, gentles and others, who are before the town of Orléans, retire in God's name to your own country. If you do not, expect to hear tidings from* The Maid *who will shortly come upon you to your very great hurt. And to you, King of England, if you do not thus, I am a chieftain of war, and whenever I meet your followers in France, I will drive them out; if they will not obey, I will put them all to death. I am sent here in God's name, the King of Heaven, to drive you body for body out of all France.*[10]

Joan apparently thought of herself as an agent of God.

Joan arrived before Orléans on April 28, 1429. Seventeen years old, she knew little of warfare and believed that if she could keep the French troops from swearing and frequenting whorehouses, victory would be theirs. On May 8, the English, weakened by disease and lack of supplies, withdrew from Orléans. Ten days later, Charles VII was crowned king at Reims. These two events marked the turning point in the war.

JOAN OF ARC *Later considered the symbol of the French state in its struggle against the English, Joan of Arc here carries a sword in one hand and a banner with the royal symbol of fleur-de-lis in the other. Her face, which scholars believe to be a good resemblance, shows inner strength and calm determination. (Archives Nationales, Paris/Giraudon)*

In 1430 England's allies, the Burgundians, captured Joan and sold her to the English. When the English handed her over to the ecclesiastical authorities for trial, the French court did not intervene. While the English wanted Joan eliminated for obvious political reasons, sorcery (witchcraft) was the ostensible charge at her trial. Witch persecution was increasing in the fifteenth century and Joan's wearing of men's clothes appeared not only aberrant but indicative of contact with the devil. Asked why she did so, Joan replied, "It is a little thing and of small importance. I did not don it by the advice of men of this world. I donned it only by the command of God and the angels."[11]

Joan of Arc's political impact on the course of the Hundred Years' War and on the development of the kingdom of France has led scholars to examine her character and behavior very closely. Besides being an excellent athlete and a superb rider, she usually dressed like a rich and elegant young nobleman. Some students maintain that Joan's manner of dress suggests uncertainty about her own sexual identity. She did not menstruate – very rare in a healthy girl of eighteen – though she was female in every external respect: many men, including several dukes, admired her beautiful breasts. Perhaps, as Joan said, wearing men's clothes meant nothing at all. On the other hand, as some writers believe, she may have wanted to assume a completely new identity. Joan always insisted that God had specially chosen her for her mission. The richness and masculinity of her clothes, therefore, emphasized her uniqueness and made her highly conspicuous.[12] In 1431 the court condemned her as a heretic – her claim of direct inspiration from God, thereby denying the authority of church officials, constituted heresy – and burned her at the stake in the marketplace in Rouen. A fresh trial in 1456 rehabilitated her name. In 1902 she was canonized and declared a holy maiden, and today she is revered as the second patron saint of France. The nineteenth-century French historian Jules Michelet extolled Joan of Arc as a symbol of the vitality and strength of the French peasant classes.

The relief of Orléans stimulated French pride and rallied French resources. In England, as the war dragged on, loss of life mounted, and money appeared to be flowing into a bottomless pit, demands for an end increased. The clergy and the intellectuals pressed for peace. Parliamentary opposition to additional war grants stiffened. Slowly the French reconquered Normandy and, finally, ejected the English from Aquitaine. At the end of the war, in 1453, only the town of Calais remained in English hands.

COSTS AND CONSEQUENCES

For both France and England, the war proved a disaster. In France, the English had slaughtered thousands of soldiers and civilians. In the years after the sweep of the Black Death, this additional killing meant a grave loss of population. The English had laid waste to hundreds of thousands of acres of rich farmland, leaving the rural economy of many parts of France in a shambles. The war had disrupted trade and the great fairs, resulting in the drastic reduction of French participation in international commerce. Defeat in battle and heavy taxation contributed to widespread dissatisfaction and aggravated peasant grievances.

In England, only the southern coastal ports experienced much destruction; yet England fared little better than France. The costs of war were tremendous: England spent over £5 million in the war effort, a huge sum in the fourteenth and fifteenth centuries. The worst loss was in manpower. Between 10 and 15 percent of the adult male population between the ages of fifteen and forty-five fought in the army or navy. In the decades after the plague, when the country was already suffering a severe manpower shortage, war losses made a bad situation frightful. Peasants serving in France as archers and pikemen were desperately needed to till the fields. The knights who ordinarily handled the work of local government as sheriffs, coroners, jurymen, and justices of the peace were abroad, and their absence contributed to the breakdown of order at the local level. The English government attempted to finance the war effort by raising taxes on the wool crop. Because of steadily increasing costs, the Flemish and Italian buyers could not afford English wool. Consequently, wool exports slumped drastically between 1350 and 1450.

Many men of all social classes had volunteered for service in France in the hope of acquiring booty and becoming rich. The chronicler Walsingham, describing the period of Crécy, tells of the tremendous prosperity and abundance resulting from the spoils of war: "For the woman was of no account who did not possess something from the spoils of . . . cities overseas in clothing, furs, quilts, and utensils . . . tablecloths and jewels, bowls of murra [semiprecious stone] and silver, linen and linen cloths."[13] Walsingham is referring to 1348, in the first generation of war. As time went on, most fortunes seem to have been squandered as fast as they were made.

If English troops returned with cash, they did not invest it in land. In the fifteenth century, returning soldiers were commonly described as beggars and vagabonds, roaming about making mischief. Even the large sums of money received from the ransom of the great – such as the £250,000 paid to Edward III for the freedom of King John of France – and the monies paid as indemnities by captured towns and castles did not begin to equal the £5 million-plus spent. England suffered a serious net loss.[14]

The long war also had a profound impact on the political and cultural lives of the two countries. Most notably, it stimulated the development of the English Parliament. Edward III's constant need for money to pay for the war compelled him to summon not only the great barons and bishops but knights of the shires and burgesses from the towns as well. Between the outbreak of the war in 1337 and the king's death in 1377, parliamentary assemblies met twenty-seven times. Parliament met in thirty-seven of the fifty years of Edward's reign.

The frequency of the meetings is significant. Representative assemblies were becoming a habit, a tradition. Knights and burgesses – or the Commons, as they came to be called – recognized their mutual interests and began to meet apart from the great lords. The Commons gradually realized that they held the country's purse strings, and a parliamentary statute of 1341 required that all nonfeudal levies have parliamentary approval. When Edward III signed the law, he acknowledged that the king of England could not tax without Parliament's consent. Increasingly, during the course of the war, money grants were tied to royal redress of grievances: if the government was to raise money, it had to correct the wrongs its subjects protested.

As the Commons met in a separate chamber – the House of Commons – it also developed its own organization. The speaker came to preside over debates in the House of Commons and to represent the Commons before the House of Lords and the king. Clerks kept a record of what transpired during discussions in the Commons.

In England theoretical consent to taxation and legislation was given in one assembly for the entire country. France had no such single assembly; instead, there were many regional or provincial assemblies. Why did a national representative assembly fail to develop in France? The initiative for convening assemblies rested with the king, who needed revenue almost as much as the English ruler. But the French monarchy found the idea of representative assemblies thoroughly distasteful. The advice of a counselor to King Charles VI (1380-1422), "above all things be sure that no great assemblies of nobles or of *communes* take place in your kingdom,"[15] was accepted. Charles VII (1422-1461) even threatened to punish those proposing a national assembly.

The English Parliament was above all else a court of law, a place where justice was done and grievances remedied. No French assembly (except that of Brittany) had such competence. The national assembly in England met frequently. In France general assemblies were so rare that they never got the opportunity to develop precise procedures or to exercise judicial functions.

No one in France wanted a national assembly. Linguistic, geographic, economic, legal, and political differences were very strong. People tended to think of themselves as Breton, Norman, Burgundian, or whatever, rather than as French. Through much of the fourteenth and early fifteenth centuries, weak monarchs lacked the power to call a national assembly. Provincial assemblies, highly jealous of their independence, did not want a national assembly. The costs of sending delegates to it would be high, and the result was likely to be increased taxation. Finally, the Hundred Year's War itself hindered the growth of a representative body. Violence on dangerous roads discouraged travel. As the fifteenth-century English jurist Sir John Fortescue wrote, "Englishmen made such war in France that the three Estates dared not come together."[16]

In both countries, however, the war did promote the growth of nationalism – the feeling of unity and identity that binds together a people who speak the same language, have a common ancestry and customs, and live in the same area. In the fourteenth century, nationalism largely took the form of hostility to foreigners. Both Philip VI and Edward III drummed up support for the war by portraying the enemy as an alien, evil people. Edward III linked his personal dynastic quarrel with England's national interests. As the Parliament Roll of 1348 states:

The Knights of the shires and the others of the Commons were told that they should withdraw together and take good counsel as to how, for with-standing the malice of the said enemy *and for the salvation of our said lord the King and his Kingdom of England ... the King could be aided.*[17]

After victories, each country experienced a surge of pride in its military strength. Just as English patriotism ran strong after Crécy and Poitiers, so French national confidence rose after Orléans. French national feeling demanded the expulsion of the enemy not merely from Normandy and Aquitaine but from French soil. Perhaps no one expressed this national consciousness better than Joan of Arc, when she exulted that the enemy had been "driven out of *France*."

VERNACULAR LITERATURE

Few developments expressed the emergence of national consciousness more vividly than the emergence of national literatures. Across Europe people spoke the language and dialect of their particular locality and class. In England, for example, the common people spoke regional English dialects, while the upper classes conversed in French. Official documents and works of literature were written in Latin or French. Beginning in the fourteenth century, however, national languages – the vernacular – came into use not only in verbal communication but in literature as well. Three masterpieces of European culture, Dante's *Divine Comedy* (1321), Chaucer's *Canterbury Tales* (1387-1400), and Villon's *Grand Testament* (1461) brilliantly manifest this new national pride.

Dante Aligheri (1265-1321) descended from an aristocratic family in Florence, where he held several positions in the city government. Dante called his work a comedy because

DANTE *In this sixteenth-century allegorical tribute to the most famous of all Florentines, the crowned poet laureate broods over the eternal conflict between the spiritual and the temporal. His right hand protects his beloved Florence, while his left hand holds the* Divine Comedy *open to paradise, which is seen in the distance surrounded by light. (National Gallery of Art, Washington, D.C. Samual H. Kress Collection 1961)*

he wrote it in Italian and in a different style from the "tragic" Latin; a later generation added the adjective "divine," referring both to its sacred subject and to Dante's artistry. The *Divine Comedy* is an allegorical trilogy of one hundred cantos (verses) whose three equal parts (1+33+33+33) each describe one of the realms of the next world, Hell, Purgatory, and Paradise. Dante recounts his imaginary journey through these regions toward God. The Roman poet Virgil, representing reason, leads Dante through Hell where he observes the torments of the damned and denounces the disorders of his own time, especially ec-

clesiastical ambition and corruption. Passing up into Purgatory, Virgil shows the poet how souls are purified of their disordered inclinations. In Paradise, home of the angels and saints, St. Bernard — representing mystic contemplation — leads Dante to the Virgin Mary. Through her intercession he at last attains a vision of God.

The *Divine Comedy* portrays contemporary and historical figures, comments on secular and ecclesiastical affairs, and draws on scholastic philosophy. Within the framework of a symbolic pilgrimage to the City of God, the *Divine Comedy* embodies the psychological tensions of the age. A profoundly Christian poem, it also contains bitter criticism of some church authorities. In its symmetrical structure and use of figures from the ancient world, such as Virgil, the poem perpetuates the classical tradition, but as the first major work of literature in the Italian vernacular it is distinctly modern.

Geoffrey Chaucer (1340–1400), the son of a London wine merchant, was an official in the administrations of the English kings Edward III and Richard II who wrote poetry as an avocation. Chaucer's *Canterbury Tales* is a collection of stories in a lengthy rhymed narrative. On a pilgrimage to the shrine of St. Thomas Becket at Canterbury (see page 362), thirty people of various social backgrounds each tell a tale. The Prologue sets the scene and describes the pilgrims, whose characters are further revealed in the story each person tells. For example, the gentle Christian Knight relates a chivalric romance; the gross Miller tells a vulgar story about a deceived husband; the earthy Wife of Bath, who earns her living as a weaver and has buried five husbands, sketches a fable about the selection of a spouse; and the elegant Prioress, who violates her vows by wearing jewelry, delivers a homily on the Virgin. In depicting the interests and behavior of all types of people, Chaucer presents a rich panorama of English social life in the fourteenth century. Like the *Divine Comedy,* the *Canterbury Tales* reflects the cultural tensions of the times. Ostensibly Christian, many of the pilgrims are also materialistic, sensual, and worldly, suggesting the ambivalence of the broader society's concern for the next world and frank enjoyment of this one.

Our knowledge of François Villon (1413–1463), probably the greatest poet of late medieval France, derives from Paris police records and his own poetry. Born to desper-ately poor parents in the year of Joan of Arc's execution, Villon was sent by his guardian to the University of Paris where he earned the Master of Arts degree. A rowdy and free-spirited student, he disliked the stuffiness of academic life. In 1455 Villon killed a man in a street brawl; banished from Paris, he joined one of the bands of wandering thieves that harassed the countryside after the Hundred Years' War. For his fellow bandits he composed ballads in thieves' jargon.

Villon's *Lais* (1456), a pun on the word *legs* (meaning "legacy"), is a series of farcical bequests to his friends and enemies. *Ballade des Pendus* (Ballad of the Hanged) was written while contemplating that fate in prison. (His execution was commuted.) Villon's greatest and most self-revealing work, the *Grand Testament,* contains another string of bequests, including a legacy to a prostitute, and describes his unshakeable faith in the beauty of life here on earth. The *Grand Testament* possesses elements of social rebellion, bawdy humor, and rare emotional depth. While the themes of Dante's and Chaucer's poetry are distinctly medieval, Villon's celebration of the human condition here on earth brands him as definitely modern. While he used medieval forms of versification, Villon's language was the despised vernacular of the poor and the criminal.

THE DECLINE OF THE CHURCH'S PRESTIGE

In times of crisis or disaster, people of all faiths have sought the consolation of religion. In the fourteenth century, however, the official Christian church offered very little solace. In fact, the leaders of the church added to the sorrow and misery of the times.

From 1309 to 1372, the popes lived in the city of Avignon in southeastern France. In order to control the church and its policies, Philip the Fair of France pressured Pope Clement V to settle in Avignon (page 383). Clement, critically ill with cancer, lacked the will to resist Philip. This period in church history is often called the Babylonian Captivity (referring to the seventy years the ancient Hebrews were held captive in Mesopotamian Babylon).

The Babylonian Captivity badly damaged papal prestige. The Avignon papacy reformed its financial administration and centralized its government. But the seven popes at Avignon concentrated on bureaucratic matters to the exclusion of spiritual objectives. Although some of the popes led austere lives at Avignon, the general atmosphere was one of luxury, splendor, and extravagance. The leadership of the church was cut off from its historic roots and the source of its ancient authority, the city of Rome. In the absence of the papacy, the Papal States in Italy lacked stability and good government. The economy of Rome had long been based on the presence of the papal court and the rich tourist trade the papacy attracted. The Babylonian Captivity left Rome poverty-stricken. As long as the French crown dominated papal policy, papal influence in England (with whom France was intermittently at war) and in Germany declined.

Many devout Christians urged the popes to return to Rome. The Dominican mystic Catherine of Siena, for example, made a special trip to Avignon to plead with the pope to return. In 1377, Pope Gregory XI brought the papal court back to Rome. Unfortunately, he died shortly after the return. At Gregory's death, Roman citizens demanded an Italian pope who would remain in Rome. Determined to influence the papal conclave (the assembly of cardinals who choose the new pope) to elect an Italian, a Roman mob surrounded St. Peter's Basilica, blocked the roads leading out of the city, and seized all boats on the Tiber River. Between the time of Gregory's death and the opening of the conclave, great pressure was put on the cardinals to elect an Italian. At the time, none of them protested this pressure.

Sixteen cardinals — eleven Frenchmen, four Italians, and one Spaniard — entered the conclave on April 7, 1378. After two ballots they unanimously chose a distinguished administrator, the archbishop of Bari, Bartolomeo Prignano, who took the name Urban VI. Each of the cardinals swore that Urban had been elected "sincerely, freely, genuinely, and canonically."

Urban VI (1378–1389) had excellent intentions for church reform: he wanted to abolish simony, pluralism (holding several church offices at the same time), absenteeism, clerical extravagance, and ostentation. These were the very abuses being increasingly criticized by Christian peoples across Europe. Unfortunately, Pope Urban went about the work of reform in a tactless, arrogant, and bullheaded manner. The day after his coronation he delivered a blistering attack on cardinals who lived in Rome while drawing their income from benefices elsewhere. His criticism was well-founded but ill-timed, and provoked opposition among the hierarchy before Urban had consolidated his authority.

In the weeks that followed Urban stepped up attacks on clerical luxury, denouncing individual cardinals by name. He threatened to strike the cardinal archbishop of Amiens. Urban even threatened to excommunicate certain cardinals, and when he was advised that such excommunications would not be lawful unless the guilty had been warned three times, he shouted, "I can do anything, if it be my will and judgment."[18] Urban's quick temper and irrational behavior have led scholars to question his sanity. Whether he was medically insane or just drunk with power is a moot point. In any case, Urban's actions brought on disaster.

In groups of two and three, the cardinals slipped away from Rome and met at Anagni. They declared Urban's election invalid because it had come about under threats from the Roman mob, and they asserted that Urban himself was excommunicated. The cardinals then proceeded to the city of Fondi between Rome and Naples and elected Cardinal Robert of Geneva, the brother of King Charles V of France, as pope. Cardinal Robert took the name Clement VII. There were thus two popes – Urban at Rome and the anti-pope Clement VII (1378–1394), who set himself up at Avignon in opposition to the legally elected Urban. So began the Great Schism, which divided Western Christendom until 1417.

THE GREAT SCHISM

The powers of Europe aligned themselves with Urban or Clement along strictly political lines. France naturally recognized the French anti-pope, Clement. England, France's historic enemy, recognized Pope Urban. Scotland, whose attacks on England were subsidized by France, followed the French and supported Clement. Aragon, Castile, and Portugal hesitated before deciding for Clement at Avignon. The German emperor, who enjoyed the title of king of the Romans and bore ancient hostility to France, recognized Urban VI. At first the Italian city-states recognized Urban; when he alienated them, they opted for Clement.

John of Spoleto, a professor at the law school at Bologna, eloquently summed up intellectual opinion of the schism:

The longer this schism lasts, the more it appears to be costing, and the more harm it does: scandal, massacres, ruination, agitations, troubles and disturbances . . . this dissention is the root of everything: divers tumults, quarrels between kings, seditions, extortions, assassinations, acts of violence, wars, rising tyranny, decreasing freedom, the impunity of villains, grudges, error, disgrace, the madness of steel and of fire given license.[19]

The scandal of competing popes "rent the seamless garment of Christ," as the church was called, and provoked horror and vigorous cries for reform. The common people, wracked by inflation, wars, and plague, were thoroughly confused about which pope was legitimate. The schism weakened the religious faith of many Christians and gave rise to instability and religious excesses. It brought the leadership of the church into serious disrepute. At a time when ordinary Christians needed the consolation of religion and confidence in their religious leaders, church officials were fighting among themselves for power.

THE CONCILIAR MOVEMENT

Calls for reform of the church were not new. A half-century before the Great Schism, in 1324, Marsiglio of Padua, then rector of the University of Paris, had published *Defensor Pacis* (*The Defender of the Peace*). Dealing as it did with the authority of the state and the church, *Defensor Pacis* proved to be one of the most controversial works written in the Middle Ages.

Marsiglio argued that the state was the great unifying power in society and that the church was subordinate to the state. He put forth the revolutionary ideas that the church had no inherent jurisdiction and should own no property. Authority in the Christian church, according to Marsiglio, should rest in a general council, made up of laymen as well as priests and superior to the pope. These ideas directly contradicted the medieval notion of a society governed by the church and the state, with the church ultimately supreme.

Defensor Pacis was condemned by the pope and Marsiglio was excommunicated. But the idea that a general council representing all of the church had a higher authority than the pope was repeated by John Gerson (1363-1429), a later chancellor of the University of Paris and influential theologian.

Even more earthshaking than the theories of Marsiglio of Padua were the ideas of the English scholar and theologian John Wyclif (1329-1384). Wyclif wrote that papal claims of temporal power had no foundation in the Scriptures, and that the Scriptures alone should be the standard of Christian belief and practice. He urged the abolition of such practices as the veneration of saints, pilgrimages, pluralism, and absenteeism. Every sincere Christian, according to Wyclif, should read the Bible for himself. Wyclif's views had broad social and economic significance. He urged that the church be stripped of its property. His idea that every Christian free of mortal sin possessed lordship was seized upon by peasants in England during a revolt in 1381 and used to justify their goals.

In advancing these views, Wyclif struck at the roots of medieval church structure and religious practices. Consequently, he has been hailed as the precursor of the Reformation of the sixteenth century. Although Wyclif's ideas were vigorously condemned by ecclesiastical authorities, they were widely disseminated by humble clerics and enjoyed great popularity in the early fifteenth century. Wyclif's followers were called Lollards. The term, meaning mumblers of prayers and psalms, refers to what they criticized. After the Czech king Wenceslaus's sister Anne married Richard II of England, members of Queen Anne's household carried Lollard principles back to Bohemia, where they were spread by John Hus, rector of the University of Prague.

While John Wyclif's ideas were being spread, two German scholars at the University of Paris, Henry of Langenstein and Conrad of Gelnhausen, produced treatises urging the summoning of a general council. Conrad wrote that the church, as the congregation of all the faithful, was superior to the pope. Although canon law held that only a pope might call a council, a higher law existed, the common good. The common good of Christendom required the convocation of a council.

In response to continued Europe-wide calls for a council, the two colleges of cardinals — one at Rome, the other at Avignon — summoned a council at Pisa in Italy in 1409. A distinguished gathering of prelates and theologians deposed both popes and selected another. Neither the Avignon pope nor the Roman pope would resign, however, and the appalling result was a threefold schism.

Finally, due to the pressure of the German emperor Sigismund, a great council met at Constance in Switzerland (1414-1418). It had three objectives: to end the schism, to reform the church "in head and members" (from top to bottom), and to wipe out heresy. The council condemned the Lollard ideas of John Hus, and he was burned at the stake. The council eventually deposed both the Roman pope and the successor of the pope chosen at Pisa, and it isolated the Avignonese anti-pope. A conclave elected a new leader, the Roman Cardinal Colonna, who took the name Martin V (1417-1431).

Martin proceeded to dissolve the council. Nothing was done about reform. The schism was over, and the conciliar movement in effect ended. For a time thereafter, the papacy concentrated on Italian problems to the exclusion of universal Christian interests. But the schism and the conciliar movement had exposed the crying need for ecclesiastical reform, thus laying the foundations for the great reform efforts of the sixteenth century.

THE LIFE OF THE PEOPLE

In the fourteenth century, economic and political difficulties, disease, and war profoundly affected the lives of European peoples. Decades of slaughter and destruction, punctuated by the decimating visits of the Black Death, made a grave economic situation virtually disastrous. In many parts of France and the Low Countries fields lay in ruin or untilled for lack of manpower. In England, as taxes increased, criticism of government policy and mismanagement multiplied. Crime, always a factor in social history, aggravated economic troubles, and throughout Europe the frustrations of the common people erupted into widespread revolts. For most people, marriage and the local parish church continued to be the center of their lives.

FUR-COLLAR CRIME

The Hundred Years' War had provided employment and opportunity for thousands of idle and fortune-seeking knights. But during periods of truce and after the war finally ended, many nobles once again had little to do. Inflation also hurt them. Although many were living on fixed incomes, their chivalric code demanded lavish generosity and an aristocratic lifestyle. Many nobles turned to crime as a way of raising money. The fourteenth and fifteenth centuries witnessed a great deal of "fur-collar crime," so-called for the miniver fur the nobility alone were allowed to wear on their collars. England provides a good case study of upper-class crime.

Fur-collar crime rarely involved such felonies as homicide, robbery, rape, and arson. Instead, nobles used their superior social status to rob and extort from the weak and then to corrupt the judicial process. Groups of noble brigands roamed the English countryside stealing from both rich and poor. Sir John de Colseby and Sir William Bussy led a gang of thirty-eight knights who stole goods worth £3,000 in various robberies. Operating exactly like modern urban racketeers, knightly gangs demanded that peasants pay "protection money" or else have their hovels burned and their fields destroyed. Members of the household of a certain Lord Robert of Payn beat up a victim and then demanded money for protection from future attack.

Attacks on the rich often took the form of kidnaping and extortion. Individuals were grabbed in their homes, and wealthy travelers were seized on the highways and held for ransom. In northern England a gang of gentry led by Sir Gilbert de Middleton abducted Sir Henry Beaumont and his brother, the bishop-elect of Durham, and two Roman cardinals in England on a peacemaking visit. Only after a ransom was paid were the victims released.[20]

Fur-collar criminals were terrorists, but like some twentieth-century white-collar criminals who commit nonviolent crimes, medieval aristocratic criminals got away with their outrages. When accused of wrongdoing, fur-collar criminals intimidated witnesses. They threatened jurors. They used "pull" or influence or cash to bribe judges. As a fourteenth-century English judge wrote to a young nobleman, "For the love of your father I have hindered charges being brought against you and have prevented execution of indictment actually made."[21]

The ballads of Robin Hood, a collection of folk legends from late medieval England, describe the adventures of the outlaw hero and his band of followers, who lived in Sherwood Forest and attacked and punished those who violated the social system and the law. Most of the villains in these simple tales are fur-collar criminals – grasping landlords, wicked sheriffs such as the famous sheriff of Nottingham, and mercenary churchmen. Robin and his merry men performed a sort of retributive justice. Robin Hood was a popular figure, because he symbolized the deep resentment of aristocratic corruption and abuse; he represented the struggle against tyranny and oppression.

Criminal activity by nobles continued decade after decade because governments were not strong enough to stop it. Then, too, much of the crime was directed against a lord's own serfs, and the line between a noble's legal jurisdiction over his peasants and criminal behavior was a very fine one indeed. Persecution by lords, coming on top of war, disease, and natural disasters, eventually drove long-suffering peasants all across Europe to revolt.

PEASANT REVOLTS

Peasant revolts occurred often in the Middle Ages. Early in the thirteenth century, the French preacher Jacques de Vitry asked rhetorically, "How many serfs have killed their lords or burnt their castles?"[22] Social and economic conditions in the fourteenth and fifteenth centuries caused a great increase in peasant uprisings.

In 1358, when French taxation for the Hundred Years' War fell heavily on the poor, the frustrations of the French peasantry exploded in a massive uprising called the *Jacquerie,* after the nickname of a supposedly happy agricultural laborer, Jacques Bonhomme (Good Fellow). Peasants in Picardy and Champagne went on the rampage.

Crowds swept through the countryside slashing the throats of nobles, burning their castles, raping their wives and daughters, killing or maiming their horses and cattle. Peasants blamed the nobility for oppressive taxes, for the criminal brigandage of the countryside, for defeat in war, and for the general misery. Artisans, small merchants, and parish priests joined the peasants. Urban and rural groups committed terrible destruction, and for several weeks the nobles were on the defensive. Then the upper class united to repress the revolt with savage and merciless ferocity. Thousands of the "Jacques," innocent as well as guilty, were cut down.

This forcible suppression of social rebellion, without some effort to alleviate its underlying causes, could only serve as a stopgap measure and drive protest underground. Between 1363 and 1484, serious peasant revolts swept the Auvergne; in 1380, uprisings occurred in the Midi; and in 1420, they erupted in the Lyonnais region of France.

The Peasants' Revolt in England in 1381, involving perhaps a hundred thousand people, was probably the largest single uprising of the entire Middle Ages. The causes were complex and varied from place to place. In general, though, the thirteenth century had witnessed the steady commutation of labor services for cash rents, and the Black Death had drastically cut the labor supply. As a result, peasants demanded higher wages and fewer manorial obligations. The parliamentary Statute of Laborers of 1351 (see page 393) declared:

Whereas to curb the malice of servants who after the pestilence were idle and unwilling to serve without securing excessive wages, it was recently ordained . . . that such servants, both men and women, shall be bound to serve in return for salaries and wages that were customary . . . five or six years earlier.[23]

THE JACQUERIE   *Because social revolt on the part of war-weary, frustrated poor seemed to threaten the natural order of Christian society, the upper classes everywhere exacted terrible vengeance on peasants and* *artisans. In this scene some* jacques *are cut down, some beheaded, and others drowned. (Bibliothèque Nationale, Paris)*

This statute was an attempt by landlords to freeze wages and social mobility.

The statute could not be enforced. As a matter of fact, the condition of the English peasantry steadily improved in the course of the fourteenth century. Some scholars believe that the peasantry in most places was better off in the period 1350–1450 than it had been for centuries before or was to be for four centuries after.

Why then was the outburst in 1381 so serious? It was provoked by a crisis of rising expectations. The relative prosperity of the la-boring classes led to demands that the upper classes were unwilling to grant. Unable to climb higher, the peasants' frustration found release in revolt. Economic grievances combined with other factors. Decades of aristocratic violence, much of it perpetrated against the weak peasantry, had bred hostility and bitterness. In France frustration over the lack of permanent victory increased. In England the social and religious agitation of the popular preacher John Ball fanned the embers of discontent. Such sayings as Ball's famous couplet

When Adam delved and Eve span
Who was then the gentleman?

reflect real revolutionary sentiment. But the lords of England believed that God had permanently fixed the hierarchical order of society and that nothing man could do would change that order. Moreover, the south of England, where the revolt broke out, had been subjected to frequent and destructive French raids. The English government did little to protect the south, and villages grew increasingly scared and insecure. Fear erupted into violence.

The straw that broke the camel's back in England was a head tax on all adult males. Although it met widespread opposition in 1380, the royal council ordered the sheriffs to collect it again in 1381 on penalty of a huge fine. Beginning with assaults on the tax collectors, the uprising in England followed much the same course as had the Jacquerie in France. Castles and manors were sacked; manorial records were destroyed. Many nobles, including the archbishop of Canterbury, who had ordered the collection of the tax, were murdered.

Although the center of the revolt was the highly populated and economically advanced south and east, sections of the north and the Midlands also witnessed rebellions. Violence took different forms in different places. The townspeople of Cambridge expressed their hostility to the university by sacking one of the colleges and building a bonfire of academic property. In towns containing skilled Flemish craftsmen, fear of competition led to their attack and murder. Urban discontent merged with rural violence. Apprentices and journeymen, frustrated because the highest positions in the guilds were closed to them, rioted.

The boy-king Richard II (1377-1399) met the leaders of the revolt, agreed to charters insuring peasants' freedom, tricked them with false promises, and then proceeded to crush the uprising with terrible ferocity. Although the nobility tried to restore ancient duties of serfdom, virtually a century of freedom had elapsed, and the commutation of manorial services continued. Rural serfdom had disappeared in England by 1550.

Conditions in England and France were not unique. In Florence in 1378, the *ciompi,* the poorest workmen, revolted. Serious social trouble occurred in Lübeck, Brunswick, and other cities of the Holy Roman Empire. In Spain in 1391, aristocratic attempts to impose new forms of serfdom combined with demands for tax relief led to massive working-class and peasant uprisings in Seville and Barcelona. These took the form of vicious attacks on Jewish communities. Rebellions and uprisings everywhere reveal deep peasant and working-class frustration and the general socioeconomic crisis of the times.

MARRIAGE

Marriage and the family provided such peace and satisfaction as most people attained. In fact, life for those who were not clerics or nuns meant marriage. Apart from sexual and emotional urgency, the community expected people to marry. For a girl, childhood was a preparation for marriage. In addition to the thousands of chores involved in running a household, girls learned obedience, or at least subordination. Adulthood meant living as a wife or widow. However, sweeping statements about marriage in the Middle Ages have limited validity. Most peasants were illiterate and left slight record of their feelings toward their spouses or about marriage as an institution. The gentry, however, often could write, and the letters exchanged between

Margaret and John Paston, upper-middle-class people who lived in Norfolk, England, in the fifteenth century, provide important evidence of the experience of one couple.

John and Margaret Paston were married about 1439, after an arrangement concluded entirely by their parents. John spent most of his time in London fighting through the law courts to increase his family properties and business interests; Margaret remained in Norfolk to supervise the family lands. Her enormous responsibilities involved managing the Paston estates, hiring workers, collecting rents, ordering supplies for the large household, hearing complaints and settling disputes among tenants, and marketing her crops. In these duties she proved herself a remarkably shrewd businessperson. Moreover, when an army of over a thousand men led by the aristocratic thug Lord Moleyns attacked her house, she successfully withstood the siege. When the Black Death entered her area, Margaret moved her family to safety.

Margaret Paston did all this on top of raising eight children (there were probably other children who did not survive childhood). Her husband died before she was forty-three, and she later conducted the negotiations for the children's marriages. Her children's futures, like her estate management, were planned with an eye toward economic and social advancement. When one daughter secretly married the estate bailiff, an alliance considered beneath her, the girl was cut off from the family as if she were dead.[24]

The many letters surviving between Margaret and John reveal slight tenderness toward their children. They seem to have reserved their love for each other, and during many of his frequent absences they wrote to express mutual affection and devotion. How typical the Paston relationship was, modern historians cannot say, but the marriage of John and Margaret, although completely arranged by

their parents, was based on respect, responsibility, and love.[25]

In the later Middle Ages, as earlier – indeed, until the late nineteenth century – economic factors, rather than romantic love or physical attraction, determined whom and when a person married. The young agricultural laborer on the manor had to wait until he had sufficient land. Thus most men had to wait until their fathers died or yielded the holding. The age of marriage was late, which in turn affected the number of children a couple had. The journeyman craftsman in the urban guild faced the same material difficulties. Prudent young men selected (or their parents selected for them) girls who would bring the most land or money to the union. Once a couple married, the union ended only with the death of one partner.

Divorce – the complete dissolution of the contract between a woman and man lawfully married – did not exist in the Middle Ages. The church held that a marriage validly entered into could not be dissolved. A valid marriage consisted of the oral consent or promise of the two parties made to each other. Church theologians of the day urged that the marriage be publicized by banns, or announcements made in the parish church, and that the couple's union be celebrated and witnessed in a church ceremony and blessed by a priest.

A great number of couples did not observe the church's regulations. Some treated marriage as a private act – they made the promise and spoke the words of marriage to each other without witnesses and then proceeded to enjoy the sexual pleasures of marriage. This practice led to a great number of disputes, because one or the other of the two parties could later deny having made a marriage agreement. The records of the ecclesiastical courts reveal many cases arising from privately made contracts. Here is a typical case heard by the ecclesiastical court at York in England in 1372:

[The witness says that] one year ago on the feast day of the apostles Philip and James just past, he was present in the house of William Burton, tanner of York. . . . when and where John Beke, saddler . . . called the said Marjory to him and said to her, "Sit with me." Acquiescing in this, she sat down. John said to her, "Marjory, do you wish to be my wife?" And she replied, "I will if you wish." And taking at once the said Marjory's right hand, John said, "Marjory, here I take you as my wife, for better or worse, to have and to hold until the end of my life; and of this I give you my faith." The said Marjory replied to him, "Here I take you John as my husband, to have and to hold until the end of my life, and of this I give you my faith." And then the said John kissed the said Marjory. . . .[26]

This was a private arrangement, made in secret and without the presence of the clergy. Evidence survives of marriages contracted in a garden, in a blacksmith's shop, at a tavern, and, predictably, in a bed. Church courts heard a great number of similar cases. The records of those courts that relate to marriage reveal that rather than suits for divorce, the great majority of petitions asked the court to enforce the marriage contract that one of the parties believed she or he had validly made. Annulments were granted in extraordinary circumstances, such as male impotence, on the grounds that a lawful marriage had never existed.

LIFE IN THE PARISH

In the later Middle Ages, the land and the parish remained the focus of life for the European peasantry. Work on the land continued to be performed collectively. All men, for example, cooperated in the annual tasks of planting and harvesting. The close association of the cycle of agriculture and the liturgy of the Christian calendar endured. The parish priest blessed the fields before the annual planting, offering prayers on behalf of the people for a good crop. If the harvest was a rich one, the priest led the processions and celebrations of thanksgiving.

How did the common people feel about their work? Since the vast majority were illiterate and inarticulate, it is difficult to say. It is known that the peasants hated the ancient services and obligations on the lords' lands and tried to get them commuted for money rents. When lords attempted to reimpose service duties, the peasants revolted.

In the thirteenth century, the craft guilds provided the small minority of men living in towns and cities with the psychological satisfaction of involvement in the manufacture of a superior product. The guild member also had economic security. The craft guilds set high standards for their merchandise. The guilds looked after the sick, the poor, the widowed, and the orphaned. Masters and journeymen worked side by side.

In the fourteenth century, those ideal conditions began to change. The fundamental objective of the craft guild was to maintain a monopoly on its product, and to do so recruitment and promotion were carefully restricted. Some guilds required a high entrance fee for apprentices; others admitted only the sons or relatives of members. Apprenticeship increasingly lasted a long time, seven years. Even after a young man had satisfied all the tests for full membership in the guild and had attained the rank of master, other hurdles had to be crossed, such as finding the funds to open his own business or special connections just to get in a guild. Restrictions limited the number of apprentices and journeymen to the anticipated openings for masters. The larger a particular business was, the greater was the likelihood that the master did not know his

MASKED MUMMERS   *People of all ages and classes enjoyed mummers' shows, which were performed by groups of masked actors who burlesqued some well-known event or person. Sometimes mummers accompanied their shows with primitive musical instruments, such as drums or tambourines. (Bibliothèque Nationale, Paris)*

employees. The separation of master and journeyman and the decreasing number of openings for master craftsmen created serious frustrations. Strikes and riots occurred in the Flemish towns, in France, and in England.

The recreation of all classes reflected the fact that late medieval society was organized for war and that violence was common. The aristocracy engaged in tournaments or jousts; archery and wrestling had great popularity among ordinary people. Everyone enjoyed the cruel sports of bullbaiting and bearbaiting. As the great French scholar Marc Bloch wrote, "Violence was an element in manners. Medieval men had little control over their immediate impulses; they were emotionally insensitive to the spectacle of pain, and they had small regard for human life..."[27] Thus, the hangings and mutilations of criminals were exciting and well-attended events, with all the festivity of a university town before a Saturday football game. Chronicles exulted in describing executions, murders, and massacres. Here a monk gleefully describes the gory execution of William Wallace in 1305:

Wilielmus Waleis, a robber given to sacrilege, arson and homicide...was condemned to most cruel but justly deserved death. He was drawn through the streets of London at the tails of horses, until he reached a gallows of unusual height, there he was suspended by a halter; but taken down while yet alive, he was mutilated, his bowels torn out and burned in a fire, his head then cut off, his body divided into four, and his quarters transmitted to four principal parts of Scotland.

Behold the end of the merciless man, who himself perished without mercy.[28]

Violence was as English as roast beef and plum pudding, as French as bread, cheese, and *potage.*

Alcohol, primarily beer or ale, provided solace to the poor, and the frequency of drunkenness reflects their terrible frustrations.

In the fourteenth and fifteenth centuries, the laity began to exercise increasing influence and control over the affairs of the parish. Churchmen were criticized. The constant quarrels of the mendicant orders (the Franciscans and Dominicans), the mercenary and grasping attitude of the parish clergy, the scandal of the Great Schism and a divided Christendom — all these did much to weaken the spiritual mystique of the clergy in the popular mind. The laity steadily took responsibility for the management of parish lands. Laymen and laywomen organized associations to vote on and purchase furnishings for the church. And ordinary lay people secured jurisdiction over the structure of the church building, its vestments, books, and furnishings. These new responsibilities of the laity reflect the increased dignity of the parishioners in the late Middle Ages.[29]

Late medieval preachers likened the crises of their times to the Four Horsemen of the Apocalypse in the Book of Revelation, who brought famine, war, disease, and death. The crises of the fourteenth and fifteenth centuries were acids that burned deeply into the fabric of traditional medieval European society. Bad weather brought poor harvests, which contributed to the international economic depression. Disease, over which people also had little control, fostered widespread psychological depression and dissatisfaction. Population losses caused by the Black Death and the

Hundred Years' War encouraged the working classes to try to profit from the labor shortage by selling their services higher: they wanted to move up the economic ladder. The socialistic ideas of thinkers like John Wyclif, John Hus, and John Ball fanned the flames of social discontent. When peasant frustrations exploded in uprisings, the frightened nobility and upper middle class crushed the revolts and condemned heretical preachers as agitators of social rebellion. But the war had heightened social consciousness among the poor.

The Hundred Years' War served as a catalyst for the development of representative government in England. The royal policy of financing the war through Parliament-approved taxation gave the middle classes an increased sense of their economic power. They would pay taxes in return for some influence in shaping royal policies.

In France, on the other hand, the war stiffened opposition to national assemblies. The disasters that wracked France decade after decade led the French people to believe that the best solutions to complicated problems lay not in an assembly but in the hands of a strong monarch. France became the model for continental countries in the evolution toward royal absolutism.

The war also stimulated technological experimentation, especially with artillery. After about 1350, the cannon, although highly inaccurate, was commonly used all over Europe.

Religion remained the cement that held society together. European culture was a Christian culture. But the Great Schism weakened the prestige of the church and people's faith in papal authority. The conciliar movement, by denying the church's universal sovereignty, strengthened the claims of secular governments to jurisdiction over all their peoples. The later Middle Ages witnessed a steady shift of basic loyalty from the Christian church to the emerging national states.

ALBRECHT DÜRER: THE FOUR HORSEMEN OF THE APOCALYPSE *From right to left, representatives of war, strife, famine, and death gallop across Christian society leaving thousands dead or in misery. The horrors of the age made this subject extremely popular in art, literature, and sermons. (Courtesy, Museum of Fine Arts, Boston)*

NOTES

1. W. H. McNeill, *Plagues and Peoples,* Doubleday, New York, 1976, pp. 151–168.

2. Quoted by P. Ziegler, *The Black Death,* Pelican Books, Harmondsworth, England, 1969, p. 20.

3. J. M. Rigg, trans., *The Decameron of Giovanni Boccaccio,* J. M. Dent & Sons, London, 1903, p. 6.

4. Ziegler, pp. 232–239.

5. N. F. Cantor, *The English: A History of Politics and Society to 1760,* Simon & Schuster, New York, 1967, p. 260.

6. J. Barnie, *War in Medieval English Society: Social Values and the Hundred Years' War,* Cornell University Press, Ithaca, N.Y., 1974, p. 6.

7. Quoted by Barnie, p. 34.

8. Ibid., p. 73.

9. Ibid., pp. 72–73.

10. W. P. Barrett, trans., *The Trial of Jeanne d'Arc,* George Routledge, London, 1931, pp. 165–166.

11. Quoted by Edward A. Lucie-Smith, *Joan of Arc,* W. W. Norton, New York, 1977, p. 32.

12. Ibid., pp. 32–35.

13. Quoted by Barnie, pp. 36–37.

14. M. M. Postan, "The Costs of the Hundred Years' War," *Past and Present* 27 (April 1964):34–53.

15. Quoted by P. S. Lewis, "The Failure of the Medieval French Estates," *Past and Present* 23 (November 1962):6.

16. Ibid., p. 10.

17. C. Stephenson and G. F. Marcham, eds., *Sources of English Constitutional History,* rev. ed., Harper & Row, New York, 1972, p. 217.

18. Quoted by J. H. Smith, *The Great Schism 1378: The Disintegration of the Papacy,* Weybright & Talley, New York, 1970, p. 141.

19. Ibid., p. 15.

20. B. A. Hanawalt, "Fur Collar Crime: The Pattern of Crime Among the Fourteenth-Century English Nobility," *Journal of Social History* 8 (Spring 1975):1–14.

21. Ibid., p. 7.

22. Quoted by M. Bloch, *French Rural History,* trans. Janet Sondheimer, University of California Press, Berkeley, 1966, p. 169.

23. Stephenson and Marcham, p. 225.

24. A. S. Haskell, "The Paston Women on Marriage in Fifteenth Century England," *Viator* 4 (1973):459–469.

25. Ibid., p. 471.

26. Quoted by R. H. Helmholz, *Marriage Litigation in Medieval England,* Cambridge University Press, Cambridge, 1974, pp. 28–29.

27. M. Bloch, *Feudal Society,* trans. L. A. Manyon, Routledge & Kegan Paul, London, 1961, p. 411.

28. A. F. Scott, ed., *Everyone a Witness: The Plantagenet Age,* Thomas Y. Crowell, New York, 1976, p. 263.

29. See E. Mason, "The Role of the English Parishioner, 1000-1500," *Journal of Ecclesiastical History* 27:1 (January 1976):17-29.

SUGGESTED READING

Students who wish further elaboration of the topics covered in this chapter should consult the following studies, on which the chapter leans extensively. For the Black Death and health generally, see W. H. McNeill, *Plagues and Peoples* (1976), a fresh, challenging, and comprehensive study; F. F. Cartwright, *Disease and History* (1972), which contains an interesting section on the Black Death; P. Ziegler, *The Black Death* (1969), a fascinating and highly readable book; and H. E. Sigerist, *Civilization and Disease* (1970), which presents a worthwhile treatment of the many social implications of disease.

The standard study of the long military conflicts of the fourteenth and fifteenth centuries remains that of E. Perroy, *The Hundred Years' War* (1959). J. Henneman, *Royal Taxation in Fourteenth Century France: The Development of War Financing, 1322-1356* (1971), is an important technical work by a distinguished historian. J. Barnie's *War in Medieval English Society: Social Values and the Hundred Years' War* (1974), treats the attitude of patriots, intellectuals, and the general public. Desmond Seward, *The Hundred Years' War: The English in France, 1337-1453* (1981), tells an exciting story, and John Keegan, *The Face of Battle* (1977), Chapter 2, "Agincourt," describes what war meant to the ordinary soldier. Barbara Tuchman, *A Distant Mirror: The Calamitous 14th Century* (1980), gives a vivid picture of many facets of fourteenth-century life, while concentrating on the war. The best treatment of the financial costs of the war is probably M. M. Postan, "The Costs of the Hundred Years' War," *Past and Present* 27 (April 1964):34-53. E. Searle and R. Burghart, "The Defense of

England and the Peasants' Revolt," *Viator* 3 (1972), is a fascinating study of the peasants' changing social attitudes.

For political and social conditions in the fourteenth and fifteenth centuries, the following studies are all useful: P. S. Lewis, *Later Medieval France: The Polity* (1968), and "The Failure of the French Medieval Estates," *Past and Present* 23 (November 1962); L. Romier, *A History of France* (1962); G. O. Sayles, *The King's Parliament of England* (1974); M. Bloch, *French Rural History* (1966); I. Kershaw, "The Great Famine and Agrarian Crisis in England, 1315-1322," *Past and Present* 59 (May 1973); B. A. Hanawalt, "Fur Collar Crime: The Pattern of Crime Among the Fourteenth-Century English Nobility," *Journal of Social History* 8 (Spring 1975): 1-17, a fascinating discussion; K. Thomas, "Work and Leisure in Pre-Industrial Society," *Past and Present* 29 (December 1964); M. Keen, *The Outlaws of Medieval Legend* (1961) and "Robin Hood – Peasant or Gentleman?," *Past and Present* 19 (April 1961):7-18; P. Wolff, "The 1391 Pogrom in Spain, Social Crisis or Not?," *Past and Present* 50 (February 1971):4-18; and R. H. Helmholz, *Marriage Litigation in Medieval England* (1974). Students are especially encouraged to consult the brilliant achievement of E. L. Ladurie, *The Peasants of Languedoc,* trans. John Day (1976).

The poetry of Dante, Chaucer, and Villon may be read in the following editions: Dorothy Sayers, trans., *Dante: The Divine Comedy,* 3 vols. (1963); Nevil Coghill, trans., *Chaucer's Canterbury Tales* (1977); Peter Dale, trans., *The Poems of Villon* (1973). The social setting of Chaucer's *Canterbury Tales* is brilliantly evoked in D. W. Robertson, Jr., *Chaucer's London* (1968).

Many of the preceding titles treat the religious history of the period. In addition, the following contain interesting and valuable information: G. Barraclough, *The Medieval Papacy* (1968), which is splendidly illustrated; W. Ullmann, *A Short History of the Papacy in the Middle Ages* (1972); E. Mason, "The Role of the English Parishioner, 1000-1500," *Journal of Ecclesiastical History* 27 (January 1976):17-29; and J. H. Smith, *The Great Schism 1378: The Disintegration of the Medieval Papacy* (1970).

CHAPTER 13

EUROPEAN SOCIETY IN THE AGE OF THE

RENAISSANCE

WHILE THE FOUR HORSEMEN of the Apocalypse carried war, plague, famine, and death across the Continent, a new culture was emerging in southern Europe. The fourteenth century witnessed the beginnings of remarkable changes in many aspects of Italian society. In the fifteenth century, these phenomena spread beyond Italy and gradually influenced society in northern Europe. These cultural changes have been collectively labeled the Renaissance. What does the term *Renaissance* mean? How did the Renaissance manifest itself in politics, government, and social organization? What developments occurred in the evolution of the nation state? Did the Renaissance involve shifts in religious attitudes? This chapter explores these questions.

THE IDEA OF THE RENAISSANCE

The Renaissance was an intellectual movement that began in Italy in the fourteenth century. It was characterized by hostility to the culture of the Middle Ages and fascination with the ancient world. Writers and artists of the Renaissance displayed great concern for individualism, a serious interest in human nature based on the study of the Greek and Latin classics, and a new excitement about life in this world. The cultural movement scholars have called the Renaissance was limited to a small, self-conscious, educated elite; it never directly involved the masses of people.

The realization that something new and unique was happening first came to men of letters of the fourteenth century, especially to the poet and humanist Francesco Petrarch (1304–1374). Petrarch thought that he was living at the start of a new age, a period of light following a long night of Gothic gloom. He believed that the first and second centuries of the Roman Empire represented the peak in the development of human civilization. The Germanic invasions had caused a sharp cultural break with the glories of Rome and inaugurated what Petrarch called "the Dark Ages." Medieval people had believed that they were continuing the glories that had been ancient Rome, and had recognized no cultural division between the world of the emperors and their own times. But for Petrarch and many of his contemporaries, the thousand-year period between the fourth and the fourteenth centuries constituted a barbarian, or Gothic, or middle age. The sculptors, painters, and writers of the Renaissance spoke contemptuously of their medieval predecessors and identified themselves with the thinkers and artists of Greco-Roman civilization. Petrarch believed he was witnessing a new golden age of intellectual achievement – a rebirth or, to use the French word that came into English, a renaissance. The division of historical time into periods is often arbitrary and done for the convenience of historians. In terms of the way most people lived and thought, no sharp division exists between the Middle Ages and the Renaissance. Nevertheless, Petrarch's categorization of time periods has had great influence. Most scholars use the word *Renaissance* to mean the artistic and cultural developments in western Europe that began in the fourteenth century and lasted into the seventeenth.

ITALIAN ORIGINS OF THE RENAISSANCE

The Renaissance began in Italy. Why did a brilliant flowering of artistic and intellectual creativity occur in Italy in the fourteenth through sixteenth centuries? This question has troubled scholars for a long time, and they still have not arrived at a definite answer. Some have offered economic explanations for Italy's cultural flowering, emphasizing the material prosperity without which the arts cannot flourish.

By the middle of the fourteenth century, the commercial classes of Florence and other Italian cities had acquired enough money that they could finance non-moneymaking activities. The cornerstone of northern Italian economic activity was international trade, commerce, and banking. The northern Italian cities had led the way in the commercial revival of the eleventh century. By the middle of the twelfth century, Venice, Genoa, Florence, and Milan were enjoying a great volume of trade with the Middle East and with northern Europe. These Italian cities fully exploited their geographical position as natural crossroads for exchange between the East and the West. Venice had profited tremendously from the Fourth Crusade. In the early fourteenth century, furthermore, Genoa and Venice made important strides in shipbuilding, allowing their ships for the first time to sail all year long. Improvements in the construction of cargo ships enabled the Venetians and Genoese to carry more bulk and to navigate the dangerous Atlantic Ocean. Most goods were purchased directly from the producers and sold a good distance away. For example, Italian merchants bought fine English wool directly from the Cistercian abbeys of Yorkshire in northern England. The wool was transported to the bazaars of North Africa either overland or by ship through the Straits of Gibraltar. The risks in such an operation were great, but the profits were enormous. These profits were continually reinvested to earn more.

It is generally agreed that the first manifestations of the Italian Renaissance – in art, ar-

BUSINESS ACTIVITIES IN A FLORENTINE BANK The Florentines early developed new banking devices. One man (left) presents a letter of credit or a bill of exchange, forerunners of the modern check, which allowed credit in distant places. A foreign merchant (right) exchanges one kind of currency for another. The bank profited from the fees it charged for these services. (Prints Division; New York Public Library; Astor, Lenox and Tilden Foundation)

chitecture, and literary creativity – appeared in Florence, and Florence possessed enormous wealth. Geography had not helped Florence; it was an inland city without easy access to water transportation. But toward the end of the thirteenth century, Florentine merchants and bankers acquired control of papal banking. From their position as tax collectors for the papacy, Florentine mercantile families began to dominate European banking on both sides of the Alps. These families had offices in Paris and London, Barcelona and Marseilles, Tunis and the North African ports, and, of course, Naples and Rome. The profits from loans, investments, and money exchanges that poured back to Florence were pumped into urban industries. Such profits contributed to the city's economic vitality.

The Florentine wool industry, however, was the major factor in the city's financial expansion and population increase. Florence purchased the best-quality wool from England and Spain, developed remarkable techniques for its manufacture, and employed thousands of workers to turn it into cloth. Florentine weavers produced immense quantities of superb woolen cloth, which brought the highest prices in the fairs, markets, and bazaars of Europe, Asia, and Africa.

By the first quarter of the fourteenth century, the economic foundations of Florence were so strong that even two severe crises could not destroy the city. In 1344, King Edward III of England repudiated his huge debts to Florentine bankers and forced some of them into bankruptcy. Florence also suffered frightfully from the Black Death, losing perhaps half its population. Still, the basic Florentine economic structure remained stable. Driving enterprise, technical know-how, and competitive spirit saw Florence through the difficult economic period of the late fourteenth century.[1]

One inconsistency in this economic explanation of the origins of the Renaissance lies in the fact that in the middle of the fourteenth century the Florentine wool and banking industries experienced a serious depression. Trade declined, affected by the Black Death and the international business slump. Moreover, such cities as Genoa, which had at one time enjoyed considerable prosperity, made no profound contribution to the Renaissance. It may be, however, that Florentine businessmen who found foreign markets closed invested instead in art, expecting a financial return from art works that increased in value.

A leading interpretation of the Italian Renaissance traces its origins to the development of civic humanism, or public pride, in Florence. In the 1380s, Florence was severely threatened by the conquests of Gian Galeazzo Visconti, duke of Milan. The Florentines put up a heroic and successful resistance, and in so doing came to appreciate the special virtues of their republican form of government – in contrast to the tyranny represented by Visconti. Awareness of their unique political heritage, which they traced back to the time of the Roman Empire, led the Florentines to take great pride in their city. Civic humanism took the form of public respect for Florence's achievements, whether in trade or architecture, education or the arts. They embarked upon a policy of beautification. This civic self-consciousness eventually spread to the other city-states of Italy.

Unlike the countries of northern Europe, Italy had never been heavily feudalized. Italian feudal lords rarely exercised the vast independent powers held by the barons of France, England, and the Holy Roman Empire. Although the volume of urban trade and the size of urban populations severely declined in the early Middle Ages, cities survived as commercial centers. In the twelfth and thirteenth centuries, northern Italian cities like Venice and Milan gained control of their surrounding territories. The wealth they steadily gained was used to acquire and solidify their independence; the Holy Roman emperors never fully exploited the wealth of the cities.

Italian society in the fourteenth century meant urban society, and this fundamental fact helps to account for the Italian origin of the Renaissance. The cities of Milan, Venice, Florence, Genoa, and Pisa were visited by traders and businessmen from all parts of the Western world. Foreigners brought with them their own customs, traditions, and values, and considerable social interchange inevitably took place. The merchant Francesco Datini, for example, was involved in commercial transactions with two hundred cities,

THE WEDDING FEAST   This picture was one of a series Botticelli produced illustrating a story in Boccaccio's Decameron. *The classical architecture with its vision of nature beyond, the pomp with which the meal is served, and the philosophical discussion at the tables — all represent the tastes and ideals of the Florentine aristocracy under the Medici. (Courtesy of Christie's)*

from Alexandria and Beirut in the south to Stockholm in the north. Italians gained an awareness of different parts of the world. They grew more refined, more sophisticated in their tastes and lifestyles, more worldly and urbane. Although Italians remained devoted sons and daughters of the church, they grew more secular in their outlook and behavior. Class distinctions remained strong in Renaissance Italy, but those distinctions were based on wealth rather than birth. And enterprise, imagination, and hard work could lead to wealth in the urban environment.

Moreover, the wealthy burghers of the cities began to strike military and marital contracts with the rural nobility of northern Italy. These alliances enabled the nobles to maintain a high standard of living in a rising money economy and gave the cities military support and protection. When the rich merchants united with the rural nobility, two significant developments occurred: the possession of land gradually came into the hands of bankers and merchants, and as a result the cities obtained political as well as economic jurisdiction over the surrounding countryside. In no other part of Europe did cities acquire such political power, primarily because the aristocratic ethos forbade feudal barons to unite with the moneygrubbing bourgeoisie. Nor did cities elsewhere have the commercial and financial strength of the Italian towns.

A foreign element also played a significant role. Beginning in the late fourteenth century, a steady stream of educated Greek refugees came from Byzantium to Italy to escape Turkish domination. Greek scholars like Manuel

Chrysoloras, John Bessarion, and Jonus Lascaris taught the Greek language and translated important Greek literary classics into Latin. Venice became the center of Greek scholarship, but Florence and Rome also gained an international reputation for Greek learning. Greek emigration to Italy broadened the intellectual horizon and enriched Italian Renaissance culture.

Finally, the Renaissance started in Italy because Italian poets, sculptors, painters, and philosophers of the fifteenth and sixteenth centuries considered themselves the natural heirs of the ancient Romans. Italy still possessed the literary manuscripts, the architectural monuments, the roads that constituted the heritage of Roman civilization. The national past of Italy was visible everywhere. Above all, Italians retained the historical memory of Roman power and imperial grandeur, and looked back on Roman antiquity as the golden age, as an ideal to be restored and reborn.

Increased wealth afforded more leisure time. Wealth in itself is usually not sufficient to satisfy the human psyche. When the physical and material needs of life are fulfilled and there is a surplus, then the spirit can be enriched by esthetic and intellectual interests.

The Renaissance, then, was an artistic and intellectual movement that began in the Italian cities and was supported and sustained by urban wealth.

HALLMARKS OF THE RENAISSANCE

The Renaissance was characterized, as we have seen, by the self-conscious awareness among fourteenth- and fifteenth-century Italians that they were living in a new era. The Renaissance also manifested itself in a new attitude toward men and women and the world – an attitude that may be described as individualism. A humanism characterized by a deep interest in the Latin classics and the deliberate attempt to revive antique lifestyles emerged, as did a bold new secular spirit.

INDIVIDUALISM

In the Middle Ages individuals thought of themselves as part of a group – as a member of a guild, as a resident of a particular area. The very few people who considered themselves so unusual that they indulged in autobiography – Saint Augustine in the fifth century and Guibert of Nogent in the twelfth, for example – were unique for that very reason. Christian humility and the concept of Western society as an organic entity encouraged people to define themselves in terms of a larger religious, economic, or social group.

This organic view of society eroded during the fourteenth and fifteenth centuries in Italy. The Renaissance witnessed the emergence of many distinctive personalities who gloried in their uniqueness. Italians of unusual abilities were self-consciously aware of their singularity, and unafraid to be unlike their neighbors; they had enormous confidence in their ability to achieve great things. Leon Battista Alberti (1404-1474), a writer, architect, and mathematician, remarked, "Men can do all things if they will."[2] Completely lacking in modesty, real or false, talented people of the Renaissance were proud of their abilities and eager for everyone to know about them. The Florentine goldsmith and sculptor Benvenuto Cellini (1500-1574) prefaced his *Autobiography* with a sonnet that declares:

My cruel fate hath warr'd with me in vain:
Life, glory, worth, and all unmeasur'd skill,
Beauty and grace, themselves in me fulfill
That many I surpass, and to the best attain.[3]

Cellini, certain of his genius, wrote so that the whole world might appreciate it.

Individualism stressed personality, genius, uniqueness, and the fullest development of capabilities and talents. Artist, athlete, painter, scholar, sculptor, whatever – a person's potential should be stretched until fully realized. Thirst for fame, a driving ambition, a burning desire for success drove such people to the complete achievement of their potential. The quest for glory was central to Renaissance individualism.

THE REVIVAL OF ANTIQUITY

In the cities of Italy, and especially in Rome, civic leaders and the wealthy populace showed phenomenal archaeological zeal for the recovery of manuscripts, statues, and monuments. Pope Nicholas V (1447-1455), a distinguished scholar, planned the Vatican Library for the nine thousand manuscripts he had collected. Pope Sixtus IV (1471-1484) built that library, which remains one of the richest repositories of ancient and medieval documents.

Patrician Italians consciously copied the lifestyle of the ancients and even searched out pedigrees dating back to ancient Rome. Aeneas Silvius Piccolomini, a native of Siena who became Pope Pius II (1458-1464), once pretentiously declared, "Rome is as much my home as Siena, for my House, the Piccolomini, came in early times from the capital to Siena, as is proved by the constant use of the names Aeneas and Silvius in my family."[4]

The revival of antiquity also took the form of profound interest in and study of the Latin classics. This feature of the Renaissance became known as the "new learning," or simply "humanism," the term of the Florentine rhetorician and historian Leonardo Bruni (1370-1444). The words *humanism* and *humanist* derive ultimately from the Latin *humanitas,* which Cicero used to mean the literary culture needed by anyone who would be considered educated and civilized. Humanists studied the Latin classics to learn what they reveal about human nature. Humanism emphasized human beings, their achievements, interests, and capabilities. Although churchmen supported the new learning, Italian humanism was a preponderantly lay phenomenon.

Appreciation for the literary culture of the Romans had never died completely in the West. Bede, Alcuin, and Einhard in the eighth century, and Ailred of Rievaulx, Bernard of Clairvaux, and John of Salisbury in the twelfth century had all studied and imitated the writings of the ancients. Medieval writers, however, had studied the ancients in order to come to know God. Medieval thinkers held that human beings are the noblest of god's creatures, and that though they have fallen, they are still capable of regeneration and thus deserving of respect. Medieval scholars interpreted the classics in a Christian sense and invested the ancients' poems and histories with Christian meaning.

Renaissance philosophers and poets also emphasized human dignity, but usually not in a Christian context. In a remarkable essay, "On the Dignity of Man," the Florentine writer Pico della Mirandola maintained that man's place in the universe may be somewhere between the beasts and the angels but that there are no limits to what he can accomplish.

Humanists tried to approach the classical texts with an open mind, to learn what the ancients had thought. They rejected the religious interpretations and systematic and formal scholastic works of the Middle Ages. They hated scholasticism because they believed it denied humanity and destroyed style.

The fourteenth- and fifteenth-century humanists loved the language of the classics and considered it superior to the corrupt Latin of the medieval schoolmen. Renaissance writers were very excited by the purity of ancient Latin. They eventually became concerned more about form than content, more about the way an idea was expressed than about the significance and validity of the idea. Literary humanists of the fourteenth century wrote each other highly stylized letters imitating ancient authors, and they held witty philosophical dialogues in conscious imitation of the Platonic Academy of the fifth century B.C. Wherever they could, Renaissance humanists heaped scorn on the "barbaric" Latin style of the medievalists. The leading humanists of the early Renaissance were rhetoricians, seeking effective and eloquent communication, both oral and written.

SECULAR SPIRIT

Secularism involves a basic concern with the material world instead of eternal and spiritual interests. A secular way of thinking tends to find the ultimate explanation of everything and the final end of human beings within the limits of what the senses can discover. In a religious society, such as the medieval, the focus is on the other-worldly, on life after death. In a secular society, attention is concentrated on the here and now, often on the acquisition of material things. The fourteenth and fifteenth centuries witnessed the slow but steady growth of secularism in Italy.

The economic changes and rising prosperity of the Italian cities in the thirteenth century worked a fundamental change in social and intellectual attitudes and values. In the Middle Ages the feudal nobility and the higher clergy had determined the dominant patterns of culture. The medieval aristocracy expressed disdain for moneymaking. Christian ideas and values infused literature, art, politics, and all other aspects of culture. In the Renaissance, by contrast, the business concerns of the urban bourgeoisie required constant and rational attention.

Worries about shifting rates of interest, shipping routes, personnel costs, and employee relations did not leave much time for thoughts about penance and purgatory. The busy bankers and merchants of the Italian cities calculated ways of making and increasing their money. Money allowed greater material pleasures, a more comfortable life, the leisure time to appreciate and patronize the arts. Money could buy many sensual gratifications, and the rich, social-climbing patricians of Venice, Florence, Genoa, and Rome came to see life more as an opportunity to be enjoyed than as a painful pilgrimage to the City of God.

In *On Pleasure,* the humanist Lorenzo Valla (1406-1457) defended the pleasures of the senses as the highest good. Scholars praise Valla as the father of modern historical criticism. His study *On the False Donation of Constantine* (1444) demonstrated by careful textual examination that an anonymous eighth-century document supposedly giving the papacy jurisdiction over vast territories in western Europe was a forgery. Medieval people had accepted the Donation of Constantine as a reality, and the proof that it was an invention seriously weakened the foundations of papal claims to temporal authority. Lorenzo Valla's work exemplifies the application of critical scholarship to old and almost sacred writings, as well as the new secular spirit of the Renaissance. The tales in the *Decameron* by the Florentine Boccaccio (1313-1375), which describe ambitious merchants, lecherous friars, and cuckolded husbands, portray a frankly acquisitive, sensual, and secular society. The "contempt of the world" theme, so pervasive in medieval literature, had disappeared. Renaissance writers justified the accumulation and enjoyment of wealth with references to ancient authors.

Nor did church leaders do much to combat the new secular spirit or set high moral standards. In the fifteenth and early sixteenth centuries, the papal court and the households of the cardinals were just as worldly as those of great urban patricians. Of course, most of the popes and higher church officials had come from the bourgeois aristocracy. The Medici pope Leo X (1513-1521), for example, supported artists and men of letters because patronage was an activity he had learned in the household of his father, Lorenzo the Magnificent. Renaissance popes beautified the city of Rome and patronized the arts. They expended enormous enthusiasm and huge sums of money on the re-embellishment of the city. A new papal chancellery, begun in 1483 and finished in 1511, stands as one of the architectural masterpieces of the High Renaissance (roughly the period 1500-1530). Pope Julius II (1503-1513) tore down the old St. Peter's Basilica and began work on the present structure in 1506. Michelangelo's dome for St. Peter's is still considered his greatest work. Papal interests, far removed from spiritual concerns, fostered rather than discouraged the new worldly attitude.

But the broad mass of the people and even the intellectuals and leaders of society remained faithful to the Christian church. Few people questioned the basic tenets of the Christian religion. Italian humanists and their aristocratic patrons were antiascetic, antischolastic, and anticlerical, but they were not agnostics or skeptics. The thousands of pious paintings, sculptures, processions, and pilgrimages of the Renaissance period prove that strong religious feeling persisted.

ART AND THE ARTIST

No feature of the Renaissance evokes greater admiration than its artistic masterpieces. The 1400s (quattrocento) and 1500s (cinquecento) witnessed a dazzling creativity in painting, architecture, and sculpture. In all the arts, the city of Florence consistently led the way. According to the Renaissance art historian Giorgio Vasari (1511-1574), the painter Perugino once asked why it was in Florence and not elsewhere that men achieved perfection in the arts. The first answer he received was, "There were so many good critics there, for the air of the city makes men quick and perceptive and impatient of mediocrity."[5]

Some historians and art critics have maintained that the Renaissance "rediscovered" the world of nature and of human beings. This is nonsense, as a quick glance at a Gothic cathedral reveals. The enormous detail applied to the depiction of animals' bodies, the careful carving of leaves, flowers, and all kinds of vegetation, the fine sensitivity frequently shown in human faces – these clearly show medieval and ancient people's appreciation for nature in all its manifestations. Saint Francis of Assisi (1181-1226) encouraged throughout his entire life an awareness of nature. No historical period has a monopoly on the appreciation of nature or beauty.

ART AND SOCIETY

Significant changes in the realm of art did occur in the fourteenth century. Art served

BOTTICELLI: *ADORATION OF THE MAGI* The *Florentine artist, biographer, and Medici courtier Giorgio Vasari (1511–1574) says that this painting contains the most faithful likenesses of Cosimo (kneel-* *ing before the Christ child) and Lorenzo (far left). Although the subject is Christian, the painting has a secular spirit, introduces individual portraits, and serves to glorify the Medici family. (Alinari/Scala)*

the newly rich middle class as well as the institutional church. The patrons of Renaissance art were more frequently laypeople than ecclesiastics. Patrician merchants and bankers supported the arts as a means of self-glorification and self-perpetuation. Art may also have been a form of financial investment. Great families, such as the Medicis in Florence, used works of art as a means of gaining and maintaining public support for their rule. A magnificent style of living, enriched by works of art, seemed to prove the greatness of the rulers.

As the fifteenth century advanced, the subject matter of art became steadily more secular. The study of classical texts and manuscripts brought deeper understanding of ancient ideas. Classical themes and motifs, such as the lives and loves of pagan gods and goddesses, figured increasingly in painting and sculpture. Religious topics, such as the Annunciation of the Virgin and the Nativity, remained popular among both patrons and artists, but frequently the patron had himself and his family portrayed in the picture. In Botticelli's *Adoration of the Magi,* for example,

Cosimo de' Medici appears as one of the Magi kneeling before the Christ child. People were conscious of their physical uniqueness, and they wanted their individuality immortalized. Paintings cost money and thus were also means of displaying wealth. Although many Renaissance paintings have classical or Christian themes, the appearance of the patron reflects the new spirit of individualism and secularism.

The style of Renaissance art was decidedly different from that of the Middle Ages. The individual portrait emerged as a distinct artistic genre. In the fifteenth century members of the newly-rich middle class often had themselves painted in a scene of romantic chivalry or in courtly society. Rather than reflecting a spiritual ideal, as medieval painting and sculpture tended to do, Renaissance portraits mirrored reality. The Florentine painter Giotto (1276-1337) led the way in the depiction of realism; his treatment of the human body and face replaced the formal stiffness and artificiality that had for so long characterized the representation of the human body. The sculptor Donatello (1386-1466) probably exerted the greatest influence of any Florentine artist before Michelangelo. His many statues express an appreciation of the incredible variety of human nature. While medieval artists had depicted the nude human body only in a spiritualized and moralizing context, Donatello revived the classical figure with its balance and self-awareness. The short-lived Florentine Masaccio (1401-1428), sometimes called the father of modern painting, inspired a new style characterized by great realism, narrative power, and remarkably effective use of light and dark.

Narrative artists depicted the body in a more scientific and natural manner. The female figure is voluptuous and sensual. The male body, as in Michelangelo's *David* and *The Last Judgment,* is strong and heroic. Renaissance glorification of the human body reveals the secular spirit of the age. Filippo Brunelleschi (1377-1446), together with Piero della Francesca (1420-1492), seems to have pioneered perspective in painting, the linear representation of distance and space on a flat surface. *The Last Supper* of Leonardo da Vinci (1452-1519), with its stress on the tension between Christ and the disciples, is an incredibly subtle psychological interpretation.

THE STATUS OF THE ARTIST

In the Renaissance the social status of the artist improved. The lower-middle-class medieval master mason had been viewed in the same light as a mechanic. The artist in the Renaissance was considered an independent intellectual worker. Some artists and architects achieved not only economic security but very great wealth. All aspiring artists received a practical (not theoretical) education in a recognized master's workshop. For example, Michelangelo (1475-1564) was apprenticed at age thirteen to the artist Ghirlandaio (1449-1494), although he later denied the fact to make it appear he never had any formal training. The more famous the artist, the more he attracted assistants or apprentices. Lorenzo Ghiberti (1378-1455) had twenty assistants during the period he was working on the bronze doors of the Baptistery in Florence, his most famous achievement.

Ghiberti's salary of two hundred florins a year compared very favorably with that of the head of the city government, who earned five hundred florins. Moreover, at a time when a man could live in a princely fashion on three hundred ducats a year, Leonardo da Vinci was making two thousand annually. Michelangelo was paid three thousand ducats for painting

HANS MEMLING: MARIA AND TOMMASO POR-
TINARI   A Florentine citizen, Tommaso Portinari
earned a fortune as representative of the Medici banking interests in Bruges, Flanders. Husband and wife
are dressed in a rich but durable black broadcloth;

Maria's necklace displays their wealth. Although both
faces show a sharp intelligence, there is a melancholy
sadness about them, suggestive of the pessimism of
northern religious piety. (The Metropolitan Museum
of Art: Bequest of Benjamin Altman, 1913)

the ceiling of the Sistine Chapel. When he
agreed to work on St. Peter's Basilica, he refused a salary; he was already a wealthy man.[6]

Renaissance society respected and rewarded
the distinguished artist. In 1537, the prolific
letter writer, humanist, and satirizer of
princes Pietro Aretino (1492-1556), wrote to
Michelangelo while he was painting the Sistine Chapel:

TO THE DIVINE MICHELANGELO:

*Sir, just as it is disgraceful and sinful to be un-
mindful of God so it is reprehensible and dishon-
ourable for any man of discerning judgement not
to honour you as a brilliant and venerable artist
whom the very stars use as a target at which to
shoot the rival arrows of their favour. You are so
accomplished, therefore, that hidden in your hands*

*lives the idea of a new king of creation, whereby
the most challenging and subtle problem of all in
the art of painting, namely that of outlines, has
been so mastered by you that in the contours of the
human body you express and contain the purpose of
art. . . . And it is surely my duty to honour you
with this salutation, since the world has many
kings but only one Michelangelo.[7]*

When the Holy Roman emperor Charles V
(1519-1556) visited the workshop of the
great Titian (1477-1576) and stooped to pick
up the artist's dropped paintbrush, the emperor was demonstrating that the patron
himself was honored in the act of honoring
the artist. The social status of the artist of
genius was immortally secured.

Renaissance artists were not only aware of

their creative power; they boasted about it. The architect Brunelleschi had his life written, and Ghiberti and Cellini wrote their autobiographies. Many medieval sculptors and painters had signed their own works; Renaissance artists almost universally did so, and many of them incorporated self-portraits, usually as bystanders, in their paintings. These actions reflect an acute consciousness of creative genius.

The Renaissance, in fact, witnessed the birth of the concept of the artist as genius. In the Middle Ages people believed that only God created, albeit through individuals; the medieval conception recognized no particular value in artistic originality. Renaissance artists and humanists came to think that a work of art was the deliberate creation of a unique personality, of an individual who goes beyond traditions, rules, and theories. A genius has a peculiar gift, which ordinary laws should not inhibit. Cosimo de'Medici described a painter, because of his genius, as "divine," implying that the artist shared in the powers of God. The word *divine* was widely applied to Michelangelo. The Renaissance thus bequeathed the idea of genius to the modern world.

The student must guard against interpreting Italian Renaissance culture in twentieth-century democratic terms. The culture of the Renaissance was that of a small mercantile elite, a business patriciate with aristocratic pretensions. Renaissance culture did not directly affect the broad middle classes, let alone the vast urban proletariat. The typical small tradesman or craftsman could not read the sophisticated Latin essays of the humanists, even if he had the time to do so. He could not afford to buy the art works of the great masters. A small, highly educated minority of literary humanists and artists created the culture of and for an exclusive elite. They cared little

for ordinary people. Castiglione, Machiavelli, and Vergerio, for example, thoroughly despised the masses. Renaissance humanists were a smaller and narrower group than the medieval clergy had ever been. High churchmen had commissioned the construction of the Gothic cathedrals, but, once finished, the buildings were for all to enjoy. The modern visitor can still see the deep ruts in the stone floors of Chartres and Canterbury where the poor pilgrims slept at night. Nothing comparable was built in the Renaissance. Insecure, social-climbing merchant princes were hardly egalitarian.[8] The Renaissance ushered in a gulf between the learned minority and the uneducated multitude that has survived for many centuries.

SOCIAL CHANGE

The Renaissance changed many aspects of Italian, and subsequently European, society. The new developments brought about real breaks with the medieval past. What impact did the Renaissance have on educational theory and practice, on political thought? How did printing, the era's most stunning technological discovery, affect fifteenth- and sixteenth-century society? Did women have a Renaissance?

EDUCATION AND POLITICAL THOUGHT

One of the central preoccupations of the humanists was education and moral behavior. Humanists poured out treatises, often in the form of letters, on the structure and goals of education and the training of rulers. In one of the earliest systematic programs for the young, Peter Paul Vergerio (1370–1444) wrote Ubertinus, the ruler of Carrara:

School of Luca della Robbia: Virgin and
Child In the late fifteenth century, della Robbia's
invention of the process of making polychrome-glazed
terracottas led contemporaries to consider him a great
artistic innovator. The warm humanity of this roun-
del (circular panel) is characteristic of della Robbia's
art. (Marion Gray. By permission of St. Anselm's
Abbey, Washington, D.C.)

The lives of men of position are passed, as it were, in public view; and are fairly expected to serve as witness to personal merit and capacity on the part of those who occupy such exceptional place amongst their fellow men. You therefore, Ubertinus, . . . the representative of a house for many generations sovereign in our ancient and most learned city of Padua, are peculiarly concerned in attaining this excellence in learning of which we speak. . . . Progress in learning . . . as in character, depends largely on ourselves.

For the education of children is a matter of more than private interest; it concerns the State, which indeed regards the right training of the young as, in certain aspects, within its proper sphere. . . . In order to maintain a high standard of purity all enticements of dancing, or suggestive spectacles, should be kept at a distance: and the society of women as a rule carefully avoided. A bad companion may wreck the character. Idleness, of mind and body, is a common source of temptation to indulgence, and unsociable, solitary temper must be disciplined, and on no account encouraged. Tutors and comrades alike should be chosen from amongst those likely to bring out the best qualities, to attract by good example, and to repress the first signs of evil. . . . Above all, respect for Divine ordinances is of the deepest importance; it should be inculcated from the earliest years. Reverence towards elders and parents is an obligation closely akin. In this, antiquity offers us a beautiful illustration. For the youth of Rome used to escort the Senators, the Fathers of the City, to the Senate House: and awaiting them at the entrance, accompany them at the close of their deliberations on their return to their homes. In this the Romans saw an admirable training in endurance and in patience. This same quality of reverence will imply courtesy towards guests, suitable greeting to elders, to friends and to inferiors. . . .

We call those studies liberal *which are worthy of a free man; those studies by which we attain and practise virtue and wisdom; that education*

which calls forth, trains and develops those highest gifts of body and of mind which ennoble men, and which are rightly judged to rank next in dignity to virtue only. . . .[9]

Part of Vergerio's treatise specifies subjects for the instruction of young men in public life: history teaches virtue by examples from the past; ethics focuses on virtue itself; and rhetoric or public speaking trains for eloquence.

No book on education achieved wider fame or broader influence than Baldassare Castiglione's *The Courtier* (1528). This treatise sought to train, discipline, and fashion the young man into the courtly ideal, the gentleman. According to Castiglione, the educated man of the upper class should have a broad background in many academic subjects, and his spiritual and physical, as well as intellectual, capabilities should be trained. The courtier should have easy familiarity with dance, music, and the arts. Castiglione envisioned a man who could compose a sonnet, wrestle, sing a song and accompany himself on an instrument, ride expertly, solve difficult mathematical problems, and, above all, speak and write eloquently. With these accomplishments, he would be the perfect Renaissance man. Whereas the medieval chivalric ideal stressed the military virtues of bravery and loyalty, the Renaissance man had to develop his artistic and intellectual potential as well as his fighting skills.

In contrast to the pattern of medieval education, the Renaissance courtier had the aristocrat's hostility to specialization and professionalism. Medieval higher education, as offered by the universities, had aimed at providing a practical grounding in preparation for a career. After exposure to the rudiments of grammar and rhetoric, which the medieval student learned mainly through memorization, he was trained for a profession

– usually law – in the government of the state or the church. Education was very functional and, by later standards, middle class.

In manner and behavior, the Renaissance courtier had traits his medieval predecessor probably had not had time to acquire. The gentleman was supposed to be relaxed, controlled, always composed and cool, elegant but not ostentatious, doing everything with a casual and seemingly effortless grace. In the sixteenth and seventeenth centuries, *The Courtier* was widely read. It influenced the social mores and patterns of conduct of elite groups in Renaissance and early modern Europe. The courtier became the model of the European gentleman.

No Renaissance book on any topic, however, has been more widely read and studied in all the centuries since its publication than the short political treatise *The Prince,* by Niccolò Machiavelli (1469–1527). Some political scientists maintain that Machiavelli was describing the actual competitive framework of the Italian states with which he was familiar. Other thinkers praise *The Prince* because it revolutionized political theory and destroyed medieval views of the nature of the state. Still other scholars consider this work a classic because it deals with eternal problems of government and society.

Born to a modestly wealthy Tuscan family, Machiavelli received a good education in the Latin classics. He entered the civil service of the Florentine government and served on thirty diplomatic missions. When the exiled Medicis returned to power in the city in 1512, they expelled Machiavelli from his position as officer of the city government. In exile he wrote *The Prince.*

The subject of *The Prince* is political power: how the ruler should gain, maintain, and increase his power. In this, Machiavelli implicitly addresses the question of the citizen's relationship to the state. As a good humanist, he explores the problems of human nature and concludes that human beings are selfish, corrupt, and out to advance their own interests. This pessimistic view leads him to maintain that the prince should manipulate the people in any way he finds necessary:

The manner in which men live is so different from the way in which they ought to live, that he who leaves the common course for that which he ought to follow will find that it leads him to ruin rather than to safety. For a man who, in all respects, will carry out only his professions of good, will be apt to be ruined amongst so many who are evil. A prince therefore who desires to maintain himself must learn to be not always good, but to be so or not as necessity may require.[10]

The prince should combine the cunning of a fox with the ferocity of a lion to achieve his goals. Asking rhetorically whether it is better for a ruler to be loved or feared, Machiavelli wrote:

A prince, therefore, should not mind the ill repute of cruelty, when he can thereby keep his subjects united and loyal; for a few displays of severity will really be more merciful than to allow, by an excess of clemency, disorders to occur, which are apt to result in rapine and murder; for these injure a whole community, whilst the executions ordered by the prince fall only upon a few individuals. And, above all others, the new prince will find it almost impossible to avoid the reputation of cruelty, because new states are generally exposed to many dangers. . . .

. . . This, then, gives rise to the question "whether it be better to be loved than feared, or to be feared than be loved." It will naturally be answered that it would be desirable to be both the one and the other; but as it is difficult to be both at the same time, it is much more safe to be feared than to be loved, when you have to choose between the

two. For it may be said of men in general that they are ungrateful and fickle, dissemblers, avoiders of danger, and greedy of gain. So long as you shower benefits upon them, they are all yours. . . . And the prince who relies upon their words, without having otherwise provided for his security, is ruined; for friendships that are won by rewards, and not by greatness and nobility of soul, although deserved, yet are not real, and cannot be depended upon in time of adversity.[11]

Medieval political theory derived ultimately from Saint Augustine's view that the state arose as a consequence of Adam's fall and people's propensity to sin. The test of good government was whether it provided justice, law and order. Political theorists and theologians from Alcuin to Marsiglio of Padua had stressed the way government ought to be; they set high moral and Christian standards for the ruler's conduct.

Machiavelli divorced government from moral and ethical considerations. He was concerned not with the way things ought to be but with the way they actually are. Consequently, the sole test of a "good" government was whether it was effective, whether the ruler increased his power. The state Machiavelli envisioned was a dynamic, amoral force.

Scholars have debated whether Machiavelli was writing a satire, trying to ingratiate himself with the Medicis, objectively describing contemporary Italian events, or advocating a fierce Italian nationalism that would achieve the unification of the peninsula. In any case, the word *Machiavellian* entered English as a synonym for devious, crafty, and corrupt politics in which the end justifies any means.

THE PRINTED WORD

Sometime in the thirteenth century, paper money and playing cards from China reached

the West. They were block printed – that is, Chinese characters or pictures were carved into a wooden block, inked, and the words or illustrations put on paper. Since each word, phrase, or picture was on a separate block, this method of reproduction was extraordinarily expensive and time-consuming.

Around 1455, probably through the combined efforts of three men – Johan Gutenberg, Johan Fust, and Peter Schoffer, all experimenting at Mainz – movable type came into being. The mirror image of each letter (rather than entire words or phrases) was carved in relief on a small block. Individual letters, easily movable, were put together to form words; words separated by blank spaces formed lines of type; and lines of type were brought together to make up a page. Once the printer had placed wooden pegs around the type for a border, and locked the whole in a frame, the page was ready for printing. Since letters could be arranged into any format, an infinite variety of texts could be printed by reusing and rearranging pieces of type.

By the middle of the fifteenth century, paper was no problem. The technologically advanced but extremely isolated Chinese knew how to manufacture paper as early as the first century A.D. This knowledge reached the West in the twelfth century, when the Arabs introduced the process into Spain. Europeans quickly learned that old rags could be shredded, mixed with water, placed in a mold, squeezed, and dried to make a durable paper, far less expensive than the vellum (calfskin) and parchment (sheepskin) on which medieval scribes had relied for centuries.

The effects of the invention of movable-type printing were not felt overnight. Nevertheless, within a half-century of the publication of Gutenberg's Bible in 1456, movable type brought about radical changes. The costs of reproducing books were drasti-

THE PRINT SHOP   Sixteenth-century printing involved a division of labor. Two persons (left) at separate benches set the pieces of type. Another (center, rear) inks the chase (or locked plate containing the set type). Another (right) operates the press which prints the sheets. The boy removes the printed pages and sets them to dry. Meanwhile, a man carries in fresh paper on his head. (BBC Hulton Picture Library)

cally reduced. It took less time and money to print a book by machine than to make copies by hand. The press also reduced the chances of error. If the type had been accurately set, all the copies would be correct no matter how many were reproduced. The greater the number of pages a scribe copied, the greater the chances for human error.

Printing stimulated the literacy of the laity. Although most of the earliest books dealt with religious subjects, students, businessmen, and upper- and middle-class people sought books on all kinds of subjects. Thus, intellectual interests were considerably broadened. International communication was enormously facilitated. The invention of printing

permitted writers and scholars of different countries to learn about one another's ideas and discoveries quickly. Intellectuals working in related fields got in touch with each other and cooperated in the advancement of knowledge.

Within the past twenty-five years, two inventions have revolutionized life for most Americans, television and the computer. By the late 1960s, the tired business executive or mechanic could return home in the evening, flip on "the tube," and while eating dinner watch battles in Vietnam or Israel that had occurred only a few hours before. The American tourist in Copenhagen or Florence or Tokyo who suddenly needs to draw on a bank account in New Orleans or Portland can have the account checked by computer in a matter of minutes. The impact of these relatively recent developments has been absolutely phenomenal. The invention of movable type likewise transformed European society in the fifteenth century.

The process of learning was made much easier by printing. In the past, students had had to memorize everything because only the cathedral, monastery, or professor possessed the book. The greater availability of books meant that students could begin to buy their own. If information was not at the tip of the tongue, it was at the tip of the fingers. The number of students all across Europe multiplied. It is not entirely accidental that between 1450 and 1517 seven new universities were established in Spain, three in France, nine in Germany, and six new colleges were set up at Oxford in England.

Printing also meant that ideas critical of the established order in state or church could be more rapidly disseminated. In the early sixteenth century, for example, the publication of Erasmus's *The Praise of Folly* helped pave the way for the Reformation. After 1517, the printing press played no small role in the spread of Martin Luther's political and social views. Cartoons and satirical engravings of all kinds proliferated. They also provoked state censorship, which had been very rare in the Middle Ages. The printed word eventually influenced every aspect of European culture: educational, economic, religious, political, and social.

WOMEN

The status of upper-class women declined during the Renaissance. If women in the High Middle Ages are compared with those of fifteenth- and sixteenth-century Italy with respect to the education they received, the kind of work they performed, their access to property and political power, and the role they played in shaping the outlook of their society, it is clear that ladies in the Renaissance ruling classes generally had less power than comparable ladies of the feudal age.

In the cities of Renaissance Italy, girls received the same education as boys. Young ladies learned their letters and studied the classics. Many read Greek as well as Latin, knew the poetry of Ovid and Virgil, and could speak one or two "modern" languages, such as French or Spanish. In this respect, Renaissance humanism represented a real educational advance for women. Girls also received some training in painting, music, and dance. What were they to do with this training? They were to be gracious, affable, charming – in short, decorative. Renaissance women were better educated than their medieval counterparts. But whereas education trained a young man to rule and to participate in the public affairs of the city, it prepared a woman for the social functions of the home. An educated lady was supposed to know how to attract artists and literati to her husband's court; she was to grace her husband's household.

A striking difference also exists between the medieval literature of courtly love, the etiquette books and romances, and the widely studied Renaissance manual on courtesy and good behavior, Castiglione's *The Courtier*. In the medieval books manners shaped the man to please the lady; in *The Courtier* the lady was to make herself pleasing to the man. With respect to love and sex, the Renaissance witnessed a downward shift in women's status. In contrast to the medieval tradition of relative sexual equality, Renaissance humanists laid the foundations for the bourgeois double standard. Men, and men alone, operated in the public sphere; women belonged in the home. Castiglione, the foremost spokesman of Renaissance love and manners, completely separated love from sexuality. For women, sex was restricted entirely to marriage. Ladies were bound to chastity, to the roles of wife and mother in a politically arranged marriage. Men, however, could pursue sensual indulgence outside marriage. The Italian Renaissance courts accepted a dual sexual standard, as the medieval courts had not. Although some noble ladies were highly educated and some exercised considerable political power, Renaissance culture did little to advance the dignity of women. They usually served as decorative objects in a male society.[12]

Popular attitudes toward rape provide another index of the status of women in the Renaissance. A careful study of the legal evidence from Venice in the years 1338–1358 is informative. The Venetian shipping and merchant elite held economic and political power and made the laws. Those laws reveal that rape was not considered a particularly serious crime against either the victim or society. Noble youths committed a higher percentage of rapes than their small numbers in Venetian society would imply, despite government-regulated prostitution. The rape of a young girl of marriageable age or a child under twelve was considered a graver crime than the rape of a married woman. Still, the punishment for rape of a noble marriageable girl was only a fine or about six months' imprisonment. In an age when theft and robbery were punished by mutilation, and forgery and sodomy by burning, this penalty was very mild indeed. When a youth of the upper class was convicted of the rape of a nonnoble girl, his punishment was even lighter.

By contrast, the sexual assault on a noblewoman by a man of working-class origin, which was extraordinarily rare, resulted in severe penalization because the crime had social and political overtones.

In the eleventh century, William the Conqueror had decreed that rapists should be castrated, thus implicitly according women protection and a modicum of respect. But in the early Renaissance, rape was treated as a minor offense. Venetian laws and their enforcement show that the populace believed that rape damaged, but only slightly, men's property – women.[13]

Evidence from Florence in the fifteenth century also sheds light on infanticide, which historians are only now beginning to study in the Middle Ages and the Renaissance. Early medieval penitentials and church councils had legislated against abortion and infanticide, though it is known that Pope Innocent III (1198–1216) was moved to establish an orphanage "because so many women were throwing their children into the Tiber."[14] In the fourteenth and early fifteenth centuries, a considerable number of children died in Florence under suspicious circumstances. Some were simply abandoned outdoors. Some were said to have been crushed to death while sleeping in the same bed with their parents. Some died from "crib death" or suffocation. These deaths occurred too frequently to have all been accidental. And far more girls than boys died thus, reflecting societal discrimination against girl children as inferior and less useful than boys. The dire poverty of parents led them to do away with unwanted children.

The gravity of the problem of infanticide, which violated both the canon law of the church and the civil law of the state, forced the Florentine government to build the Foundling Hospital. Supporters of the institution maintained that without public responsibility, "many children would soon be found dead in the rivers, sewers, and ditches, unbaptized."[15] The city fathers commissioned

TITIAN: THE RAPE OF EUROPA *According to Greek myth, the Phoenician princess Europa was carried off to Crete by the god Zeus disguised as a white bull. The story was highly popular in the Renaissance with its interests in the classics. In this masterpiece, the erotic and voluptuous female figure reveals the new interest in the human form and the secular element in Renaissance art. (Isabella Stewart Gardner Museum)*

Filippo Brunelleschi, who had recently completed the dome over the Cathedral of Florence, to design the building. (Interestingly enough, the Foundling Hospital – completed in 1445 – is the very first building to use the revitalized Roman classic design that characterizes Renaissance architecture.) The unusually large size of the hospital suggests that great numbers of children were abandoned.

BLACKS IN RENAISSANCE SOCIETY

Ever since the time of the Roman republic, a few black people had lived in Western Europe. They had come, along with white slaves, as the spoils of war. Even after the collapse of the Roman Empire, Muslim and Christian merchants continued to import them. The evidence of medieval art attests to the presence of Africans in the West and Eu-

Baldung: Adoration of the Magi Early sixteenth-century German artists produced thousands of adoration scenes depicting a black man as one of the three kings: these paintings were based on direct observation, reflecting the increased presence of blacks in Europe. The elaborate costumes, jewelry, and landscape expressed royal dignity, Christian devotion, and oriental luxury. (*Gemälde galerie. Staatliche Museen Preussischer Kulturbesitz, Berlin [West]*)

ropeans' awareness of them. In the twelfth and thirteenth centuries a large cult surrounded St. Maurice, martyred in the fourth century for refusing to renounce his Christian faith, who was portrayed as a black knight. St. Maurice received the special veneration of the nobility. The numbers of blacks, though, had always been small.

Beginning in the fifteenth century, however, hordes of black slaves entered Europe. Portuguese explorers imported perhaps a thousand a year and sold them at the markets of Seville, Barcelona, Marseilles, and Genoa. The Venetians specialized in the import of white slaves, but blacks were so greatly in demand at the Renaissance courts of northern Italy that the Venetians defied papal threats of excommunication to secure them. What roles did blacks play in Renaissance society? What image did Europeans have of Africans?

The medieval interest in curiosities, the exotic, and the marvelous continued into the Renaissance. Because of their rarity, black servants were highly prized and much sought after. In the late fifteenth century Isabella, the wife of Gian Galeazzo Sforza, took pride in the fact that she had ten blacks, seven of them females; a black lady's maid was both a curiosity and a symbol of wealth. In 1491 Isabella of Este, Duchess of Mantua, instructed her agent to secure a black girl between four and eight years old, "shapely and as black as possible." The duchess saw the child as a source of entertainment: "we shall make her very happy and shall have great fun with her." She hoped that the little girl would become "the best buffoon in the world."[16] The cruel ancient tradition of a noble household retaining a professional "fool" for the family's amusement persisted through the Renaissance — and even down to the twentieth century.

Adult black slaves filled a variety of positions. Many served as maids, valets, domestic servants; Italian aristocrats such as the Marchesa Elena Grimaldi had their portraits painted with their black page boys to indicate their wealth. The Venetians employed blacks – slave and free – as gondoliers and stevedores on the docks. Tradition, stretching back at least as far as the thirteenth century, connected blacks with music and dance. In Renaissance Spain and Italy blacks performed as dancers, as actors and actresses in courtly dramas, and as musicians, sometimes composing full orchestras.[17]

Before the sixteenth-century "discoveries" of the non-European world, Europeans had little interest in Africans and African culture. Consequently, Europeans knew little about them beyond biblical accounts. The European attitude toward Africans was ambivalent. On the one hand, Europeans perceived Africa as a remote place, the home of strange people isolated by heresy and Islam from superior European civilization. Africans' contact even as slaves with Christian Europeans could only "improve" the blacks. Most Europeans' knowledge of the black as a racial type was based entirely on theological speculation. Theologians taught that God is light. Blackness, the opposite of light, therefore represented the hostile forces of the underworld: evil, sin, and the devil. Thus the devil was commonly represented as a black man in medieval and early Renaissance art. Blackness, however, also possessed certain positive qualities. It symbolized the emptiness of worldly goods, the humility of the monastic way of life. Black clothes permitted a conservative and discreet display of wealth. Black vestments and funeral trappings indicated grief, and Christ had said that those who mourn are blessed. Until the exploration and observation of the sixteenth, seventeenth, and nineteenth centuries allowed, ever so slowly, for the development of more scientific knowledge, the Western conception of Africa and black people remained bound up with religious notions.[18]

THE ENVIRONMENT

Historians and natural scientists are only today beginning to study the attitude of peoples in earlier centuries toward their natural environment. An enormous amount of exciting research, which could improve ecological knowledge and aid in the solution of present-day problems, waits to be done. The measures the city of Florence took against water pollution in the fifteenth century provide some interesting information.

In 1450, the Florentine governing body expressed concern that fishermen and others several miles southeast of the city were using toxic substances to harvest more fish from the Arno River, which flowed through the city and was the source of much of Florence's fish. Fewer fresh fish reached the city markets. Ecclesiastical law required Christians to abstain from meat during the Fridays of the year and during the seasons of Advent and Lent. Fish was an obvious substitute, and the fishing industry was large and influential. The law of 1450 states:

Whereas it often happens, especially in parts of the Casentino and areas near there, that poisons and toxic substances are put and inserted into the neighboring rivers and waters to capture and angle fish more easily and in greater number ...

This is done where those fish are procreated and made which are called Trout, and truly noble and impressive fish they are. The result is that the said fish are destroyed and wasted.

And certainly if this were not so, our city and also other neighboring areas would continually and far more abound in the said fish. So that, therefore, the said genus of fish is preserved, and

our city and the other said areas have a copious and abundant supply of such fish, the magnificent ... lords priors ... ordain ...[19]

The citizens of Florence apparently did not understand the ecological problem and were not concerned about conservation. While they appreciated the beauty of the "noble trout," their concern was only that if upstream waters were polluted and the fish there killed, there would be fewer fish caught and brought to market in Florence. Government officials did not object to the damage to the river as a source of beauty, pleasure, and drinking water. Variations of the law of 1450 were put on the statute books in 1455, 1460, 1471, and 1477,[20] suggesting that these early conservation measures could not be enforced.

THE RENAISSANCE IN THE NORTH

In the last quarter of the fifteenth century, Renaissance thought and ideals penetrated northern Europe. Students from the Low Countries, France, Germany, and England flocked to Italy, imbibed the "new learning," and carried it back to their countries. Northern humanists interpreted Italian ideas about and attitudes toward classical antiquity, individualism, and humanism in terms of their own traditions. The cultural traditions of northern Europe tended to remain more distinctly Christian, or at least pietistic, than those of Italy. Thus while the Renaissance in Italy was characterized by a secular and pagan spirit and focused on Greco-Roman motifs and scholarship, north of the Alps the Renaissance had a religious character and emphasized biblical and early Christian themes. Scholars have termed the northern Renaissance "Christian humanism."

Christian humanists were interested in the development of an ethical way of life. To achieve it they believed that the best elements of classical and Christian cultures should be combined. For example, the classical ideals of calmness, stoical patience, and broad-mindedness should be joined in human conduct with the Christian virtues of love, faith, and hope. Northern humanists also stressed the use of reason, rather than acceptance of dogma, as the foundation for an ethical way of life. Like the Italians, they were extremely impatient with scholastic philosophy. Christian humanists had a profound faith in the power of the human intellect to bring about moral and institutional reform. They believed that although human nature had been corrupted by sin it was fundamentally good and capable of improvement through education, which would lead to piety and an ethical way of life.

This optimistic viewpoint found expression in scores of lectures, treatises, and collections of precepts. Treatises such as Erasmus's *The Education of a Christian Prince* express the naive notion that peace, harmony among nations, and a truly ethical society will result from a new system of education. This hope has been advanced repeatedly in Western history – by the ancient Greeks, by the sixteenth-century Christian humanists, by the eighteenth-century philosophers of the Enlightenment, and by nineteenth-century advocates of progress. The proposition remains highly debatable, but each time the theory has reappeared education has been further democratized.

The work of the French priest Jacques Lefèvre d'Etaples (ca 1455-1536) is one of the early attempts to apply humanistic learning to religious problems. A brilliant thinker and able scholar, he believed that more accurate texts of the Bible would lead people to live better lives. According to Lefèvre, a solid education in the Scriptures would increase piety and raise the level of behavior in Christian society. Lefèvre produced an edition of the Psalms and a commentary on Saint Paul's Epistles. In 1516, when Martin Luther lectured to his students at Wittenberg on Paul's Letter to the Romans, he relied on Lefèvre's texts.

Lefèvre's English contemporary John Colet (1466-1519) also published lectures on Saint Paul's Epistles, approaching them in the new critical spirit. Unlike the medieval theologians, who studied the Bible for allegorical meanings, Colet, who was a priest, interpreted the Pauline letters historically – that is, within the social and political context of the times when they were written. Both Colet and Lefèvre d'Etaples were later suspected of heresy, as humanistic scholarship got entangled with the issues of the Reformation.

Colet's friend and countryman Thomas More (1472-1535) towers above other figures in sixteenth-century English social and intellectual history. More's political stance at the time of the Reformation (page 492), a position that in part flowed from his humanist beliefs, got him into serious trouble with King Henry VIII and has tended to obscure his contribution to Christian humanism.

The early career of Thomas More presents a number of paradoxes that reveal the marvelous complexity of the man. Trained as a lawyer, More lived as a student in the London Charterhouse, a Carthusian monastery. He subsequently married and practiced law, but became deeply interested in the classics, and his household served as a model of warm Christian family life and a mecca for foreign and English humanists. Following the career pattern of such Italian humanists as Petrarch, he entered government service under Henry VIII and was sent as ambassador to Flanders. There More found the time to write *Utopia*

The Later Middle Ages, Renaissance, and Protestant and Catholic Reformations, 1300–1600

As is evident in this chronology, early manifestations of the Renaissance and Protestant Reformation coincided in time with major events of the Later Middle Ages.

1300–1321	Dante, *The Divine Comedy*
1304–1374	Petrarch
1309–1372	Babylonian Captivity of the papacy
1337–1453	Hundred Years' War
1347–1351	The Black Death
ca 1350	Boccaccio, *The Decameron*
1356	Golden Bull: transforms the Holy Roman Empire into an aristocratic federation
1358	The Jacquerie
ca 1376	John Wyclif publishes *Civil Dominion* attacking the church's temporal power and asserting the supremacy of Scripture
1377–1417	The Great Schism
1378	Laborers' revolt in Florence
1381	Peasants' Revolt
1385–1400	Chaucer, *Canterbury Tales*
1414–1418	Council of Constance: ends the schism, postpones reform, executes John Hus
1431	Joan of Arc is burned at the stake
1434	Medici domination of Florence begins
1438	Pragmatic Sanction of Bourges: declares autonomy of the French church from papal jurisdiction
1453	Capture of Constantinople by the Ottoman Turks, ending the Byzantine Empire
1453–1471	Wars of the Roses in England
1456	Gutenberg Bible
1492	Columbus reaches the Americas
	Unification of Spain under Ferdinand and Isabella; expulsion of Jews from Spain
1494	France invades Italy, inaugurating sixty years of war on Italian soil
	Florence expels the Medici and restores republican government

1509	Erasmus, *The Praise of Folly*
1512	Restoration of the Medici in Florence
1512–1517	Lateran Council undertakes reform of clerical abuses
1513	Balboa discovers the Pacific
	Macchiavelli, *The Prince*
1516	Concordat of Bologna between France and the papacy: rescinds the Pragmatic Sanction of 1438, strengthens French monarchy, establishes Catholicism as the national religion
	Thomas More, *Utopia*
1517	Martin Luther proclaims the 95 Theses
1519–1522	Magellan's crew circumnavigates the earth
1523	Luther's translation of the New Testament into German
1524	Peasants' Revolt in Germany
1527	Sack of Rome by mercenaries of Holy Roman Emperor Charles
1528	Castiglione, *The Courtier*
1530	Confession of Augsburg, official formulation of Lutheran theology
1534	Act of Supremacy inaugurates the English Reformation
1534–1541	Michelangelo, *The Last Judgment*
1535	Execution of Thomas More for treason
1536	John Calvin, *Institutes of the Christian Religion*
1540	Loyola founds the Society of Jesus (Jesuits)
1541	Calvin establishes a theocracy in Geneva
1543	Copernicus, *On the Revolutions of the Heavenly Spheres*
1545–1563	Council of Trent
1555	Peace of Augsburg: German princes determine the religion of their territories; no privileges for Calvinism
1572	St. Bartholemew's Day Massacre
1588	Spanish Armada
1598	Edict of Nantes grants French Protestants freedom of worship in certain towns
1603	Shakespeare, *Hamlet*
1605	Sir Francis Bacon, *The Advancement of Learning*

(1516), which presented a revolutionary view of society.

Utopia, which literally means "nowhere," describes an ideal socialistic community on a South Sea island. All its children receive a good education, primarily in the Greco-Roman classics, and learning does not cease with maturity, for the goal of all education is to develop rational faculties. Adults divide their days equally between manual labor or business pursuits (the Utopians were thoroughly familiar with advanced Flemish business practices) and various intellectual activities.

Because the profits from business and property are held strictly in common, there is absolute social equality. The Utopians use gold and silver to make chamber pots or to prevent wars by buying off their enemies. By this casual use of precious metals, More meant to suggest that the basic problems in society were caused by greed. Utopian law exalts mercy above justice. Citizens of Utopia lead an ideal and nearly perfect existence because they live by reason; their institutions are perfect.

More's ideas were profoundly original in the sixteenth century. Contrary to the long-prevailing view that vice and violence exist because women and men are basically corrupt, More maintained that *society's* flawed institutions are responsible for corruption and war. Today most people take this view so much for granted that it is difficult to appreciate how radical it was in the sixteenth century. According to More, the key to improvement and reform of the individual was reform of the social institutions that mold the individual.

Better known by his contemporaries than Thomas More was the Dutch humanist Desiderius Erasmus of Rotterdam (1469?–1536). Orphaned as a small boy, Erasmus was forced to enter a monastery. Although he intensely disliked the religious life, he developed there an excellent knowledge of the Latin language and a deep appreciation for the Latin classics. During a visit to England in 1499, Erasmus met John Colet, who decisively influenced his life's work: the application of the best humanistic learning to the study and explanation of the Bible. As a mature scholar with an international reputation stretching from Krakow to London, Erasmus could boast with truth, "I brought it about that humanism, which among the Italians . . . savored of nothing but pure paganism, began nobly to celebrate Christ."[21]

Erasmus's long list of publications includes *The Adages* (1500), a list of Greek and Latin precepts on ethical behavior; *The Education of a Christian Prince* (1504), which combines idealistic and practical suggestions for the formation of a ruler's character through the careful study of Plutarch, Aristotle, Cicero, and Plato; *The Praise of Folly* (1509), a satire on monasticism and a plea for the simple and spontaneous Christian faith of children; and, most important of all, a critical edition of the Greek New Testament (1516). In the preface to the New Testament Erasmus explained the purpose of his great work:

Only bring a pious and open heart, imbued above all things with a pure and simple faith. . . . For I utterly dissent from those who are unwilling that the sacred Scriptures should be read by the unlearned translated into their vulgar tongue, as though Christ had taught such subtleties that they can scarcely be understood even by a few theologians. . . . Christ wished his mysteries to be published as openly as possible. I wish that even the weakest woman should read the Gospel — should read the epistles of Paul. And I wish these were translated into all languages, so that they might be read and understood, not only by Scots and Irishmen, but also by Turks and Saracens. To make them understood is surely the first step. It may be that they might be ridiculed by many, but some would take them to heart. I long that the husbandman should sing portions of them to himself as he follows the plough, that the weaver should hum them to the tune of his shuttle, that the traveller should beguile with their stories the tedium of his journey. . . .

Why do we prefer to study the wisdom of Christ in men's writings rather than in the writing of Christ himself?[22]

Two fundamental themes run through all of Erasmus's scholarly work. First, education was the means to reform, the key to moral and intellectual improvement. The core of education ought to be study of the Bible and the classics. Second, the essence of Erasmus's thought is, in his own phrase, "the philosophy of Christ." By this Erasmus meant that Christianity is an inner attitude of the heart or spirit. Christianity is not formalism, special ceremonies, law; Christianity is Christ – his life and what he said and did, not what theologians and commentators have written about him. The Sermon on the Mount, for Erasmus, expressed the heart of the Christian message.

While the writings of Colet, Erasmus, and More have strong Christian themes and have drawn the attention primarily of scholars, the stories of the French humanist François Rabelais (1490?–1553) possess a distinctly secular flavor and have attracted broad readership among the literate public. Rabelais' *Gargantua* and *Pantagruel* (serialized between 1532 and 1552) belong among the great comic masterpieces of world literature. These stories' gross and robust humor introduced the adjective *Rabelasian* into the language.

Gargantua and *Pantagruel* can be read on several levels: as comic romances about the adventures of the giant Gargantua and his son Pantagruel; as a spoof on contemporary French society; as a program for educational reform; or as illustrations of Rabelais' prodigious learning. The reader enters a world of Renaissance vitality, ribald joviality, and intellectual curiosity. On his travels Gargantua meets various absurd characters, and within their hilarious exchanges there occur serious discussions on religion, politics, philosophy, and education. Rabelais had received an excellent humanistic education in a monastery, and Gargantua discusses the disorders of contemporary religious and secular life. Like More and Erasmus, Rabelais did not denounce institutions directly. Like Erasmus, Rabelais satirized hypocritical monks, pedantic academics, and pompous lawyers. But where Erasmus employed intellectual cleverness and sophisticated wit, Rabelais applied wild and gross humor. Like Thomas More, Rabelais believed that institutions molded individuals and that education was the key to a moral and healthy life. While the middle-class inhabitants of More's *Utopia* lived lives of restrained moderation, the aristocratic residents of Rabelais' Thélème lived for the full gratification of their physical instincts and rational curiosity.

Thélème, the abbey Gargantua establishes, parodies traditional religion and other social institutions. Thélème, whose motto is "Do as Thou Wilt," admits women *and* men, allows all to eat, drink, sleep, and work when they choose, provides excellent facilities for swimming, tennis, and football, and encourages sexual experimentation and marriage. Rabelais believed profoundly in the basic goodness of human beings and the rightness of instinct.

The most roguishly entertaining Renaissance writer, Rabelais was convinced that "laughter is the essence of manhood." A convinced believer in the Roman Catholic faith, he included in Gargantua's education an appreciation for simple and reasonable prayer.

JEROME BOSCH: DEATH AND THE MISER Netherlandish painters frequently used symbolism, and Bosch (ca 1450–1516) is considered the master-artist of symbolism and fantasy. Here, rats, which because of their destructiveness symbolize evil, control the miser's gold. Bosch's imagery appealed strongly to twentieth-century surrealist painters. (National Gallery of Art, Washington, D.C., Samual H. Kress Collection)

Rabelais combined the Renaissance zest for life and enjoyment of pleasure with a classical insistence on the cultivation of the body and the mind.

The distinctly religious orientation of the literary works of the Renaissance in the north also characterized northern art and architecture. Some Flemish painters, notably Jan van Eyck (1366–1441), were the equals of Italian painters. One of the earliest artists successfully to use oil on wood panels, van Eyck, in paintings such as the *Ghent Altarpiece* and the portrait of *Giovanni Arnolfini and His Bride,* shows the Flemish love for detail; the effect is great realism. Van Eyck's paintings also demonstrate remarkable attention to human personality, as do those of Hans Memling (d. 1494) in his studies of *Tommaso Portinari and His Wife.* Typical of northern piety, the Portinari are depicted in an attitude of prayer (see p. 432).

Another Flemish painter, Jerome Bosch (c. 1450–1516) frequently used religious themes, but in combination with grotesque fantasies, colorful imagery, and peasant folk legends. Many of Bosch's paintings reflect the confusion and anguish often associated with the end of the Middle Ages. In *Death and the Miser,* Bosch's dramatic treatment of the Dance of Death theme, the miser's gold, increased by usury, is ultimately controlled by diabolical rats and toads, while his guardian angel urges him to choose the crucifix.

A quasi-spiritual aura likewise infuses architectural monuments in the north. The city halls of wealthy Flemish towns like Bruges, Brussels, Louvain, and Ghent strike the viewer more as shrines to house the bones of saints than as settings for the mundane decisions of politicians and businessmen. Northern architecture was little influenced by the classical revival so obvious in Renaissance Rome and Florence.

POLITICS AND THE STATE IN THE RENAISSANCE (CA 1450–1521)

The High Middle Ages had witnessed the origins of many of the basic institutions of the modern national state. Sheriffs, inquests, juries, circuit judges, bureaucracies, and representative assemblies all trace their origins to the twelfth and thirteenth centuries (pages (351–364). The linchpin for the development of states, however, was strong monarchy, and during the period of the Hundred Years' War no ruler in western Europe was able to provide effective leadership. The resurgent power of feudal nobilities weakened the centralizing work begun earlier.

Beginning in the fifteenth century, rulers utilized the aggressive methods implied by Renaissance political ideas to rebuild their governments. First in Italy, then in France, England, and Spain, rulers began the work of reducing violence, curbing unruly nobles and troublesome elements, and establishing domestic order. Within the Holy Roman Empire of Germany, the lack of centralization helps to account for the later German distrust of the Roman papacy. Divided into scores of independent principalities, Germany could not deal with the Roman church as an equal.

The dictators and oligarchs of the Italian city-states, however, together with Louis XI of France, Henry VII of England, and Ferdinand of Spain, were tough, cynical, and calculating rulers. In their ruthless push for power and strong governments, they subordinated morality and considerations of right and wrong to the achievement of hard results. They preferred to be secure, if feared, rather than loved. Whether or not they actually read Machiavelli's *The Prince,* they acted as if they had.

Some historians have called Louis XI (1461–1483), Henry VII (1485–1509), and Ferdinand and Isabella of Spain (1474–1516) "new monarchs." The term is only partly appropriate. These monarchs were new in that they invested kingship with a strong sense of royal authority and national purpose. They stressed that monarchy was the one institution that linked all classes and peoples within definite territorial boundaries. Rulers emphasized the "royal majesty" and royal sovereignty and insisted that all must respect and be loyal to them. They ruthlessly suppressed opposition and rebellion, especially from the nobility. They loved the business of kingship and worked hard at it.

In other respects, however, the methods of these rulers, which varied from country to country, were not so new. They reasserted long-standing ideas and practices of strong monarchs in the Middle Ages. The Holy Roman emperor Frederick Barbarossa, the English Edward I, and the French King Philip the Fair had all applied ideas drawn from Roman law in the High Middle Ages. Renaissance princes also did so. They seized upon the maxim of the Justinian Code, "What pleases the prince has the force of law," to advance their authority. Some medieval rulers, such as Henry I of England, had depended heavily upon middle-class officials. Renaissance rulers too tended to rely on civil servants of middle-class background. With tax revenues, medieval rulers had built armies to crush feudal anarchy. Renaissance townspeople with commercial and business interests naturally wanted a reduction of violence and usually were willing to be taxed in order to achieve domestic order.

Scholars have often described the fifteenth-century "new monarchs" as crafty, devious, and thoroughly Machiavellian in their methods. Yet contemporaries of the Capetian Philip the Fair considered him every bit as devious and crafty as his Valois descendants, Louis XI and Francis I, were considered in the fifteenth and sixteenth centuries. Machiavellian politics were not new in the age of the Renaissance. What was new was a marked acceleration of politics, whose sole rationalization was the acquisition and expansion of power. Renaissance rulers spent precious little time seeking a religious justification for their actions. With these qualifications of the term "new monarchs" in mind, let us consider the development of national states in Italy, France, England, and Spain in the period 1450 to 1521.

THE ITALIAN CITY-STATES

In the fourteenth century, the Holy Roman emperors had made several efforts to impose imperial authority in Italy and continue the tradition begun by Charlemagne. But the German emperors, economically and militarily weak, could not defeat the powerful, though separate, city-states. The Italian city-states were thus entirely independent of the Holy Roman Empire.

In the fifteenth century, five powers dominated the Italian peninsula – Venice, Milan, Florence, the Papal States, and the kingdom of Naples (see Map 13.1). The rulers of the city-states – whether despots in Milan, patrician elitists in Florence, or oligarchs in Venice – governed as monarchs. They crushed proletarian revolts, levied taxes, killed their enemies, and used massive building programs to employ, and the arts to overawe, the masses.

Venice, with enormous trade and a vast colonial empire, ranked as an international power. Although Venice had a sophisticated constitution and was a republic in name, an oligarchy of merchant-aristocrats actually ran the city. Milan was also called a republic, but despots of the Sforza family ruled harshly and dominated the smaller cities of the north. Likewise in Florence the form of government was republican, with authority vested in several councils of state. In reality, between 1434 and 1494, power in Florence was held by the great Medici banking family. Although they did not hold public office, Cosimo (1434–1464) and Lorenzo (1469–1492) ruled from behind the scenes.

A republic is a state in which political power resides in the people and is exercised by them or their chosen representatives. The Renaissance nostalgia for the Roman form of republican government, combined with a calculating shrewdness, prompted leaders of Venice, Milan, and Florence to preserve the old forms: the people could be deceived into thinking they still possessed the decisive voice.

Central Italy consisted mainly of the Papal States, which during the Babylonian Captivity had come under the sway of important Roman families. Pope Alexander VI (1492–1503), aided militarily and politically by his son Cesare Borgia, reasserted papal authority in the papal lands. Cesare Borgia became the hero of Machiavelli's *The Prince* because he began the work of uniting the peninsula by ruthlessly conquering and exacting total obedience from the principalities making up the Papal States.

South of the Papal States was the kingdom of Naples, consisting of virtually all of southern Italy and, at times, Sicily. The kingdom of Naples had long been disputed by the Aragonese and by the French. In 1435, it passed to Aragon.

The major Italian city-states controlled the smaller ones, such as Siena, Mantua, Ferrara, and Modena, and competed furiously among themselves for territory. The large cities used

HOLY ROMAN EMPIRE

DUCHY
OF
SAVOY
• Turin

SALUZZO

DUCHY
OF
MILAN
• Milan
• Lodi
Pavia •

M. OF
MANTUA

Padua •
Venice •

REP. OF GENOA
Genoa •

D. OF
FERRARA
D. OF MODENA

REPUBLIC OF VENICE

OTTOMAN
EMPIRE

Bologna •
• Ravenna

DALMATIA

ADRIATIC SEA

REP. OF LUCCA
Pisa •

Arno
• Florence
REP. OF
FLORENCE

Urbino •

Siena •
REP. OF
SIENA

PAPAL
STATES
• Assisi

CORSICA
(to Genoa)

Tiber

• Rome

Bari •

Naples •
Salerno •

KINGDOM
OF
NAPLES

SARDINIA

M E D I T E R R A N E A N   S E A

• Palermo

KINGDOM OF
SICILY

0   50   100 Km.
0   50   100 Mi.

MAP 13.1 THE ITALIAN CITY-STATES, CA
1494   *In the fifteenth century the Italian city-states
represented great wealth and cultural sophistication.
The political divisions of the peninsula invited foreign
intervention.*

UCELLO: BATTLE OF SAN ROMANO   *The Medici commissioned this painting ca 1460 to commemorate a lucky Florentine victory over the Sienese in 1432, a victory which contributed to the rise of the Medici dynasty. Although mainly interested in perspective,* *Ucello in this unrealistic and decorative painting seems most concerned with the pageantry of war. (The National Gallery, London. Reproduced by courtesy of the Trustees.)*

diplomacy, spies, paid informers, and any other means to get information that could be used to advance their ambitions. While the states of northern Europe were moving toward centralization and consolidation, the world of Italian politics resembled a jungle where the powerful dominated the weak.

In one significant respect, however, the Italian city-states anticipated future relations among competing European states after 1500. Whenever one Italian state appeared to gain a predominant position within the peninsula, other states combined to establish a balance of power against the major threat. In 1450, for example, Venice went to war against Milan in protest against Francesco Sforza's acquisition of the title of duke of Milan. Cosimo de' Medici of Florence, a long-time supporter of a Florentine-Venetian alliance, switched his po-

sition and aided Milan. Florence and Naples combined with Milan against powerful Venice and the papacy. In the peace treaty signed at Lodi in 1454, Venice received territories in return for recognizing Sforza's right to the duchy. This pattern of shifting alliances continued until 1494.

At the end of the fifteenth century, Venice, Florence, Milan, and the papacy possessed great wealth and represented high cultural achievement. Their imperialistic ambitions at each other's expense, however, and their inability to form a common alliance against potential foreign enemies, made Italy an inviting target for invasion. When Florence and Naples entered into an agreement to acquire Milanese territories, Milan called upon France for support.

At Florence the French invasion had been

predicted by the Dominican friar Girolamo Savonarola (1452-1498). In a number of fiery sermons between 1481 and 1494, Savonarola attacked what he considered the paganism and moral vice of the city, the undemocratic government of Lorenzo de' Medici, and the corruption of Pope Alexander VI. For a time Savonarola enjoyed wide popular support among the ordinary people; he became the religious leader of Florence and as such contributed to the fall of the Medici. Eventually, however, people wearied of his moral denunciations, and he was excommunicated and executed. As an enemy of secularism, Savonarola stands as proof that the common people did not share the worldly outlook of the commercial and intellectual elite. His career also illustrates the internal instability of Italian cities such as Florence, an instability that invited foreign invasion.

The invasion of Italy in 1494 by the French king Charles VIII (1483-1498) inaugurated a new period in Italian and European power politics. Italy became the focus of international ambitions and the battleground of foreign armies. Charles swept down the peninsula with little opposition, and Florence, Rome, and Naples soon bowed before him. When Piero de' Medici, Lorenzo's son, went to the French camp seeking peace, the Florentines exiled the Medicis and restored republican government.

Charles's success simply whetted French appetites. In 1508, his son Louis XII formed the League of Cambrai with the pope and the German emperor Maximilian for the purpose of stripping rich Venice of its mainland possessions. Pope Leo X soon found the French a dangerous friend, and in a new alliance called upon the Spanish and Germans to expel the French from Italy. This anti-French combination was temporarily successful. But the French returned in 1522, and after Charles V

succeeded his grandfather Maximilian as Holy Roman emperor, there began the series of conflicts called the Habsburg-Valois wars (named for the German and French dynasties), whose battlefield was Italy.

In the sixteenth century, the political and social life of Italy was upset by the relentless competition for dominance between France and the empire. The Italian cities suffered severely from the continual warfare, especially in the frightful sack of Rome in 1527 by imperial forces under Charles V. Thus the failure of the city-states to form some federal system, or to consolidate, or at least to establish a common foreign policy, led to the continuation of the centuries-old subjection of the peninsula by outside invaders. Italy was not to achieve unification until 1870.

FRANCE

The Hundred Years' War left France badly divided, drastically depopulated, commercially ruined, and agriculturally weak. Nonetheless, the ruler whom Joan of Arc had seen crowned at Reims, Charles VII (1422-1461), revived the monarchy and France. He seemed an unlikely person to do so. Frail, ugly, feeble, hypochondriacal, mistrustful, called "the son of a madman and a loose woman," Charles VII began France's long recovery.

Charles reconciled the Burgundians and Armagnacs, who had been waging civil war for thirty years. By 1453, French armies had expelled the English from French soil except in Calais. Charles reorganized the royal council, giving increased influence to the middle-class men, and he strengthened royal finances through such taxes as the gabelle (on salt) and the taille (a land tax). These taxes remained the Crown's chief sources of state income until the Revolution of 1789.

Charles also reformed the justice system

FRENCH TRADESMEN *A bootmaker, a cloth merchant (with bolts of material on shelves), and a dealer in gold plate and silver share a stall. Through sales taxes, the French crown received a share of the profits. (Bibliothèque Municipale, Rouen/Giraudon)*

and remodeled the army. By establishing regular companies of cavalry and archers – recruited, paid, and inspected by the state – Charles created the first permanent royal army. In 1438, Charles published the Pragmatic Sanction of Bourges, asserting the superiority of a general council over the papacy, giving the French crown control over the appointment of bishops, and depriving the pope of French ecclesiastical revenues. The Pragmatic Sanction established the Gallican (or French) liberties, because it affirmed the autonomy of the French church from the Roman papacy. Greater control over the church, the army, and justice helped to consolidate the authority of the French crown.

Charles's son Louis XI, called "the Spider King" by his subjects because of his treacherous and cruel character, was very much a Renaissance prince. Facing the perpetual French problems of unification of the realm and reduction of feudal disorder, he saw money as the answer. Louis promoted new industries, such as silk weaving at Lyons and Tours. He welcomed tradesmen and foreign craftsmen, and he entered into commercial treaties with England, Portugal, and the towns of the Hanseatic League, a group of cities that played an important role in the development of towns and commercial life in northern Germany. The revenues raised through these economic activities and severe taxation were used to improve the army. With the army Louis stopped aristocratic brigandage and slowly cut into urban independence.

Luck favored his goal of expanding royal authority and unifying the kingdom. On the timely death of Charles the Bold, duke of Burgundy, in 1477 Louis invaded Burgundy and gained some territories. Three years later, the extinction of the house of Anjou brought Louis the counties of Anjou, Bar, Maine, and Provence.

Some scholars have credited Louis XI with laying the foundations for later French royal absolutism. Louis summoned only one meeting of the Estates General, and the delegates requested that they not be summoned in the future. Thereafter the king would decide. Building on the system begun by his father, Louis XI worked tirelessly to remodel the government following the debacle of the fourteenth and fifteenth centuries. In his reliance on finances supplied by the middle classes to fight the feudal nobility, Louis is typical of the new monarchs.

Two further developments strengthened the French monarchy. The marriage of Louis XII and Anne of Brittany added the large western duchy of Brittany to the state. Then, the French king Francis I and Pope Leo X reached a mutually satisfactory agreement in 1516. The new treaty, the Concordat of Bologna, rescinded the Pragmatic Sanction's assertion of the superiority of a general council over the papacy and approved the pope's right to receive the first year's income of new bishops and abbots. In return, Leo X recognized the French ruler's right to select French bishops and abbots. French kings thereafter effectively controlled the appointment and thus the policies of church officials within the kingdom.

ENGLAND

English society suffered severely from the disorders of the fifteenth century. The aristocracy dominated the government of Henry IV (1399–1413) and indulged in mischievous violence at the local level. Population, decimated by the Black Death, continued to decline. While Henry V (1413–1422) gained chivalric prestige for his military exploits in France, he was totally dependent upon the feudal magnates who controlled the royal council and Parliament. Henry V's death, leaving a nine-month-old son, the future Henry VI (1422–1461), gave the barons a perfect opportunity to entrench their power. Between 1455 and 1471, adherents of the ducal houses of York and Lancaster waged civil war, commonly called the Wars of the Roses because the symbol of the Yorkists was a white rose and that of the Lancastrians a red one. Although only a small minority of the nobility participated, the chronic disorder hurt trade, agriculture, and domestic industry. Under the pious but spineless Henry VI, the authority of the monarchy sank lower than it had been in centuries.

Edward IV (1461–1483) began establishing domestic tranquility. He succeeded in defeating the Lancastrian forces and after 1471 began to reconstruct the monarchy and consolidate royal power. Edward, his brother Richard III (1483–1485), and Henry VII of the Welsh house of Tudor worked to restore royal prestige, to crush the power of the nobility, and to establish order and law at the local level. All three rulers used methods Machiavelli would have praised – ruthlessness, efficiency, and secrecy.

The Hundred Years' War had cost the nation dearly, and the money to finance it had been raised by Parliament. Dominated by various baronial factions, Parliament had been the arena where the nobility exerted its power. As long as the monarchy was dependent on the lords and the commons for revenue, the king had to call Parliament. Thus Edward IV revived the medieval ideal that he would "live of his own," meaning on his own financial resources. He reluctantly established a policy the monarchy was to follow with rare exceptions down to 1603. Edward, and subsequently the Tudors, conducted foreign policy on the basis of diplomacy, avoiding expensive wars. Thus the English monarchy did not depend on Parliament for money, and the Crown undercut that source of aristocratic influence.

Henry VII did, however, summon several meetings of Parliament in the early years of his reign. He used these assemblies primarily to confirm laws. Parliament remained the highest court in the land, and a statute registered (approved) there by the lords, bishops, and commons gave the appearance of broad national support plus thorough judicial authority.

The center of royal authority was the royal council, which governed at the national level. There too Henry VII revealed his distrust of the nobility: although they were not completely excluded, very few great lords were among the king's closest advisers. Regular representatives on the council numbered between twelve and fifteen men, and while many gained high ecclesiastical rank (the means, as it happened, by which the Crown paid them), their origins were the lesser landowning class and their education was in law. They were in a sense middle class.

The royal council handled any business the king put before it – executive, legislative, judicial. For example, the council conducted negotiations with foreign governments and secured international recognition of the Tudor dynasty through the marriage in 1501 of Henry VII's eldest son Arthur to Catherine of Aragon, the daughter of Ferdinand and Isabella of Spain. The council prepared laws for parliamentary ratification. The council dealt with real or potential aristocratic threats through a judicial offshoot, the court of Star Chamber, so-called because of the stars painted on the ceiling of the room.

The court of Star Chamber applied principles of Roman law, and its methods were terrifying: the accused was not entitled to see evidence against him; sessions were secret; torture could be applied to extract confessions; and juries were not called. These procedures ran directly counter to English common-law precedents, but they effectively reduced aristocratic troublemaking.

Unlike the continental countries of Spain and France, England had no standing army or professional civil-service bureaucracy. The Tudors relied upon the support of unpaid local officials, the justices of the peace. These influential landowners in the shires handled all the work of local government. They apprehended and punished criminals, enforced parliamentary statutes, supervised conditions of service, fixed wages and prices, maintained proper standards of weights and measures, and even checked up on moral behavior. Justices of the peace were appointed and supervised by the council. From the royal point of view, they were an inexpensive method of government.

The Tudors won the support of the influential upper middle class because the Crown linked government policy with their interests. A commercial or agricultural upper class fears and dislikes few things more than disorder and violence. If the Wars of the Roses served any useful purpose, it was killing off dangerous nobles and thus making the Tudors' work easier. The Tudors promoted peace and social order, and the gentry did not object to arbitrary methods like the court of Star Chamber, because the government had halted the long period of anarchy.

Grave, secretive, cautious, and always thrifty, Henry VII rebuilt the monarchy. He encouraged the cloth industry and built up the English merchant marine. Both English exports of wool and the royal export tax on that wool steadily increased. Henry crushed an invasion from Ireland and secured peace with Scotland through the marriage of his daughter Margaret to the Scottish king. When Henry VII died in 1509, he left a country at peace both domestically and internationally, a fat treasury, and the dignity of the royal majesty much enhanced.

SPAIN

Political development in Spain followed a pattern different from that of France and England. The central theme in the history of medieval Spain – or, more accurately, of the separate kingdoms Spain comprised – was disunity and plurality. The various peoples who lived in the Iberian Peninsula lacked a common cultural tradition. Different languages, different laws, and different religious communities made for a rich diversity. Complementing the legacy of Hispanic, Roman, and Visigothic peoples, Muslims and Jews had made significant contributions to Spanish society.

The centuries-long *reconquista* – the attempts of the northern Christian kingdoms to control the entire peninsula – had both military and religious objectives: expulsion or conversion of the Arabs and Jews and political control of the south. By the middle of the fifteenth century, the kingdoms of Castile and Aragon dominated the weaker Navarre, Granada, and Portugal, and, with the exception of Granada, the Iberian Peninsula had been won for Christianity. The wedding in 1469 of the dynamic and aggressive Isabella, heiress of Castile, and the crafty and persistent Ferdinand, heir of Aragon, was the final major step in the unification and Christianization of Spain. This marriage, however, constituted a dynastic union of two royal houses, not the political union of two peoples. Although Ferdinand and Isabella pursued a common foreign policy, Spain under their rule remained a loose confederation of separate states. Each kingdom continued to maintain its own cortes (parliament), laws, courts, bureaucracies, and systems of coinage and taxation.

Isabella and Ferdinand determined to strengthen royal authority. In order to curb the rebellious and warring aristocracy, they revived an old medieval institution. Popular groups in the towns called *hermandades,* or brotherhoods, were given the authority to act both as local police forces and as judicial tribunals. Local communities were made responsible for raising troops and apprehending and punishing criminals. The *hermandades* repressed violence with such savage punishments that by 1498 they could be disbanded.

The second step Ferdinand and Isabella

took to curb aristocratic power was the restructuring of the royal council. Aristocrats and great territorial magnates were rigorously excluded; thus the influence of the nobility on state policy was greatly reduced. Ferdinand and Isabella intended the council to be the cornerstone of their governmental system, with full executive, judicial, and legislative power under the monarchy. The council was also to be responsible for the supervision of local authorities. The king and queen, therefore, appointed to the council only people of middle-class background. The council and various government boards recruited men trained in Roman law, a system that exalted the power of the Crown as the embodiment of the state.

In the extension of royal authority and the consolidation of the territories of Spain, the church was the linchpin. The church possessed vast power and wealth, and churchmen enjoyed exemption from taxation. Most of the higher clergy were descended from great aristocratic families, controlled armies and strategic fortresses, and fully shared the military ethos of their families.

The major issue confronting Isabella and Ferdinand was the appointment of bishops. If the Spanish crown could select the higher clergy, then the monarchy could influence ecclesiastical policy, wealth, and military resources. Through a diplomatic alliance with the papacy, especially with the Spanish pope Alexander VI, the Spanish monarchs secured the right to appoint bishops in Spain and in the Hispanic territories in America. This power enabled the "Catholic Kings of Spain," a title granted Ferdinand and Isabella by the papacy, to establish, in effect, a national church.[23]

The Spanish rulers used their power to reform the church, and they used some of its wealth for national purposes. For example, they appointed a learned and zealous churchman, Cardinal Jiménez (1436–1517), to reform the monastic and secular clergy. Jiménez proved effective in this task, and established the University of Alcalá in 1499 for the education of the clergy, although instruction did not actually begin until 1508. A highly astute statesman, Jiménez twice served as regent of Castile.

Revenues from ecclesiastical estates provided the means to raise an army to continue the *reconquista*. The victorious entry of Ferdinand and Isabella into Granada on January 6, 1492, signaled the culmination of eight centuries of Spanish struggle against the Arabs in southern Spain and the conclusion of the *reconquista* (see Map 13.2). Granada in the south was incorporated into the Spanish kingdom, and in 1512 Ferdinand conquered Navarre in the north.

Although the Arabs had been defeated, there still remained a sizable and, in the view of the Catholic sovereigns, potentially dangerous minority, the Jews. Since ancient times, governments had never tolerated religious pluralism; religious faiths that differed from the official state religion were considered politically dangerous. Medieval writers quoted the fourth-century Byzantine theologian Saint John Chrysostom, who had asked rhetorically, "Why are the Jews degenerate? Because of their odious assassination of Christ." John Chrysostom and his admirers in the Middle Ages chose to ignore two facts: that it was the Romans who had killed Christ (because they considered him a *political* troublemaker), and that Christ had forgiven his executioners from the cross. France and England had expelled their Jewish populations in the Middle Ages, but in Spain Jews had been tolerated. In fact, Jews had played a decisive role in the economic and intellectual life of the several Spanish kingdoms.

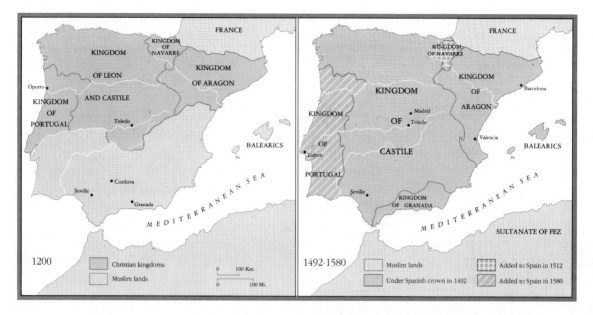

MAP 13.2   THE CHRISTIANIZATION AND UNIFICATION OF SPAIN   *The political unification of Spain was inextricably tied up with conversion or expulsion of the Muslims and the Jews. Why?*

Anti-Semitic riots and pogroms in the late fourteenth century had led many Jews to convert; they were called *conversos.* By the middle of the fifteenth century, many conversos held high positions in Spanish society as financiers, physicians, merchants, tax collectors, and even officials of the church hierarchy. Numbering perhaps 200,000 in a total population of about 7.5 million, Jews exercised an influence quite disproportionate to their numbers. Aristocratic grandees who borrowed heavily from Jews resented their financial dependence, and churchmen questioned the sincerity of Jewish conversions. At first, Isabella and Ferdinand continued the policy of royal toleration – Ferdinand himself had inherited Jewish blood from his mother. But many conversos apparently reverted to the faith of their ancestors, prompting Ferdinand and Isabella to secure Rome's permission to revive the In-

quisition, a medieval judicial procedure for the punishment of heretics.

Although the Inquisition was a religious institution established to insure the Catholic faith, it was controlled only by the Crown and served primarily as a politically unifying force in Spain. Because the Spanish Inquisition commonly applied torture to extract confessions, first from lapsed conversos, then from Muslims, and later from Protestants, it gained a notorious reputation. Thus, the word *inquisition,* meaning "any judicial inquiry conducted with ruthless severity," came into the English language. The methods of the Spanish Inquisition were cruel, though not as cruel as the investigative methods of some twentieth-century governments. In 1478 the deeply pious Ferdinand and Isabella introduced the Inquisition into their kingdoms to handle the problem of backsliding conversos. They solved the problem in a dire and drastic manner. Shortly after the reduction of the Moorish stronghold at Granada in 1492, Isabella and Ferdinand issued an edict expelling all practicing Jews from Spain. Of the community of perhaps 200,000 Jews, 150,000 fled. (Efforts were made through last-minute conversions to retain good Jewish physicians.) Absolute religious orthodoxy served as the foundation of the Spanish national state.

The diplomacy of the Catholic rulers of Spain achieved a success they never anticipated. Partly out of hatred for the French and partly to gain international recognition for their new dynasty, Ferdinand and Isabella in 1496 married their second daughter, Joanna, heiress to Castile, to the archduke Philip, heir through his mother to the Burgundian Netherlands and through his father to the Holy Roman Empire. Philip and Joanna's son, Charles V (1519–1556), thus succeeded to a vast patrimony on two continents. When Charles's son Philip II united Portugal to the Spanish crown in 1580, the Iberian Peninsula was at last politically united.

Fourteenth-century Italy witnessed the rebirth of a strong interest in the ancient world, a Renaissance whose classicizing influences affected law and literature, government, education, religion, and art. Expanding outside Italy, this movement affected the entire culture of Europe. The chief features of the Renaissance were a secular attitude toward life, a belief in individual potential, and a serious interest in the Latin classics. The printing press revolutionized communication. Meanwhile the status of women in society declined, and black people entered Europe in sizable numbers for the first time since the collapse of the Roman Empire.

These changes rested upon important economic developments. The growth of Venetian and Genoese shipping and long-distance trade, Florentine banking and manufactures, Milanese and Pisan manufactures – these activities brought into being wealthy urban classes. As commercial oligarchies, they governed their city-states. In northern Europe city merchants and rural gentry allied with rising monarchies. With taxes provided by businesspeople, kings provided a greater degree of domestic peace and order, conditions essential for trade. In Spain, France, and England, rulers also emphasized royal dignity and authority, and they utilized Machiavellian ideas to insure the preservation and continuation of their governments. Feudal monarchies gradually evolved in the direction of nation states.

NOTES

1. A. Brucker, *Renaissance Florence,* John Wiley & Sons, New York, 1969, chap. 2.

2. Quoted by J. Burckhardt, *The Civilization of the Renaissance in Italy,* Phaidon Books, London, 1951, p. 89.

3. *Memoirs of Benvenuto Cellini; A Florentine Artist; Written by Himself,* Everyman's Library, J. M. Dent & Sons, London, 1927, p. 2.

4. Quoted by Burckhardt, p. 111.

5. B. Burroughs, ed., *Vasari's Lives of the Artists,* Simon & Schuster, New York, 1946, pp. 164–165.

6. See chap. 3, "The Social Status of the Artist," in A. Hauser, *The Social History of Art,* vol. 2, Vintage Books, New York, 1959, esp. pp. 60, 68.

7. G. Bull, trans., *Aretino: Selected Letters,* Penguin Books, New York, 1976, p. 109.

8. Hauser, pp. 48–49.

9. Quoted by W. H. Woodward, *Vittorino da Feltre and Other Humanist Educators,* Cambridge University Press, Cambridge, 1897, pp. 96–97.

10. C. E. Detmold, trans., *The Historical, Political*

and Diplomatic Writings of Niccolò Machiavelli, J. R.
Osgood & Co., Boston, 1882, pp. 51–52.

11. Ibid., pp. 54–55.

12. This account rests on the excellent study of J.
Kelly-Gadol, "Did Women Have a Renaissance?"
in R. Bridenthal and C. Koonz, eds., Becoming Visible: Women in European History, Houghton Mifflin,
Boston, 1977, pp. 137–161, esp. p. 161.

13. G. Ruggiero, "Sexual Criminality in the Early
Renaissance: Venice 1338–1358," Journal of Social
History 8 (Spring 1975):18–31.

14. Quoted by R. C. Trexler, "Infanticide in
Florence: New Sources and First Results," History
of Childhood Quarterly 1:1 (Summer 1973): 99.

15. Ibid., p. 100.

16. See Jean Devisse and Michel Mollat, The Image
of the Black in Western Art, vol. II, part 2, trans.
William Granger Ryan, William Morrow and
Company, New York, 1979, pp. 187–188.

17. Ibid., pp. 190–194.

18. Ibid., pp. 255–258.

19. Quoted by R. C. Trexler, "Measures against
Water Pollution in Fifteenth-Century Florence,"
Viator 5 (1974):463.

20. Ibid., pp. 464–467.

21. Quoted by E. H. Harbison, The Christian
Scholar and His Calling in the Age of the Reformation,
Charles Scribner's Sons, New York, 1956, p. 109.

22. Quoted by F. Seebohm, The Oxford Reformers,
Everyman's Library, J. M. Dent & Sons, London,
1867, p. 256.

23. See J. H. Elliott, Imperial Spain 1469–1716,
Mentor Books, New York, 1963, esp. pp. 97–108
and p. 75.

SUGGESTED READING

There are scores of exciting studies available on
virtually all aspects of the Renaissance. In addition
to the titles given in the Notes, the curious student interested in a broad synthesis should see
J. H. Plumb, The Italian Renaissance (1965), a superbly
written book based on deep knowledge and understanding; this book is probably the best starting
point. J. R. Hale, Renaissance Europe: The Individual
and Society, 1480–1520 (1978), is an excellent treatment of individualism by a distinguished authority. F. H. New, The Renaissance and Reformation: A
Short History (1977), gives a concise, balanced, and
up-to-date account. M. P. Gilmore, The World of
Humanism (1962), is an older but sound study that
recent scholarship has not superseded on many
subjects. Students interested in the problems the
Renaissance has raised for historians should see
K. H. Dannenfeld, ed., The Renaissance: Medieval or
Modern (1959), an anthology with a variety of interpretations, and W. K. Ferguson, The Renaissance
in Historical Thought (1948), a valuable but difficult
book. For the city where much of it originated,
G. A. Brucker, Renaissance Florence (1969), gives a good
description of Florentine economic, political, social, and cultural history.

J. R. Hale, Machiavelli and Renaissance Italy
(1966), is the best short biography of Machiavelli
and broader in scope than the title would imply. G.
Bull, trans., Machiavelli: The Prince (1959), is a
readable and easily accessible edition of the political
thinker's major work. C. Singleton, trans., The
Courtier (1959), presents an excellent picture of
Renaissance court life.

The best introduction to the Renaissance in
northern Europe and a book that has greatly influenced twentieth-century scholarship is J. Huizinga, The Waning of the Middle Ages: A Study of the
Forms of Life, Thought, and Art in France and the
Netherlands in the Dawn of the Renaissance (1954).
The leading northern humanist is sensitively
treated in M. M. Philips, Erasmus and the Northern
Renaissance (1965), and in J. Huizinga, Erasmus of
Rotterdam (1952), probably the best biography. The
standard biography of Thomas More remains that of
R. W. Chambers (1935), but see also E. E. Reynolds, Thomas More (1962). Jacques LeClercq, trans.,
The Complete Works of Rabelais (1963), is easily
available.

Renaissance art has understandably inspired vast
researches. In addition to Vasari's volume of bio-

graphical sketches on the great masters referred to in the Notes, A. Martindale, *The Rise of the Artist in the Middle Ages and Early Renaissance* (1972), is a splendidly illustrated introduction. B. Berenson, *Italian Painters of the Renaissance* (1957), the work of an American expatriate who was an internationally famous art historian, has become a classic. W. Sypher, *Four Stages of Renaissance Style* (1956), relates drama and poetry to the visual arts of painting and sculpture. One of the finest appreciations of Renaissance art, written by one of the greatest art historians of this century, is E. Panofsky, *Meaning in the Visual Arts* (1955). Both Italian and northern painting are treated in the brilliant study of M. Meiss, *The Painter's Choice: Problems in the Interpretation of Renaissance Art* (1976), a collection of essays dealing with Renaissance style, form, and meaning. The splendidly illustrated work of Mary McCarthy, *The Stones of Florence* (1959), celebrates the energy and creativity of the greatest Renaissance city.

The student who wishes to study blacks in medieval and early modern European society should see the rich and original achievement of Jean Devisse and Michel Mollat, *The Image of the Black in Western Art,* vol. II: Part 1, *From the Demonic Threat to the Incarnation of Sainthood,* and Part 2, *Africans in the Christian Ordinance of the World: Fourteenth to Sixteenth Century,* trans. William Granger Ryan, William Morrow & Co., New York, 1979.

The following works are not only useful for the political and economic history of the age of the Renaissance but also contain valuable bibliographical information: A. J. Slavin, ed., *The "New Monarchies" and Representative Assemblies* (1965), a collection of interpretations; R. Lockyer, *Henry VII* (1972), a biography with documents illustrative of the king's reign; J. H. Elliott, *Imperial Spain: 1469–1716* (1966), with a balanced treatment of Isabella and Ferdinand; and I. Origo, *The Merchant of Prato* (1957), a perceptive and detailed account of one busy Florentine businessman.

CHAPTER 14

REFORM AND RENEWAL IN THE

CHRISTIAN CHURCH

THE IDEA OF REFORM is as old as Christianity itself. In his letter to the Christians of Rome, Saint Paul exhorted: "Do not model yourselves on the behavior of the world around you, but let your behavior change, reformed by your new mind. That is the only way to discover the will of God and know what is good, what it is that God wants, what is the perfect thing to do."[1] In the early fifth century, Saint Augustine of Hippo, describing the final stage of world history, wrote, "In the sixth age of the world our reformation becomes manifest, in newness of mind, according to the image of Him who created us." In the middle of the twelfth century, Saint Bernard of Clairvaux complained about the church of his day: "There is as much difference between us and the men of the primitive Church as there is between muck and gold."

The need for reform of the individual Christian and of the institutional church is central to the Christian faith. The Christian humanists of the late fifteenth and early sixteenth centuries – More, Erasmus, Lefèvre d'Etaples, and Jiménez – urged reform of the church on the pattern of the early church primarily through educational and social change. Men and women of every period believed the early Christian church represented a golden age, and critics in every period called for reform.

Sixteenth-century cries, therefore, were hardly new. Why then did sixteenth-century demands for reform lead to revolution in the Christian church and to lasting divisions in Christian society? What role did social and political factors play in the several reformations? What were the consequences of religious division? To resolve these questions, the related issue of the condition of the church within European society must first be explored.

THE CONDITION OF THE CHURCH (CA 1400–1517)

The papal conflict with the German emperor Frederick II in the thirteenth century, followed by the Babylonian Captivity and then by the Great Schism, badly damaged the prestige of church leaders. In the fourteenth and fifteenth centuries, conciliarists reflected educated public opinion when they called for the reform of the church "in head and members." The secular humanists of Italy and the Christian humanists of the north denounced corruption in the church. As Machiavelli put it, "We Italians are irreligious and corrupt above others, because the Church and her representatives set us the worst example."[2] In *The Praise of Folly,* Erasmus condemned the absurd superstitions of the parish clergy and the excessive rituals of the monks. The records of episcopal visitations of parishes, civil court records, and even such literary masterpieces as Chaucer's *Canterbury Tales* and Boccaccio's *Decameron* tend to confirm the sarcasms of the humanists.

Concrete evidence of disorder is spotty and scattered. Since a great deal of corruption may have gone unreported, the moral situation may have been worse than the evidence suggests. On the other hand, bishops' registers and public court records mention the exceptional, not the typical. The thousands of priests who quietly and conscientiously went about their duties and did not warrant correction received no mention in the documents.

The religious life of most people in early sixteenth-century Europe took place at the village or local level. Any assessment of the moral condition of the parish clergy must take into account one fundamental fact: parish priests were peasants, and they were poor. All too frequently the spiritual quality of their lives was not much better than that of the people to whom they ministered. The clergy identified religion with life; that is, they injected religious symbols and practices into everyday living. Some historians, therefore, have accused the clergy of vulgarizing religion. But if the level of belief and practice was vulgarized, still the lives of rural, isolated, and semipagan people were spiritualized.

SIGNS OF DISORDER

In the early sixteenth century, critics of the church concentrated their attacks on three disorders: clerical immorality, clerical ignorance, and clerical pluralism with the related problem of absenteeism. There was little pressure for doctrinal change; the emphasis was on moral and administrative reform.

Since the fourth century, church law had required that candidates for the priesthood accept absolute celibacy. It had always been difficult to enforce. Many priests, especially those ministering to country people, had concubines, and reports of neglect of the rule of celibacy were common. Immorality, of course, included more than sexual transgressions. Clerical drunkenness, gambling, and indulgence in fancy dress were frequent charges. There is no way of knowing how many priests were guilty of such behavior. But because such conduct was so much at odds with the church's rules and moral standards, it scandalized the educated faithful.

The bishops enforced regulations regarding the education of priests very casually. As a result, standards for ordination were shockingly low. Many priests could barely read and write, and critics laughed at the illiterate priest mumbling the Latin words of the mass, which he could not understand. Predictably, this was

the disorder the Christian humanists, with their concern for learning, particularly condemned.

Absenteeism and pluralism constituted the third major abuse. Many clerics, especially higher ecclesiastics, held several benefices (or offices) simultaneously but seldom visited their benefices, let alone performed the spiritual responsibilities those offices entailed. Instead, they collected revenues from all of them and paid a poor priest a fraction of the income to fulfill the spiritual duties of a particular local church.

Many Italian officials in the papal curia held benefices in England, Spain, and Germany. Revenues from those countries paid the Italian priests' salaries, provoking not only charges of absenteeism but nationalistic resentment. King Henry VIII's chancellor Thomas Wolsey was archbishop of York for fifteen years before he set foot in his diocese. The French king Louis XII's famous diplomat Antoine du Prat is perhaps the most notorious example of absenteeism: as archbishop of Sens, the first time he entered his cathedral was in his own funeral procession. Critics condemned pluralism, absenteeism, and the way money seemed to change hands when a bishop entered into his office.

Although royal governments strengthened their positions and consolidated their territories in the fifteenth and sixteenth centuries, rulers lacked sufficient revenues to pay and reward able civil servants. The Christian church, with its dioceses and abbeys, possessed a large proportion of the wealth of the countries of Europe. What better way to reward government officials than with high church offices? After all, the practice was sanctioned by centuries of tradition. Thus in Spain, France, England, and the Holy Roman Empire — in fact, all over Europe — because

THE CHURCH CONTRASTED *Satirical woodcuts as well as the printed word attacked conditions in the church. Here the mercenary spirit of the sixteenth-century papacy is contrasted with the attitude of Christ toward money changers: Christ drove them from the temple, but the pope kept careful records of revenues owed to the church. (Photos: Caroline Buckler)*

church officials served their monarchs, those officials were allowed to govern the church.

The broad mass of the people, in supporting the church, supported everything that churchmen did. Bishops and abbots did a lot of work for secular governments. Churchmen served as royal councilors, diplomats, treasury

officials, chancellors, viceroys, and judges. These positions had nothing whatsoever to do with spiritual matters. Bishops worked for their respective states as well as for the church, and they were paid by the church for their services to the state. It is astonishing that so many conscientiously tried to carry out their religious duties on top of their public burdens.

The prodigious wealth of the church inevitably stimulated criticism. For centuries devout laymen and laywomen had bequeathed land, money, rights, and privileges to religious institutions. By the sixteenth century, these gifts and shrewd investments had resulted in vast treasure. Some was spent in the service of civil governments. Much of it was used to alleviate the wretched condition of the poor. But some also provided a luxurious lifestyle for the church hierarchy.

In most countries except England, members of nobility occupied the highest positions in the church. The sixteenth century was definitely not a democratic age. The spectacle of proud, aristocratic prelates living in magnificent splendor contrasted very unfavorably with the simple fishermen who were Christ's first disciples. Nor did the popes of the period 1450–1550 set much of an example. They lived like secular Renaissance princes. Pius II (1458–1464), although deeply learned and a tireless worker, enjoyed a reputation as a clever writer of love stories and witty Latin poetry. Sixtus IV (1471–1484) beautified the city of Rome, built the famous Sistine Chapel, and generously supported several artists. Innocent VIII (1484–1492) made the papal court a model of luxury and scandal. All three popes used papal power and papal wealth to advance the material interests of their own families.

The court of the Spanish pope Rodrigo Borgia, Alexander VI (1492–1503), who publicly acknowledged his mistress and children, reached new heights of impropriety. Because of the prevalence of intrigue, sexual promiscuity, and supposed poisonings, the name Borgia became a synonym for moral corruption. Julius II (1503–1513), the nephew of Sixtus IV, donned military armor and personally led papal troops against the French invaders of Italy in 1506. After him, Giovanni de' Medici, the son of Lorenzo the Magnificent, carried on as Pope Leo X (1513–1521) the Medicean tradition of being a great patron of the arts.

Through the centuries, papal prestige and influence had rested heavily on the moral quality of the popes' lives – that is, on their strong fidelity to Christian teaching as revealed in the Gospel. The lives of Renaissance popes revealed little of this Gospel message.

SIGNS OF VITALITY

Calls for reform testify to the spiritual vitality of the church as well as to its problems. Before a patient can be cured of sickness, he or she must acknowledge that a problem exists. In the late fifteenth and early sixteenth centuries, both individuals and groups within the church were working actively for reform. In Spain, Cardinal Francisco Jiménez visited religious houses, encouraged the monks and friars to keep their rules and constitutions, and set high standards for the training of the diocesan clergy. Jiménez founded the University of Alcalá (1499) partly for the education of priests.

Lefèvre d'Etaples in France and John Colet in England called for a return to the austere Christianity of the early church. Both men stressed the importance of sound preaching of the Scriptures.

In Holland, beginning in the late fourteenth century, a group of pious laymen and laywomen called the Brethren of the Common Life lived in stark simplicity while daily carrying out the Gospel teaching of feeding the hungry, clothing the naked, and visiting the sick. The Brethren also established schools for the education of the young, their most famous pupil being Erasmus of Rotterdam. The spirituality of the Brethren of the Common Life found its finest expression in the classic *The Imitation of Christ* by Thomas à Kempis. As its title suggests, *The Imitation of Christ* urges ordinary Christians to take Christ as their model and to seek perfection in a simple way of life. The movement, which spread to Germany, France, and Italy, was a real religious revival.

So too were the activities of the Oratories of Divine Love in Italy. The oratories were groups of priests living in communities who worked to revive the church through prayer and preaching. They did not withdraw from the world as medieval monks had done, but devoted themselves to pastoral and charitable activities such as founding hospitals and orphanages. Oratorians served God in an active ministry.

If external religious observances are a measure of depth of heartfelt conviction, Europeans in the early sixteenth century remained deeply pious and loyal to the Roman Catholic church. Villagers participated in processions honoring the local saints. Middle-class people made pilgrimages to the great national shrines, as the enormous wealth of Saint Thomas Becket's tomb at Canterbury in England and the shrine of Saint James de Compostella in Spain testify. The upper classes continued to remember the church in their wills. In England, for example, between 1480 and 1490 almost £30,000, a prodigious sum in those days, was bequeathed to religious foundations. People of all social classes devoted an enormous amount of their time and

GRUNEWALD: CRUCIFIXION The bloodless hands, tortured face, and lacerated body reveal profound sorrow for Christ's physical agony and suggest the intense piety of northern Europe. Grunewald, court painter to Albert of Brandenburg, shows in this painting (ca 1510) his strong attraction to Luther's ideas. (National Gallery of Art, Washington, D.C. Samual H. Kress Collection)

income to religious causes and foundations. Sixteenth-century society remained deeply religious; all across Europe people sincerely yearned for salvation.

The papacy also expressed concern for reform. Pope Julius II summoned an ecumenical (universal) council, which met in the church of St. John Lateran in Rome from 1512 to 1517. Since most of the bishops were Italian and did not represent a broad cross-section of international opinion, the term *ecumenical* is not appropriate. Nevertheless, the bishops and theologians present strove earnestly to reform the church. They criticized the ignorance of priests, lamenting that only 2 percent of the clergy could understand the Latin of the liturgical books. The Lateran Council also condemned superstitions believed by many of the laity. The council recommended higher standards for education of the clergy and instruction of the common people. The bishops placed the responsibility for eliminating bureaucratic corruption squarely on the papacy and suggested significant doctrinal reforms. But many obstacles stood in the way of ecclesiastical change. Nor did the actions of an obscure German friar immediately force the issue.

MARTIN LUTHER AND THE BIRTH OF PROTESTANTISM

As the result of a personal religious struggle, a German Augustinian friar, Martin Luther (1483–1546), launched the Protestant Reformation of the sixteenth century. Luther was not a typical person of his time; miners' sons who become professors of theology are never typical. But Luther is representative of his time in the sense that he articulated the widespread desire for reform of the Christian church and the deep yearning for salvation. In the sense that concern for salvation motivated Luther and other reformers, the sixteenth-century Reformation was in part a continuation of the medieval religious search.

LUTHER'S EARLY YEARS

Martin Luther was born at Eisleben in Saxony, the second son of a hardworking and ambitious copper miner. At considerable sacrifice, his father sent him to school and then to the University of Erfurt, where Martin earned a master's degree with distinction at the young age of twenty-one. Hans Luther intended his son to proceed to the study of law and a legal career, which had since Roman times been the steppingstone to public office and material success. Badly frightened during a thunderstorm, however, Martin Luther vowed to become a friar. Without consulting his father, he entered the monastery of the Augustinian friars at Erfurt in 1505. Luther was ordained a priest in 1507, and after additional study earned the doctorate of theology. From 1511 until his death in 1546, he served as professor of Scripture at the new University of Wittenberg.

Martin Luther was exceedingly scrupulous in his monastic observances and devoted to prayer, penances, and fasting; nevertheless, the young friar's conscience troubled him constantly. The doubts and conflicts felt by any sensitive young person who has just taken a grave step were especially intense in young Luther. He had terrible anxieties about sin and worried continually about his salvation. Luther intensified his monastic observances but still found no peace of mind.

A recent psychological interpretation of Luther's early life suggests that he underwent a severe inner crisis in the years 1505–1515. Luther had disobeyed his father, thus viola-

YOUNG LUTHER   Lucas Cranach, court painter to Elector Frederick of Saxony and a friend of Luther's, captured the piety, the strength, and the intense struggle of the young friar. (Photo: Caroline Buckler)

ting one of the Ten Commandments, and serious conflict persisted between them. The religious life seemed to provide no answers to his mental and spiritual difficulties. Three fits that he suffered in the monastic choir during those years may have been outward signs of his struggle.[3] Luther was grappling, as had thousands of medieval people before him, with the problem of salvation and thus the meaning of life. He was also searching for his life's work.

Luther's wise and kindly confessor, Staupitz, directed him to the study of Saint Paul's letters. Gradually, Luther arrived at a new understanding of the Pauline letters and of all Christian doctrine. He came to believe that salvation comes not through external observances and penances but through a simple faith in Christ. Faith is the means by which God sends humanity his grace, and faith is a free gift that cannot be earned. Thus Martin Luther discovered himself, God's work for him, and the centrality of faith in the Christian life.

THE NINETY-FIVE THESES

An incident illustrative of the condition of the church in the early sixteenth century propelled Martin Luther onto the stage of history and brought about the Reformation in Germany. The University of Wittenberg lay within the ecclesiastical jurisdiction of the archdiocese of Magdeburg. The twenty-seven-year-old archbishop of Magdeburg, Albert, was also administrator of the see of Halberstadt and had been appointed archbishop of Mainz. To hold all three offices simultaneously – blatant pluralism – required papal dispensation. At that moment Pope Leo X was anxious to continue the construction of St. Peter's Basilica, but was hard pressed for funds. Archbishop Albert borrowed money from the Fuggers, a wealthy banking family of Augsburg, to pay for the papal dispensation allowing him to hold the several episcopal benefices. Only a few powerful financiers and churchmen knew the details of the arrangement, but Leo X authorized Archbishop Albert to sell indulgences, or pardons, in Germany. With the proceeds the archbishop could repay the Fuggers.

Wittenberg was in the political jurisdiction of Frederick of Saxony, one of the seven electors of the Holy Roman Empire. When Frederick forbade the sale of indulgences within his duchy, people of Wittenberg, including some of Professor Luther's students, streamed across the border from Saxony into Jüteborg in Thuringia to buy indulgences.

What was an indulgence? According to Catholic theology, individuals who sin alienate themselves from God and his love. In order to be reconciled to God, the sinner must confess his or her sins to a priest and do the penance assigned. For example, the man who steals must first return the stolen goods and then perform the penance given by the priest, usually certain prayers or good works. This is known as the temporal (or earthly) penance, since no one knows what penance God will ultimately require.

The doctrine of indulgence rested on three principles. First, God is merciful, but he is also just. Second, Christ and the saints, through their infinite virtue, established a "treasury of merits," which the church, through its special relationship with Christ and the saints, can draw upon. Third, the church has the authority to grant to sinners the spiritual benefits of those merits. Originally, an indulgence was a remission of the temporal (priest-imposed) penalties for sin. Beginning in the twelfth century, the papacy and bishops had given Crusaders such indulgences. By the later Middle Ages people widely believed that an indulgence secured total remission of penalties for sin – on earth or in purgatory – and assured swift entry into heaven.

Archbishop Albert hired the Dominican friar John Tetzel to sell the indulgences. Tetzel mounted a blitz advertising campaign. One of his slogans – "As soon as coin in coffer rings, the soul from purgatory springs" – brought phenomenal success. Men and women could buy indulgences not only for themselves but for deceased parents, relatives, or friends. Tetzel even drew up a chart with specific prices for the forgiveness of particular sins. The

massive amounts of junk that "sophisticated" Americans buy today should make one cautious in condemning the gullibility of sixteenth-century German peasants. Who wouldn't want a spiritual insurance policy?

Luther was severely troubled that ignorant people believed that they had no further need for repentance once they had purchased an indulgence. Accordingly, in the academic tradition of the times, on the eve of All Saints' Day (October 31) 1517, he attached to the door of the church at Wittenberg castle a list of ninety-five theses (or propositions) on indulgences. By this act Luther intended only to start a theological discussion of the subject and to defend the theses publicly.

Some of the theses challenged the pope's power to grant indulgences, and others criticized papal wealth: "Why does not the Pope, whose riches are at this day more ample than those of the wealthiest of the wealthy, build the one Basilica of St. Peter's with his own money, rather than with that of poor believers . . . ?"[4] Luther at first insisted that the pope had not known about the traffic in indulgences, for if he had known, he would have put a stop to it.

The theses were soon printed and read by Germans all over the empire. Immediately, broad theological issues were raised. When questioned, Luther insisted that Scripture persuaded him of the invalidity of indulgences. He rested his fundamental argument on the principle that there was no biblical basis for indulgences. But, replied Luther's opponents, to deny the legality of indulgences was to deny the authority of the pope who had authorized them. The issue was drawn: where did authority lie in the Christian church?

Through 1518 and 1519, Luther studied the history of the papacy. Gradually, he gained the conviction, like Marsiglio and Hus before him (pages 408–409), that ultimate authority in the church belonged not to the papacy but to a general council. Then, in 1519, in a large public disputation with the Catholic debater John Eck at Leipzig, Luther denied both the authority of the pope and the infallibility of a general council. The Council of Constance, he said, had erred when it condemned John Hus in 1415.

The papacy responded with a letter condemning some of Luther's propositions, ordering that his books be burned, and giving him two months to recant or be excommunicated. Luther retaliated by publicly burning the letter. Shortly afterward – January 3, 1521 – his excommunication became final. By this time the controversy involved more than theological issues. The papal legate wrote, "All Germany is in revolution. Nine-tenths shout 'Luther' as their war-cry; and the other tenth cares nothing about Luther, and cries 'Death to the court of Rome.' "[5]

In this highly charged atmosphere the twenty-one-year-old emperor Charles V held his first diet (assembly of the Estates of the empire) at Worms and summoned Luther to appear before it. When ordered to recant, Luther replied in language that rang all over Europe:

Unless I am convinced by the evidence of Scripture or by plain reason – for I do not accept the authority of the Pope or the councils alone, since it is established that they have often erred and contradicted themselves – I am bound by the Scriptures I have cited and my conscience is captive to the Word of God. I cannot and will not recant anything, for it is neither safe nor right to go against conscience. God help me. Amen.[6]

Luther was declared an outlaw of the empire, which meant that he was denied legal protection.

Between 1520 and 1530, Luther worked out the basic theological tenets that became the articles of faith for his new church and subsequently for all Protestant groups. The word *Protestant* derives from the protest drawn up by a small group of reforming German princes at the Diet of Speyer in 1529. The princes "protested" the decisions of the Catholic majority. At first Protestant meant Lutheran, but with the appearance of many protesting sects it became a general term applied to all non-Catholic Christians. Lutheran Protestant thought was officially formulated in the Confession of Augsburg in 1530.

Ernst Troeltsch, a German student of the sociology of religion, has defined Protestantism as a "modification of Catholicism, in which the Catholic formulation of questions was retained, while a different answer was given to them." Luther provided new answers to four old, basic theological issues.

First, how is a person to be saved? Traditional Catholic teaching held that salvation was achieved by both faith *and* good works. Luther held that salvation comes by *faith alone*. Women and men are saved, said Luther, by the arbitrary decision of God, irrespective of good works or the sacraments.

Second, where does religious authority reside? Christian doctrine had long maintained that authority rests both in the Bible and in the traditional teaching of the church. Luther maintained that authority rests in the Word of God as revealed in the Bible alone and as interpreted by an individual's conscience. He urged that each person read and reflect upon the Scriptures.

Third, what is the church? Luther reemphasized the Catholic teaching that the church consists of the entire community of

Christian believers. The medieval church had tended to identify the church with the clergy. Luther insisted upon the priesthood of all believers.

Finally, what is the highest form of Christian life? The medieval church had stressed the superiority of the monastic and religious life over the secular. Luther argued that all vocations have equal merit, whether ecclesiastical or secular, and that every person should serve God in his or her individual calling.[7] Protestantism, in sum, represented a reformulation of the Christian heritage.

THE SOCIAL IMPACT OF LUTHER'S BELIEFS

In the sixteenth century, religion infused many aspects of life, and theological issues had broad social implications. The Lutheran movement started a religious revolution, which soon led to social revolt. As early as 1521, Luther had a vast following. Every encounter with ecclesiastical or political authorities attracted attention to him. Pulpits and printing presses spread his message all over Germany. By the time of his death, people of all social classes had become "Lutheran."

What was the immense appeal of Luther's religious ideas? Historians have puzzled over this question for centuries. It is always difficult to distinguish between spiritual and altruistic motives and materialistic, self-serving ones. The attraction of the German peasants to Lutheran beliefs was logical and almost predictable. Luther himself came from a peasant background, and he knew their ceaseless toil. The peasants must have admired Luther's defiance of the authority of the church. Moreover, they thrilled to the words Luther used in his treatise *On Christian Liberty* (1520): "A Christian man is the most free lord of all and

subject to none." Taken by themselves, these words easily contributed to social unrest.

In the early sixteenth century, the economic condition of the peasantry varied from place to place, but was generally worse than it had been in the fifteenth century and was continuing to deteriorate. Although the lords did not attempt to reimpose or increase servile obligations that had been set aside after the Black Death, nevertheless rising prices hurt people living on fixed incomes. A huge number of beggars swelled the populations of the towns. At Hamburg, for example, perhaps 20 percent of the people were paupers.

The upper classes viewed the peasants and their wretched conditions with contempt. Nobles looked upon peasants as little more than animals, "the ox without horns." Luther's fellow professor and colleague in reform at Wittenberg, Philip Melanchthon, enjoyed a great reputation as a Christian humanist, yet dismissed the peasants with the words "the ass *will* have blows and the people *will* be ruled by force."

In June 1524, a massive revolt broke out near the Swiss frontier and swept into the Rhineland, Swabia, Franconia, and Saxony. As many townspeople as farm laborers participated. Urban proletariat and agricultural laborers poured their grievances into the *Twelve Articles,* published in 1525. The peasants wanted complete abolition of serfdom, an end to oppressive taxes and tithes, reform of the clergy, confiscation of church property, and such basic privileges as the right to cut wood in the lords' forests. The slogans of the crowds that swept across Germany came directly from Luther's writings. "God's righteousness" and "the Word of God" were invoked in the effort to secure social and economic justice.[8]

The poor who expected Luther's support

THE PEASANTS' REVOLT   The peasants were attracted to Luther's faith because it seemed to give religious support to their economic grievances. Carrying the banner of the Peasants' League and armed with pitchforks and axes, a group of peasants surround a knight. (Photo: Caroline Buckler)

were soon disillusioned. Background, education, and monastic observance all inclined him toward obedience to political authority and respect for social superiors. Luther had written of the "freedom" of the Christian, but he had meant the freedom to obey the Word of God, for in sin men and women lose their freedom and break their relationship with God. Freedom for Luther meant independence from the authority of the Roman church; it did *not* mean opposition to legally established secular powers. Accordingly he tossed off a tract, *Against the Murderous, Thieving Hordes of the Peasants,* calling upon the nobility to put down the unlawful revolt. The German nobility crushed it with ferocity. Historians have estimated that as many as a hundred thousand peasants were slaughtered.

Luther took literally these words of Saint Paul's letter to the Romans: "Let every soul be subject to the higher powers. For there is no power but of God: the powers that be are established by God. Whosoever resists the power, resists the ordinance of God: and they that resist shall receive to themselves damnation."[9] As it developed, Lutheran theology exalted the state, subordinated the church to the state, and everywhere championed "the powers that be." The consequences for German society were profound and have redounded into the twentieth century. After the revolt, the condition of the working classes worsened, and their religion taught complete obedience to divinely appointed authority, the state.

Scholars in many disciplines have attributed Luther's fame and success to the new invention of the printing press, which rapidly reproduced and made known his ideas. Equally important is Luther's incredible skill with language. Some thinkers have lavished praise on the Wittenberg reformer; others have bitterly condemned him. But, in the words of psychologist Erik Erikson:

The one matter on which professor and priest, psychiatrist and sociologist, agree is Luther's immense gift for language: his receptivity for the written word; his memory for the significant phrase; and his range of verbal expression (lyrical, biblical, satirical, and vulgar) which in English is paralleled only by Shakespeare.[10]

Language proved to be the weapon with which this peasant's son changed the world.

Educated people and humanists, like the peasants, were much attracted by Luther's words. He advocated a simpler, personalized religion based on faith, a return to the spirit of the early church, the centrality of the Scriptures in the liturgy and in the Christian life, the abolition of elaborate ceremonial — precisely the reforms the northern Christian humanists had been calling for. Ulrich Zwingli (1483–1531), for example, a humanist of Zurich, was strongly influenced by Luther's writings; they stimulated Zwingli's reforms in that Swiss city. The nobleman Ulrich von Hutton (1488–1523), who had published several humanistic tracts, in 1519 dedicated his life to the advancement of Luther's reformation. And as we shall see, the Frenchman John Calvin (1509–1564), often called the organizer of Protestantism, owed a great deal to Luther's thought.

The publication of Luther's German translation of the New Testament in 1523 democratized religion. His insistence that everyone should read and reflect upon the Scriptures attracted the literate and thoughtful middle classes partly because Luther appealed to their intelligence. Moreover, the business classes, preoccupied with making money, envied the church's wealth, disapproved of the luxurious lifestyle of some churchmen, and resented tithes and ecclesiastical taxation. Luther's doctrines of salvation by faith and the priesthood of all believers not only raised the religious status of the commercial classes but protected their pocketbooks as well.

Martin Luther's attitude toward women became the standard for German and Protestant women for centuries. Luther believed that marriage was a woman's career. A student recorded Luther as saying, early in his public ministry, "Let them bear children until they are dead of it; that is what they are for." A happy marriage to the ex-nun Katharine von Bora mellowed him, and another student later quoted him as saying, "Next to God's Word there is no more precious treasure than holy matrimony. God's highest gift on earth is a pious, cheerful, God-fearing, home-keeping wife, with whom you may live peacefully, to whom you may entrust your goods, and body and life."[11] Although Luther deeply loved his "dear Katie," he believed that women's concerns revolved exclusively around the children, the kitchen, and the church. A happy woman was a patient wife, an efficient manager, and a good mother.

Luther's viewpoint reflected contemporary values: German women were no more oppressed than Italian, Spanish, or even French ones. But few men considered women intelligent enough to handle a profession outside the home.

GERMANY AND THE PROTESTANT REFORMATION

The history of the Holy Roman Empire in the later Middle Ages is a story of dissension, disintegration, and debility. Unlike Spain, France, and England, the empire lacked a strong central power. The Golden Bull of 1356 created government by an aristocratic federation. Each of seven electors – the archbishops of Mainz, Trier, and Cologne, the margrave of Brandenburg, the duke of Saxony, the count palatine of the Rhine, and the king of Bohemia – gained virtual sovereignty in his own territory. The agreement ended disputed elections in the empire; it also reduced the central authority of the emperor. Thereafter, Germany was characterized by weak borders, localism, and chronic disorder. The nobility strengthened their territories, while imperial power declined.

Against this background of decentralization and strong local power, Martin Luther had launched a movement to reform the church. Two years after Luther posted the Ninety-Five Theses, the electors chose as emperor a nineteen-year-old Habsburg prince, who ruled as Charles V. How did the goals and interests of the emperor influence the course of the Reformation in Germany? What impact did the upheaval in the Christian church have on the political condition in Germany?

THE RISE OF THE HABSBURG DYNASTY

The marriage in 1477 of Maximilian I of the house of Habsburg and Mary of Burgundy was a decisive event in early modern European history. Through this union with the rich and powerful duchy of Burgundy, the Austrian house of Habsburg became the strongest ruling family within the empire. Its fortunes became permanently linked to those of the empire.

In the fifteenth and sixteenth centuries, as in the Middle Ages, relations among states continued to be greatly affected by the connections of royal families. Marriage often determined the diplomatic status of states. The Habsburg-Burgundian marriage angered the French, who considered Burgundy part of French territory. Louis XI of France repeatedly ravaged parts of the Burgundian Netherlands until he was able to force Maximilian to accept French terms: the Treaty of Arras (1482) emphatically declared Burgundy a part of the kingdom of France. The Habsburgs, however, never really renounced their claim to Burgundy, and intermittent warfare over it continued between France and Maximilian. Within the empire, German principalities that resented Austria's pre-eminence began to see that they shared interests with France. The marriage of Maximilian and Mary was to inaugurate two centuries of conflict between the Austrian house of Habsburg and the Valois kings of France. And Germany was to be the chief arena of the struggle.

"Other nations wage war; you, Austria, marry." Historians dispute the origins of the adage, but no one questions its accuracy. The heir of Mary and Maximilian, Philip of Burgundy, married Joanna of Castile, daughter of Ferdinand and Isabella of Spain. Philip and Joanna's son Charles V (1500–1558) fell heir to a vast conglomeration of territories. Through a series of accidents and unexpected deaths, Charles inherited Spain from his mother, together with her possessions in the New World and the Spanish dominions in

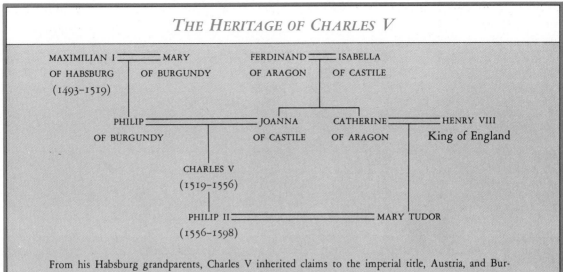

THE HERITAGE OF CHARLES V

MAXIMILIAN I — MARY	FERDINAND — ISABELLA
OF HABSBURG OF BURGUNDY	OF ARAGON OF CASTILE
(1493–1519)	

PHILIP ═══════════════ JOANNA   CATHERINE ═══════════ HENRY VIII
OF BURGUNDY   OF CASTILE   OF ARAGON   King of England

CHARLES V
(1519–1556)

PHILIP II ═══════════════════════════ MARY TUDOR
(1556–1598)

From his Habsburg grandparents, Charles V inherited claims to the imperial title, Austria, and Burgundy; through his mother, Charles acquired Spain, the Spanish territories in Italy, and the vast uncharted Spanish possessions in the New World.

Italy, Sicily, Sardinia, and Naples. From his father he inherited the Habsburg lands in Austria, southern Germany, the Low Countries, and Franche-Comté in east central France.

Charles's inheritance was an incredibly diverse collection of states and peoples, each governed in a different manner and held together only by the person of the emperor. Charles's Italian adviser, the grand chancellor Gattinara, told the young ruler: "God has set you on the path towards world monarchy." Charles not only believed this; he was convinced that it was his duty to maintain the political and religious unity of Western Christendom. In this respect Charles V was the last medieval emperor.

Charles needed and in 1519 secured the imperial title. Forward-thinking Germans proposed governmental reforms. They urged placing the administration in the hands of an imperial council whose president, the emperor's appointee, would have ultimate executive power. Reforms of the imperial finances, the army, and the judiciary were also recommended. Such ideas did not interest the young emperor at all. When he finally arrived in Germany from Spain and opened his first diet at Worms in January 1521, he naively announced that "the empire from of old has had not many masters, but one, and it is our intention to be that one." Charles went on to say that he was to be treated as of greater account than his predecessors because he was more powerful than they had been. In view of the long history of aristocratic power, Charles's notions were pure fantasy.

Charles continued the Burgundian policy of his grandfather Maximilian. That is, German revenues and German troops were subordinated to the needs of other parts of the empire, first Burgundy and then Spain. Habs-

EMPEROR CHARLES V Sometimes called a second Charlemagne, Charles V unsuccessfully tried to unite millions of people divided by geography, custom, language, and centuries of historical development under his family rule. The full beard partially conceals the long jutting jaw, a Habsburg family trait. (Photo: Caroline Buckler)

burg international interests came before the need for reform in Germany.

THE POLITICAL IMPACT OF LUTHER'S BELIEFS

In the sixteenth century, the practice of religion remained a public matter. Everyone participated in the religious life of the community, just as almost everyone shared in the local agricultural work. Whatever spiritual convictions individuals held in the privacy of their consciences, the emperor, king, prince, magistrate, or other civil authority determined the official form of religious practice within his jurisdiction. Religion had too many social implications to be left to individual judgment. Almost everyone believed that the presence of a faith different from that of the majority represented a political threat to the security of the state. Only a tiny minority, and certainly none of the princes, believed in religious liberty.

Against this background, the religious storm launched by Martin Luther swept across northern and central Germany. Several elements in his religious reformation stirred patriotic feelings. Anti-Roman sentiment ran high. Humanists lent eloquent intellectual support. And Luther's translation of the New Testament into German evoked national pride. Lutheranism contributed to the development of German nationalism.

For decades devout laymen and churchmen had called on the German princes to reform the church. In 1520, Luther took up the cry in his *Appeal to the Christian Nobility of the German Nation.* Unless the princes destroyed papal power in Germany, Luther argued, reform was impossible. He urged the princes to confiscate ecclesiastical wealth and to abolish indulgences, dispensations, pardons, and clerical celibacy. He told them that it was their public duty to bring about the moral reform of the church. Luther based his argument in part on the papacy's financial exploitation of Germany:

Now that Italy is sucked dry, they come into Germany, and begin, oh so gently. But let us beware, or Germany will soon become like Italy. Already we have some cardinals; what the Romans seek by that the "drunken Germans" are not to understand until we have not a bishopric, a monastery, a living, a benefice, a mite or a penny left. . . . They skim the cream off the bishoprics, monasteries, and benefices, and because they do not yet venture to turn them all to shameful use, as they have done in Italy, they only practice for the present the sa-

cred trickery of coupling together ten or twenty prelacies and taking a yearly portion from each of them so as to make a tidy sum after all. The priory of Würzburg yields a thousand gulden; that of Bamberg, something; Mainz, Trier, and the others, something more; and so . . . that a cardinal might live at Rome like a rich king.

How comes it that we Germans must put up with such robbery and such extortion of our property at the hands of the pope? If the Kingdom of France has prevented it, why do we Germans let them make such fools and apes of us? It would all be more bearable if in this way they only stole our property; but they lay waste the churches and rob Christ's sheep of their pious shepherds, and destroy the worship and the Word of God. Even if there were not a single cardinal, the Church would not go under. As it is they do nothing for the good of Christendom; they only wrangle about the incomes of bishoprics and prelacies, and that any robber could do. . . .

Since we here come to the heart of the matter, we will pause a little, and let it be seen that the Germans are not quite such gross fools as not to note or understand the sharp practices of the Romans. I do not now complain that at Rome God's command and Christian law are despised; for such is the state of Christendom, and particularly of Rome, that we may not now complain of such high matters. Nor do I complain that natural or temporal law and reason count for nothing. The case is worse even than that. I complain that they do not keep their own self-devised canon law, though it is, to be sure, mere tyranny, avarice, and temporal splendor, rather than law. . . .[12]

These words fell on welcome ears and itchy fingers. Luther's appeal to German patriotism gained him strong support, and national feeling influenced many princes otherwise confused by or indifferent to the complexities of the religious issues.

The church in Germany possessed great

wealth. And, unlike other countries, Germany had no strong central government to check the flow of gold to Rome. Rejection of Roman Catholicism and adoption of Protestantism would mean the legal confiscation of lush farmlands, rich monasteries, and wealthy shrines. Some German princes, such as the prince-archbishop of Cologne, Hermann von Wied, were sincerely attracted to Lutheranism, but many civil authorities realized that they had a great deal to gain by embracing the new faith. A steady stream of duchies, margraviates, free cities, and bishoprics secularized church property, accepted Lutheran theological doctrines, and adopted simpler services conducted in German. The decision reached at Worms in 1521 to condemn Luther and his teaching was not enforced because the German princes did not want to enforce it.

Charles V was a vigorous defender of Catholicism, and contemporary social and political theory denied the possibility of two religions coexisting peacefully in one territory. Thus, many princes used the religious issue to extend their financial and political independence. When doctrinal differences became linked to political ambitions and financial receipts, the results proved unfortunate for the improvement of German government. The Protestant movement ultimately proved a political disaster for Germany.

Charles V must share blame with the German princes for the disintegration of imperial authority in the empire. He neither understood nor took an interest in the constitutional problems of Germany, and he lacked the material resources to oppose Protestantism effectively there. Throughout his reign he was preoccupied with his Flemish, Spanish, Italian, and American territories.

Five times between 1521 and 1555, Charles V went to war with the Valois kings of France. The issue each time was the Habsburg lands acquired by the marriage of Maximilian and Mary of Burgundy. Much of the fighting occurred in Germany. The cornerstone of French foreign policy in the sixteenth and seventeenth centuries was the desire to keep the German states divided. Thus Europe witnessed the paradox of the Catholic king of France supporting the Lutheran princes in their challenge to his fellow Catholic, Charles V. French policy was successful. The long dynastic struggle commonly called the Habsburg-Valois wars advanced the cause of Protestantism and promoted the political fragmentation of the German empire.

Charles's efforts to crush the Lutheran states were unsuccessful. Finally in 1555 he agreed to the Peace of Augsburg, which, in accepting the status quo, officially recognized Protestantism. Each prince was permitted to determine the religion of his territory. Most of northern and central Germany became Lutheran, while the south remained Roman Catholic. There was no freedom of religion, however. Princes or town councils established state churches to which all subjects of the area had to belong. Dissidents, whether Lutheran or Catholic, had to convert or leave. The political difficulties Germany inherited from the Middle Ages had been compounded by the religious crisis of the sixteenth century.

THE GROWTH OF THE PROTESTANT REFORMATION

The printing press publicized Luther's defiance of the Roman church and spread his theological ideas all over Europe. Working people discovered in Luther's ideas the economic theories they wanted to find. Christian humanists believed initially that Luther supported their own educational and intellectual goals. Princes steadily read in Luther's theories an expansion of state power and authority. What began as one man's religious search in a small corner of Germany soon became associated with many groups' interests and aspirations.

By 1555, much of northern Europe had broken with the Roman Catholic church. All of Scandinavia, England, Scotland, and such self-governing cities as Geneva and Zurich in Switzerland and Strasbourg in eastern France had rejected the religious authority of Rome and adopted new faiths. In that a common religious faith had been the one element uniting all of Europe for almost a thousand years, the fragmentation of belief led to profound changes in European life and society. The most significant new form of Protestantism was Calvinism, of which the Peace of Augsburg had made no mention at all.

JOHN CALVIN *The lean, ascetic face with the strong jaw reflects the iron will and determination of the organizer of Protestantism. The fur collar represents his training in law. (Photo: Caroline Buckler)*

CALVINISM

In 1509, while Luther was studying for the doctorate at Wittenberg, John Calvin (1509–1564) was born in Noyon in northwestern France. Luther inadvertently launched the Protestant Reformation. Calvin, however, had the greater impact on future generations. His theological writings profoundly influenced the social thought and attitudes of Europeans and English-speaking peoples all over the world, especially in Canada and the United States. Although he had originally intended to have an ecclesiastical career, Calvin studied law, which had a decisive impact on his mind and later thought. In 1533, he experienced a religious crisis, as a result of which he converted to Protestantism.

Calvin believed that God had delegated him to reform the church. Accordingly, he accepted an invitation to assist in the reformation of the Swiss city of Geneva. There, beginning in 1541, Calvin established a theocracy, which was, according to contemporary theory, a society ruled by God through reformed ministers and civil magistrates. Geneva, "a city that was a Church," became the model of a Christian community for sixteenth-century Protestant reformers.

To understand Calvin's Geneva, it is necessary to understand Calvin's ideas. These he embodied in *The Institutes of the Christian Re-*

ligion, first published in 1536 and definitively issued in 1559. The cornerstone of Calvin's theology was his belief in the absolute sovereignty and omnipotence of God and the total weakness of humanity. Before the infinite power of God, he asserted, men and women are as insignificant as grains of sand:

Our souls are but faint flickerings over against the infinite brilliance which is God. We are created, he is without beginning. We are subject to ignorance and shame. God in his infinite majesty is the summation of all virtues. Whenever we think of him we should be ravished with adoration and astonishment. . . . The chief end of man is to enjoy the fellowship of God and the chief duty of man is to glorify God. . . .[13]

Predestination

Calvin did not grant free will to human beings, because that would detract from the sovereignty of God. Men and women cannot actively work to achieve salvation; rather, God in his infinite wisdom decided at the beginning of time who would be saved and who damned. This viewpoint constitutes the theological principle called predestination:

Predestination we call the eternal decree of God, by which he has determined in himself, what he would have become of every individual of mankind. For they are not all created with a similar destiny; but eternal life is foreordained for some, and eternal damnation for others. . . .

In conformity, therefore, to the clear doctrine of the Scripture, we assert, that by an eternal and immutable counsel, God has once for all determined, both whom he would admit to salvation, and whom he would condemn to destruction. We affirm that this counsel, as far as concerns the elect, is founded on his gratuitous mercy, totally irrespective of human merit; but that to those whom he devotes to condemnation, the gate of life

is closed by a just and irreprehensible, but incomprehensible, judgment.

How exceedingly presumptuous it is only to inquire into the causes of the Divine will; which is in fact, and is justly entitled to be, the cause of everything that exists. . . . For the will of God is the highest justice; so that what he wills must be considered just, for this very reason, because he wills it.[14]

Many people have found this a pessimistic view of the nature of God, who revealed himself in the Old and New Testaments as merciful as well as just. Calvin's response was that although individuals cannot know whether they will be saved — and the probability is that they will be damned — still, good works are a "sign" of election. In any case, people should concentrate on worshiping God and doing his work and not waste time worrying about salvation.

While Luther subordinated the church to the state, Calvin made the state subordinate to the church, and he succeeded in arousing Genevans to a high standard of public and private behavior. For Calvin, God was perpetually active, vigilant, and busy, and he selected certain individuals to do his work. Calvin, convinced that he was one of those individuals, worked tirelessly to transform Geneva into the perfect Christian community. Those who denied predestination were banished.

Austere living, religious instruction for all, public fasting, and evening curfew became the order of the day. Dancing, card playing, fashionable clothes, and heavy drinking were absolutely prohibited. The ministers investigated the private morals of citizens but were unwilling to punish the town prostitutes as severely as Calvin would have preferred.

Calvin reserved his harshest condemnation for religious dissenters. He declared:

If anybody slanders a mortal man he is punished and shall we permit a blasphemer of the living God to go unscathed? If a prince is injured, death appears to be insufficient for vengeance. And now when God, the sovereign Emperor, is reviled by a word, is nothing to be done? God's glory and our salvation are so conjoined that a traitor to God is also an enemy to the human race and worse than a murderer because he brings souls to perdition. Some object that since the offense consists only in words, there is no need for severity. But we muzzle dogs, and shall we leave men free to open their mouths as they please? Those who object are dogs and swine. They murmur that they will go to America where nobody will bother them.

God makes plain that the false prophet is to be stoned without mercy. We are to crush beneath our heel all affections of nature when His honor is concerned. The father should not spare his child, nor brother his brother, nor husband his own wife or the friend who is dearer to him than life. No human relationship is more than animal unless it be grounded in God[15]

Calvin translated his words into action. In the 1550s, the Spanish humanist Michael Servetus had gained international notoriety for his publications denying the Christian dogma of the Trinity, which holds that God is three divine persons, Father, Son, and Holy Spirit. Servetus had been arrested by the Spanish Inquisition, but escaped to Geneva, where he hoped for support. He was promptly rearrested. At his trial he not only held to his belief that there is no scriptural basis for the Trinity but rejected child baptism and insisted that a person under twenty cannot commit a mortal sin. The city fathers considered this last idea dangerous to public morality, "especially in these days when the young are so corrupted." Although Servetus begged that he be punished by banishment, Calvin and the

town council maintained that the denial of child baptism and the Trinity amounted to a threat to all society. Whispering "Jesus, Son of the eternal God, have pity on me," Servetus was burned at the stake.

To many sixteenth-century Europeans, Calvin's Geneva seemed "the most perfect school of Christ since the days of the Apostles." Religious refugees from France, England, Spain, Scotland, and Italy poured into the city. Subsequently, Calvin's church served as the model for the Presbyterian church in Scotland, the Huguenot church in France, and Puritan churches in England and New England.

Calvinism became the compelling force in international Protestantism. The Calvinist ethic of the "calling" dignified all work with a religious aspect. Hard work, well done, was pleasing to God. This doctrine encouraged an aggressive, vigorous social activism. In the *Institutes* Calvin provided a systematic theology for Protestantism. The reformed church of Calvin had a strong and well-organized machinery of government. These factors, together with the social and economic applications of Calvin's theology, made Calvinism the most dynamic force in sixteenth- and seventeenth-century Protestantism.

THE ANABAPTISTS

The name *Anabaptist* derives from a Greek word meaning "to baptize again." The Anabaptists, sometimes described as "the left wing of the Reformation," believed that only adults could make a free choice about religious faith, baptism, and entry into the Christian community. Thus they considered the practice of baptizing infants and children preposterous and claimed there was no scriptural basis for it. They wanted to rebaptize believers who had been baptized as children.

Anabaptists took the Gospel and, at first, Luther's teachings absolutely literally and favored a return to the kind of church that had existed among the earliest Christians – a voluntary association of believers who had experienced an inner light.

Anabaptists maintained that only a few people would receive the inner light. This position meant that the Christian community and the Christian state were not identical. In other words, Anabaptists believed in the separation of church and state and in religious tolerance. They almost never tried to force their values on others. In an age that believed in the necessity of state-established churches, Anabaptist views on religious liberty were far ahead of their time.

Each Anabaptist community or church was entirely independent; it selected its own ministers and ran its own affairs. In 1534 the community at Münster in Germany, for example, established a legal code that decreed the death penalty for insubordinate wives. Moreover, the Münster community also practiced polygamy and forced all women under a certain age to marry or face expulsion or execution.

Anabaptist attitudes toward women were sexist and discriminatory, although Anabaptists admitted women to the priesthood. They shared goods as the early Christians had done, refused all public offices, and would not serve in the armed forces. In fact, they laid great stress on pacifism. A favorite Anabaptist scriptural quotation was "By their fruits you shall know them," meaning that if Christianity was a religion of peace, the Christian should not fight. Good deeds were the sign of Christian faith, and to be a Christian meant to imitate the meekness and mercy of Christ. With such beliefs Anabaptists were inevitably a minority. Anabaptism attracted the poor,

the unemployed, the uneducated. Geographically, Anabaptists drew their members from depressed urban areas – from among the followers of Zwingli in Zurich, and from Basel, Augsburg, and Nuremberg.

Ideas such as absolute pacifism and the distinction between the Christian community and the state brought down upon these unfortunate people fanatical hatred and bitter persecution. Zwingli, Luther, Calvin, and Catholics all saw – quite correctly – the separation of church and state as leading ultimately to the complete secularization of society. The powerful rulers of Swiss and German society immediately saw the connection between religious heresy and economic dislocation. Civil authorities feared that the combination of religious differences and economic grievances would lead to civil disturbances. In Saxony, in Strasbourg, and in the Swiss cities, Anabaptists were either banished or cruelly executed by burning, beating, or drowning. Their ideas, however, survived.

Later, the Quakers with their gentle pacifism; the Baptists with their emphasis on an inner spiritual light, the Congregationalists with their democratic church organization; and, in 1789, the authors of the United States Constitution with their concern for the separation of church and state – all these trace their origins in part to the Anabaptists of the sixteenth century.

THE ENGLISH REFORMATION

As on the Continent, the Reformation in England had social and economic causes as well as religious ones. As elsewhere, too, Christian humanists had for decades been calling for the purification of the church. When the political matter of the divorce of King Henry VIII (1509-1547) became enmeshed with other issues, a complete break with Rome resulted.

Demands for ecclesiastical reform dated back to the fourteenth century. The Lollards (pages 409–410) had been driven underground in the fifteenth century, but survived in parts of London, East Anglia, west Kent, and southern England. Working-class people, especially cloth workers, were attracted to their ideas. The Lollards stressed the individual's reading and interpretation of the Bible, which they considered the only standard of Christian faith and holiness. Consequently, they put no stock in the value of the sacraments and were vigorously anticlerical. Lollards opposed ecclesiastical wealth, the veneration of the saints, prayers for the dead, and all war. Although they had no notion of justification by faith, like Luther they insisted upon the individual soul's direct responsibility to God.

The work of the English humanist William Tyndale (ca 1494–1536) stimulated cries for reform. Tyndale visited Luther at Wittenberg in 1524, and a year later at Antwerp he began printing an English translation of the New Testament. From Antwerp merchants carried the New Testament into England, where it was distributed by Lollards. Fortified with copies of Tyndale's English Bible and some of Luther's ideas, the Lollards represented the ideal of "a personal, scriptural, non-sacramental, and lay-dominated religion."[16] Thus, in this manner, doctrines that would later be called Protestant flourished underground in England before any official or state-approved changes.

In the early sixteenth century the ignorance of much of the parish clergy, and the sexual misbehavior of some, compared unfavorably with the education and piety of lay people. In 1510 Dr. William Melton, an official of York Cathedral, exhorted the newly ordained priests of the diocese:

. . . from this darkness of ignorance . . . arises that great and deplorable evil throughout the whole Church of God, that everywhere throughout town and countryside there exists a crop of oafish and boorish priests, some of whom are engaged in ignoble and servile tasks, while others abandon themselves to tavern haunting, swilling and drunkenness. Some cannot get along without their wenches; others pursue their amusement in dice and gambling and other such trifling all day long. . . . This is inevitable, for since they are completely ignorant of good literature, how can they obtain improvement or enjoyment in reading and study. Nay rather, they throw aside their books in contempt and everywhere they return to the wretched and unlovely life I have mentioned. . . . We must avoid and keep far from ourselves that grasping, deadly plague of avarice for which practically every priest is accused and held in disrepute before the people, when it is said that we are greedy for rich promotions, or harsh and grasping in retaining and amassing money. . . .[17]

Even more than the ignorance and lechery of the lower clergy, the wealth of the English church fostered resentment and anticlericalism. The church controlled perhaps 20 percent of the land, and also received an annual tithe of the produce of lay people's estates. Since the church had jurisdiction over wills, the clergy also received mortuary fees, revenues paid by the deceased's relatives. Mortuary fees led to frequent lawsuits, since the common lawyers nursed a deep jealousy of the ecclesiastical courts.

The career of Thomas Wolsey (1474?–1530) provides an extreme example of pluralism in the English church in the early sixteenth century. The son of a butcher, Wolsey became a priest and in 1507 secured an

HENRY VIII'S "VICTORY" *This cartoon shows Henry VIII, assisted by Cromwell and Cranmer, triumphing over Pope Clement VII. Although completely removed from the historical facts, such illustrations were effectively used to promote antipapal feeling in late sixteenth-century England. (Photo: Caroline Buckler)*

appointment as chaplain to Henry VII. In 1509 Henry VIII made Wolsey a privy councillor, where his remarkable ability and energy won him rapid advancement. In 1515 he became a cardinal and lord chancellor, and in 1518 papal legate. As chancellor, Wolsey dominated domestic and foreign policy, prosecuted the rich in the royal courts, and attacked the nobility in Parliament. As papal legate he ruled the English church, with final authority in all matters relating to marriage, wills, the clergy, and ecclesiastical appointments. Wolsey had more power than any previous royal minister, and he used that power to amass a large number of church offices, including the archbishopric of York, the rich bishoprics of Winchester and Lincoln, and the abbacy of St. Albans. He displayed the vast wealth these positions brought him with ostentation and arrogance, which in turn fanned the embers of anticlericalism. The divorce of Henry VIII ignited all these glowing coals.

Having fallen in love with Anne Boleyn, sister of his cast-off mistress Mary Boleyn, Henry wanted to divorce his wife Catherine of Aragon. Legal, diplomatic, and theological problems stood in his way, however. Catherine had first been married to Henry's brother Arthur. Contemporaries doubted that Arthur's union with Catherine had been consumated during the short time Arthur lived, and theologians therefore believed that no true marriage existed between them. When Henry married Catherine in 1509, he boasted that she was a virgin. According to custom, and in order to eliminate all doubts and legal technicalities about Catherine's marriage to Arthur, Henry secured a dispensation from Pope Julius II. For eighteen years Catherine and Henry lived together in what contemporaries thought a happy marriage. Catherine produced six children, but only the princess Mary survived childhood.

Precisely when Henry lost interest in his wife as a woman is unknown, but around 1527 he began to quote from a passage in the Old Testament Book of Leviticus: "You must not uncover the nakedness of your brother's wife; for it is your brother's nakedness. . . . The man who takes to wife the wife of his brother: that is impurity; he has uncovered his brother's nakedness, and they shall be childless."[18] Henry insisted that God was denying him a male heir to punish him for marrying his brother's widow. Henry claimed that he wanted to spare England the dangers of a disputed succession. The anarchy and disorders of the Wars of the Roses would surely be repeated if a woman, the princess Mary, inherited the throne. Although Henry contended that the succession was the paramount issue in his mind, his behavior suggests otherwise.

Henry went about the business of insuring a peaceful succession in a most extraordinary manner. He petitioned Pope Clement VII for an annulment of his marriage to Catherine. Henry wanted the pope to declare that a legal marriage with Catherine had never existed, in which case Princess Mary was illegitimate and thus ineligible to succeed to the throne. The pope was an indecisive man whose attention at the time was focused on the Lutheran revolt in Germany and the Habsburg-Valois struggle for control of Italy. Clement delayed acting on Henry's request. The capture and sack of Rome in 1527 by the emperor Charles V, Queen Catherine's nephew, thoroughly tied the pope's hands. Charles could hardly allow the pope to grant the annulment, thereby acknowledging that Charles's aunt, the queen of England, was a loose woman who had lived in sin with Henry VIII.

Accordingly, Henry determined to get his divorce in England. The convenient death of the archbishop of Canterbury allowed Henry to appoint a new archbishop, Thomas Cranmer (1489-1556). Cranmer heard the case in his archiepiscopal court, granted the annulment, and thereby paved the way for Henry's marriage to Anne Boleyn. English public opinion was against this marriage and strongly favored Queen Catherine as a woman much wronged. By rejecting Catherine, Henry ran serious political risks, and all for a woman whom contemporaries found neither very intelligent nor very attractive. The only distinguishing feature they noticed was a sixth finger on her right hand. The marriage between Henry and Anne was publicly announced on May 28, 1533. In September the princess Elizabeth was born.

Since Rome had refused to support Henry's matrimonial plans, he decided to remove the English church from papal jurisdiction. Henry used Parliament to legalize the Reformation in England. The Act in Restraint of Appeals (1533) declared that:

Where, by divers sundry old authentic histories and chronicles, it is manifestly declared and expressed that this realm of England is an empire, and so hath been accepted in the world, governed by one supreme head and king having the dignity and royal estate of the imperial crown of the same (he being also institute and furnished by the goodness and sufferance of Almighty God with plenary, whole, and entire power, pre-eminence, authority, prerogative, and jurisdiction to render and yield justice and final determination to all manner of folk residents or subjects within this his realm, in all causes, matters, debates, and contentions happening to occur, insurge, or begin within the limits thereof, without restraint or provocation to any foreign princes or potentates of the world. . . .).[19]

The act went on to forbid all judicial appeals to the papacy, thus establishing the Crown as the highest legal authority in the land. In effect, the Act in Restraint of Appeals placed sovereign power in the king. The Act for the Submission of the Clergy (1534) required churchmen to submit to the king and forbade the publication of all ecclesiastical laws without royal permission. The Supremacy Act of 1534 declared the king the supreme head of the Church of England.

Englishmen had long criticized ecclesiastical abuses. Sentiment for reform was strong, and a minority of people held distinctly Protestant doctrinal views. Still, it is difficult to gauge the degree of popular support for Henry's break with Rome. Scholars have pointed out that the king had to bribe, threaten, and intimidate the House of Commons to get his legislation passed. Some opposed the king. John Fisher, the bishop of Rochester, a distinguished scholar and humanist who had preached the oration at the funeral of Henry VII, lashed the clergy with scorn for their cowardice. Another humanist, Thomas More, resigned the chancellorship to protest the passage of the Act for the Submission of the Clergy and would not take an oath recognizing Anne's heir. Fisher, More, and other dissenters were beheaded.

When Anne Boleyn failed in her second attempt to produce a male child, Henry VIII charged her with adulterous incest and in 1536 had her beheaded. Parliament promptly proclaimed the princess Elizabeth illegitimate and, with the royal succession thoroughly confused, left the throne to whomever Henry chose. His third wife, Jane Seymour, gave Henry the desired son, Edward, and then died in childbirth. Henry went on to three more wives. Before he passed to his reward in 1547, he got Parliament to reverse the decision of 1536, relegitimating Mary and Elizabeth and fixing the succession first in his son and then in his daughters.

Between 1535 and 1539, under the influence of his chief minister, Thomas Cromwell, Henry decided to dissolve the English monasteries because, he charged, they were economically mismanaged and morally corrupt. Actually, he wanted their wealth. Justices of the peace and other local officials who visited religious houses throughout the land found the contrary. Ignoring their reports, the king ended nine hundred years of English monastic life, dispersed the monks and nuns, and confiscated their lands. Hundreds of properties were later sold to the middle and upper classes and the proceeds spent on war. The dissolution of the monasteries did not achieve a more equitable distribution of land and wealth or advance the cause of social justice. Rather, the "bare ruined choirs where late the

HOLBEIN: SIR THOMAS MORE *This powerful portrait (1527), revealing More's strong character and humane sensitivity, shows Holbein's complete mastery of detail—down to the stubble on More's chin. The chain was an emblem of More's service to Henry VIII. (© The Frick Collection, New York)*

sweet birds sang" – as Shakespeare described the desolate religious houses – testified to the loss of a valuable esthetic and cultural force in English life.

The English Reformation under Henry VIII was primarily a matter of political, social, and economic issues, rather than religious ones. In fact, the Henrician Reformation retained such traditional Catholic practices and doctrines as confession to a priest, clerical celibacy, and transubstantiation (the doctrine of the real presence of Christ in the bread and wine of the Eucharist). On the other hand, Protestant literature circulated, Protestant doctrines captured increasing numbers of people, and Henry approved the selection of men with known Protestant sympathies as tutors for his son. Until late in the century the religious situation remained fluid.

The nationalization of the church and the dissolution of the monasteries led to important changes in governmental administration. Vast tracts of land came temporarily under the Crown's jurisdiction, and new bureaucratic machinery had to be developed to manage those properties. New departments had to be coordinated with old ones. Medieval government had been household government: all branches of the state were associated with the person and personality of the monarch. In finances, for example, no distinction was made between the king's personal income and state revenues. Each branch of government was supported with funds from a specific source; if the source had a bad year, that agency suffered while other branches of government were well in the black. Massive confusion and overlapping of responsibilities existed.

Thomas Cromwell reformed and centralized the king's household, the council, the secretariats, and the Exchequer. New departments of state were set up. Surplus funds from all departments went into a liquid fund to be applied to areas where there were deficits. This balancing resulted in greater efficiency and economy. In Henry VIII's reign can be seen the growth of the modern centralized bureaucratic state.

For several decades after Henry's death in 1547, the English church shifted left and right. In the short reign of Henry's sickly son Edward VI (1547-1553), the strongly Protestant ideas of Archbishop Thomas Cranmer exerted a significant influence on the religious life of the country. Cranmer drastically simplified the liturgy, invited Protestant theologians to England, and prepared the first *Book of Common Prayer* (1549). In stately and dignified English, the *Book of Common Prayer* included, together with the Psalter, the order for all services of the Church of England.

The equally brief reign of Mary Tudor (1553-1558) witnessed a sharp move back to Catholicism. The devoutly Catholic daughter of Catherine of Aragon, Mary rescinded the Reformation legislation of her father's reign and fully restored Roman Catholicism. Mary's marriage to her cousin Philip of Spain, son of the emperor Charles V, proved highly unpopular in England, and her persecution and execution of several hundred Protestants further alienated her subjects. During her reign many Protestants fled to the Continent. Mary's death raised to the throne her sister Elizabeth (1558-1603) and inaugurated the beginnings of religious stability.

For a long time, Elizabeth's position as queen was insecure. Although the populace cheered her accession, many questioned her legitimacy. On the one hand, Catholics wanted a Roman Catholic ruler. On the other hand, a vocal number of returned English exiles wanted all Catholic elements in the Church of England destroyed. The latter, because they wanted to "purify" the church, were called Puritans.

Elizabeth had been raised a Protestant, but if she had genuine religious convictions she kept them to herself. Probably one of the shrewdest politicians in English history, Elizabeth chose a middle course between Catholic and Puritan extremes. She insisted upon dignity in church services and political order in the land. She did not care what people believed as long as they kept quiet about it. Avoiding precise doctrinal definitions, Elizabeth had herself styled "Supreme Governor of the Church of England, Etc.," and left it to her subjects to decide what the "Etc." meant.

The parliamentary legislation of the early years of Elizabeth's reign – laws sometimes labeled the "Elizabethan Settlement" – required outward conformity to the Church of England and uniformity in all ceremonies. Everyone had to attend Church of England services; those who refused were fined. In 1563, a convocation of bishops approved the Thirty-Nine Articles, a summary in thirty-nine short statements of the basic tenets of the Church of England. During Elizabeth's reign, the Anglican church (for the Latin *Ecclesia Anglicana*), as the Church of England was called, moved in a moderately Protestant direction. Services were conducted in English, monasteries were not re-established, and the clergy were allowed to marry. But the bishops remained as church officials, and apart from language, the services were quite traditional.

THE ESTABLISHMENT OF THE CHURCH OF SCOTLAND

Reform of the church in Scotland did not follow the English model. In the early sixteenth century, the church in Scotland presented an extreme case of clerical abuse and corruption, and Lutheranism initially attracted sympathetic support. In Scotland as elsewhere, political authority was the decisive influence in reform. The monarchy was very weak, and factions of virtually independent nobles competed for power. King James V and his daughter Mary, Queen of Scots (1560–1567), staunch Catholics and close allies of Catholic France, opposed reform. The Scottish nobles supported it. One man, John Knox (1505?–1572) dominated the movement for reform in Scotland.

In 1559, Knox, a dour, narrow-minded, and fearless man with a reputation as a passionate preacher, set to work reforming the church. He had studied and worked with Calvin in Geneva, and was determined to structure the Scottish church after the model of Calvin's Geneva. In 1560, Knox persuaded the Scottish parliament, which was dominated by reform-minded barons, to enact legislation ending papal authority. The mass was abolished and attendance at it forbidden under penalty of death. Knox then established the Presbyterian Church of Scotland, so named because presbyters, or ministers – not bishops – governed it. The Church of Scotland was strictly Calvinist in doctrine, adopted a simple and dignified service of worship, and laid great emphasis on preaching. Knox's *Book of Common Order* (1564) became the liturgical directory for the church. The Presbyterian Church of Scotland was a national, or state, church, and many of its members maintained close relations with English Puritans.

PROTESTANTISM IN IRELAND

To the ancient Irish hatred of English political and commercial exploitation, the Reformation added the bitter antagonism of religion. Henry VIII wanted to "reduce that realm to the knowledge of God and obedience to us." English rulers in the sixteenth century regarded the Irish as barbarians, and a policy of complete extermination was rejected only because "to enterprise [attempt] the whole extirpation and total destruction of all the Irishmen in the land would be a marvelous sumptious charge and great difficulty."[20] In other words, it would have cost too much.

In 1536, on orders from London, the Irish parliament, which represented only the English landlords and the people of the Pale (the area around Dublin), approved the English laws severing the church from Rome and making the English king sovereign over ecclesiastical organization and practice. The Church of Ireland was established on the English pattern, and the (English) ruling class adopted the new reformed faith. Most of the Irish, probably for political reasons, defiantly remained Roman Catholic. Monasteries were secularized. Catholic property was confiscated and sold, and the profits shipped to England. With the Roman church driven underground, the Catholic clergy acted as national as well as religious leaders.

LUTHERANISM IN SWEDEN, NORWAY, AND DENMARK

In Sweden, Norway, and Denmark the monarchy took the initiative in the religious reformation. The resulting institutions were Lutheran state churches. Since the late fourteenth century, the Danish kings had ruled Sweden and Norway as well as Denmark. In 1520, the Swedish nobleman Gustavus Vasa led a successful revolt against Denmark, and Sweden became independent. As king, Gustavus Vasa seized church lands and required the bishops' loyalty to the Swedish crown. The Wittenberg-educated Swedish reformer Olaus Petri (1493–1552) translated the New Testament into Swedish and, with the full support of Gustavus Vasa, organized the church along strict Lutheran lines. This consolidation of the Swedish monarchy in the

sixteenth century was to have a profound effect on Germany in the seventeenth century.

In Denmark, King Christian III (1534–1559) secularized church property and set up a Lutheran church. Norway, which was governed by Denmark until 1814, became Lutheran under Danish influence.

THE CATHOLIC AND THE COUNTER REFORMATIONS

Between 1517 and 1547, the reformed versions of Christianity known as Protestantism made remarkable advances. All of England, Scotland, Scandinavia, half of Germany, and sizable parts of France and Switzerland adopted the creeds of Luther, Calvin, and other reformers. Still, the Roman Catholic church made a significant comeback. After about 1540, no new large areas of Europe, except for the Netherlands, accepted Protestant beliefs (see Map. 14.1).

Historians distinguish between two types of reform within the Catholic church in the sixteenth and seventeenth centuries. The Catholic Reformation began before 1517 and sought renewal basically through the stimulation of a new spiritual fervor. The Counter Reformation started in the 1530s as a reaction to the rise and spread of Protestantism. The Counter Reformation involved Catholic efforts to convince dissidents or heretics to return to the church lest they corrupt the entire community of Catholic believers. Fear of the "infection" of all Christian society by the religious dissident was a standard sixteenth-

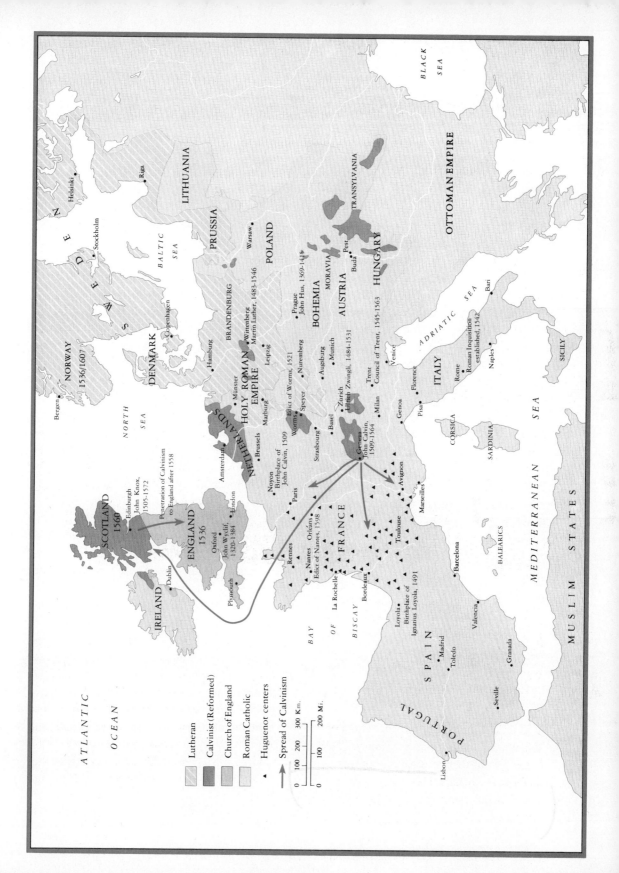

ATLANTIC
OCEAN

BLACK
SEA

OTTOMAN EMPIRE

NORWAY
1536/1607

SWEDEN

Helsinki

Bergen

Stockholm

Riga

LITHUANIA

PRUSSIA

Warsaw

POLAND

TRANSYLVANIA

BALTIC
SEA

DENMARK

Copenhagen

BRANDENBURG

Hamburg

Wittenberg
Martin Luther, 1483–1546

Leipzig

Prague

John Hus, 1369–1415

Pest

Buda

HUNGARY

Münster

HOLY ROMAN
EMPIRE

Nuremberg

BOHEMIA

MORAVIA

AUSTRIA

ADRIATIC
SEA

Bari

NORTH
SEA

Brussels

Marburg

Worms
Edict of Worms, 1521

Speyer

Augsburg

Munich

Trent
Council of Trent, 1545–1563

Venice

Roman Inquisition
established, 1542

Amsterdam

NETHERLANDS

Strasbourg

Basel

Zürich
Ulrich Zwingli, 1484–1531

Milan

Genoa

ITALY

Florence

Rome

SICILY

Naples

Noyon
Birthplace of
John Calvin, 1509

Paris

Geneva
John Calvin,
1509–1564

Avignon

Pisa

CORSICA

SARDINIA

MEDITERRANEAN
SEA

SCOTLAND
1560

Edinburgh
John Knox,
1505–1572

Penetration of Calvinism
to England after 1558

ENGLAND
1536

Oxford
John Wyclif,
1320–1384

London

Dublin

IRELAND

Plymouth

Rennes

Nantes
Edict of Nantes, 1598

Orléans

FRANCE

Toulouse

Marseilles

La Rochelle

Bordeaux

BAY   OF   BISCAY

Loyola
Birthplace of
Ignatius Loyola, 1491

Barcelona

BALEARICS

MUSLIM   STATES

SPAIN

Madrid

Toledo

Valencia

Granada

Seville

PORTUGAL

Lisbon

Lutheran

Calvinist (Reformed)

Church of England

Roman Catholic

▲ Huguenot centers

Spread of Calvinism

0   100   200   300 Km.

0   100   200 Mi.

century attitude. If the heretic could not be persuaded to reconvert, counter-reformers believed it necessary to call upon temporal authorities to defend Christian society by expelling or eliminating the dissident. The Catholic Reformation and the Counter Reformation were not mutually exclusive; in fact, after about 1540 they progressed simultaneously.

What factors influenced the attitudes and policies of the papacy? Why did church leaders wait so long before dealing with the issues of schism and reform? How did the Catholic church succeed in reforming itself and in stemming the tide of Protestantism?

THE SLOWNESS OF INSTITUTIONAL REFORM

The Renaissance princes who sat on the throne of Saint Peter were not blind to the evils that existed. Modest reform efforts had begun with the Lateran Council called in 1512 by Pope Julius II. The Dutch pope Adrian VI (1522–1523) had instructed his legate in Germany to

say that we frankly confess that God permits this [Lutheran] persecution of his church on account of the sins of men, especially those of the priests and prelates. . . . We know that in this Holy See now for some years there have been many abominations, abuses in spiritual things, excesses in things commanded, in short that all has become perverted. . . . We have all turned aside in our ways, nor was there, for a long time, any who did right — no, not one.[21]

Why did the popes, spiritual leaders of the Western church, move so slowly? The answers lie in the personalities of the popes themselves, their preoccupation with political affairs in Italy, and the awesome difficulty of

reforming so complicated a bureaucracy as the Roman curia.

Pope Leo X (1513–1521), who opened his pontificate with the words "Now that God has given us the papacy, let us enjoy it," typified the attitude of the Renaissance papacy. Leo concerned himself with artistic beauty and sensual pleasures. He first dismissed the Lutheran revolution as "a monkish quarrel," and by the time he finally acted with a letter condemning Luther, much of northern Germany had already rallied around the sincere Augustinian.

Adrian VI tried desperately to reform the church and to check the spread of Protestantism. His reign lasted only thirteen months, however, and the austerity of his life and his Dutch nationality provoked the hostility of pleasure-loving Italian curial bureaucrats.

Clement VII, a true Medicean, was far more interested in elegant tapestries and Michelangelo's painting of the Last Judgment than in theological disputes in barbaric Germany. Indecisive and vacillating, Pope Clement must bear much of the responsibility for the great spread of Protestantism. While Emperor Charles V and the French king Francis I competed for the domination of divided Italy, the papacy worried about the security of the Papal States. Clement tried to follow a middle course, backing first the emperor and then the French ruler. At the battle of Pavia in 1525, Francis I suffered a severe defeat and was captured. In a reshuffling of diplomatic alliances, the pope switched from Charles and the Spaniards to Francis I. The emperor was victorious once again, however, and in 1527 his Spanish and German mercenaries sacked and looted Rome and captured the pope. Obviously, papal concern about Italian affairs and the Papal States diverted attention from reform.

The idea of reform was closely linked to the idea of a general council representing the entire church. Early in the sixteenth century, Ferdinand of Spain appointed a committee of Spanish bishops to draft materials for conciliar reform of the church. In France, the University of Paris also pressed for a council. (French monarchs subsequently used this academic demand to support their military intervention in Italy.) The emperor Charles V, increasingly disturbed by the Lutheran threat, called for "a free Christian council in German lands." German Catholic bishops drew up lists of "oppressive disorders" that needed reform. A strong contingent of countries from beyond the Alps – from Spain, Germany, and France – wanted to reform the vast bureaucracy of Latin officials, reducing offices, men, and revenues.

Popes from Julius II to Clement VII, remembering fifteenth-century conciliar attempts to limit papal authority, resisted calls for a council. The papal bureaucrats who were the popes' intimates warned the popes against a council, fearing loss of power and prestige. Five centuries before, Saint Bernard of Clairvaux had anticipated the situation: "The most grievous danger of any Pope lies in the fact that, encompassed as he is by flatterers, he never hears the truth about his own person and ends by not wishing to hear it."[22]

THE COUNCIL OF TRENT

In the papal conclave that followed the death of Clement VII, Cardinal Alexander Farnese promised two German cardinals that if he were elected pope he would summon a council. He won the election and ruled as Pope Paul III (1534-1549). This Roman aristocrat, humanist, and astrologer, who immediately made his teenage grandsons cardinals, seemed an unlikely person to undertake serious reform. Yet Paul III appointed as cardinals several learned churchmen, such as Caraffa (later Pope Paul IV), established the Inquisition in the Papal States and – true to his word – called a council, which finally met at Trent in northern Italy.

The Council of Trent met intermittently from 1545 to 1563. It was called not only to reform the church but to secure reconciliation with the Protestants. Lutherans and Calvinists were invited to participate, but their insistence that the Scriptures be the sole basis for discussion made reconciliation impossible. Other problems bedeviled all the sessions of the council. International politics repeatedly cast a shadow over the theological debates. Charles V opposed discussions on any matter that might further alienate his Lutheran subjects, fearing the loss of additional imperial territory to Lutheran princes. Meanwhile, the French kings worked against the reconciliation of Roman Catholicism and Lutheranism: as long as religious issues divided the German states, the empire would be weakened, and a weak and divided empire meant a stronger France.

Trent had been selected as the site for the council because of its proximity to Germany. The city's climate, small size, and poor accommodations, the advanced age of many bishops, the difficulties of travel in the sixteenth century, and the refusal of Charles V and Henry II of France to allow their national bishops to attend certain sessions – these factors drastically reduced attendance. Portugal, Poland, Hungary, and Ireland sent representatives, but very few German bishops attended.

Another problem was the persistence of the conciliar theory of church government. Some bishops wanted a concrete statement asserting the supremacy of a church council over the

The Representation of the Fathers assembled in the
Council of Trent: begun about the end of the year 1545.
Concluded towards the end of 1563. under ÿ Pontificate
of Paul III. Iulius III. Marcel II. Paul IV. and Pius IV.
There were XXV. Sessions, in which were present
VII. Cardinals. V. whereof were the Popes Legates.
XVI. Ambassadours from Kings, Princes & Repub-
licks. CCL. Patriarchs, Archbishops, Bishops,
Abbots and Generals of Orders. All Divines
and Doctours of the Civil and Canon Law.

THE COUNCIL OF TRENT *This seventeenth-
century engraving depicts one of the early and sparsely
attended sessions of the Council of Trent. The tridentine sessions of 1562–63 drew many more bishops and
laymen, but there were never many representatives
from northern Europe. (Photo: Caroline Buckler)*

papacy. The adoption of the conciliar principle could have led to a divided church. The bishops had a provincial and national outlook; only the papacy possessed an international perspective. Fortunately, the centralizing tenet was established that all acts of the council required papal approval.

In spite of the obstacles, the achievements of the Council of Trent are impressive. It dealt with both doctrinal and disciplinary matters. The council gave equal validity to the Scriptures and to tradition as sources of religious truth and authority in the church. It reaffirmed the seven sacraments and the traditional Catholic teaching on transubstantiation – the belief in the conversion of the bread and wine used in the Mass into the actual body and blood of Christ. Thus, Lutheran and Calvinist positions were rejected.

The council tackled the problems arising from ancient abuses by strengthening ecclesiastical discipline. Tridentine (from *Tridentum,* the Latin word for Trent) decrees required bishops to reside in their own dioceses, suppressed pluralism and simony, and forbade the sale of indulgences. Clerics who kept concubines were to be warned to give them up and, if they refused, stripped of all ecclesiastical income. The jurisdiction of bishops over all the clergy of their dioceses was made almost absolute, and bishops were ordered to visit every religious house within the diocese at least once every two years. In a highly original canon, the council required every diocese to establish a seminary for the education and training of the clergy; the council even prescribed the curriculum and insisted that preference for admission be given to sons of the poor. Finally, great emphasis was laid on preaching and instructing the laity, especially the uneducated.

The Council of Trent did not meet everyone's expectations. Reconciliation with Protestantism was not achieved, nor was reform brought about immediately. Nevertheless, the Tridentine decrees laid a solid basis for the spiritual renewal of the church and for the enforcement of correction. For four centuries the doctrinal and disciplinary legislation of Trent served as the basis for Roman Catholic faith, organization, and practice.

NEW RELIGIOUS ORDERS

The establishment of new religious orders within the church reveals a central feature of the Catholic Reformation. These new orders developed in response to one crying need: to raise the moral and intellectual level of the clergy. Education was a major goal of them all.

The Ursuline order of nuns founded by Angela Merici (1474-1540) attained enormous prestige for the education of women. The daughter of a country gentleman, Angela Merici worked for many years among the poor, sick, and uneducated around her native Brescia in northern Italy. In 1535 she established the Ursuline order to combat heresy through Christian education. The first religious order concentrating exclusively on teaching young girls, the Ursulines sought to re-Christianize society by training future wives and mothers. Approved as a religious community by Paul III in 1544, the Ursulines rapidly grew and spread to France and the New World. Their schools in North America, stretching from Quebec to New Orleans, provided superior education for young women and inculcated the spiritual ideals of the Catholic Reformation.

The Society of Jesus, founded by Ignatius Loyola (1491-1556), a former Spanish soldier, played a powerful international role in resisting the spread of Protestantism, converting Asians and Latin American Indians to Catholicism, and spreading Christian education all over Europe. While recuperating from a severe battle wound in his legs, Loyola studied a life of Christ and other religious books and decided to give up his military career and become a soldier of Christ. During a year spent in seclusion, prayer, and personal mortification, he gained the religious insights that went into his great classic, *Spiritual Exercises.* This work, intended for study during a four-week period of retreat, directed the individual imagination and will to the reform of life and a new spiritual piety.

Loyola was apparently a man of considerable personal magnetism. After study at the universities in Salamanca and Paris, he gathered a group of six companions and in 1540 secured papal approval of the new Society of Jesus, whose members were called Jesuits. Their goals were the reform of the church primarily through education, preaching the Gospel to pagan peoples, and fighting Protestant heresy. Within a short time, the Jesuits had attracted many recruits.

The Society of Jesus was a highly centralized, tightly knit organization. Candidates underwent a two-year novitiate, in contrast to the usual one-year probation. Although new members took the traditional vows of poverty, chastity, and obedience, the emphasis was on obedience. Carefully selected members made a fourth vow of obedience to the pope and the governing members of the society. As faith was the cornerstone of Luther's life, so obedience became the bedrock of the Jesuit tradition.

The Jesuits had a modern, quasi-military quality; a sort of ecclesiastical Green Berets, they achieved phenomenal success for the papacy and the reformed church. Jesuit schools adopted modern teaching methods, and while they first concentrated on the children of the poor, they were soon educating the sons of the nobility. As confessors and spiritual directors to kings, Jesuits exerted great political influence. Operating on the principle that the end sometimes justifies the means, they were not above spying. Indifferent to physical comfort and personal safety, they carried Christianity to the Moluccan Islands, Ceylon, and Japan before 1550, to Brazil and the Congo in the seventeenth century. Within Europe, the Jesuits brought southern Germany and much of eastern Europe back to Catholicism.

THE SACRED CONGREGATION OF THE HOLY OFFICE

In 1542, Pope Paul III established the Sacred Congregation of the Holy Office with jurisdiction over the Roman Inquisition, which became a powerful instrument of the Counter Reformation. The Inquisition was a committee of six cardinals with judicial authority over all Catholics and with the power to arrest, imprison, and execute. Under the direction of the fanatical Cardinal Caraffa, it vigorously attacked heresy.

The Roman Inquisition operated under the principles of Roman law. It accepted hearsay evidence, was not obliged to inform accused people of the charges against them, and sometimes applied torture. Echoing one of Calvin's remarks about heresy, Cardinal Caraffa wrote, "No man is to lower himself by showing toleration towards any sort of heretic, least of all a Calvinist."[23] The Holy Office published the *Index of Prohibited Books,* a catalog of forbidden reading that included the publications of many printers.

Within the Papal States in central Italy, the Inquisition effectively destroyed heresy (and many heretics). Outside the papal territories, however, its influence was slight. Governments had their own judicial systems for the suppression of treasonable activities, as religious heresy was then considered. The republic of Venice is a good case in point.

In the sixteenth century, Venice was one of the great publishing centers of Europe. The Inquisition and the Index could have badly damaged the Venetian book trade. Authorities there cooperated with the Holy Office only when heresy became a great threat to the security of the republic. The Index had no influence on scholarly research in nonreligious areas, such as law, classical literature, and mathematics. Venetians and Italians, as a result of the Inquisition, were not cut off from the main currents of European learning.[24]

———◆———

The age of the Reformation presents very real paradoxes. The break with Rome and the rise of Lutheran, Anglican, Calvinist, and other faiths destroyed the unity of Europe as an organic Christian society. Saint Paul's exhortation, "There should be no schism in the body [of the church].... You are all one in Christ,"[25] was gradually ignored. On the other hand, religious belief remained tremendously strong. In fact, the strength of religious convictions caused political fragmentation. In the later sixteenth century and through most of the seventeenth, religion and religious issues continued to play a major role in the lives of individuals and in the policies and actions of governments. Religion, whether Protestant or Catholic, decisively influenced the growth of national states.

For almost a thousand years, the church had taught Europeans "to believe in order that you may know." In the seventh through ninth centuries, European peoples had been led in massive numbers to the waters of Christian baptism. The Christian faith and Christian practices, however, meant little to the pagan barbarians of the early Middle Ages.

Many centuries passed before the church had a significantly Christianizing impact on those peoples. Therein lies another paradox. At the moment when literature, sermons, and especially art were expressing the widespread desire for individual and emotional experience within a common spiritual framework, the schism brought confusion, divisiveness, and destruction. The Reformation was, ironically, a tribute to the successful educational work of the medieval church.

Finally, scholars have maintained that the sixteenth century witnessed the beginnings of the modern world. They are both right and wrong. The sixteenth-century revolt from the church paved the way for the eighteenth-century revolt from the Christian God, one of the strongest supports of life in Western culture. In this respect, the Reformation marked the beginning of the modern world, with its secularism and rootlessness. At the same time, it can equally be argued that the sixteenth century represented the culmination of the Middle Ages. Martin Luther's anxieties about salvation show him to be very much a medieval man. His concerns had deeply troubled serious individuals since the time of Saint Augustine. Modern people tend to be less troubled by this issue. The sixteenth century was a definite watershed.

NOTES

1. Romans 12:2–3.

2. Quoted by J. Burckhardt, *The Civilization of the Renaissance in Italy,* Phaidon Books, London, 1951, p. 262.

3. See E. Erickson, *Young Man Luther: A Study in Psychoanalysis and History,* W. W. Norton, New York, 1962, passim.

4. T. C. Mendenhall et al., eds., *Ideas and Institu-*

tions in European History: 800–1715, Henry Holt, New York, 1948, p. 220.

5. Quoted by O. Chadwick, *The Reformation,* Penguin Books, Baltimore, 1976, p. 55.

6. Quoted by E. H. Harbison, *The Age of Reformation,* Cornell University Press, Ithaca, N.Y., 1963, p. 52.

7. I have leaned heavily here on Harbison, pp. 52–55.

8. H. Hillerbrand, *Men and Ideas in the Sixteenth Century,* Rand McNally, Chicago, 1969, p. 28.

9. Romans 13:1–2.

10. Erickson, p. 47.

11. Quoted by J. Atkinson, *Martin Luther and the Birth of Protestantism,* Penguin Books, Baltimore, 1968, pp. 247–248.

12. *Martin Luther: Three Treatises,* Muhlenberg Press, Philadelphia, 1947, pp. 28–31.

13. Quoted by R. Bainton, *The Travail of Religious Liberty,* Harper & Brothers, New York, 1958, p. 65.

14. J. Allen, trans., *John Calvin: The Institutes of the Christian Religion,* Westminster Press, Philadelphia, 1930, book 3, chap. 21, paras. 5, 7.

15. Quoted by Bainton, pp. 69–70.

16. A. G. Dickens, *The English Reformation,* Schocken Books, New York, 1964, p. 36.

17. A. G. Dickens and Dorothy Carr, eds., *The Reformation in England to the Accession of Elizabeth I,* Edward Arnold, London, 1969, pp. 15–16.

18. Leviticus 18:16, 20, 21.

19. C. Stephenson and G. F. Marcham, *Sources of English Constitutional History,* Harper & Row, New York, 1937, p. 304.

20. Quoted by P. Smith, *The Age of the Reformation,* rev. ed., Henry Holt, New York, 1951, p. 346.

21. Ibid., p. 84.

22. Quoted by H. Jedin, *A History of the Council of Trent,* Nelson & Sons, London, 1957, 1.126.

23. Quoted by Chadwick, p. 270.

24. See P. Grendler, *The Roman Inquisition and the Venetian Press, 1540–1605,* Princeton University Press, Princeton, N.J., 1977.

25. I Corinthians 1:25, 27.

SUGGESTED READING

There are many lucidly written and easily accessible studies of the religious reformations of the sixteenth century. O. Chadwick, *The Reformation* (1976); E. H. Harbison, *The Age of Reformation* (1963); R. Bainton, *The Reformation of the Sixteenth Century* (1961); and H. Hillerbrand, *Men and Ideas in the Sixteenth Century* (1969), are all good general introductions. P. Smith's *The Age of the Reformation,* rev. ed. (1951) is an older but comprehensive and often amusing treatment. The recent work of Steven Ozment, *The Age of Reform, 1250–1550: An Intellectual and Religious History of Late Medieval and Reformation Europe* (1980), provides a sophisticated survey of the ideas of the period.

Students who wish to explore aspects of Luther's life and work in greater detail should see, in addition to the titles in the Notes, R. Bainton, *Here I Stand* (1960); J. Atkinson, *Martin Luther and the Birth of Protestantism* (1968); and the sensitively scholarly work of H. Boehmer, *Martin Luther: Road to Reformation* (1960), a well-balanced book by a distinguished Protestant theologian. The perceptive study of H. G. Haile, *Luther: An Experiment in Biography* (1980), focuses on the character of the mature and aging reformer. The pioneering work of Gerald Strauss, *Luther's House of Learning: The Indoctrination of the Young in the German Reformation* (1978), describes how plain people were imbued with Reformation ideas and behavior. The best biography of the central political figure in the period of the German Reformation remains K. Brandi, *Charles V* (1954), while G. Barraclough, *The Origins of Modern Germany* (1952), gives a closet Marxist treatment.

The best introduction to Calvin as a man and theologian is probably the balanced account of F. Wendel, *Calvin: The Origins and Development of His Thought,* trans. P. Mairet (1963). J. T. McNeill, *History and Character of Calvinism* (1954), presents useful and previously inaccessible information. W. E. Monter, *Calvin's Geneva* (1967), is an excellent account of the impact of Calvinism on the social and economic life of that Swiss city. R. T. Kendall,

Calvinism and English Calvinism to 1649 (1981), treats English conditions, while Robert M. Mitchell, *Calvin and the Puritan's View of the Protestant Ethic* (1979), provides a good interpretation of the socioeconomic implications of Calvin's thought. Students interested in the left wing of the Reformation should see the profound work of G. H. Williams, *The Radical Reformers* (1962).

For England, in addition to the fundamental works by Dickens cited in the Notes, see S. T. Bindoff, *Tudor England* (1959), a good short synthesis. The marital trials of Henry VIII are treated in both the sympathetic study of G. Mattingly, *Catherine of Aragon* (1949), and H. A. Kelly, *The Matrimonial Trials of Henry VIII* (1975). A persuasive treatment of Henry VIII's possible syphilis and its effects on his children is given in F. S. Cartwright, *Disease and History* (1972). The legal implications of Henry VIII's divorces have been thoroughly analyzed by J. J. Scarisbrick, *Henry VIII* (1968), an almost definitive biography. On the dissolution of the English monasteries, see D. Knowles, *The Religious Orders in England,* vol. 3 (1959), one of the finest examples of historical prose in English written in the twentieth century. Knowles's *Bare Ruined Choirs* (1976) is an attractively illustrated abridgement of *Religious Orders.* G. R. Elton, *The Tudor Revolution in Government* (1959), discusses the modernization of English government under Thomas Cromwell.

P. Janelle, *The Catholic Reformation* (1951), is a fine comprehensive treatment of the Catholic reformation from a Catholic point of view, and A. G. Dickens, *The Counter Reformation* (1969), gives the Protestant standpoint in a beautifully illustrated book. The definitive study of the Council of Trent was written by H. Jedin, *A History of the Council of Trent,* 3 vols. (1957-1961).

CHAPTER 15

THE AGE OF RELIGIOUS WARS

AND EUROPEAN EXPANSION

THE RENAISSANCE and the reformations of the fifteenth and sixteenth centuries drastically altered intellectual, political, religious, and social life in Europe. But even before Martin Luther initiated the movement to reform the church, European peoples had been involved in overseas activities that had profound consequences for the domestic life of Europe and for the rest of the world. In the middle of the fifteenth century, Europeans began to confront ancient civilizations in Africa, Asia, and the Americas. These confrontations led first to conquest, then to exploitation, and finally to significant changes in both Europe and the conquered territories. European expansion took place amidst domestic and international conflict.

For much of the period 1560–1648, war and religious issues dominated the politics of European states. Wars were fought for power and territorial expansion, although religion was commonly used to rationalize those wars. Meanwhile Europeans carried their political, religious, and social attitudes to the new continents they subdued. This chapter seeks to explore the following questions. Why, in the sixteenth and seventeenth centuries, did European peoples expand overseas? How were a relatively small number of people living on the edge of the Eurasian landmass able to gain control of the major sea-lanes of the world and establish economic and political hegemony on distant continents far from home? What effect did overseas expansion have on Europe and on conquered societies?

DISCOVERY, RECONNAISSANCE, AND EXPANSION

Historians have variously called the period 1450–1650 "The Age of Discovery," "The

WORLD MAP OF VESCONTE MAGGIOLI, 1511 *Renaissance geographers still accepted the Greco-Egyptian Ptolemy's theory (second century A.D.) that the earth was one continuous land mass. Cartographers could not subscribe to the idea of a new, separate continent. Thus, this map, inaccurate when it was drawn, shows America as an extension of Asia. (John Carter Brown Library, Brown University, Providence)*

Age of Reconnaissance," and "The Age of Expansion." All three labels are appropriate. "The Age of Discovery" refers to the era's phenomenal advances in geographical knowledge and in technology, often achieved through trial and error. In 1350, it took as long to sail from the eastern end of the Mediterranean to the western end as it had taken a thousand years earlier, in 350. Even in the fifteenth century, Europeans knew little more about the earth's surface than the Romans had known. By 1650, however, Europeans had made an extensive reconnaissance – or preliminary exploration – and had sketched fairly accurately the physical outline of the whole earth. Much of the geographical information they had gathered was tentative and not fully understood – hence the appropriateness of the term "The Age of Reconnaissance."

The designation of the era as "The Age of Expansion" refers to the migration of Europeans to other parts of the world. This colonization resulted in political control of much of South America and North America, coastal regions of Africa, India, China, Japan, and many Pacific islands. Political hegemony was accompanied by economic exploitation, religious domination, and the introduction of European patterns of social and intellectual life. The sixteenth-century expansion of European society launched a new age in world history.

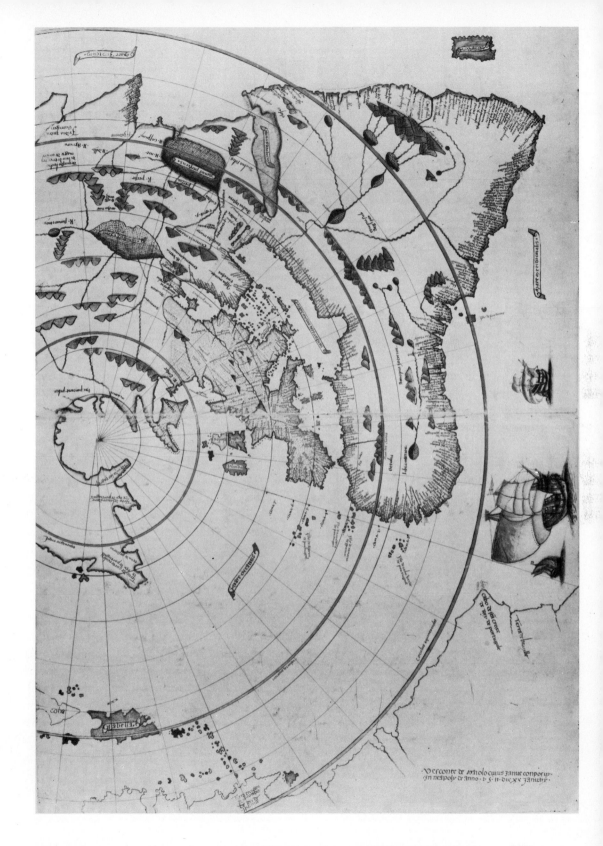

The outward expansion of Europe began with the Viking voyages across the Atlantic in the tenth and eleventh centuries. Under Eric the Red and Leif Ericson, the Vikings discovered Greenland and the eastern coast of North America. They may even have traveled down the New England coast as far south as Boston. The Crusades of the eleventh through thirteenth centuries were another phase in Europe's attempt to explore, Christianize, and exploit territories and peoples on the periphery of the Continent. But these early thrusts outward resulted in no permanent settlements. The Vikings made only quick raids in search of booty. Lacking stable political institutions in Scandinavia, they had no workable forms of government to impose on distant continents. In the twelfth and thirteenth centuries, the lack of a strong territorial base, weak support from the West, and sheer misrule combined to make the medieval Crusader kingdoms short-lived. Even in the mid-fifteenth century, Europe seemed ill-prepared for international ventures. By 1450, a grave new threat had appeared in the East – the Ottoman Turks.

Combining excellent military strategy with efficient administration of their conquered territories, the Turks had subdued most of Asia Minor and begun to settle on the Western side of the Bosporus. The Ottoman Turks under Sultan Mohammed II (1451–1481) captured Constantinople in 1453, pressed southwest into the Balkans, and by the early sixteenth century controlled the eastern Mediterranean. The Turkish menace badly frightened Europeans. In France in the fifteenth and sixteenth centuries, twice as many books were printed about the Turkish threat as about the American discoveries. The Turks imposed a military blockade on eastern Europe, thus forcing Europeans' attention westward. Yet the fifteenth and sixteenth centuries witnessed a fantastic continuation, on a global scale, of European expansion: great discoveries led to overseas empires.

Political centralization in Spain, France, and England helps to explain those countries' outward push. In the fifteenth century, Isabella and Ferdinand had consolidated their several kingdoms to achieve a united Spain. The Catholic rulers slashed the powers of the nobility, revamped the Spanish bureaucracy, and humbled dissident elements, notably the Muslims and the Jews. The Spanish monarchy was stronger than ever before, and in a position to support foreign ventures; it could bear the costs and dangers of exploration. But Portugal, situated on the extreme southwestern edge of the European continent, got the start on the rest of Europe.

Portugal's taking of Ceuta, an Arab city in northern Morocco, in 1415 marked the beginning of European exploration and control of overseas territory. The objectives of Portuguese policy included the historic Iberian crusade to Christianize Muslims, and the search for gold, for an overseas route to the spice markets of India, and for the mythical Christian ruler of Ethiopia, Prester John.

In the early phases of Portuguese exploration, Prince Henry (1394–1460), called "the Navigator" because of the annual expeditions he sent down the western coast of Africa, played the leading role. In the fifteenth century, most of the gold that reached Europe came from the Sudan in West Africa and from Ashanti blacks living near the gold coast. Muslim caravans brought the gold from the African cities of Niani and Timbuktu and carried it north across the Sahara to Mediterranean ports. Then the Portuguese muscled in on this commerce in gold. Prince Henry's carefully planned expeditions succeeded in reaching Guinea, and under King John II (1481-1495), the Portuguese established trading posts and forts on the Guinea coast and penetrated into the continent all the way to Timbuktu (see Map 15.1). Portuguese ships transported gold to Lisbon, and by 1500 Portugal controlled the flow of gold to Europe. The golden century of Portuguese prosperity had begun.

Still the Portuguese pushed farther south down the west coast of Africa. In 1487, Bartholomew Diaz rounded the Cape of Good Hope at the southern tip, but storms and a threatened mutiny forced him to turn back. On a second expedition (1497-1499), the Portuguese mariner Vasco da Gama reached India and returned to Lisbon loaded with samples of Indian wares (see Map 15.1). King Manuel (1495-1521) promptly dispatched thirteen ships under the command of Pedro Alvares Cabral, assisted by Diaz, to set up trading posts in India. On April 22, 1500, the coast of Brazil in South America was sighted and claimed for the crown of Portugal. Cabral then proceeded south and east around the Cape of Good Hope and reached India. Half the fleet was lost on the return voyage, but the six spice-laden vessels that dropped anchor in Lisbon harbor in July 1501 more than paid for the entire expedition. Thereafter, convoys were sent out every March. Lisbon became the entrance port for Asian goods into Europe – but not without a fight.

For centuries the Muslims had controlled the rich spice trade of the Indian Ocean, and they did not surrender it willingly. Portuguese commercial activities were accompanied by the destruction or seizure of strategic Muslim coastal forts, which later served Portugal as both trading posts and military bases.

Alfonso de Albuquerque, whom the Portuguese crown appointed as governor of India (1509-1515), decided that these bases and not inland territories should control the Indian Ocean. Accordingly, his cannon blasted open the ports of Calicut, Ormuz, Goa, and Malacca, the vital centers of Arab domination of south Asian trade. This bombardment laid the foundation for Portuguese imperialism in the sixteenth and seventeenth centuries: a strange way to bring Christianity to "those who were in darkness." As one scholar wrote about the opening of China to the West, "while Buddha came to China on white elephants, Christ was borne on cannon balls."[1]

In March 1493, between the first and second voyages of Vasco da Gama, Spanish ships entered Lisbon harbor bearing a triumphant Italian explorer in the service of the Spanish monarchy. Christopher Columbus (1451-1506), a Genose mariner, had secured Spanish support for an expedition to the East. He sailed from Palos, Spain, to the Canary Islands and crossed the Atlantic to the Bahamas, landing in October 1492 on an island that he named San Salvador and believed to be the coast of India.

Columbus explained the motives for his expedition in the journal of his voyage, entitled *Book of the First Navigation and Discovery of the Indies:*

And Your Highnesses, as Catholic Christians and Princes devoted to the Holy Christian Faith and the propagators thereof, and enemies of the sect of Mahomet and of all idolatries and heresies, resolved to send me Christopher Columbus to the said regions of India, to see the said princes and peoples and lands and [to observe] the disposition of them and of all, and the manner in which may be undertaken their conversion to our Holy Faith, and ordained that I should not go by land (the usual

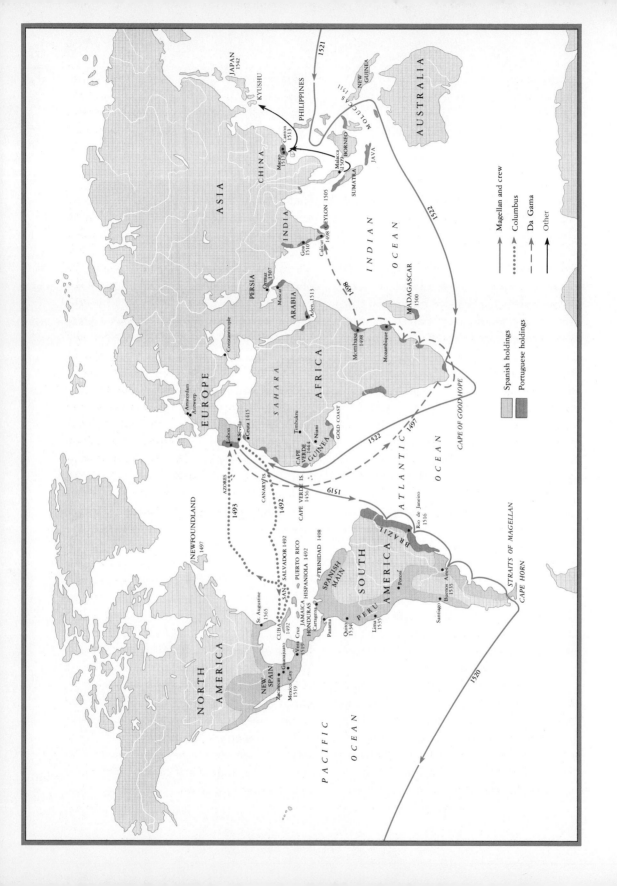

JAPAN
1542

KYUSHU

PHILIPPINES

NEW
GUINEA

MOLUCCAS 1511

AUSTRALIA

1521

Canton
1513

Macao
1517

Malacca
1509

BORNEO

JAVA

CHINA

ASIA

INDIA

Goa
1510

Calicut
1498

CEYLON 1505

SUMATRA

1522

INDIAN

OCEAN

Magellan and crew

Columbus

Da Gama

Other

PERSIA

Ormuz
1507

Muscat

ARABIA

Aden 1513

MADAGASCAR
1500

1498

EUROPE

Constantinople

Mombasa
1498

Mozambique

CAPE OF GOOD HOPE

Spanish holdings

Portuguese holdings

Amsterdam
Antwerp

SAHARA

AFRICA

Lisbon
Seville
Ceuta 1415

Timbuktu

Niani

1522

1497

GOLD COAST

CAPE
VERDE
1444

GUINEA

ATLANTIC

OCEAN

AZORES
1493

CANARY IS.
1492

CAPE VERDE IS.
1456

1519

NEWFOUNDLAND
1497

St. Augustine
1565

CUBA
1492

SAN
SALVADOR 1492

PUERTO RICO
1492

JAMAICA

HONDURAS
HISPANIOLA 1492

TRINIDAD 1498

SPANISH MAIN

Rio de Janeiro
1516

BRAZIL

STRAITS OF MAGELLAN

NORTH

AMERICA

NEW
SPAIN

Zacatecas
Guanajuato
Mexico City
1519
Vera
Cruz 1519

Cartagena

Panama

Quito
1534

SOUTH
AMERICA

PERU

Potosí

Lima
1535

Santiago

Buenos
Aires
1535

CAPE HORN

1520

PACIFIC

OCEAN

MAP 15.1 OVERSEAS EXPLORATION AND CON-
QUEST, FIFTEENTH AND SIXTEENTH CEN-
TURIES *The voyages of discovery marked another
phase in the centuries-old migrations of European
peoples. Consider the major contemporary significance
of each of the three voyages depicted on the map.*

*way) to the Orient, but by the route of the Oc-
cident, by which no one to this day knows for sure
that anyone has gone.*[2]

Like most people of his day, Christopher Columbus was a deeply religious man. The crew
of his flagship, *Santa Maria,* recited vespers
every night and sang a hymn to the Virgin,
the "Salve Regina," before going to bed.
Nevertheless, the Spanish fleet, sailing westward to find the East, sought wealth as well as
souls to convert to Christianity.

Between 1492 and 1502, Columbus made
four voyages to America, discovering all the
major islands of the Caribbean – Haiti
(which he called Dominica and the Spanish
named Hispaniola), San Salvador, Puerto
Rico, Jamaica, Cuba, Trinidad – and Honduras in Central America. Columbus believed
until he died that the islands he found were
off the coast of India. In fact, he had opened
up for the rulers of Spain a whole new world.
The Caribbean islands – the West Indies –
represented to Spanish missionary zeal millions of Indian natives for conversion to
Christianity. Hispaniola, Cuba, and Puerto
Rico also offered gold.

Forced labor, disease, and starvation in the
Spaniards' gold mines rapidly killed off the
Indians of Hispaniola. When Columbus arrived in 1493, the population had been approximately 100,000; in 1570, 300 people
survived. Indian slaves from the Bahamas and
black Africans from Guinea were then imported to do the mining.

The search for precious metals determined

the direction of Spanish exploration and expansion into South America. When it became
apparent that placer mining in the Caribbean
islands was slow and the rewards slim, new
routes to the East and new sources of gold
and silver were sought.

In 1519, the Spanish ruler Charles V commissioned Ferdinand Magellan (1480–1521)
to find a direct route to the Moluccan Islands
off the southeast coast of Asia. Magellan sailed
southwest across the Atlantic to Brazil, and
proceeded south around Cape Horn into the
Pacific Ocean (see Map 15.1). He crossed the
Pacific, sailing west, to the Malay Archipel-
ago, which he called the Western Isles. (These
islands were conquered in the 1560s and
named the Philippines for Philip II of Spain.)

Although Magellan was killed, the expedition continued, returning to Spain in 1522
from the east by way of the Indian Ocean, the
Cape of Good Hope, and the Atlantic. Terrible storms, mutiny, starvation, and disease
haunted this voyage. Nevertheless, it verified
Columbus's theory that the earth was round
and brought information about the vastness
of the Pacific. Magellan also proved that the
earth was much larger than Columbus and
others had believed.

In the West Indies, the slow recovery of
gold, the shortage of a healthy labor force,
and sheer restlessness speeded up Spain's
search for wealth. In 1519, the year Magellan
departed on his worldwide expedition, a brash
and determined Spanish adventurer Hernando
Cortez (1485–1547), crossed from Hispaniola
to mainland Mexico with six hundred men,
seventeen horses, and ten canon. Within three
years, Cortez had conquered the fabulously
rich Aztec empire, taken captive the Aztec
emperor Montezuma, and founded Mexico
City as the capital of New Spain. The subjugation of northern Mexico took longer, but
between 1531 and 1550 the Spanish gained

COLUMBUS LANDS ON SAN SALVADOR The printed page and illustrations, such as this German woodcut, spread reports of Columbus's voyage all over Europe. According to Columbus, a group of naked Indians greeted the Spaniards' arrival. Pictures of the Indians as "primitive" and "uncivilized" instilled prejudices which centuries have not erased. (Photo: Caroline Buckler)

control of Zacatecas and Guanajuato, where rich silver veins were soon tapped.

Another Spanish conquistador, Francisco Pizzaro (1470–1541), repeated Cortez's feat in Peru. Between 1531 and 1536, with even fewer resources, Pizzaro crushed the Inca empire in northern South America and established the Spanish viceroyalty of Peru with its center at Lima. In 1545, Pizzaro opened at Potosí in the Peruvian highlands what became the richest silver mines in the New World.

Between 1525 and 1575, the riches of the Americas poured into the Spanish port of Seville and the Portuguese capital of Lisbon. For all their new wealth, however, Lisbon and Seville did not become important trading centers. It was the Flemish city of Antwerp, although controlled by the Spanish Habsburgs, that developed into the great entrepôt for overseas bullion and Portuguese spices and served as the commercial and financial capital of the entire European world.

Since the time of the great medieval fairs, cities of the Low Countries – so called because much of the land lies below sea level – had been important sites for the exchange of products from the Baltic and Italy. Antwerp, ideally situated on the Scheldt River at the intersection of many trading routes, steadily expanded as the chief intermediary for international commerce and finance. English woolens, Baltic wheat, fur, and timber, Portuguese spices, German iron and copper, Spanish fruit, French wines and dyestuffs, Italian silks, marbles, and mirrors, together with vast amounts of cash, were exchanged at Antwerp. The city's harbor could dock 2,500 vessels at once, and 5,000 merchants from many nations gathered daily in the bourse (or exchange). Spanish silver was drained to the Netherlands to pay for food and luxury goods. Even so, the desire for complete economic independence from Spain was to play a major role in the Netherlands' revolt in the late sixteenth century.

By the end of the century, Amsterdam had overtaken Antwerp as the financial capital of Europe. The Dutch had also embarked on foreign exploration and conquest. The Dutch East India Company, founded in 1602, became the major organ of Dutch imperialism and within a few decades expelled the Portuguese from Ceylon and other East Indian islands. By 1650, the Dutch West India Company had successfully horned in on the Spanish possessions in America and gained control of much of the African and American trade.

English and French explorations lacked the immediate and sensational results of the Spanish and Portuguese. In 1497 John Cabot, a Genoese merchant living in London, sailed for Brazil but discovered Newfoundland. The next year he returned and explored the New England coast and perhaps as far south as Delaware. Since these expeditions found no spices or gold, the English king Henry VII lost interest in exploration. Between 1534 and 1541, the Frenchman Jacques Cartier made several voyages and explored the St. Lawrence region of Canada, but the first permanent French settlement, at Quebec, was not founded until 1608.

COLONIAL ADMINISTRATION

Columbus, Cortez, and Pizzaro claimed the lands they had "discovered" for the crown of Spain. How were they to be governed? According to the Spanish theory of absolutism, the Crown was entitled to exercise full authority over all imperial lands. In the sixteenth century the Crown divided its New World territories into four viceroyalties or administrative divisions: New Spain, which consisted of Mexico, Central America, and present-day California, Arizona, New Mexico, and Texas, with the capital at Mexico City; Peru, originally all the lands in continental South America, later reduced to the territory of modern Peru, Chile, Bolivia, and Equador, with the viceregal seat at Lima; New Granada, including present-day Venezuela, Colombia, Panama, and after 1739 Ecuador, with Bogata as its administrative center; and La Plata, consisting of Argentina, Uruguay, and Paraguay,

with Buenos Aires as the capital. Within each territory, the viceroy or imperial governor exercised broad military and civil authority as the direct representative of the sovereign in Madrid. The viceroy presided over the *audiencia,* a board of twelve to fifteen judges, which served as his advisory council and the highest judicial body. The enlightened Spanish king Charles III (1716-1788) introduced the system of intendants. These royal officials possessed broad military, administrative, and financial authority within their intendancy, and were responsible not to the viceroy but to the Crown in Madrid.

From the early sixteenth century to the beginning of the nineteenth, the Spanish monarchy acted on the mercantilist principle that the colonies existed for the financial benefit of the mother country. The mining of gold and silver was always the most important industry in the colonies. The Crown claimed the *quinto,* one-fifth of all precious metals mined in South America. Gold and silver yielded the Spanish monarchy 25 percent of its total income. In return, it shipped manufactured goods to America and discouraged the development of native industries.

The Portuguese governed their colony of Brazil in a similar manner. After the union of the crowns of Portugal and Spain in 1580, Spanish administrative forms were introduced. Local officials called *corregidores* held judicial and military powers. Mercantilist policies placed severe restrictions on Brazilian industries that might compete with those of Portugal. In the seventeenth century the use of black slave labor made possible the cultivation of coffee and cotton, and in the eighteenth century Brazil led the world in the production of sugar. The unique feature of colonial Brazil's culture and society was its thoroughgoing intermixture of Indians, whites, and blacks.

THE ECONOMIC EFFECTS OF SPAIN'S DISCOVERIES IN THE NEW WORLD

The sixteenth century has often been called the golden century of Spain. The influence of Spanish armies, Spanish Catholicism, and Spanish wealth was felt all over Europe. This greatness rested largely upon the influx of precious metals from the New World.

The mines at Zacatecas and Guanajuato in Mexico and Potosí in Peru poured out huge quantities of precious metals. To protect this treasure from French and English pirates, armed convoys transported it each year to Spain. Between 1503 and 1650, 16 million kilograms of silver and 185,000 kilograms of gold entered the port of Seville. Scholars have long debated the impact of all this bullion on the economies of Spain and Europe as a whole. Spanish predominance, however, proved temporary.

In the sixteenth century, Spain experienced a steady population increase, creating a sharp rise in the demand for food and goods. Spanish colonies in the Americas also represented a demand for products – olive oil, wine, wool, steel cutlery, and a variety of luxury goods. Since Spain had expelled some of the best farmers and businessmen, the Muslims and the conversos, in the fifteenth century, the Spanish economy was already suffering and could not meet the new demands. Prices rose. Because the costs of manufacturing cloth and other goods increased, Spanish products could not compete in the international market with cheaper products made elsewhere. The textile industry was badly hurt. Prices spiraled upward, faster than the government could levy taxes to dampen the economy. (Higher taxes would have cut the public's buying power; with fewer goods sold, prices would have come down.)

Several times between 1557 and 1647, Philip II and his successors were forced to repudiate the state debt, which in turn undermined confidence in the government. The enormous flow of silver and gold from the Americas thus contributed to the destruction of Spanish agriculture and industry. When the flow declined in the seventeenth century, the economy was in a shambles.

As Philip II paid his armies and foreign debts with silver bullion, the Spanish inflation was transmitted to the rest of Europe. Between 1560 and 1600, much of Europe experienced large price increases. Prices doubled and in some cases quadrupled. Spain suffered most severely, but all European countries were affected. People who lived on fixed incomes, such as the continental nobles, were badly hurt because their money bought less. Those who owed fixed sums of money, such as the middle class, prospered: in a time of rising prices, debts had less value each year. Food costs rose most sharply, and the poor fared worst of all.

TECHNOLOGICAL STIMULI TO EXPLORATION

Technological developments were the key to Europe's remarkable outreach. By 1350, cannon – iron or bronze guns that fired iron or stone balls – had been fully developed in western Europe. These pieces of artillery emitted frightening noises and great flashes of fire and could batter down fortresses and even city walls. Sultan Mohammed II's siege of Constantinople in 1453 provides a classic illustration of the effectiveness of cannon fire.

Constantinople had the strongest walled fortifications in the West. The sultan secured the services of a Western technician who built fifty-six small cannon and a gigantic gun that could hurl stone balls weighing about eight hundred pounds. The gun could be moved only by several hundred oxen, and loaded and fired only by about a hundred men working together. Reloading took two hours. This awkward but powerful weapon breached the walls of Constantinople before it cracked on the second day of the bombardment. Lesser cannon finished the job.

Early cannon posed serious technical difficulties. Iron cannon were cheaper than bronze to construct, but they were difficult to cast effectively and were liable to crack and injure the artillerymen. Bronze guns, made of copper and tin, were less subject than iron to corrosion, but they were very expensive. All cannon were extraordinarily difficult to move, required considerable time for reloading, and were highly inaccurate. They thus proved inefficient for land warfare. However, they could be used at sea.

The mounting of cannon on ships and improved techniques of shipbuilding gave impetus to European expansion.[3] Since ancient times, most seagoing vessels had been narrow open boats called galleys, propelled by manpower. Slaves or convicts who had been sentenced to the galleys manned the oars of the ships that sailed the Mediterranean, and both cargo and warships carried soldiers for defense. Although well suited to the placid and thoroughly explored waters of the Mediterranean, galleys could not withstand the rough winds and uncharted shoals of the Atlantic. The need for sturdier craft, as well as population losses caused by the Black Death, forced the development of a new style of ship that would not require soldiers for defense.

In the course of the fifteenth century, the Portuguese developed the caravel, a small, light, three-masted sailing ship. Although somewhat slower than the galley, the caravel held more cargo and was highly maneuverable. When fitted with cannon, it could dominate larger vessels, such as the round ships commonly used as merchantmen. The substitution of windpower for manpower, and artillery fire for soldiers, signaled a great technological advance and gave Europeans navigational and fighting ascendancy over the rest of the world.[4]

Other fifteenth-century developments in navigation helped make possible the conquest of the Atlantic. The magnetic compass enabled sailors to determine their direction and position at sea. The astrolabe, an instrument used to determine the altitude of the sun and other celestial bodies, permitted mariners to plot their latitude, or position north or south of the equator. Steadily improved maps and sea charts provided information about distance, sea depths, and general geography.

THE EXPLORERS' MOTIVES

The expansion of Europe was not motivated by demographic pressures. The Black Death had caused serious population losses from which Europe had not recovered in 1500. Few Europeans emigrated to North or South America in the sixteenth century. Half of those who did sail to begin a new life in America died en route; half of those who reached the New World eventually returned to their homeland. Why, then, did explorers brave the Atlantic and Pacific oceans, risking their lives to discover new continents and spread European culture?

The reasons are varied and complex. People of the sixteenth century were still basically medieval, in the sense that their attitudes and values were shaped by religion and expressed in religious terms. In the late fifteenth century, crusading fervor remained a basic part of the Portuguese and Spanish national ideal. The desire to Christianize Muslims and pagan peoples played a central role in European expansion. Queen Isabella of Spain, for example, showed a fanatical zeal for converting the Muslims to Christianity, but she concentrated her efforts on the Arabs in Granada. After the abortive crusading attempts of the thirteenth century, Isabella and other rulers realized full well that they lacked the material resources to mount the full-scale assault on Islam necessary for victory. Crusading impulses thus shifted from the Muslims to the pagan peoples of Africa and the Americas.

Government sponsorship and encouragement of exploration also help to account for the results of the various voyages. Mariners and explorers could not afford, as private individuals, the massive sums needed to explore mysterious oceans and to control remote continents. The strong financial support of Prince Henry the Navigator led to Portugal's phenomenal success in the spice trade. Even the grudging and modest assistance of Isabella and Ferdinand eventually brought untold riches – and complicated problems – to Spain. The Dutch in the seventeenth century, through such government-sponsored trading companies as the Dutch East India Company, reaped enormous wealth, and although the Netherlands was a small country in size, it dominated the European economy in 1650. In England, by contrast, Henry VII's lack of interest in exploration delayed English expansion for a century.

Scholars have frequently described the European discoveries as a manifestation of Renaissance curiosity about the physical universe, the desire to know more about the geography and peoples of the world. There is truth to this explanation. Cosmography, natural history, and geography aroused enormous interest among educated people in the fifteenth and sixteenth centuries. Just as science fiction and speculation about life on other planets excite readers today, quasi-scientific literature about Africa, Asia, and the Americas captured the imaginations of literate Europeans. Oviedo's *General History of the Indies,* a detailed eyewitness account of plants, animals, and peoples, was widely read.

Spices were another important incentive to undertake voyages of discovery. Introduced into western Europe by the Crusaders in the twelfth century, nutmeg, mace, ginger, cinnamon, and pepper added flavor and variety to the monotonous diet of Europeans. Spices were also used in the preparation of medicinal drugs and in the manufacture of incense for religious ceremonies. In the late thirteenth century, the Venetian Marco Polo (1254?–1324?), the greatest of the medieval travelers, had visited the court of the Chinese emperor. The widely publicized account of his travels in the *Book of Various Experiences* stimulated a rich trade in spices between Asia and Italy. The Venetians came to hold a monopoly of the spice trade in western Europe.

Spices were grown in India and China, shipped across the Indian Ocean to ports on the Persian Gulf, and then transported by Arabs across the Arabian Desert to Mediterranean ports. But the rise of the Ming dynasty in China in the late fourteenth century resulted in the expulsion of foreigners. And the steady penetration of the Ottoman Turks into the eastern Mediterranean and of hostile Muslims across North Africa forced Europeans to seek a new route to the Asian spice markets.

The basic reason for European exploration and expansion, however, was the quest for material profit. Mariners and explorers frankly admitted this. As Bartholomew Diaz put it, his motives were "to serve God and His Majesty, to give light to those who were in darkness and to grow rich as all men desire to do." When Vasco da Gama reached the port of Calicut, India, in 1498, a native asked what the Portuguese wanted. Da Gama replied, "Christians and spices."[5] The bluntest of the Spanish conquistadors, Hernando Cortez, announced as he prepared to conquer Mexico, "I have come to win gold, not to plow the fields like a peasant."[6]

Spanish and Portuguese explorers carried the fervent Catholicism and missionary zeal of the Iberian Peninsula to the New World, and once in America they urged home governments to send clerics "to bring light to those who were in darkness." At bottom, however, wealth was the driving motivation. A sixteenth-century diplomat, Ogier Gheselin de Busbecq, summed up this paradoxical attitude well: in expeditions to the Indies and the Antipodes, he said, "religion supplies the pretext and gold the motive."[7] The mariners, explorers, and conquistadors were religious and "medieval" in justifying their actions, materialistic and "modern" in their behavior.

POLITICS, RELIGION, AND WAR

In 1559, France and Spain signed the Treaty of Cateau-Cambrésis, which ended the long conflict known as the Habsburg-Valois wars. This event marks a decisive watershed in early modern European history. Spain was the victor. France, exhausted by the struggle, had to acknowledge Spanish dominance in Italy, where much of the war had been fought. Spanish governors ruled in Sicily, Naples, and Milan, and Spanish influence was strong in the Papal States and Tuscany.

The emperor Charles V had divided his attention between the Holy Roman Empire and Spain. Under his son Philip II (1556–1598), however, the center of the Habsburg empire and the political center of gravity for all of Europe shifted westward to Spain. Before 1559, Spain and France had fought bitterly for control of Italy; after 1559, the two Catholic powers aimed their guns at Protestantism. The Treaty of Cateau-Cambrésis ended an era of dynastic wars and initiated a period of conflicts in which religion played a dominant role.

Because a variety of issues were stewing, it is not easy to generalize about the wars of the late sixteenth century. Some were continuations of struggles between the centralizing goals of monarchies and the feudal reactions of nobilities. Some were crusading battles between Catholics and Protestants. Some were struggles for national independence or for international expansion.

These wars differed considerably from earlier wars. Sixteenth- and seventeenth-century armies were bigger than medieval ones; some forces numbered as many as fifty thousand men. Because large armies were expensive, governments had to reorganize their administrations to finance them. The use of gunpowder altered both the nature of war and popular attitudes toward it. Guns and cannon killed and wounded from a distance, indiscriminately. Writers scorned gunpowder as a coward's weapon that allowed a common soldier to kill a gentleman. The Italian poet Ariosto lamented:

Through thee is martial glory lost, through
Thee the trade of arms becomes a worthless art:
And at such ebb are worth and chivalry that
The base often plays the better part.[8]

Gunpowder destroyed the notion, common during the Hundred Years' War, that warfare was an ennobling experience. Governments had to utilize propaganda, pulpits, and the printing press to arouse public opinion to support war.[9]

Late-sixteenth-century conflicts fundamentally tested the medieval ideal of a unified Christian society governed by one political ruler, the emperor, to whom all rulers were theoretically subordinate, and one church, to which all people belonged. The Protestant Reformation had killed this ideal, but few people recognized it as dead. Catholics continued to believe that Calvinists and Lutherans could be reconverted; Protestants persisted in thinking that the Roman church should be destroyed. Catholics and Protestants alike feared people of the other faith living in their midst. The settlement finally achieved in 1648, known as the Peace of Westphalia, signaled the end of the medieval ideal.

THE ORIGINS OF DIFFICULTIES IN FRANCE (1515–1559)

In the first half of the sixteenth century, France continued the recovery begun under Louis XI (page 457). The population losses caused by the plague and the disorders accompanying the Hundred Years' War had created such a labor shortage that serfdom virtually disappeared. Cash rents replaced feudal rents and servile obligations. This development clearly benefited the peasantry. Meanwhile, the declining buying power of money hurt the nobility. The steadily increasing French population brought new lands under cultivation, but the division of property among sons meant that most peasant holdings were very small. Domestic and foreign trade picked up; mercantile centers such as Rouen and Lyons expanded; and in 1517 a new port city was founded at Le Havre.

ROSSO AND PRIMATICCIO: THE GALLERY OF FRANCES I   Flat paintings alternating with rich sculpture provide a rhythm that directs the eye down the long gallery at Fontainebleau, the construction of which occupied much of Francis I's attention from 1530 to 1540. He sought to re-create in France the elegant Renaissance lifestyle he had discovered in Italy. (Giraudon)

The charming and cultivated Francis I (1515–1547) and his athletic, emotional son Henry II (1547–1559) governed through a small, efficient council. Great nobles held titular authority in the provinces as governors, but Paris-appointed officials, the baillis and seneschals, continued to exercise actual fiscal and judicial responsibility (pages 353–354). In 1539, Francis issued an ordinance that placed all France under the jurisdiction of the royal law courts and made French the language of those courts. This act had a powerful centralizing impact. The taille, a tax on land, provided such strength as the monarchy had and supported a strong standing army. Unfortunately, the tax base was too narrow for France's extravagant promotion of the arts and ambitious foreign policy.

Deliberately imitating the Italian Renaissance princes, the Valois monarchs lavished money on a magnificent court and vast building program, and on Italian artists. Francis I commissioned the Paris architect Pierre Lescot to rebuild the palace of the Louvre. Francis secured the services of Michelangelo's star pupil, Il Rosso, who decorated the wing of the Fontainebleau chateau, subsequently called the Gallery Francis I, with rich scenes of classical and mythological literature. After acquiring Leonardo da Vinci's Mona Lisa, Francis brought Leonardo himself to France, where he soon died. Henry II built a castle at Dreux for his mistress, Diana de Poitiers, and a palace in Paris, the Tuileries, for his wife, Catherine de' Medici. Art historians credit

Francis I and Henry II with importing Italian Renaissance art and architecture to France. Whatever praise these monarchs deserve for their cultural achievement, they spent far more than they could afford.

The Habsburg-Valois wars, waged intermittently through the first half of the sixteenth century, also cost more than the government could afford. Financing the war posed problems. In addition to the time-honored practices of increasing taxes and heavy borrowing, Francis I tried two new devices to raise revenue: the sale of public offices and a treaty with the papacy. The former proved to be only a temporary source of money. The offices sold tended to become hereditary within a family, and once a man bought an office he and his heirs were tax-exempt. The sale of public offices thus created a tax-exempt class called the nobility of the robe, which held positions beyond the jurisdiction of the Crown.

The treaty with the papacy was the Concordat of Bologna (page 457), in which Francis agreed to recognize the supremacy of the papacy over a universal council. In return, the French crown gained the right to appoint all French bishops and abbots. This understanding gave the monarchy a rich supplement of money and offices and a power over the church that lasted until the Revolution of 1789. The Concordat of Bologna helps to explain why France did not later become Protestant: it in effect established Catholicism as the national religion. Because they possessed control over appointments and had a vested financial interest in Catholicism, French rulers had no need to revolt from Rome.

However, the Concordat of Bologna perpetuated disorders within the French church. Ecclesiastical offices were used primarily to pay and reward civil servants. Churchmen in France, as elsewhere, were promoted to the hierarchy not for any special spiritual qualifications but because of their services to the state. Such bishops were unlikely to work to elevate the intellectual and moral standards of the parish clergy. Few of the many priests in France devoted scrupulous attention to the needs of their parishioners. The teachings of Luther and Calvin, as the presses disseminated them, found a receptive audience.

Luther's tracts first appeared in France in 1518, and his ideas attracted some attention. After the publication of Calvin's *Institutes* in 1536, sizable numbers of French people were attracted to the "reformed religion," as Calvinism was called. Because Calvin wrote in French, rather than Latin, his ideas gained wide circulation. Initially, Calvinism drew converts from among reform-minded members of the Catholic clergy, the industrious middle classes, and from artisan groups. Most Calvinists lived in major cities, such as Paris, Lyons, Meaux, and Grenoble.

In spite of condemnation by the universities, government bans, and massive burnings at the stake, the numbers of Protestants grew steadily. When Henry II died in 1559, there were 40 well-organized and 2,150 mission churches in France. Perhaps one-sixth of the population had become Calvinist.

RELIGIOUS RIOTS AND CIVIL WAR IN FRANCE (1559–1589)

For thirty years, from 1559 to 1589, violence and civil war divided and shattered France. The feebleness of the monarchy was the seed from which the weeds of civil violence germinated. The three weak sons of Henry II who occupied the throne could not provide the necessary leadership. Francis II (1559–1560) died after seventeen months. Charles IX (1560–1574) succeeded at the age of ten and was thoroughly dominated by his opportunis-

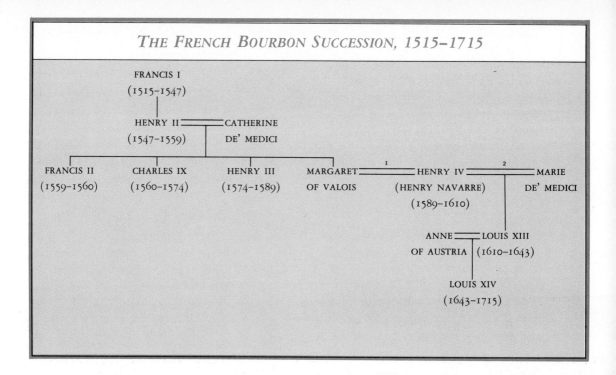

FRANCIS I
(1515–1547)

HENRY II ═══════ CATHERINE
(1547–1559)   DE' MEDICI

FRANCIS II   CHARLES IX   HENRY III   MARGARET ══════ 1 ══════ HENRY IV ══════ 2 ══════ MARIE
(1559–1560)   (1560–1574)   (1574–1589)   OF VALOIS   (HENRY NAVARRE)   DE' MEDICI
                                                                                    (1589–1610)

                                                                      ANNE ═══════ LOUIS XIII
                                                                      OF AUSTRIA │ (1610–1643)

                                                                            LOUIS XIV
                                                                            (1643–1715)

tic mother, Catherine de' Medici, who would support any party or position to maintain her influence. The intelligent and cultivated Henry III (1574–1589) divided his attention between debaucheries with his male lovers and frantic acts of repentance.

The French nobility took advantage of this monarchial weakness. In the second half of the sixteenth century, between two-fifths and half of the nobility at one time or another became Calvinist. Just as German princes in the Holy Roman Empire had adopted Lutheranism as a means of opposition to the emperor Charles V, so French nobles frequently adopted the "reformed religion" as a religious cloak for their independence. No one believed that peoples of different faiths could coexist peacefully within the same territory. The Reformation thus led to a resurgence of feudal disorder. Armed clashes between Catholic royalist lords and Calvinist antimonarchial lords occurred in many parts of France.

Among the upper classes the Catholic-Calvinist conflict was the surface issue, but the fundamental object of the struggle was power. Working-class crowds composed of skilled craftsmen and the poor wreaked terrible violence on people and property. Both Calvinists and Catholics believed that the others' books, services, and ministers polluted the community. Preachers incited violence, and ceremonies like baptisms, marriages, and funerals triggered it. Protestant pastors encouraged their followers to destroy statues and liturgical objects in Catholic churches. Catholic priests urged their flocks to shed the blood of the Calvinist heretics.

In 1561 in the Paris church of St.-Médard, a Protestant crowd cornered a baker guarding a box containing the consecrated Eucharistic bread. Taunting "Does your God of paste protect you now from the pains of death?"[10] the mob proceeded to kill the poor man. Calvinists believed that the Catholic emphasis on symbols in their ritual desecrated what was truly sacred and promoted the worship of images. In scores of attacks on Catholic churches religious statues were knocked down, stained-glass windows smashed, and sacred vestments, vessels, and Eucharistic elements defiled. In 1561, a Catholic crowd charged a group of just-released Protestant prisoners, killed them, and burned their bodies in the street. Hundreds of Huguenots, as French Calvinists were called, were tortured, had their tongues or throats slit, were maimed or murdered.

In the fourteenth and fifteenth centuries, crowd action – attacks on great nobles and rich prelates – had expressed economic grievances. Religious rioters of the sixteenth century believed that they could assume the power of public magistrates and rid the community of corruption. Municipal officials criticized the crowds' actions, but the participation of pastors and priests in these demonstrations lent riots a sort of legitimacy.[11]

A savage Catholic attack on Calvinists in Paris on August 24, 1572 (Saint Bartholomew's Day) followed the usual pattern. The occasion was a religious ceremony, the marriage of the king's sister Margaret of Valois to the Protestant Henry of Navarre. Among the many Calvinists present for the wedding festivies was the admiral de Coligny, head of one of the great noble families of France and leader of the Huguenot party. Coligny had recently replaced Catherine in influence over the young king Charles IX. When, the night before the wedding, the leader of the Catholic aristocracy, Henry of Guise, had Coligny murdered, rioting and slaughter followed. The Huguenot gentry in Paris were massacred, and religious violence spread to the provinces. Between August 25 and October 3, perhaps twelve thousand Huguenots perished at Meaux, Lyons, Orléans, and Paris. The contradictory orders of the unstable Charles IX worsened the situation.

The Saint Bartholomew's Day massacre launched the War of the Three Henrys, a civil conflict among factions led by the Catholic Henry of Guise, the Protestant Henry of Navarre, and King Henry III, who succeeded the tubercular Charles IX in 1574. Although he remained Catholic, King Henry realized that the Catholic Guise group represented his greatest danger. The Guises wanted, through an alliance of Catholic nobles called the Holy League, not only to destroy Calvinism but also to replace Henry III as king with a member of the Guise family. Violence continued. France suffered fifteen more years of religious rioting and domestic anarchy. Agriculture in many areas was destroyed; commercial life declined severely; starvation and death haunted the land.

What ultimately saved France was a small group of Catholic moderates called *politiques* who believed that only the restoration of strong monarchy could reverse the trend toward collapse. No religious creed was worth the incessant disorder and destruction. Therefore the *politiques* supported religious toleration. The death of Catherine de' Medici, followed by the assassinations of Henry of Guise and King Henry III, paved the way for the accession of Henry of Navarre, who became Henry IV (1589–1610).

This glamorous prince, "who knew how to fight, to make love and to drink," as a contemporary remarked, wanted above all a strong and united France. He knew too that the majority of the French were Roman Catholics. Declaring "Paris is worth a mass," Henry knelt before the archbishop of Bourges and was received into the Roman Catholic church. Henry's willingness to sacrifice religious principles to political necessity saved France. The Edict of Nantes, which Henry published in 1598, granted to Huguenots liberty of conscience and liberty of worship in certain specified towns, such as La Rochelle. The reign of Henry IV and the Edict of Nantes prepared the way for French absolutism in the seventeenth century by helping to restore internal peace in France.

THE NETHERLANDS UNDER CHARLES V

In the last quarter of the sixteenth century, the political stability of England, the international prestige of Spain, and the moral influence of the Roman papacy all became mixed up with the religious crisis in the Low Countries. The Netherlands was the pivot around which European money, diplomacy, and war revolved. What began as a movement for the reformation of the church developed into a struggle for Dutch independence.

The emperor Charles V (1519–1556) had inherited the seventeen provinces that compose present-day Belgium and Holland (pages 480–481). Ideally situated for commerce between the Rhine and Scheldt rivers, the great towns of Bruges, Ghent, Brussels, Arras, and Amsterdam made their living by trade and industry. The French-speaking southern towns produced fine linens and woolens, while the wealth of the Dutch-speaking northern cities rested on fishing, shipping, and international banking. The city of Antwerp was the largest port and the greatest money market in Europe. In the cities of the Low Countries trade and commerce had produced a vibrant cosmopolitan atmosphere, which was well personified by the urbane Erasmus of Rotterdam.

Each of the seventeen provinces of the Netherlands possessed historic liberties: each was self-governing and enjoyed the right to make its own laws and collect its own taxes. Only the recognition of a common ruler in the person of the emperor Charles V united the provinces. Delegates from each province met together in the Estates General, but important decisions had to be referred back to each province for approval. In the middle of the sixteenth century, the seventeen provinces had a limited sense of federation.

In the Low Countries as elsewhere, corruption in the Roman church and the critical spirit of the Renaissance provoked pressure for reform. Lutheran tracts and Dutch translations of the Bible flooded the seventeen provinces in the 1520s and 1530s, attracting many people to Protestantism. Charles V's government responded with condemnation and mild repression. This policy was not particularly effective, however, because ideas circulated freely in the cosmopolitan atmosphere of the commercial centers. But Charles's personality checked the spread of Lutheranism. Charles had been born in Ghent and raised in the Netherlands; he was Flemish in language and culture. He identified with the Flemish and they with him.

In 1556, however, Charles V abdicated, dividing his territories between his brother Ferdinand, who received Austria and the Holy Roman Empire, and his son Philip, who inherited Spain, the Low Countries, and the Spanish possessions in America. Charles delivered his abdication speech before the Estates General at Brussels. The emperor was then fifty-five years old, white-haired, and so crippled in the legs that he had to lean for support on the young Prince William of Orange. According to one account:

His under lip, a Burgundian inheritance, as faithfully transmitted as the duchy and county, was heavy and hanging, the lower jaw protruding so far beyond the upper that it was impossible for him to bring together the few fragments of teeth which still remained, or to speak a whole sentence in an intelligible voice.[12]

Charles spoke in Flemish. His small, shy, and sepulchral son Philip responded in Spanish; he could speak neither French nor Flemish. The Netherlanders had always felt Charles one of themselves. They were never to forget that Philip was a Spaniard.

THE REVOLT OF THE NETHERLANDS (1556–1587)

By the 1560s, there was a strong, militant minority of Calvinists in most of the cities of the Netherlands. The seventeen provinces possessed a large middle-class population, and the "reformed religion," as a contemporary remarked, had a powerful appeal "to those who had grown rich by trade and were therefore ready for revolution."[13] Calvinism appealed to the middle classes because of its intellectual seriousness, moral gravity, and emphasis on any form of labor well done. It took deep root among the merchants and financiers in Amsterdam and the northern provinces. Working-class people were also converted, partly because their employers would hire only fellow Calvinists. Well-organized and with the backing of rich merchants, Calvinists quickly gained a wide following. Lutherans taught respect for the powers that be; the "reformed religion," however, tended to encourage opposition to "illegal" civil authorities.

In 1559, Philip II appointed his half-sister Margaret as regent of the Netherlands (1559–1567). A proud, energetic, and strong-willed woman who once had Ignatius Loyola as her confessor, Margaret pushed Philip's orders to wipe out Protestantism. She introduced the Inquisition. Her more immediate problem, however, was revenue to finance the government of the provinces. Charles V had steadily increased taxes in the Low Countries. When Margaret appealed to the Estates General, they claimed that the Low Countries were more heavily taxed than Spain. Nevertheless, Margaret raised taxes. In so doing, she quickly succeeded in uniting the opposition to the government's fiscal policy with the opposition to official repression of Calvinism.

In August 1566, fanatical Calvinists, primarily of the poorest classes, embarked upon a rampage of frightful destruction. As in France, Calvinist destruction in the Low Countries was incited by popular preaching, and attacks were aimed at religious images as symbols of false doctrines, not at people. The Cathedral of Notre Dame at Antwerp was the first target. Begun in 1124 and finished only in 1518, this church stood as a monument to the commercial prosperity of Flanders, the piety of the business classes, and the artistic genius of centuries. On six successive summer evenings, crowds swept through the nave. While the town harlots held tapers to the greatest concentration of art works in northern Europe, people armed with axes and sledgehammers smashed altars, statues, paintings, books, tombs, ecclesiastical vestments, missals, manuscripts, ornaments, stained-glass windows, and sculptures. Before the havoc was over, thirty more churches had been sacked and irreplaceable libraries burned. From Antwerp the destruction spread to Brussels and Ghent and north to the provinces of Holland and Zeeland.

From Madrid, Philip II sent twenty thousand Spanish troops under the duke of Alva to pacify the Low Countries. Alva interpreted

TO PURIFY THE CHURCH *The destruction of pictures and statues representing biblical events, Christian doctrine, or sacred figures was a central feature of the Protestant Reformation. Here Dutch Protestant soldiers destroy what they consider idols in the belief that they are purifying the church. (Fotomas Index)*

"pacification" to mean the ruthless extermination of religious and political dissidents. On top of the Inquisition he opened his own tribunal, soon called the Council of Blood. On March 3, 1568, fifteen hundred men were executed. Even Margaret was sickened and resigned her regency. Alva resolved the financial crisis by levying a 10 percent sales tax on every transaction, which in a commercial society

caused widespread hardship and confusion.

For ten years, between 1568 and 1578, civil war raged in the Netherlands between Catholics and Protestants and between the seventeen provinces and Spain. A series of Spanish generals could not halt the fighting. In 1576, the seventeen provinces united under the leadership of Prince William of Orange, called "the Silent" because of his remarkable discretion. In 1578, Philip II sent his nephew Alexander Farnese, duke of Parma, to crush the revolt once and for all. A general with a superb sense of timing, an excellent knowledge of the geography of the Low Countries, and a perfect plan, Farnese arrived with an army of German mercenaries. Avoiding pitched battles, he fought by patient sieges. One by one the cities of the south fell – Maastricht, Tournai, Bruges, Ghent, and finally the financial capital of northern Europe, Antwerp. Calvinism was forbidden in these territories, and Protestants were compelled to convert or leave. The collapse of Antwerp marked the farthest extent of Spanish jurisdiction and the political division of the Netherlands.

The ten southern provinces, the Spanish Netherlands (the future Belgium), remained under the control of the Spanish Habsburgs. The seven northern provinces, led by Holland, formed the Union of Utrecht, and in 1581 declared their independence from Spain. Thus was born the United Provinces of the Netherlands (see Map 15.2).

Geography, language and sociopolitical structure differentiated the two countries. The northern provinces were ribboned with sluices and canals and therefore were highly defensible. Several times the Dutch had broken the dikes and flooded the countryside to halt the advancing Farnese. In the southern provinces the Ardennes mountains interrupt the otherwise flat terrain. The Dutch spoken in the north was akin to German, while the Flemish spoken in the south was close to French. In the north the commercial aristocracy possessed the predominant power; in the south the landed nobility had the greater influence. The north was Protestant; the south remained Catholic.

Philip II and Alexander Farnese did not accept this geographical division, and the struggle continued after 1581. The United Provinces repeatedly begged the Protestant Queen Elizabeth of England for assistance.

The crown on the head of Elizabeth I (pages 494–495) did not rest easily. She had steered a moderately Protestant course between the Puritans, who sought the total elimination of Roman Catholic elements in the English church, and the Roman Catholics, who wanted full restoration of the old religion. Elizabeth survived a massive uprising by the Catholic north in 1569–1570. She survived two serious plots against her life. In the 1570s, the presence in England of Mary, Queen of Scots, a Roman Catholic and the legal heir to the English throne, produced a very embarrassing situation. Mary was the rallying point of all opposition to Elizabeth, yet the English sovereign hesitated to set the terrible example of regicide by ordering Mary executed.

Elizabeth faced a grave dilemma. If she responded favorably to Dutch pleas for military support against the Spanish, she would antagonize Philip II. The Spanish king had the steady flow of silver from the Americas at his disposal, and Elizabeth, lacking such treasure, wanted to avoid war. But if she did not help the Protestant Netherlands and they were crushed by Farnese, the likelihood was that the Spanish would invade England.

Three developments forced Elizabeth's hand. First, the wars in the Low Countries – the chief market for English woolens – badly hurt the English economy. When wool was not exported, the Crown lost valuable customs revenues. Second, the murder of William the Silent in July 1584 eliminated not only a great Protestant leader but the chief military check on the Farnese advance. Third, the collapse of Antwerp appeared to signal a

Catholic sweep throughout the Netherlands. The next step, the English feared, would be a Spanish invasion of their island. For these reasons, Elizabeth pumped £250,000 and two thousand troops into the Protestant cause in the Low Countries between 1585 and 1587. Increasingly fearful of the plots of Mary, Queen of Scots, Elizabeth finally signed her death warrant. Mary was beheaded on February 18, 1587. Sometime between March 24 and 30, the news of Mary's death reached Philip II.

PHILIP II AND THE SPANISH ARMADA

Philip pondered the Dutch and English developments at the Escorial northwest of Madrid. Begun in 1563 and completed under the king's personal supervision in 1584, the Monastery of Saint Lawrence of the Escorial served as a monastery for Jeromite monks, a tomb for the king's Habsburg ancestors, and a royal palace for Philip and his family. The vast buildings resemble a gridiron, the instrument on which Saint Lawrence (d. 258) had supposedly been roasted alive. The royal apartments were in the center of the Italian Renaissance building complex. King Philip's tiny bedchamber possessed a concealed sliding window that opened directly onto the high altar of the monastery church so he could watch the services and pray along with the monks. In this somber atmosphere, surrounded by a community of monks and close to the bones of his ancestors, the Catholic ruler of Spain and of much of the globe passed his days.

Philip of Spain considered himself the international defender of Catholicism and the heir to the medieval imperial power. Hoping to keep England within the Catholic church when his wife Mary Tudor died, Philip had asked Elizabeth to marry him; she had em-

MAP 15.2 THE NETHERLANDS, 1578–1609 *Although small in geographical size, the Netherlands held a strategic position in the religious struggles of the sixteenth century. Why?*

phatically refused. Several popes had urged him to move against England. When Pope Sixtus V (1585–1590) heard of the death of the queen of Scots, he promised to pay Philip 1 million gold ducats the moment Spanish troops landed in England. Alexander Farnese had repeatedly warned that to subdue the Dutch, he would have to conquer England and cut off the source of Dutch support. Philip worried that the vast amounts of South American silver he was pouring into the conquest of the Netherlands seemed to be going down a bottomless pit. Two plans for an expedition were considered. Philip's naval adviser recommended that a fleet of 150 ships sail from Lisbon, attack the English navy in the Channel, and invade England. In Antwerp, Farnese urged Philip to assemble a collection of barges and troops in Flanders to stage a cross-Channel assault. With the "inevitable" support of English Catholics, Spain would achieve a great victory.

Philip compromised. He prepared a vast armada to sail from Lisbon to Flanders, fight off Elizabeth's navy *if* it attacked, rendezvous with Farnese, and escort his barges across the English Channel. The expedition's purpose was to transport the Flemish army.

On May 9, 1588, *la felicissima armada* — "the most fortunate fleet," as it was ironically called in official documents — sailed from Lisbon harbor on the last medieval crusade. The Spanish fleet of 130 vessels carried 123,790 cannon balls and perhaps 30,000 men, every one of whom had confessed his sins and received the Eucharist. An English fleet of about 150 ships met the Spanish in the Channel. It was composed of smaller, faster, more maneuverable ships, many of which had greater firing power. A combination of storms and squalls, spoiled food and rank water, inadequate Spanish ammunition, and, to a lesser extent, English fire ships that caused the Spanish to panic and scatter, gave England the victory. Many Spanish ships went to the bottom of the ocean; perhaps 65 managed to crawl home by way of the North Sea.

The battle in the Channel has frequently been described as one of the decisive battles in the history of the world. In fact, it had mixed consequences. Spain soon rebuilt its navy, and after 1588 the quality of the Spanish fleet improved. The destruction of the Armada did not halt the flow of silver from the New World. More silver reached Spain between 1588 and 1603 than in any other fifteen-year period. The war between England and Spain dragged on for years.

The defeat of the Spanish Armada was decisive, however, in the sense that it prevented Philip II from reimposing unity on western Europe by force. He did not conquer England, and Elizabeth continued her financial and military support of the Dutch. In the Netherlands, however, neither side gained significant territory. The borders of 1581 tended to become permanent. In 1609, Philip III of Spain (1598–1621) agreed to a truce, in effect recognizing the independence of the United Provinces.

THE THIRTY YEARS' WAR (1618–1648)

While Philip II dreamed of building a second armada and Henry IV began the reconstruction of France, the political-religious situation in central Europe deteriorated. An uneasy truce had prevailed in the Holy Roman Empire since the Peace of Augsburg of 1555 (page 484). The Augsburg settlement, in recognizing the independent power of the German princes, had destroyed the authority of the central government. The Habsburg ruler in Vienna enjoyed the title of emperor but had no power.

According to the Augsburg settlement, the faith of the prince determined the religion of his subjects. Later in the century, though, Catholics grew alarmed because Lutherans, in violation of the Peace of Augsburg, were steadily acquiring north German bishoprics. The spread of Calvinism further confused the issue. The Augsburg settlement had pertained only to Lutheranism and Catholicism, but Calvinists ignored it and converted several princes. Lutherans feared that the Augsburg principles would be totally undermined by

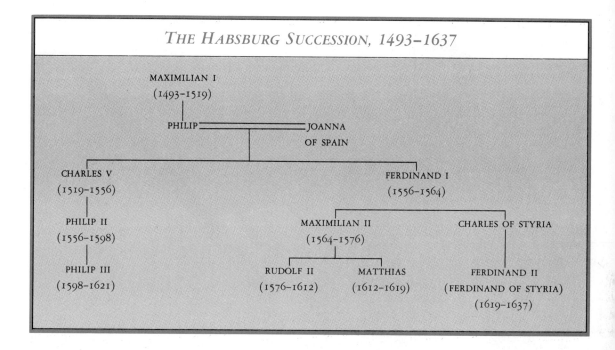

THE HABSBURG SUCCESSION, 1493–1637

MAXIMILIAN I
(1493–1519)

PHILIP ══════════════ JOANNA
OF SPAIN

CHARLES V
(1519–1556)

FERDINAND I
(1556–1564)

PHILIP II
(1556–1598)

MAXIMILIAN II
(1564–1576)

CHARLES OF STYRIA

PHILIP III
(1598–1621)

RUDOLF II
(1576–1612)

MATTHIAS
(1612–1619)

FERDINAND II
(FERDINAND OF STYRIA)
(1619–1637)

Catholic and Calvinist gains. Also, the militantly active Jesuits had reconverted several Lutheran princes to Catholicism. In an increasingly tense situation, Lutheran princes formed the Protestant Union (1608) and Catholics retaliated with the Catholic League (1609). Each alliance was determined that the other should make no religious (that is, territorial) advance. The empire was composed of two armed camps.

Dynastic interests were also involved in the German situation. When Charles V abdicated in 1556, he had divided his possessions between his son Philip II and his brother Ferdinand I. This partition began the Austrian and Spanish branches of the Habsburg family. Ferdinand inherited the imperial title and the Habsburg lands in central Europe, including Austria, Bohemia, and Hungary. Ferdinand's

grandson, Matthias, had no direct heirs and promoted the candidacy of his fanatically Catholic cousin, Ferdinand of Styria. The Spanish Habsburgs strongly supported the goals of their Austrian relatives: the unity of the empire and the preservation of Catholicism within it.

In 1617, Ferdinand of Styria secured election as king of Bohemia, a title that gave him jurisdiction over Silesia and Moravia as well as Bohemia. The Bohemians were Czech and German in nationality, and Lutheran, Calvinist, Catholic, and Hussite in religion; all these faiths enjoyed a fair degree of religious freedom. When Ferdinand proceeded to close some Protestant churches, the heavily Protestant Estates of Bohemia protested. On May 23, 1618, Protestants hurled two of Ferdinand's officials from a castle window in

SIXTEENTH-CENTURY GERMAN BATTLE HAMMER   Held in the hand with the leather thong secured around the wrist, a powerful blow from this battle hammer could instantly crush a skull or smash a rib cage. (Photo: Caroline Buckler)

SEVENTEENTH-CENTURY BATTLE ARMOR   Armor remained a symbol of the noble's high social status and military profession, although armor gave much less protection after the invention of gun powder. The maker had a sense of humor. (Photo: Caroline Buckler)

Prague. They fell seventy feet but survived: Catholics claimed that angels had caught them; Protestants said the officials fell on a heap of soft horse manure. Called "the defenestration of Prague," this event marked the beginning of the Thirty Years' War.

Historians traditionally divide the war into four phases. The first or Bohemian phase (1618–1625) was characterized by civil war in Bohemia between the Catholic League, led by Ferdinand, and the Protestant Union, headed by Prince Frederick of the Palatinate. The Bohemians fought for religious liberty and independence from Habsburg rule. In 1618, the Bohemian Estates deposed Ferdinand and gave the crown of Bohemia to Frederick, thus uniting the interests of German Protestants with those of the international enemies of the Habsburgs. Frederick wore his crown only a few months. In 1620, he was totally defeated by Catholic forces at the battle of the White Mountain. Ferdinand, who had recently been elected Holy Roman emperor as Ferdinand II, followed up his victories by wiping out Protestantism in Bohemia through forcible conversions and the activities of militant Jesuit missionaries. Within ten years, Bohemia was completely Catholic.

The second or Danish phase of the war (1625–1629) – so called because of the participation of King Christian IV of Denmark (1588–1648), the ineffective leader of the Protestant cause – witnessed additional Catholic victories. The Catholic imperial army led by Albert of Wallenstein scored smashing victories. It swept through Silesia, north through Schleswig and Jutland to the Baltic, and east into Pomerania. Wallenstein had made himself indispensable to the emperor Ferdinand, but he was an unscrupulous opportunist who used his vast riches to build an army loyal only to himself. The general

seemed interested more in carving out an empire for himself than in aiding the Catholic cause. He quarreled with the Catholic League, and soon the Catholic forces were badly divided. Religion was eclipsed as a basic issue of the war.

The year 1629 marked the peak of Habsburg power. The Jesuits persuaded the emperor to issue the Edict of Restitution, whereby all Catholic properties lost to Protestantism since 1552 were to be restored and only Catholics and Lutherans (*not* Calvinists, Hussites, or other sects) were to be allowed to practice their faiths. Ferdinand appeared to be embarked on a policy to unify the empire. When Wallenstein began ruthless enforcement of the edict, Protestants throughout Europe feared a complete collapse of the balance of power in north central Europe.

The third or Swedish phase of the war (1630–1635) began with the arrival in Germany of the Swedish king Gustavus Adolphus (1594–1632). The ablest administrator of his day and a devout Lutheran, Gustavus Adolphus intervened to support the oppressed Protestants within the empire and to assist his relatives, the exiled dukes of Mecklenburg. Cardinal Richelieu, the chief minister of King Louis XIII of France (1610–1643) subsidized the Swedes, hoping to weaken Habsburg power in Europe. In 1631, with a small but well-disciplined army equipped with superior muskets and warm uniforms, Gustavus Adolphus won a brilliant victory at Breitenfeld. Again in 1632, he was victorious at Lützen, although he was fatally wounded in the battle.

The participation of the Swedes in the Thirty Years' War proved decisive for the future of Protestantism and of later German history. When Gustavus Adolphus landed on German soil, he had already brought Denmark, Poland, Finland, and the smaller Baltic states under Swedish influence. The Swedish victories ended the Habsburg ambition of uniting all the German states under imperial authority.

The death of Gustavus Adolphus, followed by the defeat of the Swedes at the battle of Nördlingen in 1634, prompted the French to enter the war on the side of the Protestants. Thus began the French, or international, phase of the Thirty Years' War (1635–1648). For almost a century French foreign policy had been based on opposition to the Habsburgs, because a weak empire divided into scores of independent principalities enhanced France's international stature. In 1622, when the Dutch had resumed the war against Spain, the French had supported Holland. Now, in 1635, Cardinal Richelieu declared war on Spain and again sent financial and military assistance to the Swedes and the German Protestant princes. The war dragged on. French, Dutch, and Swedes, supported by Scots, Finns, and German mercenaries, burned, looted, and destroyed German agriculture and commerce. The Thirty Years' War lasted so long because neither side had the resources to win a quick, decisive victory. Finally, in October 1648, peace was achieved.

The treaties signed at Münster and Osnabrück, commonly called the Peace of Westphalia, mark a turning point in European political, religious, and social history. The treaties recognized the sovereign independent authority of the German princes. Each ruler could govern his particular territory and make war and peace as well. With power in the hands of more than three hundred princes, with no central government, courts, or means of controlling unruly rulers, the Holy Roman Empire as a real state was effectively destroyed (see Map 15.3).

The independence of the United Provinces of the Netherlands was acknowledged. The

MAP 15.3 EUROPE IN 1648 *Which country emerged from the Thirty Years War as the strongest European power? What dynastic house was that country's major rival in the early modern period?*

international stature of France and Sweden was also greatly improved by the Peace of Westphalia. The political divisions within the empire, the weak German frontiers, and the acquisition of the province of Alsace increased France's size and prestige. The treaties allowed France to intervene at will in German affairs. Sweden received a large cash indemnity and jurisdiction over German territories along the Baltic Sea. The powerful Swedish presence in northeastern Germany subsequently posed a major threat to the future kingdom of Brandenburg-Prussia. The treaties also denied the papacy the right to participate in German religious affairs – a restriction symbolizing the reduced role of the Roman Catholic church in European politics.

In religion the Westphalian treaties stipulated that the Augsburg agreement of 1555 should stand permanently. The sole modification was that Calvinism, along with Catholicism and Lutheranism, would become a legally permissible creed. In practice the north German states remained Protestant, the south German states Catholic. The war settled little. Both sides had wanted peace, and with remarkable illogic they fought for thirty years to get it.

GERMANY AFTER THE THIRTY YEARS' WAR

The Thirty Years' War was a disaster for the German economy and society, probably the most destructive event in German history before the twentieth century. Population losses were frightful. Perhaps one-third of the urban residents and two-fifths of the inhabitants of

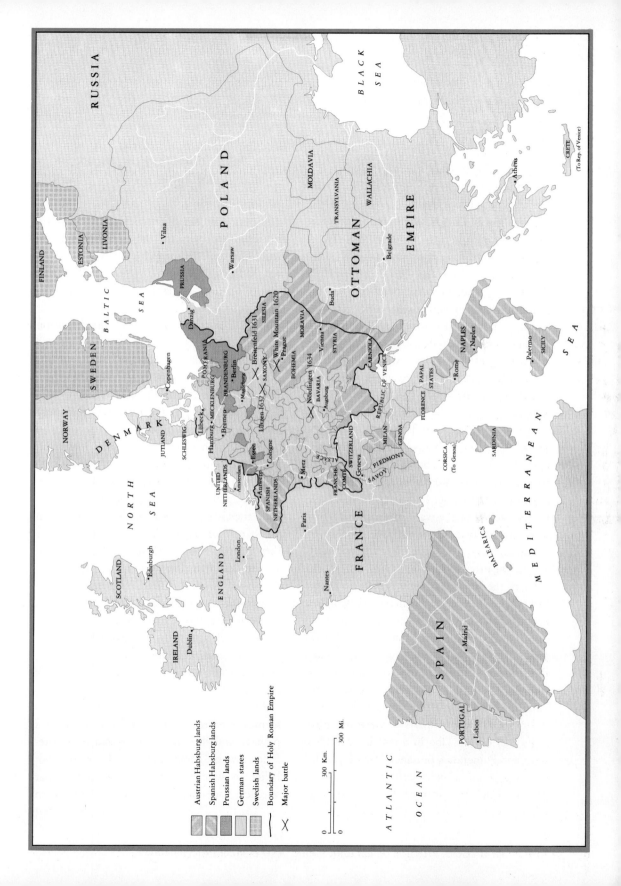

RUSSIA

FINLAND

ESTONIA

LIVONIA

• Vilna

POLAND

MOLDAVIA

WALLACHIA

BLACK SEA

CRETE
(To Rep. of Venice)

• Athens

SWEDEN

BALTIC SEA

PRUSSIA

• Danzig

• Warsaw

OTTOMAN EMPIRE

• Belgrade

NORWAY

DENMARK

NORTH SEA

Copenhagen •

JUTLAND

SCHLESWIG

Lübeck •

Hamburg •

Bremen •

POMERANIA

MECKLENBURG

BRANDENBURG

• Berlin

Magdeburg •

SILESIA

White Mountain 1620

Breitenfeld 1631

SAXONY

Lützen 1632

BOHEMIA

Prague •

MORAVIA

Nördlingen 1634

BAVARIA

Augsburg •

Vienna •

STYRIA

Buda •

TRANSYLVANIA

CARNIOLA

REPUBLIC OF VENICE

NAPLES

• Naples

SICILY

• Palermo

MEDITERRANEAN SEA

SCOTLAND

Edinburgh •

IRELAND

Dublin •

ENGLAND

London •

UNITED NETHERLANDS

Amsterdam •

Antwerp •

SPANISH NETHERLANDS

Essen •

Cologne •

Metz •

ALSACE

FRANCHE COMTÉ

SWITZERLAND

Geneva •

MILAN

PIEDMONT

SAVOY

GENOA

FLORENCE

PAPAL STATES

Rome •

CORSICA
(To Genoa)

SARDINIA

Paris •

FRANCE

Nantes •

SPAIN

• Madrid

BALEARICS

PORTUGAL

Lisbon •

ATLANTIC OCEAN

Austrian Habsburg lands
Spanish Habsburg lands
Prussian lands
German states
Swedish lands
Boundary of Holy Roman Empire
Major battle

0   300 Km.
0   300 Mi.

rural areas died. Entire areas of Germany were depopulated, partly by military actions, partly by disease – typhus, dysentery, bubonic plague, and syphilis accompanied the movements of armies – and partly by the thousands of refugees who fled to safer areas.

In the late sixteenth and early seventeenth centuries, all Europe experienced an economic crisis primarily caused by the influx of silver from South America. Because the Thirty Years' War was fought on German soil, these economic difficulties were badly aggravated in the empire. Scholars still cannot estimate the value of losses in agricultural land and livestock, in trade and commerce. The trade of southern cities like Augsburg, already hard hit by the shift in transportation routes from the Mediterranean to the Atlantic, was virtually destroyed by the fighting in the south. Meanwhile, towns like Lübeck, Hamburg, and Bremen in the north and Essen in the Ruhr actually prospered because of the many refugees they attracted. The destruction of land and foodstuffs, compounded by the flood of Spanish silver, brought on a severe price rise. During and after the war, inflation was worse in Germany than anywhere else in Europe.

Agricultural areas suffered catastrophically. The population decline caused a rise in the value of the labor, and owners of great estates had to pay more for agricultural workers. Farmers who needed only small amounts of capital to restore their lands started over again. Many small farmers, however, lacked the revenue to rework their holdings and had to become day laborers. Nobles and landlords bought up many small holdings and acquired great estates. In some parts of Germany, especially east of the Elbe in areas like Mecklenburg and Pomerania, peasants' loss of land led to the rise of a new serfdom.[14] Thus the Thirty Years' War contributed to the legal

and economic decline of the largest segment of German society.

THE GREAT EUROPEAN WITCH-HUNT

The period of the religious wars witnessed a startling increase in the phenomenon of witch-hunting, whose prior history was long but sporadic. "A witch," according to Chief Justice Coke of England, "was a person who hath conference with the Devil to consult with him or to do some act." This definition by the highest legal authority in England demonstrates that educated people, as well as the ignorant, believed in witches. Belief in witches – individuals who could mysteriously injure other people, for instance by causing them to become blind or impotent, and who could harm animals, for example by preventing cows from giving milk – dates back to the dawn of time. For centuries tales had circulated about old women who made nocturnal travels on greased broomsticks to "sabbats," or assemblies of witches, where they participated in sexual orgies and feasted on the flesh of infants. In the popular imagination witches had definite characteristics: the vast majority were married women or widows between fifty and seventy years old, crippled or bent with age, with pockmarked skin; they often practiced midwifery or folk medicine, and most had sharp tongues and were quick to scold.

In the sixteenth century religious reformers' extreme notions of the devil's powers, and the insecurity created by the religious wars, contributed to the growth of belief in witches. The idea developed that witches made pacts with the devil in return for the power to work mischief on their enemies. Since pacts with the devil meant the renunciation of God, witchcraft was considered heresy, and all religions persecuted it.

Fear of witches took a terrible toll of innocent lives in parts of Europe. In southwestern Germany 3,229 witches were executed between 1561 and 1670, most by burning. The communities of the Swiss Confederation tried 8,888 persons between 1470 and 1700 and executed 5,417 of them as witches. In all the centuries before 1500 witches in England had been suspected of causing perhaps "three deaths, a broken leg, several destructive storms and some bewitched genitals." Yet between 1559 and 1736 witches were thought to have caused thousands of deaths, and in that period almost 1,000 witches were executed in England.[15]

Historians and anthropologists have offered a variety of explanations for the great European witch-hunt. Some scholars maintain that charges of witchcraft were a means of accounting for inexplicable misfortunes. Just as the English in the fifteenth century had blamed their military failures in France on Joan of Arc's sorcery, so in the seventeenth century the English Royal College of Physicians attributed undiagnosable illnesses to witchcraft. Some scholars hold that in small communities, which typically insisted on strict social conformity, charges of witchcraft were a means of attacking and eliminating the nonconformist; witches, in other words, served the collective need for scapegoats. The evidence of witches' trials, some writers suggest, shows that women were not accused because they harmed or threatened their neighbors; rather, their communities believed such women worshiped the devil, engaged in wild sexual activities with him, and ate infants. Other scholars argue the exact opposite:

that people were tried and executed as witches because their neighbors feared their evil powers. Finally, there is the theory that the unbridled sexuality of which witches were accused was a psychological projection on the part of their accusers, resulting from Christianity's repression of sexuality. The reasons for the persecution of witches probably varied from place to place. Perhaps witches, symbolizing unacceptable ideas or practices, were "victims of society's constant pressure towards intellectual conformity."[16]

SEXISM, RACISM, AND SKEPTICISM

The age of religious wars revealed extreme and violent contrasts. It was a deeply religious period in which men fought passionately for their beliefs; seventy percent of the books printed dealt with religious subjects. Yet the times saw the beginnings of religious skepticism. Europeans explored new continents, partly with the missionary aim of Christianizing the peoples they encountered. Yet the Spanish, Portuguese, Dutch, and English proceeded to enslave the Indians and blacks they encountered. While Europeans indulged in gross sensuality, the social status of women declined. Sexism, racism, and skepticism had all originated in ancient times. But late in the sixteenth century they began to take on their familiar modern forms.

THE STATUS OF WOMEN

The decades between 1560 and 1648 witnessed another decline in the status of women in European society. The Reformation did not help women. The early reformers had urged study of the Bible as the means of improving human conduct. Scriptural study, however, tended to revive Saint Paul's notion that women are the source of sin and vice in the world. Also, the violence and upheaval of the religious wars was followed by a period of reaction and retrenchment. While early humanists such as Erasmus and Zwingli had allowed divorce on grounds of insanity and extreme cruelty, by 1600 all faiths firmly opposed divorce on any grounds. In England, for example, only an act of Parliament could dissolve a marriage.

Although private opinions and public laws relating to the social position of women varied widely, the weight of evidence from the sixteenth and seventeenth centuries indicates that women were considered to be decidedly inferior beings. Their social value rested on their ability to produce heirs. A few women, of course, had power and influence. Margaret of Austria, Charles V's aunt, and Louise of Savoy, Francis I's mother — they cannot be identified apart from their male relatives — conducted the diplomatic negotiations that in 1529 led to the Peace of Cambrai and the end of the second phase of the Habsburg-Valois wars. Jeanne d'Albret, the mother of Henry of Navarre (later Henry IV of France), legalized Calvinism in her domain and aided its spread through France; she was known as "the Saint of the Reform." Likewise, Mary Tudor reestablished Catholicism in England. All these women, however, were of royal blood.

The great majority of women were treated either as grown-up children to be teasingly indulged or as hopelessly irrational. The attitude of John Knox, the Calvinist reformer of the Scottish church, was not atypical: "Nature doth paint them forth to be weak, frail, impatient, feeble and foolish, and experience hath declared them to be unconstant, variable, cruel, and void of the spirit of council and regiment." (Knox had in mind the Catholic

Mary, Queen of Scots, whom he had good political reasons for fearing.) In 1595, the professors at Wittenberg University solemnly debated whether or not women are human beings. Humanists repeated the ancient story of woman the temptress and cause of sin in the world.

Artists' drawings of plump, voluptuous women and massive, muscular men reveal the contemporary standards of physical beauty. It was a sensual age that gloried in the delights of the flesh. Some people, such as the humanist-poet Aretino, found sexual satisfaction with both sexes. Reformers and public officials simultaneously condemned and condoned sexual "sins." The oldest profession had many practitioners, and when in 1566 Pope Pius IV expelled all the prostitutes from Rome, so many people left and the city suffered such a loss of revenue that in less than a month the pope was forced to rescind the order. Scholars debated Saint Augustine's notion that whores serve a useful social function by preventing worse sins. Prostitution was common, because desperate poverty forced women and young men into it. The general public took it for granted. Consequently, civil authorities in both Catholic and Protestant countries licensed houses of public prostitution. These establishments were intended for the convenience of single men, and some Protestant cities, such as Geneva and Zurich, installed officials in the brothels with the ex-

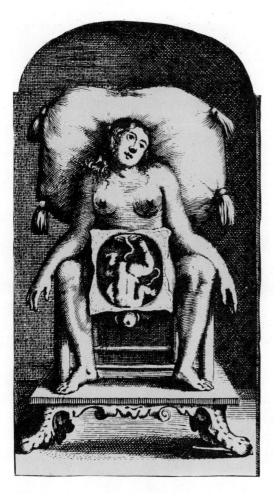

WOMAN IN LABOR *The production of male heirs was women's major social responsibility. Long into modern times a sitting or squatting position for the delivery of babies was common, because it allowed the mother to push. The calm and wistful look on the mother's face suggests a remarkably easy delivery; it is the artist's misconception of the process. (Photo: Caroline Buckler)*

press purpose of preventing married men from patronizing them.

Marriage for all social classes remained a serious business, entered into primarily to advance the economic interests of the parties. There are some remarkable success stories. Elizabeth Hardwick, the orphaned daughter of an obscure English country squire, made four careful marriages, each of which brought her more property and carried her higher up the social ladder. She managed her estates, amounting to more than a hundred thousand acres, with a degree of business sense rare in any age. The two great mansions she built, Chatsworth and Hardwick, stand today as monuments to her acumen. As countess of Shrewsbury, "Bess of Hardwick" so thoroughly enjoyed the trust of Queen Elizabeth that Elizabeth appointed her jailer of Mary, Queen of Scots. Having established several aristocratic dynasties, the countess of Shrewsbury died in 1608, past her eightieth year, one of the richest people in England.[17]

While the Catholic church held up the ideal of celibacy and the religious life as the highest form of Christian life, Protestantism exalted the dignity of marriage. Luther insisted that absolute celibacy was impossible. In the Middle Ages, and later in Catholic countries, the religious life provided a career option for women who did not choose or could not afford to marry. For Protestant women, marriage became the only professional possibility. Protestant marriages took on the form of a contract, whereby each partner promised the other support, understanding, and sharing of material goods. Within marriage many women certainly controlled their own destinies, but there was no question of social or legal equality: wives were subordinate to their husbands.

If some nuns in the later Middle Ages

lacked a religious vocation, and if some religious houses witnessed moral laxness and financial mismanagement, nevertheless convents provided the only scope for the literary, artistic, and administrative talents of unmarried women. In abolishing the religious houses, Protestantism threw out the baby with the bathwater. Marriage became virtually the only occupation for Protestant women, which helps to explain why Anglicans, Calvinists, and Lutherans established communities of religious women in the eighteenth and nineteenth centuries.

Many sixteenth-century reformers, including Luther, Erasmus, and several popes, believed polygamy less of an evil than divorce. (By polygamy they meant a man having several wives at the same time, not a woman having more than one husband.) Theologians found scriptural justification for their position on polygamy. Except among the Anabaptists, however, polygamy was rarely practiced.

If the partners to a monogamous marriage found themselves unsuited, there was virtually no socially acceptable way out. In Catholic countries as well as Protestant ones, a woman could not secure a divorce on grounds of extreme cruelty, desertion, adultery, or complete incompatibility. Women's social and legal position became steadily more confined, and, apart from the upper classes, that position would not change much before the nineteenth century. Death alone dissolved a legitimate marriage. When a spouse died, the great majority of survivors remarried.[18]

ORIGINS OF NORTH AMERICAN RACISM: THE AFRICAN SLAVE TRADE

The Age of Discovery opened up vast new continents for European exploration and exploitation. Once across the Atlantic, the major problem European settlers faced was a shortage of labor. As early as 1495, the Spanish solved the problem by enslaving the native Indians. In the sixteenth and seventeenth centuries, the Portuguese, the Dutch, and the English followed suit.

Unaccustomed to any form of manual labor, and certainly to panning gold for more than twelve hours a day in the broiling sun, the Indians died "like fish in a bucket," as one Spanish settler reported.[19] In 1515, a Spanish missionary, Bartholomé de Las Casas (1474-1566), who had seen the evils of Indian slavery, urged Emperor Charles V to end Indian slavery in his American dominions. Las Casas recommended the importation of blacks from Africa, both because church law did not strictly forbid black slavery and because blacks could better survive under South American conditions. The emperor agreed, and in 1518 the African slave trade began.

Several European nations participated in the African slave trade. Spain brought the first slaves to Brazil; by 1600, 44,000 were being imported annually. Between 1619 and 1623, the Dutch West India Company, with the full support of the government of the United Provinces, transported 15,430 Africans to Brazil. Only in the late seventeenth century, with the chartering of the Royal African Company, did the English get involved. Thereafter, large numbers of African blacks poured into the North American colonies. In 1790, there were 757,181 Negroes in a total United States population of 3,929,625. When the first census was taken in Brazil in 1798, Negroes numbered about 2 million in a total population of 3.25 million.

Almost all peoples in the world have engaged in slavery at some time in their histories. Since ancient times, victors in battle had enslaved conquered peoples. European slavers found slavery widespread in Africa when they arrived in the sixteenth and seventeenth centuries, and they had no difficulty finding Africans willing to sell their captured tribal enemies for cloth, jewelry, guns and whiskey. In seeking slaves in Africa, Europeans encouraged more slave hunting.

Almost as soon as the institution of black slavery was introduced into the New World, controversy arose about it. Las Casas and others soon became disgusted with the Spanish treatment of blacks, and criticized black slavery on the same grounds as Indian slavery: it was inhumane. By the late seventeenth century, abolitionist movements existed in both South and North America.

European settlers brought to the New World the racial attitudes they had absorbed in Europe. North American attitudes derive basically from England. On the eve of the Age of Discovery, the English were overwhelmingly a rural people. Tough, sober, accustomed to unending hard work relieved by few physical comforts, a quarrelsome but rarely violent people, they accepted life with stoical patience. The age was cruel, and the English were not compassionate. The public execution of criminals and the stoning of wretches tied up in the village stocks were major occasions for public entertainment. When a good workman fell from a ladder and was permanently disabled, his community was more concerned that he would become a public charge than about his misfortune.[20]

Early Christian writers in the fourth and fifth centuries had identified blackness with sin and corruption. This notion had become deep-rooted over the centuries. Thus in 1550, when the first black Africans appeared on the streets of London, the concept of blackness was already loaded with emotional meaning. Black meant "deeply stained with dirt, soiled,

THE SPANISH IN AMERICA   The Spanish used barbaric methods to frighten and subdue the Indians. Based on the eyewitness accounts of the Spanish missionary Bartholomew de las Casas, illustrations of Spanish cruelties satisfied Europeans' curiosity about the New World, gratified appetites for bizarre tortures, and promoted anti-Spanish and anti-Catholic feelings. (Photo: Caroline Buckler)

dirty, foul . . . malignant, having dark or deadly purposes."[21] White, on the other hand, connoted purity and virginity, goodness and cleanliness. Physical beauty to the English meant an almost alabaster white skin tinged with pink. The Negro's black skin, "disfigured" facial features, and curled hair seemed the exact opposite of the physical ideal.

Art and literature had already given English people some acquaintance with "Ethiopians," as black Africans had been called since Roman times. In the sixteenth and seventeenth centuries, the English were still extremely curious about Africans' lives and customs, and slavers' accounts were extraordinarily popular. Travel literature depicted Africans as savages because of their eating habits, morals, clothing, and social customs; as barbarians because of their language and methods of war; and as heathens because they were not Christian. English people saw similarities between apes and Africans; thus, the terms "bestial" and "beastly" were frequently applied to Africans. Africans were believed to possess a potent sexuality and to be extremely lustful. One seventeenth-century observer considered Africans "very lustful and impudent, . . (for a Negroes hiding his members, their extraordinary greatness) is a token of their lust." African women were considered sexually aggressive and "possessed of a temper hot and lascivious."[22]

The English used the heathenism of the Africans as a justification for enslaving them.

Africans appeared to suit the agricultural needs of the underpopulated continent of North America. Unlike the North American Indians, who were armed, however primitively, and had the psychological support of their tribes, the Africans, stripped of their languages and tribal cultures, were powerless in the New World. Moreover, in spite of the dangers of the trade in Africa and the frightful loss of life among both traders and slaves, the profits in slavery were enormous.

In the seventeenth and eighteenth centuries, English colonists in North America continued to believe in these supposed social characteristics of Africans. Gradually they became part of the American mental furniture. The myths of black savagery, barbarism, and lechery became the classic stereotypes of modern American racial attitudes.

THE ORIGIN OF MODERN SKEPTICISM: MICHEL DE MONTAIGNE

The decades of religious fanaticism, bringing in their wake death, famine, and civil anarchy, caused both Catholics and Protestants to doubt that any one faith contained absolute truth. The late sixteenth and early seventeenth centuries witnessed the beginnings of modern skepticism. Skepticism is a school of thought founded on doubt that total certainty or definitive knowledge is ever attainable. The skeptic is cautious and critical, and suspends judgment. Perhaps the finest representative of early modern skepticism is the Frenchman Michel de Montaigne (1533–1592).

Montaigne came from a bourgeois family that had made a fortune selling salted herring and in 1477 had purchased the title and property of Montaigne in Gascony. Montaigne received a classical education before studying law and securing a judicial appointment in 1554. Although a member of the nobility, in

embarking on a judicial career he identified with the new nobility of the robe. He condemned the ancient nobility of the sword for being more concerned with war and sports than with the cultivation of the mind.

At the age of thirty-eight, Montaigne resigned his judicial post, retired to his estate, and devoted the rest of his life to study, contemplation, and the effort to understand himself. Like the Greeks, he believed that the object of life was to "know thyself," for self-knowledge teaches men and women how to live in accordance with nature and God. Montaigne developed a new literary genre, the essay – from the French *essayer,* meaning to test or try – to express his thoughts and ideas.

Montaigne's *Essays* provide insight into the mind of a remarkably humane, tolerant, and civilized man. He was a humanist; he loved the Greek and Roman writers and was always eager to learn from them. In his essay "On Solitude," he quoted the Roman poet Horace:

Reason and sense remove anxiety,
Not villas that look out upon the sea

Ambition, avarice, irresolution, fear, and lust do not leave us when we change our country.

Some said to Socrates that a certain man had grown no better by his travels. "I should think not," he said; "he took himself along with him. . . ."
   We should have wife, children, goods, and above all health, if we can; but we must not bind ourselves to them so strongly that our happiness depends on them. We must reserve a back shop all our own, entirely free, in which to establish our real liberty and our principal retreat and solitude. . . .[23]

From the ancient authors, especially the Roman stoic Seneca, Montaigne acquired a sense of calm, inner peace, and patience. The ancient authors also inculcated in him a tolerance and broad-mindedness. Montaigne had grown up during the French civil wars, perhaps the worst kind of war. Religious ideology had set family against family, even brother against brother. He wrote:

In this controversy . . . France is at present agitated by civil wars, the best and soundest side is undoubtedly that which maintains both the old religion and the old government of the country. However, among the good men who follow that side (for I speak not of those who use it as a pretext either to wreak their private vengeances, or to supply their avarice, or to pursue the favor of princes; but of those who follow it out of true zeal toward their religion and a holy concern for maintaining the peace and the status of their fatherland) – of these, I say, we see many whom passion drives outside the bounds of reason, and makes them sometimes adopt unjust, violent, and even reckless courses. . . .[24]

Although he remained a Catholic, Montaigne possessed a detachment, an independence, an openness of mind, and a willingness to look at all sides of a question. As he wrote, "I listen with attention to the judgment of all men; but so far as I can remember, I have followed none but my own. Though I set little value upon my own opinion, I set no more on the opinions of others."

In a violent and cruel age, Montaigne was a gentle and sensitive man. In his famous essay "On Cruelty," he said:

Among other vices, I cruelly hate cruelty, both by nature and by judgment, as the extreme of all vices. . . .

I live in a time when we abound in incredible examples of this vice, through the license of our civil wars; and we see in the ancient histories nothing more extreme than what we experience of

this every day. But that has not reconciled me to it at all.[25]

In the book-lined tower where Montaigne passed his days, he became a deeply learned man. Yet he was not ignorant of the world of affairs, and he criticized scholars and bookworms who ignored the life around them. Montaigne's essay "On Cannibals" reflects the impact of overseas discoveries on Europeans' consciousness. His tolerant mind rejected the notion that one culture is superior to another:

I long had a man in my house that lived ten or twelve years in the New World, discovered in these latter days, and in that part of it where Villegaignon landed [Brazil]. . . .

I find that there is nothing barbarous and savage in [that] nation, by anything that I can gather, excepting, that every one gives the title of barbarism to everything that is not in use in his own country. As, indeed, we have no other level of truth and reason, than the example and idea of the opinions and customs of the place wherein we live: there is always the perfect religion, there is perfect government, there the most exact and accomplished usage of all things. . . .[26]

In his belief in the nobility of human beings in the state of nature, uncorrupted by organized society, and in his cosmopolitan attitude toward different civilizations, Montaigne anticipated many eighteenth-century thinkers.

The thought of Michel de Montaigne marks a sharp break with the past. Faith and religious certainty had characterized the intellectual attitudes of Western society for a millennium. Montaigne's rejection of any kind of dogmatism, his secularism, and his skepticism thus represent a basic change. In his own time, and throughout the seventeenth century, few would have agreed with him. The publication of his ideas, however, anticipated a basic shift in attitudes. Montaigne inaugurated an era of doubt. "Wonder," he said, "is the foundation of all philosophy, research is the means of all learning, and ignorance is the end."[27]

ELIZABETHAN AND JACOBEAN LITERATURE

The age of the religious wars and European expansion also experienced an extraordinary degree of intellectual ferment. In addition to the development of the essay as a distinct literary genre, the late sixteenth and early seventeenth centuries fostered remarkable creativity in other branches of literature. England, especially, in the latter part of Elizabeth's reign and the first years of her successor James I (1603–1625), witnessed unparalleled brilliance. The terms *Elizabethan* and *Jacobean* (referring to the reign of James) are used to designate the English music, poetry, prose, and drama of this period. The poetry of Sir Philip Sidney (1554–1586), such as *Astrophel and Stella,* strongly influenced later poetic writing. *The Faerie Queene* of Edmund Spenser (1552–1599) endures as one of the greatest moral epics in any language. The rare poetic beauty of the plays of Christopher Marlowe (1564–1593), such as *Tamburlaine* and *The Jew of Malta,* paved the way for the work of Shakespeare. Above all, the immortal dramas of Shakespeare and the stately prose of the Authorized or King James Bible mark the Elizabethan and Jacobean periods as the golden age of English literature.

William Shakespeare (1564–1616), the son of a successful glove manufacturer who rose to the highest municipal office in the Warwickshire town of Stratford-on-Avon, chose a career on the London stage. By 1592 he had gained recognition as an actor and playwright.

Between 1599 and 1603 Shakespeare performed in the Lord Chamberlain's Company and became co-owner of the Globe Theater, which after 1603 presented his plays.

Shakespeare's genius lies in the originality of his characterizations, the diversity of his plots, his understanding of human psychology, and his unexcelled gift for language. Shakespeare was a Renaissance man in his deep appreciation for classical culture, individualism, and humanism. Such plays as *Julius Caesar, Pericles,* and *Antony and Cleopatra* deal with classical subjects and figures. Several of his comedies have Italian Renaissance settings. The nine history plays, including *Richard II, Richard III,* and *Henry IV,* enjoyed the greatest popularity among Shakespeare's contemporaries. Written during the decade after the defeat of the Spanish Armada, the history plays express English national consciousness; lines such as these from *Richard II* reflect this sense of national greatness with unparalleled eloquence:

This royal Throne of Kings, this scepter'd Isle,
This earth of Majesty, this seat of Mars,
This other Eden, demi-paradise,
This fortress built by Nature for herself,
Against infection and the hand of war:
This happy breed of men, this little world,
This precious stone, set in the silver sea,
Which serves it in the office of a wall,
Or as a moat defensive to a house,
Against the envy of less happier Lands,
This blessed plot, this earth, this Realm, this
    England. . .

Shakespeare's later plays, above all the tragedies *Hamlet, Othello,* and *Macbeth,* explore an enormous range of human problems and are capable of an almost infinite variety of interpretations. *Othello,* which the nineteenth-century historian Thomas Macaulay called "perhaps the greatest work in the world,"

A ROYAL PICNIC   The English court imitated the Italian Renaissance devotion to nature. (See Bellini's Feast of the Gods — *in first color section.) In this pastoral atmosphere suggestive of classical mythology, Queen Elizabeth interrupts the day's hunt for a picnic in the forest. The meal seems to consist of fowl, bread, wine, and perhaps pastries. (The Huntington Library, San Marino, California)*

portrays an honorable man destroyed by a flaw in his own character and the satanic evil of his supposed friend Iago. *Macbeth's* central theme is exorbitant ambition. Shakespeare analyzes the psychology of sin in the figures of Macbeth and Lady Macbeth whose mutual love under the pressure of ambition leads to their destruction. The central figure in *Hamlet,* a play suffused with individuality, wrestles with moral problems connected with revenge and with man's relationship to life and death. The soliloquy in which Hamlet debates suicide is perhaps the most widely quoted passage in English literature:

To be, or not to be: that is the question:
Whether 'tis nobler in the mind to suffer
The slings and arrows of outrageous fortune,
Or to take arms against a sea of troubles,
And by opposing end them? To die: to sleep;
No more; and by a sleep to say we end
The heart-ache and the thousand natural shocks
That flesh is heir to, 'tis a consummation
Devoutly to be wish'd.

Hamlet's sad cry, "There is nothing either good or bad but thinking makes it so," expresses the anguish and uncertainty of modern man. *Hamlet* has always enjoyed great popularity, because in his many-faceted personality people have seen an aspect of themselves.

Shakespeare's dynamic language bespeaks his extreme sensitivity to the sounds and meanings of words. Perhaps no phrase better summarizes the reason for his immortality than this line, slightly modified, from *Antony and Cleopatra:* "Age cannot wither [him], nor custom stale/[his] infinite variety."

The other great masterpiece of the Jacobean period was the *Authorized Bible.* At a theological conference in 1604, a group of Puritans urged James I to support a new translation of the Bible. The king in turn assigned the task to a committee of scholars, who published their efforts in 1611. Based on the best scriptural research of the time and divided into chapters and verses, the Authorized Version is actually a revision of earlier Bibles more than an original work. Yet it provides a superb expression of the mature English vernacular in the early seventeenth century. Thus, Psalm 37:

Fret not thy selfe because of evill doers, neither bee
*   thou envious against the workers of iniquitie.*
For they shall soone be cut downe like the grasse;
*   and wither as the greene herbe.*
Trust in the Lord, and do good, so shalt thou
*   dwell in the land, and verely thou shalt be*
*   fed.*
Delight thy selfe also in the Lord; and he shall
*   give thee the desires of thine heart.*
Commit thy way unto the Lord: trust also in him,
*   and he shall bring it to passe.*
And he shall bring forth thy righteousness as the
*   light, and thy judgement as the noone day.*

The Authorized Version, so-called because it was produced under royal sponsorship – it had no official ecclesiastical endorsement – represented the Anglican and Puritan desire to encourage lay people to read the Scriptures. It quickly achieved great popularity and displaced all earlier versions. British settlers carried this Bible to the North American colonies, where it became known as the *King*

James Bible. For centuries the *King James Bible* has had a profound influence on the language and lives of English-speaking peoples.

———◆———

In the sixteenth and seventeenth centuries, Europeans explored and for the first time gained access to large parts of the globe. European peoples had the intellectual curiosity, the driving ambition, and the scientific technology to attempt feats that were as difficult and expensive then as is going to the moon in our own time. Exploration and exploitation contributed to a more sophisticated standard of living, in the form of spices and Asian luxury goods, and to a terrible international inflation resulting from the influx of South American silver and gold. Governments, the upper classes, and the peasantry were badly hurt by the inflation. Meanwhile the middle class of bankers, shippers, financiers, and manufacturers prospered for much of the seventeenth century.

European expansion and colonization took place against a background of religious conflict and budding national consciousness. The seventeenth century was by no means a secular period. Although the medieval religious framework had broken down, people still thought largely in religious terms. Europeans explained what they did politically and economically in terms of religious doctrine. Religious ideology served as a justification for a variety of goals: the French nobles' opposition to the Crown, the Dutch struggle for political and economic independence from Spain. In Germany religious pluralism and foreign ambitions added to political difficulties. After 1648, the divisions between Protestant and Catholic tended to become permanent. Religious skepticism and racial attitudes were harbingers of developments to come.

NOTES

1. Quoted by C. M. Cipolla, *Guns, Sails, and Empires: Technological Innovation and the Early Phases of European Expansion, 1400–1700,* Minerva Press, New York, 1965, pp. 115–116.

2. Quoted by S. E. Morison, *Admiral of the Ocean Sea: A Life of Christopher Columbus,* Little, Brown, Boston, 1946, p. 154.

3. Cipolla, pp. 90–131.

4. J. H. Parry, *The Age of Reconnaissance,* Mentor Books, New York, 1963, chaps. 3 and 5.

5. Quoted by Cipolla, p. 132.

6. Quoted by F. H. Littell, *The Macmillan Atlas History of Christianity,* Macmillan, New York, 1976, p. 75.

7. Quoted by Cipolla, p. 133.

8. Quoted by J. Hale, "War and Public Opinion in the Fifteenth and Sixteenth Centuries," *Past and Present* 22 (July 1962):29.

9. See ibid., pp. 18–32.

10. Quoted by N. Z. Davis, "The Rites of Violence: Religious Riot in Sixteenth Century France," *Past and Present* 59 (May 1973):59.

11. See ibid., pp. 51–91.

12. Quoted by J. L. Motley, *The Rise of the Dutch Republic,* David McKay, Philadelphia, 1898, 1.109.

13. Quoted by P. Smith, *The Age of the Reformation,* Henry Holt, New York, 1951, p. 248.

14. H. Kamen, "The Economic and Social Consequences of the Thirty Years' War," *Past and Present* 39 (April 1968):44–61.

15. Norman Cohn, *Europe's Inner Demons: An Enquiry Inspired by the Great Witch-Hunt,* Basic Books, New York, 1975, pp. 253–254; Keith Thomas, *Religion and the Decline of Magic,* Charles Scribner's Sons, New York, 1971, pp. 450–455.

16. See Keith Thomas, op. cit., pp. 435–446; Cohn, op. cit., pp. 258–263.

17. See D. Durant, *Bess of Hardwick: Portrait of an Elizabethan Dynast,* Weidenfeld & Nicolson, London, 1977.

18. S. M. Wyntjes, "Women in the Reformation Era," in *Becoming Visible: Women in European History,* ed. R. Bridenthal and C. Koonz, Houghton Mifflin, Boston, 1977, p. 187.

19. Quoted by D. P. Mannix, *Black Cargoes: A History of the Atlantic Slave Trade,* Viking, New York, 1968, p. 5.

20. W. Notestein, *The English People on the Eve of Colonization,* Harper & Brothers, New York, 1954, p. 14.

21. Quoted by W. D. Jordan, *The White Man's Burden: Historical Origins of Racism in the United States,* Oxford University Press, New York, 1974, p. 6.

22. Ibid., p. 19.

23. Quoted by D. M. Frame, trans., *The Complete Works of Montaigne,* Stanford University Press, Stanford, Calif., 1958, pp. 175-176.

24. Ibid., p. 177.

25. Ibid., p. 306.

26. Quoted by C. Cotton, trans., *The Essays of Michel de Montaigne,* A. L. Burt, New York, 1893, pp. 207, 210.

27. Ibid., p. 523.

SUGGESTED READING

Perhaps the best starting point for the study of European society in the age of exploration is J. H. Parry, *The Age of Reconnaissance* (1963), which treats the causes and consequences of the voyages of discovery. Parry's splendidly illustrated *The Discovery of South America* (1979) examines Europeans' reactions to the maritime discoveries and treats the entire concept of new *discoveries.* The urbane studies of C. M. Cipolla present fascinating material on technological and sociological developments written in a lucid style: *Guns, Sails, and Empires: Technological Innovation and the Early Phases of European Expansion, 1400-1700* (1965); *Clocks and Culture, 1300-1700* (1967); *Cristofano and the Plague: A Study in the History of Public Health in the Age of Galileo* (1973); and *Public Health and the Medical Profession in the Renaissance* (1976). S. E. Morison, *Admiral of the Ocean Sea: A Life of Christopher Columbus* (1946), is the standard biography of the great discoverer.

For the religious wars, in addition to the references in the Suggested Reading for Chapter 14 and in the Notes to this chapter, see J. H. M. Salmon, *Society in Crisis: France in the Sixteenth Century* (1975), which traces the fate of French institutions during the civil wars. A. N. Galpern, *The Religions of the People in Sixteenth-Century Champagne* (1976), is a useful case study in religious anthropology, and William A. Christian, Jr., *Local Religion in Sixteenth Century Spain* (1981) traces the attitudes and practices of ordinary people.

A beautifully illustrated introduction to Holland is K. H. D. Kaley, *The Dutch in the Seventeenth Century* (1972). The best comprehensive treatment of the religious strife and civil wars in the Low Countries remains that of J. L. Motley, *The Rise of the Dutch Republic,* 3 vols. (1898). The student who reads French will find a wealth of material in H. Hauser, *La prépondérance espagnole, 1559-1660* (1948).

Of the many biographies of Elizabeth of England, Wallace T. MacCaffrey, *Queen Elizabeth and the Making of Policy, 1572-1588* (1981), examines the problems posed by the Reformation and how Elizabeth solved them. J. E. Neale, *Queen Elizabeth I* (1957), remains valuable, and L. B. Smith, *The Elizabethan Epic* (1966), is a splendid evocation of the age of Shakespeare with Elizabeth at the center.

Nineteenth- and early twentieth-century historians described the defeat of the Spanish Armada as a great victory for Protestantism, democracy, and capitalism, which those scholars tended to link together. Recent historians have treated the event in terms of its contemporary significance. G. Mattingly, *The Armada* (1959), combines superb readability with the highest scholarly standards: this is history at its best. M. Lewis, *The Spanish Armada* (1972), tells a good story from the English perspective; David Howarth, *The Voyage of the Armada: the Spanish Story* (1981), presents the other side in an exciting narrative. C. V. Wedgwood, *The*

Thirty Years' War (1961), must be qualified in light of recent research on the social and economic effects of the war, but it is still a good (if detailed) starting point on a difficult period. A variety of opinions on the causes and results of the war are given in T. K. Rabb's anthology, *The Thirty Years' War* (1981). The following articles, all of which appear in the scholarly journal *Past and Present,* provide some of the latest important findings: H. Kamen, "The Economic and Social Consequences of the Thirty Years' War," no. 39 (1968); J. Hale, "War and Public Opinion in the Fifteenth and Sixteenth Centuries," no. 22 (1962); J. V. Polišenský, "The Thirty Years' War and the Crises and Revolutions of Sixteenth Century Europe," no. 39 (1968); and for the overall significance of Sweden, M. Roberts, "Queen Christina and the General Crisis of the Seventeenth Century," no. 22 (1962).

As background to the intellectual changes instigated by the Reformation, D. C. Wilcox, ed., *In Search of God and Self: Renaissance and Reformation Thought* (1975), contains perceptive articles, and T. Ashton, ed., *Crisis in Europe, 1560–1660* (1967), is fundamental. On witches and witchcraft, see, in addition to the titles by Norman Cohn and Keith Thomas in the Notes, Jeffrey B. Russell, *Witchcraft in the Middle Ages* (1976); Montague Summers, *The History of Witchcraft and Demonology* (1973); and H. R. Trevor-Roper, *The European Witch-Craze of the Sixteenth and Seventeenth Centuries* (1967), a brilliant collection of essays. Among the fascinating studies on North American racism, the interested student should consult W. D. Jordan, *The White Man's Burden: Historical Origins of Racism in the United States* (1974), and D. P. Mannix in collaboration with M. Cowley, *Black Cargoes: A History of the Atlantic Slave Trade* (1968), a hideously fascinating account. South American conditions may be contrasted in C. R. Boxer, *Four Centuries of Portuguese Expansion* (1969). The leading authority on Montaigne is D. M. Frame. See his *Montaigne's Discovery of Man* (1955), and his translation, *The Complete Works of Montaigne* (1958).

CHAPTER 16

ABSOLUTISM AND CONSTITUTIONALISM

IN WESTERN EUROPE (CA 1589–1715)

THE SEVENTEENTH CENTURY was a period of revolutionary transformation. Some of its most profound developments were political: the seventeenth century has been called the century when government became modern. The sixteenth century had witnessed the emergence of the nation-state. The long series of wars fought in the name of religion – but actually contests between royal authority and aristocratic power – brought social dislocation and agricultural and commercial disaster. Increasingly, strong national monarchy seemed the only solution. Spanish and French monarchs gained control of the major competing institution in their domains, the Roman Catholic church. In England and some of the German principalities, where rulers could not completely regulate the church, they set up national churches. In the German Empire the Treaty of Westphalia placed territorial sovereignty in the hands of the princes. The kings of France, England, and Spain claimed the basic loyalty of their subjects. Monarchs made laws, to which everyone within their borders was subject. These powers added up to something close to sovereignty.

A nation may be termed sovereign when it possesses a monopoly over the instruments of justice and the use of force within clearly defined boundaries. In a sovereign state no system of courts, such as ecclesiastical tribunals, competes with state courts in the dispensation of justice; and private armies, such as those of feudal lords, present no threat to royal authority because the national army is stronger. Royal law touches all persons within the country. Sovereignty had been evolving in the late sixteenth century. Seventeenth-century governments now faced the problem of *which* authority within the state would possess sovereignty – the Crown or the nobility.

In the period between roughly 1589 and 1715, two basic patterns of government emerged in Europe: absolute monarchy and the constitutional state. Almost all subsequent governments have been modeled on one or the other of these patterns. How were these forms of government "modern"? How did they differ from the feudal and dynastic monarchies of earlier centuries? Which countries best represent the new patterns of political organization? This chapter will be concerned with these political questions.

ABSOLUTISM

In the absolutist state, sovereignty is embodied in the person of the ruler. The ruler is not restrained by any legal authority. Absolute kings claimed to rule by divine right, meaning that they were responsible to God alone. (Medieval kings had governed "by the grace of God," but invariably they acknowledged that they had to respect and obey the law.) Absolute monarchs in the seventeenth and eighteenth centuries were not checked by national assemblies. Estates general and parliaments met at the wish and in response to the needs of kings. Because these meetings provided opportunities for opposition to the Crown to coalesce, absolute monarchs eventually stopped summoning them.

Absolute rulers effectively controlled all competing jurisdictions, all institutions or interest groups within their territories. They regulated religious sects. They abolished the liberties (privileges) long held by certain areas, groups, or provinces. Absolute kings also secured mastery over the one class that historically had posed the greatest threat to monarchy, the nobility. Medieval governments had been able to do none of these things. They had been restrained by the church, by the feudal nobility, and by their own financial limitations.

In some respects the key to the power and success of absolute monarchs lay in how they solved their financial problems. The solution was the creation of new state bureaucracies, which directed the economic life of the country in the interests of the king, raising ever higher taxes or devising other methods of raising revenue.

Bureaucracies were composed of career officials, appointed by and solely accountable to the king. The backgrounds of these civil servants varied. Absolute monarchs sometimes drew on the middle class, as in France, or utilized members of the nobility, as in Spain and eastern Europe. Where there was no middle class or an insignificant one, as in Austria, Prussia, Spain, and Russia, the government of the absolutist state consisted of an interlocking elite of monarchy, aristocracy, and bureaucracy.

Royal agents in medieval kingdoms had used their public offices and positions to benefit themselves and their families. In England, for example, Crown servants from Thomas Becket to Thomas Wolsey had treated their high offices as their personal private property, and reaped considerable profit from the positions they held. The most striking difference between seventeenth-century bureaucracies and their medieval predecessors was that seventeenth-century civil servants served the state as represented by the king. Bureaucrats recognized that the offices they held were public, or state, positions. The state paid them salaries to handle revenues that belonged to the Crown, and they were not supposed to use their official positions for private gain. Bureaucrats gradually came to distinguish between public duties and private property.

Absolute monarchs also maintained permanent standing armies. Medieval armies had been raised by feudal lords for particular wars or campaigns, after which the troops were disbanded. In the seventeenth century, monarchs alone recruited and maintained armies – in peacetime as well as during war. Kings deployed their troops both inside and outside the country in the interests of the monarchy. Armies became basic features of absolutist, and modern, states. Absolute rulers also invented new methods of compulsion. They concerned themselves with the private lives of potentially troublesome subjects, often through the use of secret police.

Thus rule of absolute monarchs was not all-embracing because they lacked the financial and military resources and the technology to make it so. Thus the absolutist state was not the same as a totalitarian state. Totalitarianism is a twentieth-century phenomenon; it seeks to direct all facets of a state's culture – art, education, religion, the economy, and politics – in the interests of the state. By definition totalitarian rule is *total* regulation. By twentieth-century standards, the ambitions of an absolute monarch were quite limited: he sought the exaltation of himself as the embodiment of the state. When King Louis XIV of France declared, "L'état, c'est moi!" ("I am the state!"), he meant that he personally was the incarnation of France. Yet the absolutist state did foreshadow recent totalitarian regimes in two fundamental respects: in the glorification of the state over all other aspects of the national culture, and in the use of war and an expansionist foreign policy to divert attention from domestic ills.

All of this is best illustrated by the experience of France, aptly known as the model of absolute monarchy.

THE FOUNDATIONS OF ABSOLUTISM IN FRANCE: HENRY IV AND SULLY

The ingenious Huguenot-turned-Catholic, Henry IV (pages 524–525), ended the French religious wars with the Edict of Nantes. The first of the Bourbon dynasty, and probably the first French ruler since Louis IX in the thirteenth century genuinely to care about the French people, Henry IV and his great minister Sully (1560–1641) laid the foundations of later French absolutism. Henry denied influence on the royal council to the nobility, which had harassed the countryside for half a century. Maintaining that "if we are without compassion for the people, they must succumb and we all perish with them," Henry also lowered the severe taxes on the overburdened peasantry.

Sully proved himself a financial genius. He not only reduced the crushing royal debt but began to build up the treasury. He levied an annual tax, the *paulette,* on people who had purchased financial and judicial offices and had consequently been exempt from royal taxation. One of the first French officials to appreciate the significance of overseas trade, Sully subsidized the Company for Trade with the Indies. He started a countrywide highway system and even dreamed of an international organization for the maintenance of peace.

In twelve short years Henry IV and Sully restored public order in France and laid the foundations for economic prosperity. By late-sixteenth-century standards, Henry IV's government was both progressive and promising. His murder in 1610 by a crazed fanatic plunged the country into civil war and threatened to undo his work.

THE CORNERSTONE OF FRENCH ABSOLUTISM: LOUIS XIII AND RICHELIEU

After the death of Henry IV, the queen-regent Marie de' Medici led the government for the child-king Louis XIII (1610–1643), but in fact feudal nobles and princes of the blood dominated the political scene. In 1624, Marie de' Medici secured the appointment of Armand Jean du Plessis – Cardinal Richelieu (1585–1642) – to the council of ministers. It was a remarkable appointment. The next year Richelieu became president of the council, and after 1628 he was first minister of the French crown and the actual ruler of France. Richelieu used his strong influence over King Louis XIII to exalt the French monarchy as the embodiment of the French state. One of the greatest servants of the French state, Richelieu set in place the cornerstone of French absolutism, and his work served as the basis for France's cultural domination of Europe in the later seventeenth century.

Richelieu's policy was the total subordination of all groups and institutions to the French monarchy. The French nobility, with its selfish and independent interests, had long constituted the foremost threat to the centralizing goals of the Crown and to a strong national state. Therefore, Richelieu broke the power of the nobility. He leveled castles, long the symbol of feudal independence. He crushed aristocratic conspiracies with quick executions. For example, when the duke de Montmorency, the first peer of France and the godson of Henry IV, became involved in a revolt in 1632, he was summarily put to death. Richelieu abolished the great medieval military dignities that had exalted the prestige and local power of some great nobles. He banned dueling. He prevented the great lords from sitting in the king's council.

The constructive genius of Cardinal Richelieu is best reflected in the administrative system he established. He extended the use of royal commissioners called intendants. France was divided into thirty-two *généralités* (districts), in each of which a royal intendant had complete responsibility for justice, police, and finances. The intendants were authorized "to decide, order and execute all that they see good to do." Usually members of the upper middle class or minor nobility, the intendants were appointed directly by the monarch, to whom they were solely responsible. They had complete power in their districts and were to use that power for two related purposes: to enforce royal orders in the *généralités* of their jurisdiction and to weaken the power and influence of the regional nobility. The system of government by intendants derived from Philip Augustus's baillis and seneschals, and ultimately from Charlemagne's *missi dominici*. As the intendants' power grew during Richelieu's administration, so did the power of the centralized state.

Although Richelieu succeeded in building a rational and centralized political machine in the intendant system, he was not the effective financial administrator Sully had been. France lacked a sound system of taxation, a method of raising sufficient revenue to meet the needs of the state. Richelieu reverted to the old device of selling offices. He increased the number of sinecures, tax exemptions, and benefices that were purchasable and inheritable. In 1624, this device brought in almost 40 percent of royal revenues.

The rising cost of foreign and domestic policies led to the auctioning of tax farms, the system whereby a man bought the right to collect taxes. Tax farmers kept a very large part of the receipts they collected. The sale of offices and this antiquated system of tax collection were improvisations that promoted confusion and corruption. Even worse, state offices, once purchased, were passed on to heirs, which meant that a family that held a state office was eternally exempt from taxation. Richelieu's inadequate and temporary solutions created grave financial problems for the future.

The cardinal perceived that Protestantism all too often served as a cloak for the political intrigues of ambitious lords. When the Huguenots revolted in 1625, under the duke de Rohan, Richelieu personally supervised the siege of their walled city, La Rochelle, and forced it to surrender. Thereafter, fortified places of security were abolished. Huguenots were allowed to practice their faith, but they no longer possessed armed strongholds or the means to be an independent party in the state. Another aristocratic prop was knocked down.

French foreign policy under Richelieu was aimed at the destruction of the fence of Habsburg territories that surrounded France. Consequently, Richelieu supported the Habsburgs' enemies. In 1631, he signed a treaty with the Lutheran king Gustavus Adolphus promising French support against the Catholic Habsburgs in what has been called the Swedish phase of the Thirty Years' War (page 533). French influence became an important factor in the political future of the German empire. Richelieu added Alsace in the east (1639) and Arras in the north (1640) to French territory.

Richelieu's efforts at centralization extended even to literature. In 1635 he gave official recognition to a group of philologists who were interested in grammar and rhetoric. Thus was born the French Academy. With Richelieu's encouragement, the Academy began the preparation of a *dictionary* to standardize the French language; it was completed in 1694. The French Academy survives as a prestigious learned society, whose membership has been broadened to include people outside the field of literature.

Richelieu personified the increasingly secular spirit of the seventeenth century. Although a bishop of the Roman Catholic church, he gave his first loyalty to the French state. Although a Roman Catholic cardinal, he gave strong support to the Protestant Lutherans of Germany. The portrait of Richelieu by Philippe de Champaigne – with its penetrating eyes, expression of haughty and imperturbable cynicism, and dramatic sweep of rich red robes – reveals the authority, grandeur, and power the cardinal wanted to convey as first minister of France. Just before Richelieu died in 1642, worn out with work and ulcers, the curé of St.-Eustache asked him to forgive his enemies. Richelieu replied, characteristically, that he had no enemies save those of the king and the state.

Richelieu had persuaded Louis XIII to appoint his protegé Jules Mazarin (1602-1661) as his successor. An Italian diplomat of great charm, Mazarin served on the Council of State under Richelieu, acquiring considerable political experience. He became a cardinal in 1641 and a French citizen in 1643. When Louis XIII followed Richelieu to the grave in 1643 and a regency headed by Queen Anne of Austria governed for the child-king Louis XIV, Mazarin became the dominant power in the government. He continued the antifeudal and centralizing policies of Richelieu, but his attempts to increase royal revenues led to the civil wars known as the Fronde.

The word *fronde* means slingshot or catapult, and a *frondeur* was originally a street urchin who threw mud at the passing carriages of the rich. The term came to be used for anyone who opposed the policies of the government. Richelieu had stirred up the bitter resentment of the aristocracy, who felt its constitutional status and ancient privileges threatened. He also bequeathed to the Crown a staggering debt, and when Mazarin tried to impose financial reforms the monarchy incurred the enmity of the middle classes. Both groups plotted against Anne and Mazarin. Most historians see the Fronde as the last serious effort by the French nobility to oppose the monarchy by force. When in 1648 Mazarin proposed new methods for raising income, bitter civil war ensued between the monarchy on the one side and the frondeurs

(the nobility and the upper-middle classes) on the other. Riots and public turmoil wracked Paris and the nation. The violence continued intermittently for almost twelve years. Factional disputes among the nobles led to their ultimate defeat.

The conflicts of the Fronde had two significant results for the future: a badly disruptive effect on the French economy and a traumatic impact on the young Louis XIV. The king and his mother were frequently threatened and sometimes treated as prisoners by aristocratic factions. On one occasion a mob broke into the royal bedchamber to make sure the king was actually there; it succeeded in giving him a bad fright. Louis never forgot such humiliations. The period of the Fronde formed the cornerstone of his political education and of his unalterable conviction that the sole alternative to anarchy was absolute monarchy.

THE ABSOLUTE MONARCHY OF LOUIS XIV

According to the court theologian Bossuet, the clergy at the coronation of Louis XIV in Reims Cathedral asked God to cause the splendors of the French court to fill all who beheld it with awe. God subsequently granted that prayer. In the reign of Louis XIV (1643-1715), the longest in European history, the French monarchy reached the peak of absolutist development. In the magnificence of his court, in his absolute power, in the brilliance of the culture over which he presided and which permeated all of Europe, and in his remarkably long life, Louis XIV dominated his age. No wonder scholars have characterized the second half of the seventeenth century as "The Grand Century," "The Age of Magnificence," and, echoing the eighteenth-century philosopher Voltaire, "The Age of Louis XIV."

COMBAT BETWEEN CARNIVAL AND LENT (above) Pieter Bruegel the Elder (ca 1525–1559). One of the most original Flemish painters of the sixteenth century, Bruegel concentrated on scenes of peasant life. He treated many subjects satirically. In this conflict be-tween gluttony and asceticism, a common Reformation theme, Bruegel suggests that neither side is a perfect model of Christian living. (Courtesy, Museum of Fine Arts, Boston.)

FEAST OF THE GODS (above) Giovanni Bellini (1430?–1516). In this pastoral scene based on a story of the Roman poet Ovid, Olympian gods picnic in a wooded grove as satyrs and nymphs serve them. The light filtering through the window represents a technical achievement and the secular appreciation for the world of nature and of man. The pagan theme, the appreciation for perspective and nature, and the sensual atmosphere make this painting a fine example of Italian Renaissance classicism. (National Gallery of Art, Washington, D.C.)

A WOMAN PEELING APPLES (below left) Pieter de Hooch (1629–1677). Stability, seriousness, and thrift are idealized in this Dutch domestic scene. The light filtering through the window represents a technical achievement and the secular appreciation for the world of nature and of man. The pagan theme, the appreciation for perspective and nature, and the sensual atmosphere make this painting a fine example of Italian Renaissance classicism. (Reproduced by permission of the Trustees of the Wallace Collection.)

GEORG GISZE (below, right) Hans Holbein (1497–1543). Born in Danzig, Gisze became a rich London merchant. Here he is portrayed with quill and ink, seal, scales, and business letters hung on racks behind him. The Caucasian rug covering the desk was probably woven in Asia Minor in the fifteenth century. (Gemäldegalerie, Berlin.)

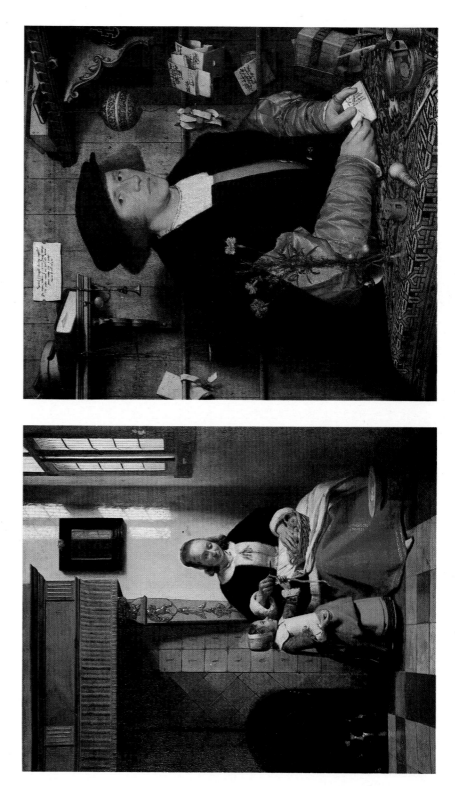

THE BURY ST. EDMUNDS' CROSS (above, left) Probably made for the English abbot Samson of Bury St. Edmunds' (1181–1211) and used in ceremonial processions, this walrus ivory cross, 2 ft. high and 14 in. across, contains 8 scenes, 108 figures, and 60 inscriptions from the Old and New Testaments. A superb example of late twelfth-century craftsmanship, piety, and, some inscriptions imply, anti-Semitic attitudes. (The Metropolitan Museum of Art; The Cloisters Collection, 1963.)

LES TRÈS RICHES HEURES DU JEAN, DUC DE BERRY (above, right) This illustrates March in a book of calendar miniatures produced for the duke of Berry, brother of the king of France. With exquisite detail the artists capture four scenes of agricultural life in the early fifteenth century. A shepherd with a dog guards a flock of sheep. Three peasants prune vines while another works in a different field. And an aged farmer guides a wheeled plow and oxen. Symbolically, the vast castle of Lusignan dominates the landscape. (Chantilly, Musée Condé/Giraudon.)

THE CAMPIN ALTARPIECE (ca 1425–1428), by Robert Campin (d. 1444). This 4-by 2-ft. painting in oil on wood was intended to hang behind the altar, facing the people. The Annunciation scene in the center panel occurs in the house of a Flemish burgher. Every detail has significance. For example, the serious, modestly dressed middle-class donors in the left panel are memorialized observing the mystery, the lilies on the table in the center panel represent the Virgin's chastity, and Joseph in front of a delicately painted view of a fifteenth-century city in the right panel carves a mousetrap, symbolizing Christ, the bait set to catch the devil. (The Metropolitan Museum of Art, The Cloisters Collection.)

ATHENIAN WOMEN AT A FOUNTAIN HOUSE
(left) The Greeks often decorated their vases with
scenes from daily life. Here five well-dressed Athenian women are seen filling their water jugs at a
fountain house. They used the occasion to chat and
exchange information. Scenes such as this one suggest that Athenian women were not so sheltered as
they are often portrayed. (Courtesy, Museum of Fine
Arts, Boston.)

BLACKSMITH'S SHOP (right) One blacksmith
holds the heated metal in tongs while his husky
companion wields a hammer. Hanging from the wall
is one man's cloak, a water jug, and knives and axes
that the smiths have made or repaired. In the winter
the blacksmith's shop, kept warm by a constant fire,
was a favorite place for the men to chat and to come
in from the cold. (Courtesy, Museum of Fine Arts,
Boston.)

PALESTRINA MOSAIC (below) Fish and birds
abound as boatsmen steer among rocks and try their
hand at spearing fish. The Nile was legendary for its
fertility and the exotic animals that could be encountered along its course. Mosaics such as this
were common in the ancient world and could be
found in temples and the homes of the wealthy.
(Scala/EPA.)

ART: A MIRROR OF SOCIETY

Art reveals the interests and values of society and frequently gives intimate and unique glimpses of how people actually lived. In portraits and statues, whether of saints, generals, philosophers, popes, poets, or merchants, it preserves the memory and fame of men and women who shaped society. In paintings, drawings, and carvings, it also shows how people worked, played, relaxed, suffered, and triumphed. Art, therefore, is extremely useful to the historian, especially for periods such as the ancient and medieval, when written records are scarce. Every work of art and every part of it has meaning and has something of its own to say.

Ancient and medieval art, apart from splendid public buildings, temples, cathedrals, and monasteries, was created by and for an aristocratic elite. It reflected the tastes and the interests of the aristocracy. Only a wealthy Greek could afford to buy a richly painted vase or wine cup. Only a wealthy Roman family could decorate the floors of their house with dazzling mosaics. The Royal Standard of Ur, below, shows aspects of Sumerian society in peacetime. The upper band of the standard, a triangular box on a pole used on ceremonial occasions, depicts a royal banquet, with the king and his nobles drinking and listening to music. In the lower band herdsmen lead animals. (By courtesy of the British Museum.) Art was also created primarily for the aristocracy in the Middle Ages, when upper-class people commissioned mosaics, illuminated manuscripts, carved and jewelled objects, and miniatures and paintings. Furthermore, in the Middle Ages the primary function of art was to teach. Most medieval artists were clerics or monks, their subject matter was religious, and consequently religious themes pervade their art.

Art also manifests the changes and continuity of European life. Scenes of agricultural work and commerce were popular both in antiquity and in the Middle Ages. As values changed in Europe, so did major artistic themes. The religious art of the early Middle Ages replaced the sensuous pagan art of antiquity. In turn, the art of the later Middle Ages, a time which saw the emergence of a rich urban middle class, increasingly displayed secular interests. Europeans of the sixteenth and seventeenth centuries remained deeply religious but showed a new interest in the world around them: their middle-class attitudes and concerns were harbingers of developments to come.

Who was this phenomenon of whom it was said that when Louis sneezed, all Europe caught cold? Born in 1638, king at the age of five, he entered into personal, or independent, rule in 1661. One of his first recorded remarks reveals the astonishing sense of self that was to awe French people and foreigners alike. Taken as a child to his father's deathbed, he identified himself as "Louis Quatorze" ("Louis the fourteenth").

In old age Louis claimed that he had grown up learning very little, and many historians have agreed. He knew little Latin and only the rudiments of arithmetic, and was thus by Renaissance standards not well educated. On the other hand, he learned to speak Italian and Spanish fluently; he knew some French history, and more European geography than the ambassadors accredited to his court. He imbibed the devout Catholicism of his mother Anne of Austria, and throughout his long life scrupulously performed his religious duties. Religion, Anne, and Mazarin all taught Louis that God had established kings as His rulers on earth. The royal coronation consecrated him to God's service, and he was certain – to use Shakespeare's phrase – that there was a divinity that doth hedge a king. Although kings were a race apart, they could not do as they pleased: they must obey God's laws and rule for the good of the people.

Louis's education was more practical than formal. Under Mazarin's instruction he studied state papers as they arrived, and he attended council meetings and sessions at which French ambassadors were dispatched abroad and foreign ambassadors received. He learned by direct experience and gained professional training in the work of government. Above all, the misery he suffered during the Fronde gave Louis an eternal distrust of the nobility and a profound sense of his own isolation. Accordingly, silence, caution, and secrecy became political tools for the achievement of his goals. His characteristic answer to requests of all kinds became the enigmatic "Je verrai" ("I shall see").

Louis grew up with an absolute sense of his royal dignity. Tall and distinguished in appearance, he was inclined to fatness because of the gargantuan meals in which he indulged. Seduced by one of his mother's maids when he was sixteen, the king matured into a highly sensual man easily aroused by an attractive female face and figure. It is to his credit, however, that neither his wife, Queen Maria Theresa, whom he married as the result of a diplomatic agreement with Spain, nor his mistresses ever possessed any political influence. Extraordinarily selfish, Louis doted on flattery, which he interpreted as glory.

Whatever his negative qualities, Louis XIV worked extremely hard and succeeded in being "every moment and every inch a king." Because he so thoroughly relished the role of king, historians have had difficulty distinguishing the man from the monarch. Louis XIV was a consummate actor, and his "terrifying majesty" awed all who saw him.

The reign of Louis XIV witnessed great innovations in style but few in substance; Louis extended and intensified earlier practices and trends. The most significant development was his acquisition of absolute control over the French nobility. Indeed, it is often said that Louis achieved the complete "domestication" of the nobility.

Louis XIV turned the royal court into a fixed institution. In the past the king of France and the royal court had traveled constantly, visiting the king's properties, the great noblemen, and his *bonnes villes* or good towns. Since the time of Louis IX, or even Charlemagne, rulers had traveled to maintain order in distant parts of the realm, to impress humbler subjects with the royal dignity and

AERIAL VIEW OF VERSAILLES Awe-inspiring, monumental, and over a quarter of a mile long, Versailles is the supreme example of classical baroque architecture in the service of absolute monarchy. The vast formal gardens with their geometric regularity pro-vided the outdoor setting for Louis XIV's festivities, while the three avenues radiating from the palace symbolize the king as source of all power. (French Government Tourist Office)

magnificence, and in so doing to bind the country together through loyalty to the king. Since the early Middle Ages, the king's court had consisted of his family, trusted advisers and councilors, a few favorites, and servants. Except for the very highest officials of the state, members of the council had changed constantly.

Louis XIV installed the court at Versailles, a small town ten miles from Paris. He required all the great nobility of France, at the peril of social, political, and sometimes economic disaster, to come live at Versailles for at least part of the year. Today, Versailles stands as the best surviving museum of a vanished society on earth. In the seventeenth century, it became a model of rational order, the center of France and thus the center of Western civilization, the perfect symbol of the king's absolute power.

Louis XIII had begun Versailles as a hunting lodge, a retreat from a queen he did not

HALL OF MIRRORS AT VERSAILLES This long and magnificently impressive room takes up much of the central block of Versailles. The hundreds of mirrors, which give the illusion of width, reflected the court spectacles and the king's glory. The splendor of *this hall and many other adjacent palace rooms was a far cry, however, from the cramped conditions that many nobles were forced to live with at the royal court. (French Government Tourist Office)*

like. His son's architects, Le Nôtre and Le Vau, turned what Saint-Simon called "the most dismal and thankless of sights" into a veritable paradise. Wings were added to the original building to make the palace U-shaped. Everywhere at Versailles the viewer has a sense of grandeur, vastness, and incredible elegance. Enormous state rooms became display galleries for inlaid tables, Italian marble statuary, Gobelin tapestries woven at the state factory in Paris, silver ewers, and beauti-

ful (if uncomfortable) furniture. If genius means attention to detail, Louis XIV and his designers had it: the décor was perfected down to the last doorknob and keyhole. In the gigantic Hall of Mirrors, which was later to reflect so much of German as well as French history, hundreds of candles illuminated the domed ceiling, where allegorical paintings celebrated the king's victories.

The Ambassador's Staircase is of brilliantly colored marble, with part of the railing gold-plated. The staircase is dominated by a great bust of the king, which when completed so overwhelmed a courtier that he exclaimed to the sculptor Bernini, "Don't do anything more to it, it's so good I'm afraid you might spoil it." The statue, like the staircase – and the entire palace – succeeded from the start in its purpose: it awed.

The formal, carefully ordered, and perfectly landscaped gardens at Versailles express at a glance the spirit of the age of Louis XIV. Every tree, every bush, every foot of grass, every fountain, pool, and piece of statuary within three miles is perfectly laid out. The vista is of the world made rational and absolutely controlled. Nature itself was subdued to enhance the greatness of the king.

Under the vast terrace stands one of the great architectural splendors of France, the Orangerie. Designed to house the king's twelve hundred potted palms and orange trees, the Orangerie is a huge vaulted space, so large that when it was completed in 1686 several operas could be performed there simultaneously without inconvenience. The Siamese ambassador is reputed to have said that the magnificence of Louis XIV must indeed be great, since he had raised so superb a palace simply for his orange trees.

Against this background of magnificent splendor, as the great aristocrat Saint-Simon describes, Louis XIV

reduced everyone to subjection, and brought to his court those very persons he cared least about. Whoever was old enough to serve did not dare demur. It was still another device to ruin the nobles by accustoming them to equality and forcing them to mingle with everyone indiscriminately....

... To keep everyone assiduous and attentive, the King personally named the guests for each festivity, each stroll through Versailles, and each trip. These were his rewards and punishments. He

knew there was little else he could distribute to keep everyone in line. He substituted idle rewards for real ones and these operated through jealousy, the petty preferences he showed many times a day, and his artfulness in showing them. No one was more ingenious than him in nourishing the hopes and satisfactions to which these petty preferences and distinctions gave birth....

... Upon rising, at bedtime, during meals, in his apartments, in the gardens of Versailles, everywhere the courtiers had a right to follow, he would glance right and left to see who was there; he saw and noted everyone; he missed no one, even those who were hoping they would not be seen.... For the most distinguished persons, it was a demerit not to put in a regular appearance at court. It was just as bad for those of lesser rank to come but rarely, and certain disgrace for those who never, or almost never, came....

... Louis XIV took great pains to inform himself on what was happening everywhere, in public places, private homes, and even on the international scene.... Spies and informers of all kinds were numberless....

... But the King's most vicious method of securing information was opening letters....[1]

Through ritual and ceremony the king turned the proud and ancient nobility into a pack of trained seals. He destroyed their ancient right to advise and counsel the monarch. Operas, fetes, and balls occupied the nobles' time and attention. They become solely instruments of the king's pleasure. Louis XIV may have had limited native intelligence, but through painstaking attention to detail and precisely calculated showmanship, he emasculated the major threat to his absolute power. He separated power from grandeur: the nobility enjoyed the grandeur in which they lived; the king alone enjoyed the power.

The art and architecture of Versailles served as fundamental tools of state policy under

Louis XIV. Architecture was the device the king used to overawe his subjects and foreign visitors. Versailles was seen as a reflection of French genius. Thus the Russian czar Peter the Great imitated Versailles in the construction of his palace, Peterhof, as did the Prussian emperor Frederick the Great in his palace at Potsdam outside Berlin.

As in architecture, so too in language. Beginning in the reign of Louis XIV, French became the language of polite society and the vehicle of diplomatic exchange. French also gradually replaced Latin as the language of international scholarship and learning. The wish of other kings to ape the courtly style of Louis XIV and the imitation of French intellectuals and artists spread the French language all over Europe. The royal courts of Sweden, Russia, Poland, and Germany all spoke French. In the eighteenth century, the great Russian aristocrats were more fluent in French than in Russian. In England the First Hanoverian king, George I, spoke French but no English. France inspired a cosmopolitan European culture in the late seventeenth century, and that culture was inspired by the king. That is what Voltaire meant when he called the period "The Age of Louis XIV."

Louis dominated the court, and the court was the center of France. In the king's scheme of things, the court was more significant than the government. Louix XIV made no innovations in the government of France. He continued the system of the intendants, appointing them entirely from the middle class. By curbing the power of the local aristocracy and gentry, the intendants advanced royal sovereignty in the provinces. Members of the royal councils – such as the Council of State, which dealt with diplomacy, war, and peace – were drawn from the class Saint-Simon called "the bookkeepers," the middle class.

Louis feared and distrusted the nobility, and so he eliminated them from government. Throughout his long reign, and in spite of increasing financial problems, he never called the French nobility together in a meeting of the Estates General. The nobility, therefore, had no means of united expression or action. Nor did Louis have a first minister, freeing him from worry about the inordinate power of a Richelieu. Louis's use of terror – a secret police force, a system of informers, and the practice of opening private letters – foreshadowed some of the devices of the modern state. French government remained highly structured, bureaucratic, centered in Paris, and responsible to Louis XIV.

ECONOMIC MANAGEMENT UNDER LOUIS XIV: COLBERT AND MERCANTILISM

As controller-general of finances, the king named Jean Baptiste Colbert. The son of a draper of Reims, Colbert (1619–1683) came to manage the entire royal administration and proved himself a financial genius. Colbert's central principle was that the economy and the wealth of France should serve the state. He did not invent the economic system or program called mercantilism, but he rigorously applied it to France.

Mercantilism is a system for the regulation of economic activities, especially commercial activities, by and for the state. In seventeenth- and eighteenth-century economic theory, a nation's international power was thought to be based on its wealth, specifically its gold supply. To accumulate gold, a country should always sell abroad more than it bought. Colbert believed that a successful economic policy meant more than a favorable balance of trade. He insisted that the French sell abroad and buy *nothing* back. France should be self-sufficient, able to produce within its borders everything the subjects of the French king needed. Consequently, the outflow of gold would be halted and the power and prestige of the state enhanced.

Colbert attempted to accomplish self-sufficiency through state support for both old industries and newly created ones. He subsidized the established cloth industries at Abbeville, St.-Quentin, and Carcassonne. He granted special royal privileges to the rug and tapestry industries at Paris, Gobelin, and Beauvais. New factories at St.-Antoine in Paris manufactured mirrors to replace Venetian imports. Looms at Chantilly and Alençon competed with English lacemaking, and foundries at St.-Etienne made steel and firearms that cut Swedish imports. To insure a high-quality finished product, Colbert set up a system of state inspection and regulation. To insure order within every industry he compelled all craftsmen to organize into guilds, and within every guild he gave the masters absolute power over their workers. Colbert encouraged skilled foreign craftsmen and manufacturers to immigrate to France, and he gave them special privileges. To protect French products, Colbert enacted high tariffs, which prevented foreign goods from competing with French ones.

Colbert's most important work was the creation of a powerful merchant marine to transport French goods. He gave bonuses to French shipowners and builders, and established a method of maritime conscription, arsenals, and academies for the training of sailors. In 1661, France possessed 18 unseaworthy vessels; by 1681, France had 276 frigates, galleys, and ships of the line. Colbert tried to organize and regulate the entire French economy for the glory of the French state as embodied in the king.

Colbert hoped to make Canada – rich in untapped minerals and some of the best agricultural land in the world – part of a vast French empire. He gathered four thousand peasants from western France and shipped them to Canada, where they peopled the province of Quebec. (In 1608, one year after the English arrived at Jamestown, Virginia, Sully had established the city of Quebec, which became the capital of French Canada.) Subsequently, the Jesuit Marquette and the merchant Joliet sailed down the Mississippi River and took possession of the land on both sides as far south as present-day Arkansas. In 1684, the French explorer La Salle continued down the Mississippi to its mouth and claimed vast territories and the rich delta for Louis XIV. The area was called, naturally, Louisiana.

Nothing did more to destroy Colbert's system of commercial and colonial regulation than the revocation of the Edict of Nantes – an event that, on the surface at least, had little to do with economic life. For almost a century the edict had granted equal political and some religious rights to the Huguenots of France. Scholars have debated at length the reasons for Louis XIV's revocation of it in 1685. Was the revocation due to the powerful influence of the king's Catholic wife, Madame de Maintenon? Was it the result of pressure from Catholic business interests who resented the competition of the clever Huguenots? Did Louis abolish freedom of religion because of his pride and religious intolerance, which could not countenance the existence in France of a sizable group with a faith different from his own? Or was it sheer ignorance of the large numbers of his Calvinist subjects and their social and economic importance to the state, an ignorance attributable to the isolation of the court? Whatever the exact causes of the revocation, its consequences proved disastrous.

Perhaps 300,000 French citizens chose to emigrate rather than convert. Some of the best craftsmen, businessmen, soldiers, and sailors fled to England, Holland, and Prussia. They left their goods behind but carried their skills and hatred of Louis XIV with them. The loss of so many experts and the taxes they represented – on top of Louis's chronic need for money – severely aggravated the national financial situation. After 1685, the French government had to resort again to the expediency of creating offices and selling them on a broad scale. This stopgap measure paid for the present by mortgaging the future, since officeholders and their descendants paid no taxes.

Most catastrophic of all, the revocation of the Edict of Nantes provoked domestic turmoil within France and fear and hatred abroad. Calvinist peasants in Languedoc revolted, for example, and Louis was ultimately forced to back down. The Protestant states of northern Europe – Holland, Brandenburg, and Sweden – united against Louis XIV, and from 1688 until his death France was almost continually at war. With some justification, historians have called the revocation of the Edict of Nantes the greatest error the Bourbon dynasty committed.

FRENCH CLASSICISM

Scholars characterize the art and literature of the age of Louis XIV as French Classicism. By this they mean that the artists and writers of the late seventeenth century deliberately imitated the subject matter and style of classical antiquity; that their work resembles that of Renaissance Italy; and that French art possessed the classical qualities of discipline, balance, and restraint. Classicism was the official style of Louis's court. In painting, however, French classicism had already reached its peak before 1661, the beginning of the king's personal government.

Nicholas Poussin (1593-1665) is generally considered the finest example of French classicist painting. Poussin spent all but eighteen months of his creative life in Rome because he found the atmosphere in Paris uncongenial. Deeply attached to classical antiquity, he believed that the highest aim of painting was to represent noble actions in a logical and orderly, but not realistic, way. His masterpiece, "The Rape of the Sabine Women," exhibits these qualities. Its subject is an incident in Roman history; the figures of people and horses are ideal representations, and the emotions expressed are studied, not spontaneous. Even the buildings are exact architectural models of ancient Roman structures.

While Poussin selected grand and "noble" themes, Louis Le Nain (1593-1648) painted genre scenes of peasant life. At a time when artists favored Biblical and classical allegories, Le Nain's paintings are unique for their depiction of peasants. The highly realistic group assembled in "The Peasant Family" have great human dignity. The painting itself is reminiscent of portrayals of peasants by seventeenth-century Dutch painters.

Le Nain and Poussin, whose paintings still had individualistic features, did their work before 1661. After Louis's accession to power, the principles of absolutism molded the ideals of French classicism. Individualism was not allowed, and artists' efforts were directed to the glorification of the state as personified by the king. Precise rules governed all aspects of culture, with the goal of formal and restrained perfection.

Contemporaries said that Louis XIV never

ceased playing the role of grand monarch on the stage of his court. If the king never fully relaxed from the pressures and intrigues of government, he did enjoy music and theater and used them as a backdrop for court ceremonial. Louis favored Jean-Baptiste Lully (1632–1687), whose orchestral works combine lively animation with the restrained austerity typical of French classicism. Lully also composed court ballets, and his operatic productions achieved a powerful influence throughout Europe. Louis supported Francois Couperin (1668–1733), whose harpsicord and organ works possess the regal grandeur the king loved, and Marc-Antoine Charpentier (1634–1704), whose solemn religious music entertained him at meals. Charpentier received a pension for the *Te Deums,* hymns of thanksgiving he composed to celebrate French military victories.

Louis XIV loved the stage, and in the plays of Molière and Racine his court witnessed the finest achievements in the history of the French theater. When Jean-Baptiste Poquelin (1622–1673), the son of a prosperous tapestry maker, refused to join his father's business and entered the theater, he took the stage name Molière. As playwright, stage manager, director, and actor, Molière produced comedies that exposed the hypocrisies and follies of society though brilliant caricature. *Tartuffe* satirized the religious hypocrite, *Le Bourgeois Gentilhomme (The Would-Be Gentleman)* attacked the social parvenu, and *Les Femmes savantes (The Learned Women)* mocked the fashionable pseudo-intellectuals of the day. In structure Molière's plays followed classical models, but they were based on careful social observation. Molière made the bourgeoisie the butt of his ridicule; he stopped short of criticizing the nobility, thus reflecting the policy of his royal patron.

While Molière dissected social mores, his

Considered the greatest French painter of the seventeenth century, Poussin in this dramatic work (ca 1636) shows his complete devotion to the ideals of classicism. The heroic figures are superb physical specimens, but hardly life-like. (Metropolitan Museum of Art, New York [Dick Fund, 1946])

contemporary Jean Racine (1639–1699) analyzed the power of love. Racine based his tragic dramas on Greek and Roman legends, and his persistent theme is the conflict of good and evil. Several plays – *Andromache, Berenice, Iphigenie,* and *Phedre* – bear the names of women and deal with the power of passion in women. Louis preferred *Mithridates* and *Brittanicus* because of the "grandeur" of their themes. For simplicity of language, symmetrical structure, and calm restraint, the plays of Racine represent the finest examples of French classicism. His tragedies and Molière's comedies are still produced today.

LOUIS XIV'S WARS

Just as the architecture and court life at Versailles served to reflect the king's glory, and as the economy of the state under Colbert was managed to advance the king's prestige, so did Louis XIV use war to exalt himself above the other rulers and nations of Europe. He visualized himself as a great military hero. "The character of a conqueror," he remarked, "is regarded as the noblest and highest of titles." Military glory was his aim. In 1666, Louis appointed François le Tellier (later Marquis de Louvois) as secretary of war. Louvois created a professional army, which was modern in the sense that the French state, rather than private nobles, employed the soldiers.

Because of the justifiable fear that an army of native French soldiers would turn on their oppressors, the army of Louis XIV was re-

cruited heavily from Swiss, German, and Irish mercenaries. Officers were French, the ranks largely foreign. A foreign mercenary army could more easily be employed against rebellious peasants whose language they did not speak. It is one of the ironies of Louis' wars that a French army of Protestant Swiss and German troops was sent against the Protestant Dutch.

A commissariat was established to feed the troops, in place of the ancient practice of living off the countryside. An ambulance corps was designed to look after the wounded. Uniforms and weapons were standardized. Finally, a rational system of recruitment, training, discipline, and promotion was imposed. With this new military machine, for the first time in Europe's history one national state, France, was able to dominate the politics of Europe.

Louis continued on a broader scale the expansionist policy begun by Cardinal Richelieu. In 1667, using a dynastic excuse, he invaded Flanders, part of the Spanish Netherlands, and Franche-Comté in the east. In consequence he acquired twelve towns, including the important commercial centers of Lille and Tournai (see Map 16.1). Five years later, Louis personally led an army of over a hundred thousand men into Holland, and the Dutch ultimately saved themselves only by opening the dikes and flooding the countryside. This war, which lasted six years and eventually involved the German empire and Spain, was concluded by the Treaty of Nijmegen (1678). Louis gained additional Flemish towns and the whole of Franche-Comté.

Encouraged by his successes, by the weakness of the German empire, and by divisions among the other European powers, Louis continued his aggression. In 1684 he seized the city of Trier, and the province of Lorraine was permanently occupied by France. At that moment, the king seemed invincible.

In fact, Louis had reached the limit of his expansion at Nijmegen. The wars of the 1680s and 1690s brought him no additional territories. In 1689, the Dutch prince William of Orange, a bitter foe of Louis XIV, became king of England. William joined the League of Augsburg – which included the German emperor, the kings of Spain and Sweden, and the electors of Bavaria, Saxony, and the Palatinate – adding British resources and men to the alliance. Neither the French nor the league won any decisive victories. The alliance served instead as preparation for the long-expected conflict known as the War of the Spanish Succession.

This struggle (1701-1713), provoked by the territorial disputes of the past century, also involved the dynastic question of the succession to the Spanish throne. It was an open secret in Europe that the king of Spain, Charles II (1665-1700), was mentally defective and sexually impotent. In his will Charles left his territories to his grandnephew, Philip of Anjou, who was also Louis XIV's grandson. When Charles died on November 1, 1700, the line of the Spanish Habsburgs ended. Immediately, Louis claimed the Spanish throne on behalf of his grandson.

The union of the French and Spanish crowns would have totally upset the European balance of power, and Louis's declaration that "the Pyrenees no longer exist" provoked the long-anticipated crisis. In May 1702 England, Holland, and the Holy Roman Empire declared war on France. They claimed that they were fighting to prevent France from becoming too strong in Europe, but during the previous half-century overseas maritime rivalry among France, Holland, and England had created serious international tension. The secondary motive of the Allied Powers was to check France's expanding commercial power in North America, Asia, and Africa. In the

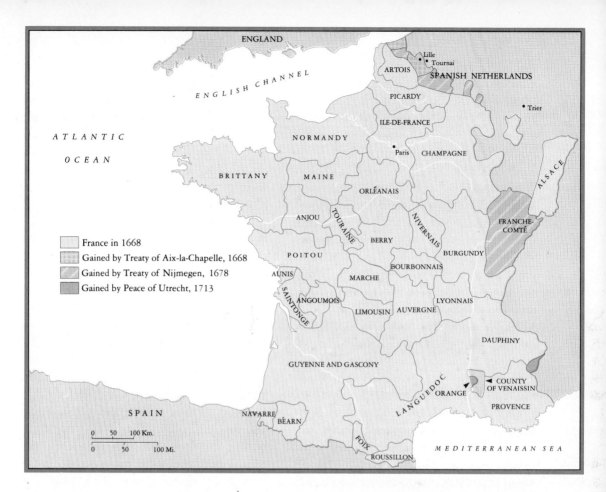

MAP 16.1   THE ACQUISITIONS OF LOUIS XIV, 1668–1713   The desire for glory and the weakness of his German neighbors encouraged Louis' expansionist policy. But he paid a high price for his acquisitions.

ensuing series of conflicts, two great soldiers dominated the alliance against France: Eugene, prince of Savoy, representing the Holy Roman Empire, and the Englishman John Churchill, subsequently duke of Marlborough. Eugene and Churchill inflicted a crushing defeat on Louis in 1704 at Blenheim in Bavaria. Marlborough followed with another victory at Romilles near Namur in Brabant.

The war was finally concluded at Utrecht in 1713, where the principle of partition was applied. Louis's grandson Philip became the first Bourbon king of Spain on the understanding that the French and Spanish crowns would never be united. France surrendered Newfoundland, Nova Scotia, and the Hudson Bay territory to England, which also acquired Gibraltar, Minorca, and the *asiento,* or control of the African slave trade from Spain. The Dutch received little because the former Spanish Netherlands was given to Austria.

The Peace of Utrecht had important international consequences. It represented the balance-of-power principle in operation, setting limits on the extent to which any one power, in this case France, could expand. The treaty completed the decline of Spain as a great power. It vastly expanded the British Empire. Finally, Utrecht gave European powers experience in international cooperation and thus prepared them for the great alliances against France at the end of the eighteenth century.

For Louis XIV, Utrecht was a severe defeat. He had waged his wars in the quest for glory. He had gained little (see Map 16.1). Utrecht marked the end of French expansion. To raise revenue for the wars, forty thousand additional offices had been sold, thus increasing the number of families exempt from future taxation. Constant war had disrupted trade, which meant the state could not tax the profits of trade. Widespread starvation in the provinces provoked peasant revolts, especially in Brittany. In 1714, France hovered on the brink of financial bankruptcy. Louis had exhausted the country without much compensation. It is no wonder that when he died on September 1, 1715, Saint-Simon wrote, "Those . . . wearied by the heavy and oppressive rule of the King and his ministers, felt a delighted freedom. . . . Paris . . . found relief in the hope of liberation. . . . The provinces . . . quivered with delight . . . [and] the people, ruined, abused, despairing, now thanked God for a deliverance which answered their most ardent desires."[2]

THE DECLINE OF ABSOLUTIST SPAIN IN THE SEVENTEENTH CENTURY

Spanish absolutism and greatness had preceded that of the French. In the sixteenth century, Spain had developed the standard features of absolute monarchy: a permanent bureaucracy staffed by professionals employed in the various councils of state, a standing army, and national taxes, the *servicios,* which fell most heavily on the poor.

France depended upon financial and admin-

VELAZQUEZ: THE MAIDS OF HONOR The Infanta Margarita painted in 1656 with her maids and playmates has invaded the artist's studio, while her parents' image is reflected in the mirror on the back wall. Velazquez (extreme left), who powerfully influenced nineteenth-century impressionist painters, imbued all of his subjects, including the pathetic dwarf (right, in black) with a sense of dignity. (Giraudon)

istrative unification within its national borders; Spain had developed an international absolutism on the basis of silver bullion from Peru. Spanish gold and silver, Spanish armies, and Spanish glory had dominated the continent of Europe for most of the sixteenth century, but by the 1590s the seeds of disaster were sprouting. While France in the seventeenth century represented the classic model of the modern absolute state, Spain was experiencing steady decline and decay. Fiscal disorder, political incompetence, population decline, intellectual isolation, and psychological malaise — all combined to reduce Spain, by 1715, to the rank of a second-rate power.

The fabulous and seemingly inexhaustible flow of silver from Mexico and Peru had led Philip II (page 529) to assume the role of defender of Roman Catholicism in Europe. In order to humble the Protestant Dutch and to control the Spanish Netherlands, Philip believed that England, the Netherlands' greatest supporter, had to be crushed. He poured millions of Spanish ducats and all of Spanish hopes into the vast fleet that sailed in 1588. When the "Invincible Armada" went down in the North Sea, a century of Spanish pride and power went with it. After 1590, a spirit of defeatism and disillusionment crippled almost all efforts at reform.

Philip II's Catholic crusade had been financed by the revenues of the Spanish-Atlantic economy. These included, in addition to silver and gold bullion, the sale of cloth,

grain, oil, and wine to the colonies. In the early seventeenth century, the Dutch and English began to trade with the Spanish colonies, cutting into the revenues that had gone to Spain. Mexico and Peru themselves developed local industries, further lessening their need to buy from Spain. Between 1610 and 1650, Spanish trade with the colonies fell 60 percent.

At the same time the native Indians and African slaves, who worked the South American silver mines under conditions that would have disgraced the ancient Egyptian pharaohs, suffered frightful epidemics of disease. Moreover, the lodes started to run dry. Consequently, the quantity of metal produced for Spain steadily declined. Nevertheless, in Madrid royal expenditures constantly exceeded income. The remedies applied in the face of a mountainous state debt and declining revenues were devaluation of the coinage and declarations of bankruptcy. In 1596, 1607, 1627, 1647, and 1680 Spanish kings found no solution to the problem of an empty treasury other than cancellation of the national debt. Naturally, public confidence in the state deteriorated.

Spain, in contrast to the other countries of western Europe, had only a tiny middle class. Disdain for money, in a century of increasing commercialism and bourgeois attitudes, reveals a significant facet of the Spanish national character. Public opinion, taking its cue from the aristocracy, condemned moneymaking as vulgar and undignified. Those with influence or connections sought titles of nobility and social prestige. Thousands entered economically unproductive professions and became priests, monks, and nuns: there were said to be nine thousand monasteries in the province of Castile alone. The flood of gold and silver had produced severe inflation, pushing the

costs of production in the textile industry higher and higher, to the point that Castilian cloth could not compete in colonial and international markets. Many manufacturers and businessmen found so many obstacles in the way of profitable enterprise that they simply gave up.[3]

Spanish aristocrats, attempting to maintain an extravagant lifestyle they could no longer afford, increased the rents on their estates. High rents and heavy taxes in turn drove the peasants from the land. Agricultural production suffered and the peasants departed for the large cities, where they swelled the ranks of unemployed beggars.

Their most Catholic majesties, the kings of Spain, had no solutions to these dire problems. The portraits of Philip III (1598–1622), Philip IV (1622–1665), and Charles II hanging in the Prado, the Spanish national museum in Madrid, reflect the increasing weakness of the dynasty. Their faces – the small beady eyes, the long noses, the jutting Habsburg jaws, the constipated and pathetically stupid expressions – tell a story of excessive inbreeding and decaying monarchy. These Spanish kings all lacked force of character. Philip III, a pallid, melancholy, and deeply pious man "whose only virtue appeared to reside in a total absence of vice," handed the government over to the lazy duke of Lerma, who used it to advance his personal and familial wealth. Philip IV left the management of his several kingdoms to Count Olivares.

Olivares was an able administrator. He did not lack energy and ideas; he devised new sources of revenue. But he clung to the grandiose belief that the solution to Spain's difficulties rested in a return to the imperial tradition. Unfortunately, the imperial tradition demanded the revival of war with the Dutch at the expiration of a twelve-year truce in 1622 and a long war with France over Mantua (1628–1659). These conflicts on top of an empty treasury brought disaster.

In 1640, Spain faced serious revolts in Naples and Portugal, and in 1643 the French inflicted a crushing defeat on a Spanish army in Belgium. By the Treaty of the Pyrenees of 1659, which ended the French-Spanish wars, Spain was compelled to surrender extensive territories to France. This treaty marked the end of Spain as a great power.

Seventeenth-century Spain was the victim of its past. It could not forget the grandeur of the sixteenth century and look to the future. The bureaucratic councils of state continued to function as symbols of the absolute Spanish monarchy. But because those councils were staffed by aristocrats, it was the aristocracy that held the real power. Spanish absolutism had been built largely on slave-produced gold and silver. When the supply of bullion decreased, the power and standing of the Spanish state declined.

The most cherished Spanish ideals were military glory and strong Roman Catholic faith. In the seventeenth century, Spain lacked the finances and the manpower to fight the expensive wars in which it foolishly got involved. Spain also ignored the new mercantile ideas and scientific methods, because they came from heretical nations, Holland and England. The incredible wealth of South America destroyed the tiny Spanish middle class and created contempt for business and manual labor.

The decadence of the Habsburg dynasty and the lack of effective royal councilors also contributed to Spanish failure. Spanish leaders seemed to lack the will to reform. Pessimism and fatalism permeated national life. In the reign of Philip IV, a royal council was appointed to plan the construction of a canal linking the Tagus and Manzanares rivers in Spain. After interminable debate, the committee decided that "if God had intended the rivers to be navigable, He would have made them so."

In the novel *Don Quixote,* the Spanish writer Cervantes (1547–1616) produced one of the great masterpieces of world literature. The main character, Don Quixote, lives in a world of dreams, traveling about the countryside seeking military glory. From the title of this book English has borrowed the word *quixotic.* Meaning idealistic but impractical, it characterizes seventeenth-century Spain.

CONSTITUTIONALISM

The seventeenth century, which witnessed the development of absolute monarchy, also saw the appearance of the constitutional state. While France and later Prussia, Russia, and Austria solved the question of sovereignty with the absolutist state, England and Holland evolved toward the constitutional state. What is constitutionalism? Is it the same as democracy?

Constitutionalism is the limitation of government by law. Constitutionalism also implies a balance between the authority and power of the government on the one hand, and the rights and liberties of the subjects on the other. The balance is often very delicate.

A nation's constitution may be written or unwritten. In may be embodied in one basic document, occasionally revised by amendment or judicial decision, like the Constitution of the United States. Or a constitution may be partly written and partly unwritten and include parliamentary statutes, judicial decisions, and a body of traditional procedures and practices, like the English and Canadian constitutions. Whether written or unwritten, a constitution gets its binding force from the government's acknowledgment that it must respect that constitution – that is, that the state must govern according to the laws. Likewise, in a constitutional state, the people look upon the law and the constitution as the protectors of their rights, liberties, and property.

Modern constitutional governments may take either a republican or a monarchial form. In a constitutional republic, the sovereign power resides in the electorate and is exercised by the electorate's representatives. In a constitutional monarchy, a king or queen serves as the head of state and possesses some residual political authority, but again the ultimate or sovereign power rests in the electorate.

A constitutional government is not, however, quite the same as a democratic government. In a complete democracy, *all* the people have the right to participate either directly, or indirectly through their elected representatives, in the government of the state. Democratic government, therefore, is intimately tied up with the franchise (the vote). Most men could not vote until the late nineteenth century. Even then, women – probably the majority in Western societies – lacked the franchise; they gained the right to vote only in the twentieth century. Consequently, although constitutionalism developed in the seventeenth century, full democracy was achieved only in very recent times.

THE DECLINE OF ROYAL ABSOLUTISM IN ENGLAND (1603–1649)

In the late sixteenth century the French monarchy was powerless; a century later the king's power was absolute. In 1588, Queen Elizabeth I of England exercised very great personal power; by 1689, the English monarchy was severely circumscribed and limited. Change in England was anything but orderly: England in the seventeenth century displayed as much political stability as some African states in the twentieth. They executed one king, experienced a bloody civil war, experimented with military dictatorship, then restored the son of the murdered king, and finally, after a bloodless revolution, established a constitutional monarchy. Political stability came only in the 1690s. How do we account for the fact that after such a violent and tumultuous century, England laid the foundations for a constitutional monarchy? What combination of political, socioeconomic, and religious factors brought on first a civil war in 1642–1649 and then the constitutional settlement of 1688–1689?

The extraordinary success of Elizabeth I had rested on her political shrewdness and flexibility, her careful management of finances, her wise selection of ministers, her clever manipulation of Parliament, and her sense of royal dignity and devotion to hard work. The aging queen had always refused to discuss the succession. After her Scottish cousin James Stuart succeeded her as James I (1603–1625), Elizabeth's strengths seemed even greater than they actually had been. The Stuarts lacked every quality Elizabeth had possessed.

King James was well educated and learned but lacking in common sense – he was once called "the wisest fool in Christendom." He also lacked the common touch. Urged to wave at the crowds who waited to greet their new ruler, James complained that he was tired, and threatened to drop his breeches "so they can cheer at my arse." Having left barbarous and violent Scotland for rich and prosperous England, James believed he had entered "the Promised Land." As soon as he got to London, the new English king went to see the Crown jewels.

Abysmally ignorant of English law and of the English Parliament, but sublimely arrogant, James was devoted to the theory of the divine right of kings. He expressed his ideas about divine right in his essay "The Trew Law of Free Monarchy." According to James I, a monarch has a divine (or God-given) right to his authority, and is responsible only to God. Rebellion is the worst of political crimes. If a king orders something evil, the subject should respond with passive disobedience but should be prepared to accept any penalty for non-compliance.

James substituted political theorizing and talk for real work. He lectured the House of Commons: "There are no privileges and immunities which can stand against a divinely appointed King." This notion, implying total royal jurisdiction over the liberties, persons, and properties of English men and women, formed the basis of the Stuart concept of absolutism. Such a view ran directly counter to the long-standing English idea that a person's property could not be taken away without due process of law. James's expression of such views before the English House of Commons constituted a grave political mistake.

The House of Commons guarded the pocketbook of the nation, and James and later Stuart kings badly needed to open that pocketbook. Elizabeth had bequeathed to James a sizable royal debt. Through prudent management the debt could have been gradually reduced, but James I looked upon all revenues as a happy windfall to be squandered on a lavish court and favorite courtiers. In fact, the extravagance and licentiousness of James' court, and the public flaunting of his male lovers, weakened respect for the monarchy.

Elizabeth had also left to her Stuart successors a House of Commons that appreciated its

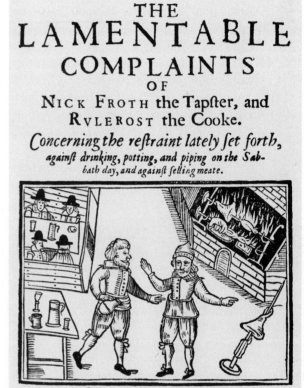

THE
LAMENTABLE
COMPLAINTS
OF
NICK FROTH the Tapſter, and
RVLEROST the Cooke.
Concerning the reſtraint lately ſet forth,
againſt drinking, potting, and piping on the Sab-
bath day, and againſt ſelling meate.

Printed in the yeare, 1641.

PURITAN IDEALS OPPOSED The Puritans preached sober living and abstention from alcoholic drink, rich food, and dancing. This pamphlet reflects the common man's hostility to such restraints. "Potting" refers to tankards of beer; "piping" means making music. (The British Museum)

own financial strength and intended to use that strength to acquire a greater say in the government of the state. The knights and burgesses who sat at Westminster in the early seventeenth century wanted to discuss royal expenditures, religious reform, and foreign affairs. In short, the Commons wanted what amounted to sovereignty.

Profound social changes had occurred since the sixteenth century. The English House of Commons during the reigns of James I and his son Charles I (1625-1649) was very different from the assembly Henry VIII had terrorized into passing his Reformation legislation. A social revolution had brought about the change. The dissolution of the monasteries and the sale of monastic land had enriched many people. Agricultural techniques like the draining of wasteland and the application of fertilizers improved the land and its yield. Old manorial common land had been enclosed and turned into sheep runs; breeding was carefully supervised, and the size of the flocks increased. In these activities, as well as in renting and leasing parcels of land, precise accounts were kept.

Many men invested in commercial ventures at home, such as the expanding cloth industry, and in partnerships and joint stock companies engaged in foreign enterprises. They made prudent marriages. All these developments led to a great deal of social mobility. Both in commerce and in agriculture, the English in the late sixteenth and early seventeenth centuries were capitalists, investing their profits to make more money. Although the international inflation of the period hit everywhere, in England commercial and agricultural income rose faster than prices. Wealthy country gentry, rich city merchants, and financiers invested abroad.

The typical pattern was for the commercially successfully to set themselves up as country gentry, thus creating an elite group that possessed a far greater proportion of land and of the national wealth in 1640 than had been the case in 1540. Small wonder that in 1640 someone could declare in the House of Commons, probably accurately, "We could buy the House of Lords three times over." Increased wealth had also produced a better-educated and more articulate House of Commons. Many members had acquired at least a

smattering of legal knowledge, and they used that knowledge to search for medieval precedents from which to argue against the king. The class that dominated the Commons wanted political power corresponding to its economic strength.

In England, unlike France, there was no social stigma attached to paying taxes. Members of the House of Commons were willing to tax themselves provided they had some say in the expenditure of those taxes and in the formulation of state policies. The Stuart kings, however, considered such ambitions intolerable presumption and a threat to their divine-right prerogative. Consequently, at every Parliament between 1603 and 1640 bitter squabbles erupted between the Crown and the wealthy, articulate, and legal-minded Commons. Charles I's attempt to govern without Parliament (1629-1640), and to finance his government by arbitrary nonparliamentary levies, brought the country to a crisis.

An issue graver than royal extravagance and Parliament's desire to make the law also disturbed the English and embittered relations between the king and the House of Commons. That problem was religion. In the early seventeenth century, increasing numbers of English men and women felt dissatisfied with the Church of England established by Henry VIII and reformed by Elizabeth. Many believed the Reformation had not gone far enough. They wanted to "purify" the Anglican church of Roman Catholic elements — elaborate vestments and ceremonial, the position of the altar at the east end of the church, even the giving and wearing of wedding rings. These people were called Puritans.

It is very difficult to establish what proportion of the English population was Puritan. It is clear, however, that many English men and women were attracted by the socioeconomic implications of John Calvin's theology. Calvinism emphasized hard work, sobriety, thrift, competition, and postponement of pleasure, and tended to link sin and poverty with weakness and moral corruption. These attitudes fit in precisely with the economic approaches and practices of many (successful) businessmen and farmers. These values have frequently been called the Protestant, or middle-class, or capitalist, ethic. While it is hazardous to identify capitalism and progress with Protestantism – there were many successful Catholic capitalists – the "Protestant virtues" represented the prevailing values of the great majority of members of the House of Commons.

James I and Charles I both gave the impression of being highly sympathetic to Roman Catholicism. Charles supported the policies of William Laud, archbishop of Canterbury (1573-1645), who tried to impose elaborate ritual and rich ceremonial on all churches. Laud insisted on complete uniformity of church services, and enforced that uniformity through an ecclesiastical court called High Commission. People believed the country was being led back to Roman Catholicism. When in 1639 Laud attempted to impose a new prayer book, modeled on the Anglican Book of Common Prayer, on the Presbyterian Scots, the Scots revolted. In order to finance an army to put down the Scots, King Charles was compelled to summon Parliament in November 1640.

For eleven years Charles I had ruled without Parliament, financing his government through extraordinary stopgap levies, considered illegal by most English people. For example, the king revived a medieval law requiring coastal districts to help pay the cost of ships for defense, but levied the tax, called ship money, on inland as well as coastal counties. When the issue was tested in the courts, the judges, having been suborned, decided in the king's favor.

Most members of Parliament believed that such taxation without consent amounted to arbitrary and absolute despotism. Consequently, they were not willing to trust the king with an army. Accordingly, this Parliament, commonly called the Long Parliament because it sat from 1640 to 1660, proceeded to enact legislation that limited the power of the monarch and made arbitrary government impossible.

In 1641, the Commons passed the Triennial Act, which compelled the king to summon Parliament every three years. The Commons impeached Archbishop Laud and abolished the House of Lords and the Court of High Commission. It went further and threatened to abolish the institution of episcopacy. King Charles, fearful of a Scottish invasion – the original reason for summoning Parliament – accepted these measures. Understanding and peace were not achieved, however, partly because radical members of the Commons pushed increasingly revolutionary propositions, partly because Charles maneuvered to rescind those he had already approved. An uprising in Ireland precipitated civil war.

Ever since Henry II had conquered Ireland in 1171, English governors had mercilessly ruled the Irish, and English landlords had ruthlessly exploited them. The English Reformation had made a bad situation worse: because the Irish remained Catholic, religious differences became united with economic and political oppression. Without an army, Charles I could neither come to terms with the Scots nor put down the Irish rebellion, and the Long Parliament remained unwilling to place an army under a king it did not trust.

Charles thus instigated military action against parliamentary forces. He recruited an army drawn from the nobility and their cavalry staff, the rural gentry, and mercenaries. The Parliamentary army was composed of the militia of the City of London, country squires with business connections, and men with a firm belief in the spiritual duty of serving.

The English Civil War (1642–1646) tested whether sovereignty in England was to reside in the king or in Parliament. The Civil War did not resolve that problem, although it ended in 1649 with the execution of King Charles on the charge of high treason – a severe blow to royal power. The period between 1649 and 1660, called the Interregnum because it separated two monarchial periods, saw England's one experience of military dictatorship.

PURITANICAL ABSOLUTISM IN ENGLAND: CROMWELL AND THE PROTECTORATE

The problem of sovereignty was vigorously debated in the middle years of the seventeenth century. In *Leviathan,* the English philosopher and political theorist Thomas Hobbes (1588–1679) maintained that sovereignty is ultimately derived from the people, who transfer it to the monarchy by implicit contract. The power of the ruler is absolute, but kings do not hold their power by divine right. This view pleased no one in the seventeenth century.

When Charles I was beheaded on January 30, 1649, the kingship was abolished. A commonwealth, or republican form of government, was proclaimed. Theoretically, legislative power rested in the surviving members of Parliament and executive power in a council of state. In fact, the army that had defeated the royal forces controlled the government, and Oliver Cromwell controlled the army.

Although called the Protectorate, the rule of Cromwell (1653–1658) constituted military dictatorship.

Oliver Cromwell (1599–1658) came from the country gentry, the class that dominated the House of Commons in the early seventeenth century. He himself had sat in the Long Parliament. Cromwell rose in the parliamentary army, and achieved nationwide fame by infusing the army with his Puritan convictions and molding it into the highly effective military machine, called the New Model Army, that defeated the royalist forces.

Parliament had written a constitution, the Instrument of Government (1653), that invested executive power in a lord protector (Cromwell) and a council of state. The Instrument provided for triennial parliaments and gave Parliament the sole power to raise taxes. But after repeated disputes Cromwell tore the document up. He continued the standing army and proclaimed quasi-martial law. He divided England into twelve military districts, each governed by a major general. On the issue of religion Cromwell favored broad toleration, and the Instrument of Government gave all Christians, except Roman Catholics, the right to practice their faith. Toleration meant state protection of many different Protestant sects, and most English people had no enthusiasm for such a notion; the idea was far ahead of its time. Cromwell identified Irish Catholicism with sedition. In 1649 he crushed rebellion there with merciless savagery, leaving a legacy of Irish hatred for England that has not yet subsided. The state rigorously censored the press, forbade sports, and kept the theaters closed.

Cromwell's regulation of the nation's economy had features typical of seventeenth-century absolutism. The lord protector's policies were mercantilist, similar to those Colbert established in France. Cromwell enforced a navigation act requiring that English goods be transported on English ships. The navigation act was a great boost to the development of an English merchant marine, and brought about a short but successful war with the commercially threatened Dutch. Cromwell also welcomed the immigration of Jews, because of their skills, and they began to return to England in larger numbers after four centuries of absence.

Absolute government collapsed when Cromwell died in 1658. Absolutism failed because the English got fed up with military rule. They longed for a return to civilian government, restoration of the common law, and social stability. Moreover, the strain of creating a community of puritanical saints proved too psychologically exhausting. Government by military dictatorship was an unfortunate experiment that English men and women never forgot and never repeated. By 1660, they were ready to restore the monarchy.

THE RESTORATION OF THE ENGLISH MONARCHY

The Restoration of 1660 re-established the monarchy in the person of Charles II (1660–1685), eldest son of Charles I. At the same time both houses of Parliament were restored, together with the established Anglican church, the courts of law, and the system of local government through justices of the peace. The Restoration failed to resolve two serious problems. What was to be the attitude of the state toward Puritans, Catholics, and dissenters from the established church? And what was to be the constitutional position of the king – that is, what was to be relationship between the king and Parliament?

About the first of these issues, Charles II, a relaxed, easygoing, and sensual man, was basically indifferent. He was not interested in

THE HOUSE OF COMMONS *This seal of the Commonwealth shows the small House of Commons in session with the speaker presiding; the legend "in the third year of freedom" refers to 1651, three years after the abolition of the monarchy. In 1653, however, Cromwell abolished this "Rump Parliament" — so-called because it consisted of the few surviving members elected before the Civil War — and he and the army governed the land. (The British Museum)*

doctrinal issues. Parliamentarians were, and they proceeded to enact a body of laws that sought to compel religious uniformity. Those who refused to receive the sacrament of the Church of England could not vote, hold public office, preach, teach, attend the universities, or even assemble for meetings, according to the Test Act of 1673. These restrictions could not be enforced. When the Quaker William Penn held a meeting of his friends and was arrested, the jury refused to convict him.

In politics, Charles II was determined "not to set out in his travels again," which meant that he intended to get along with Parliament. Charles II's solution to the problem of the relationship between the king and the House of Commons had profound importance for later constitutional development. Generally good rapport existed between the king and the strongly royalist Parliament that had restored him. This rapport was due largely to the king's appointment of a council of five men who served both as his major advisers and as members of Parliament, thus acting as liaison agents between the executive and the legislature. This body – known as the Cabal from the names of its five members (Clifford, Arlington, Buckingham, Ashley-Cooper and Lauderdale) – was an ancestor of the later cabinet system. It gradually came to be accepted that the Cabal was answerable in Parliament for the decisions of the king. This development gave rise to the concept of ministerial responsibility: royal ministers must answer to the Commons.

Harmony between the Crown and Parliament rested on the understanding that Charles would summon frequent parliaments and that Parliament would vote him sufficient revenues. However, although Parliament believed Charles had a virtual divine right to govern, it did not grant him an adequate income. Accordingly, Charles entered into a secret agreement with Louis XIV. The French king would give Charles £200,000 annually, and in return Charles would relax the laws against Catholics, gradually re-Catholicize England, and support French policy against the Dutch.

When the details of this secret treaty leaked out, a great wave of anti-Catholic fear swept England. This fear was compounded by a crucial fact: although Charles had produced several bastards, he had no legitimate children. It therefore appeared that his brother and heir, James, Duke of York, who had publicly acknowledged his Catholicism, would inaugu-

rate a Catholic dynasty. The combination of hatred for the French absolutism embodied in Louis XIV, hostility to Roman Catholicism, and fear of a permanent Catholic dynasty produced virtual hysteria. The Commons passed an exclusion bill denying the succession to a Roman Catholic, but Charles quickly dissolved Parliament and the bill never became law.

James II (1685–1688) did succeed his brother, and almost at once the worst English anti-Catholic fears were realized. In direct violation of the Test Act, James appointed Roman Catholics to positions in the army, the universities, and local government. When these actions were tested in the courts, the judges, whom James had appointed, decided for the king. The king was suspending the law at will, and appeared to be reviving the absolutism of his father and grandfather. He went further. Attempting to broaden his base of support with Protestant dissenters and nonconformists, James issued a declaration of indulgence granting religious freedom to all.

Two events gave the signals for revolution. First, seven bishops of the Church of England petitioned the king that they not be forced to read the declaration of indulgence because of their belief it was an illegal act. They were imprisoned in the Tower of London but subsequently acquitted amid great public enthusiasm. Second, in June 1688, James's queen produced a male heir. A Catholic dynasty seemed assured. The fear of a Roman Catholic monarchy, supported by France and ruling outside the law, prompted a group of eminent persons to offer the English throne to James's Protestant daughter Mary and her Dutch husband, Prince William of Orange. In November 1688, James II, his queen, and infant son fled to France and became pensioners of Louis XIV.

The English call the events of 1688 the Glorious Revolution. The revolution was indeed glorious in the sense that it replaced one king with another with a minimum of bloodshed. It also represented the destruction, once and for all, of the idea of divine-right monarchy. William and Mary accepted the English throne from Parliament, and in so doing explicitly recognized the supremacy of Parliament. The revolution of 1688 established the principle that sovereignty, the ultimate power in the state, rested in Parliament, and that the king ruled with the consent of the governed.

The men who had brought about the revolution quickly framed their intentions in the Bill of Rights, which is the cornerstone of the modern British constitution. The basic principles of the Bill of Rights were formulated in direct response to Stuart absolutism. Law was to be made in Parliament; once made, the law could not be suspended by the Crown. Parliament had to be called at least every three years. Both elections to and debate in Parliament were to be free in the sense that the Crown was not to interfere in them; this aspect of the Bill was widely disregarded in the eighteenth century. Judges would hold their offices "during good behavior," which assured the independence of the judiciary. No longer could the Crown get the judicial decisions it wanted by threats of removal. There was to be no standing army in peacetime – a limitation designed to prevent the repetition of either Stuart or Cromwellian military government. The Bill of Rights granted "that the subjects which are Protestants may have arms for their defense suitable to their conditions and as al-

lowed by law,"[4] meaning that Catholics could not possess firearms because the Protestant majority feared them. Additional parliamentary legislation granted freedom of worship to Protestant dissenters and nonconformists and required that the English monarch always be Protestant in faith.

The Glorious Revolution found its best defense in the political philosopher John Locke's "Second Treatise on Civil Government" (1690). A spokesman for the great land-owning class that had brought about the revolution, Locke (1632-1704) maintained that men set up civil governments in order to defend property. Thus the purpose of government is to protect life, liberty, and property. Locke's ideas, though not profound, had great influence throughout the eighteenth century.

However glorious, the events of 1688-1690 did not constitute a *democratic* revolution. The revolution placed sovereignty in Parliament, and Parliament represented the upper classes. The great majority of English people acquired no say in their government. The English revolution established a constitutional monarchy; it also inaugurated an age of aristocratic government, which lasted at least until 1832 and probably until 1914.

In the course of the eighteenth century, the cabinet system of government evolved. The term *cabinet* refers to the small private room in which English rulers consulted their chief ministers. In a cabinet system the leading ministers, who must have seats in and the support of a majority of the House of Commons, formulate common policy and conduct the business of the country. During the administration of one royal minister, Sir Robert Walpole (1721-1742), the idea developed that the cabinet was responsible to the House of Commons. The king normally presided at cabinet meetings, but because the Hanoverian king George I (1714-1727) did not understand enough English to follow the discussions, he stopped attending cabinet sessions. George II (1727-1760) followed that precedent. The influence of the Crown in decision making accordingly declined. Walpole enjoyed the favor of the monarchy and of the House of Commons, and came to be called the king's first, or prime, minister. In the English cabinet system both legislative and executive power are held by the leading ministers, who form the government.

THE DUTCH REPUBLIC IN THE SEVENTEENTH CENTURY

The seventeenth century witnessed an unparalled flowering of Dutch scientific, artistic, and literary achievement. In this period, often called "the golden age of the Netherlands," Dutch ideas and attitudes played a profound role in shaping a new and modern worldview. At the same time the Republic of the United Provinces of the Netherlands represents another model of the development of the modern state.

In the late sixteenth century, the seven northern provinces of the Netherlands, of which Holland and Zeeland were the most prosperous, succeeded in throwing off Spanish domination. This success was based on their geographical lines of defense, the wealth of the cities, the brilliant military strategy of William the Silent, the preoccupation of Philip II of Spain with so many other concerns, and the northern provinces' vigorous Calvinism. In 1581 the seven provinces of the Union of Utrecht had formed the United Provinces (page 528). Philip II continued to try to crush the Dutch with the Armada but in 1609 his son Philip III agreed to a truce that implicitly recognized the independence of the United Provinces. At the time neither side

expected the peace to be permanent. The Peace of Westphalia in 1648, however, confirmed the Dutch republic's independence.

Within each province an oligarchy of wealthy merchants called regents handled domestic affairs in the local Estates. The provincial Estates held virtually all the power. A federal assembly, or States General, handled matters of foreign affairs, such as war. But the States General did not possess sovereign authority, since all issues had to be referred back to the local Estates for approval. The States General appointed a representative, the stadholder, in each province. As the highest executive there, the stadholder carried out ceremonial functions and was responsible for defense and good order. The sons of William the Silent, Maurice and William Louis, held the office of stadholder in all seven provinces. The regents in each province jealously guarded local independence and resisted efforts at centralization. Nevertheless, Holland, which had the largest navy and the most wealth, dominated the republic and the States General. Significantly, the Estates assembled at Holland's capital, The Hague.

The government of the United Provinces fits none of the standard categories of seventeenth-century political organization. The Dutch were not monarchial, but fiercely republican. The government was controlled by wealthy merchants and financiers. Although rich, their values were not aristocratic but strongly middle-class, emphasizing thrift, hard work, and simplicity in living. The Dutch republic was not a strong federation but a confederation – that is, a weak union of strong provinces. The provinces were a temptation to powerful neighbors, yet the Dutch resisted the long Spanish effort at reconquest and withstood both French and English attacks in the second half of the century. Louis XIV's hatred of the Dutch was proverbial. They

MODEL OF A SEVENTEENTH-CENTURY FLUYT
The Dutch surpassed all nations in the design of fast-sailing ships. The fluyt *or fluteship was cheap to construct, carried a large cargo, and required only a small crew. It gave the Dutch a great advantage, resulting in their notable commercial success. (Photo: Caroline Buckler)*

represented all that he despised – middle-class values, religious toleration, and political independence.

The political success of the Dutch rested on the phenomenal commercial prosperity of the Netherlands. The moral and ethical bases of that commercial wealth were thrift, frugality, and religious toleration. John Calvin had written, "From where do the merchant's profits come except from his own diligence and industry"; this attitude undoubtedly encouraged a sturdy people who had waged a centuries-old struggle against the sea.

Alone of all European peoples in the seventeenth century, the Dutch practiced religious toleration. Peoples of all faiths were welcome within their borders. It is a striking testimony to the urbanity of Dutch society that in a century when patriotism was closely identified with religious uniformity, the Calvinist province of Holland allowed its highest official, Jan van Oldenbarneveldt, to continue to practice his Roman Catholic faith. As long as a businessman conducted his religion in private, the government did not interfere with him.

Toleration also paid off: it attracted a great deal of foreign capital and investment. Deposits at the Bank of Amsterdam were guaranteed by the city council, and in the middle years of the century the bank became Europe's best source of cheap credit and commercial intelligence, and the main clearinghouse for bills of exchange. Men of all races and creeds traded in Amsterdam, at whose docks on the Amstel River five thousand ships, half the merchant marine of the United Provinces, were berthed. Joost van den Vondel, the poet of Dutch imperialism, exulted:

God, God, the Lord of Amstel cried, hold every conscience free;
And Liberty ride, on Holland's tide, with billowing sails to sea,
And run our Amstel out and in; let freedom gird the bold,
And merchant in his counting house stand elbow deep in gold.[5]

The fishing industry was the cornerstone of the Dutch economy. For half the year, from June to December, fishing fleets combed the dangerous English coast and the North Sea, raking in tiny herring. Profits from herring stimulated shipbuilding, and even before 1600 the Dutch were offering the lowest shipping rates in Europe. Although Dutch cities became famous for their exports – diamonds, linen from Haarlem, pottery from Delft – Dutch wealth depended less on exports than on transport. The merchant marine was the largest in Europe.

In 1602, a group of the regents of Holland formed the Dutch East India Company, a joint stock company. Each investor received a percentage of the profits proportional to the amount of money he had put in. Within half a century, the Dutch East India Company had cut heavily into Portuguese trading in the Far East. The Dutch seized the Cape of Good

Hope, Ceylon, and Malacca, and established trading posts in each place. In the 1630s, the Dutch East India Company was paying its investors about 35 percent return annually on their investments. The Dutch West India Company, founded in 1621, traded extensively with Latin America and Africa.

Although the initial purpose of both companies was commercial – the import of spices and silks to Europe – the Dutch found themselves involved in the imperialistic exploitation of large parts of the Pacific and Latin America. Amsterdam, the center of a worldwide Dutch empire, became the commercial and financial capital of Europe. During the seventeenth century the Dutch translated their commercial acumen and flexibility into political and imperialist terms with striking success. But war with France and England in the 1670s hurt the United Provinces. The long War of the Spanish Succession, in which the Dutch supported England against France, was a costly drain on Dutch manpower and financial resources. The peace signed in 1715 to end the war marked the beginning of Dutch economic decline.

According to Thomas Hobbes, the central drive in every man is "a perpetual and restless desire of Power, after Power, that ceaseth only in Death." The seventeenth century solved the problem of *sovereign power* in two fundamental

ways, absolutism and constitutionalism. The France of Louis XIV witnessed the emergence of the fully absolutist state. The king commanded all the powers of the state: judicial, military, political, and to a great extent ecclesiastical. France developed a centralized bureaucracy, a professional army, a state-directed economy, all of which Louis personally supervised. For the first time in history all the institutions and powers of the national state were effectively controlled by a single person. The king saw himself as the representative of God on earth, and it has been said that "to the seventeenth century imagination God was a sort of image of Louis XIV."[6]

As Louis XIV personifies absolutism, so Stuart England exemplifies the evolution of the first modern constitutional state. The conflicts between Parliament and the first two Stuart rulers, James I and Charles I, tested where sovereign power would rest in the state. The resulting Civil War did not solve the problem. The Instrument of Government, the document produced in 1653 by the victorious parliamentary army, provided for a balance of governmental authority and recognition of popular rights; as such, the Instrument has been called the first modern constitution. Unfortunately, it lacked public support. James II's absolutist tendencies brought on the Revolution of 1688, and the people who made that revolution settled three basic issues. Sovereign power was divided between king and parliament, with parliament enjoying the greater share. Government was to be based on the rule of law. And the liberties of English people were made explicit in written form, in the Bill of Rights. The framers of the English constitution left to later generations the task of making constitutional government work.

The models of governmental power established by seventeenth-century England and

France strongly influenced other states then and ever since. As the Mississippi novelist William Faulkner wrote, "The past isn't dead; it's not even past."

NOTES

1. S. de Gramont, ed., *The Age of Magnificence: Memoirs of the Court of Louis XIV by the Duc de Saint-Simon,* Capricorn Books, New York, 1964, pp. 141–145.

2. Ibid., p. 183.

3. S. H. Elliott, *Imperial Spain, 1469–1716,* Mentor Books, New York, 1963, pp. 306–308.

4. C. Stephenson and G. F. Marcham, *Sources of English Constitutional History,* Harper & Row, New York, 1937, p. 601.

5. Quoted by D. Maland, *Europe in the Seventeenth Century,* Macmillan, New York, 1967, pp. 198–199.

6. Quoted by Carl J. Friedrich and Charles Blitzer, *The Age of Power,* Cornell University Press, Ithaca, New York, 1957, p. 112.

SUGGESTED READING

Students who wish to explore the problems presented in this chapter in greater depth will easily find a rich and exciting literature with many titles available in paperback editions. Geoffrey Parker, *Europe in Crisis, 1598–1618* (1980), provides a readable introduction to the religious, social, and economic tensions of the period. C. Friedrich, *The Age of the Baroque, 1610–1660* (1962), is a good survey. Perhaps the best recent study of absolutism is P. Anderson, *Lineages of the Absolutist State* (1974), a Marxist interpretation of absolutism in western and eastern Europe. The short study of M. Beloff, *The Age of Absolutism* (1967), concentrates on the social forces that underlay administrative change. H. Rosenberg, "Absolute Monarchy and Its Legacy," in *Early Modern Europe, 1450–1650* (1967), ed. N. F. Cantor and S. Werthman, is a seminal study. T. Aston, ed., *Crisis in Europe, 1560–1660* (1967), contains stimulating essays by leading authorities. The classic treatment of constitutionalism remains that of C. H. McIlwain, *Constitutionalism: Ancient and Modern* (1940), written by a great scholar during the rise of German fascism. S. B. Crimes, *English Constitutional History* (1967), is an excellent survey with valuable chapters on the sixteenth through eighteenth centuries.

Louis XIV and his age have seduced the attention of many scholars. The best contemporary biography is J. Wolf, *Louis XIV* (1968), which stresses Louis' contribution to the development of the modern bureaucratic state. For a variety of opinions about Louis, see William F. Church, ed., *Louis XIV in Historical Thought* (1978). Two works of W. H. Lewis, *The Splendid Century* (1957) and *The Sunset of the Splendid Century* (1963), make delightful reading and contain useful material on social history. R. Hatton, *Europe in the Age of Louis XIV* (1979), is a splendidly illustrated survey of many aspects of European culture in the seventeenth century. O. Ranum, *Paris in the Age of Absolutism* (1968), describes the geographical, political, economic, and architectural significance of the cultural capital of Europe. R. Mousnier, *Peasant Uprisings in Seventeenth-Century France, Russia, and China* (1970), an important study in comparative history, treats agrarian relationships and social stratification. V. L. Tapie, *The Age of Grandeur: Baroque Art and Architecture* (1960), is a magnificently illustrated book that emphasizes the relationship between art and politics. Part 4 of L. Romier, *A History of France,* trans. A. L. Rowse (1962), offers an intelligible and nationalistic narrative. For Spain, J. H. Elliott, *Imperial Spain, 1469–1716,* rev. ed. (1977), is a sensitively written and authoritative study.

G. M. Trevelyan, *England Under the Stuarts* (1960), is a good starting point for English social and political history. Brief accounts of many facets of English culture are contained in M. Ashley, *England in the Seventeenth Century* (1961), and J. H. Plumb, *England in the Eighteenth Century* (1961). M. Weber, *The Protestant Ethic and the Spirit of Capitalism* (1958), traces the relationship between Protestantism and socioeconomic developments. W. Haller, *The Rise of Puritanism* (1957), is the best treatment of English Puritanism, but it is for the advanced student. For the background to the Civil War and the war itself, see C. V. Wedgwood, *The King's Peace* (1969) and *The King's War* (1959), both highly readable; the old but scholarly biography of Cromwell by C. Firth, *Oliver Cromwell* (1956); and the recent popular study by A. Fraser, *Cromwell* (1975). C. Brinton, *The Anatomy of Revolution* (1952), contains an interesting analysis of the English Civil War and contrasts it with the French and Russian revolutions. L. Stone, *The Crisis of the Aristocracy, 1558–1641* (1967), is broader in scope than the title implies and in fact treats many aspects of English social history. Stone is a leading authority on English family history.

On Holland, the best introduction to the relationship between commercial development and the growth of democratic ideas and institutions remains Henri Pirenne, *Early Democracies in the Low Countries* (1963), especially chapters X and XI. C. R. Boxer, *The Dutch Seaborne Empire* (1980), and the appropriate chapters of D. Maland, *Europe in the Seventeenth Century* (1967), are useful for Dutch overseas expansion and the reasons for Dutch prosperity. K. H. D. Haley, *The Dutch in the Seventeenth Century* (1972), is a splendidly illustrated appreciation of Dutch commercial and artistic achievements. No recent work has replaced the well-written, thorough narrative of J. L. Motley, *The Rise of the Dutch Republic,* 3 vols., (1898).

CHAPTER 17

ABSOLUTISM IN EASTERN EUROPE

TO 1740

THE SEVENTEENTH CENTURY witnessed a struggle between constitutionalism and absolutism in eastern Europe. With the notable exception of the kingdom of Poland, monarchial absolutism was everywhere triumphant in eastern Europe; constitutionalism was decisively defeated. Absolute monarchies emerged in Austria, Prussia, and Russia. This was a development of great significance: these three monarchies exercised enormous influence until 1918, and they created a strong authoritarian tradition that is still dominant in eastern Europe.

Although the monarchs of eastern Europe were greatly impressed by Louis XIV and his model of royal absolutism, their states differed in several important ways from their French counterpart. Louis XIV built French absolutism on the heritage of a well-developed medieval monarchy and a strong royal bureaucracy. And when Louis XIV came to the throne the powers of the nobility were already somewhat limited, the French middle class was relatively strong, and the peasants were generally free from serfdom. Eastern absolutism rested upon a very different social reality: a powerful nobility, a weak middle class, and an oppressed peasantry condemned to serfdom.

These differences in social conditions raise three major questions. First, why did the basic structure of society in eastern Europe move away from that of western Europe in the early modern period? Second, how and why, in their different social environments, did the rulers of Austria, Prussia, and Russia manage to build powerful absolute monarchies, which proved more durable than that of Louis XIV? Finally, how did the absolute monarchs' interaction with artists and architects contribute to the splendid achievements of baroque culture? These are the questions this chapter seeks to answer.

LORDS AND PEASANTS IN EASTERN EUROPE

When absolute monarchy took shape in eastern Europe in the seventeenth century, it built on social and economic foundations laid between roughly 1400 and 1650. In those years the princes and the landed nobility of eastern Europe rolled back the gains made by the peasantry during the High Middle Ages and reimposed a harsh serfdom on the rural masses. The nobility also reduced the importance of the towns and the middle classes. This process differed profoundly from developments in western Europe at the same time. In the west peasants won greater freedom and the urban capitalistic middle class continued its rise. Thus, the east that emerged contrasted sharply with the west — another aspect of the shattered unity of medieval Latin Christendom.

THE MEDIEVAL BACKGROUND

Between roughly 1400 and 1650, nobles and rulers re-established serfdom in the eastern lands of Bohemia, Silesia, Hungary, eastern Germany, Poland, Lithuania, and Russia. The east — the land east of the Elbe River in Germany, which historians often call "East Elbia" — gained a certain social and economic unity in the process. But eastern peasants lost their rights and freedoms. They became bound first to the land they worked and then, by degrading obligations, to the lords they served.

This development was a tragic reversal of trends in the High Middle Ages. The period from roughly 1050 to 1300 had been a time of general economic expansion characterized by the growth of trade, towns, and population. Expansion also meant clearing the forests and colonizing the frontier beyond the Elbe River. Anxious to attract German settlers to their sparsely populated lands, the rulers and nobles of eastern Europe had offered potential newcomers attractive economic and legal incentives. Large numbers of incoming settlers obtained land on excellent terms and gained much greater personal freedom. These benefits were also gradually extended to the local Slavic populations, even those of central Russia. Thus by 1300 there had occurred a very general improvement in peasant conditions in eastern Europe. Serfdom all but disappeared. Peasants bargained freely with their landlords and moved about as they pleased. Opportunities and improvements east of the Elbe had a positive impact on western Europe, where the weight of serfdom was also reduced between 1100 and 1300.

After about 1300, however, as Europe's population and economy both declined grievously, mainly because of the Black Death, the east and the west went in different directions. In both east and west there occurred a many-sided landlord reaction, as lords sought to solve their tough economic problems by more heavily exploiting the peasantry. Yet this reaction generally failed in the west. In many western areas by 1500 almost all of the peasants were completely free, and in the rest of western Europe serf obligations had declined greatly. East of the Elbe, however, the landlords won. By 1500, eastern peasants were well on their way to becoming serfs again.

Throughout eastern Europe, as in western Europe, the drop in population and prices in the fourteenth and fifteenth centuries caused severe labor shortages and hard times for the nobles. Yet rather than offer better economic and legal terms to keep old peasants and attract new ones, eastern landlords used their political and police power to turn the tables on the peasants. They did this in two ways.

First, the lords made their kings and princes issue laws that restricted or eliminated the peasants' precious, time-honored right of free movement. Thus, a peasant could no longer leave to take advantage of better opportunities elsewhere without the lord's permission, and the lord had no reason to make such concessions. In Prussian territories by 1500, the law required that runaway peasants be hunted down and returned to their lords; a runaway servant was to be nailed to a post by one ear and given a knife to cut himself loose. Until the middle of the fifteenth century, medieval Russian peasants had been free to move wherever they wished and seek the best landlord. Thereafter this freedom was gradually curtailed, so that by 1497 a Russian peasant had the right to move only during a two-week period after the fall harvest. Eastern peasants were losing their status as free and independent men and women.

Second, lords steadily took more and more of their peasants' land and imposed heavier and heavier labor obligations. Instead of being independent farmers paying reasonable, freely negotiated rents, peasants tended to become forced laborers on the lords' estates. By the early 1500s, lords in many territories could command their peasants to work for them without pay as many as six days a week. A German writer of the mid-sixteenth century described peasants in eastern Prussia who "do not possess the heritage of their holdings and have to serve their master whenever he wants them."[1]

The gradual erosion of the peasantry's economic position was bound up with manipulation of the oppressive legal system. The local lord was also the local prosecutor, judge, and jailer. As a matter of course, he ruled in his own favor in disputes with his peasants. There were no independent royal officials to provide justice or uphold the common law.

Between 1500 and 1650, the social, legal, and economic conditions of peasants in eastern Europe continued to decline. Free peasants lost their freedom and became serfs. In Poland, for example, nobles gained complete control over their peasants in 1574, after which they could legally inflict the death penalty on their serfs whenever they wished. In Prussia a long series of oppressive measures reached their culmination in 1653. Not only were all the old privileges of the lords reaffirmed, but peasants were assumed to be in "hereditary subjugation" to their lords unless they could prove the contrary in the lords' courts, which was practically impossible. Prussian peasants were serfs tied to their lords as well as to the land.

In Russia the right of peasants to move from a given estate was "temporarily" suspended in the 1590s and permanently abolished in 1603. In 1649, a new law code completed the process. At the insistence of the lower nobility, the Russian tsar lifted the nine-year time limit on the recovery of runaways. Henceforth, runaway peasants were to be returned to their lords whenever they were caught, as long as they lived. The last small hope of escaping serfdom was gone. Control of serfs was strictly the lords' own business, for the new law code set no limits on the lords' authority over their peasants. Although the political development of the various eastern states differed, the legal re-establishment of permanent hereditary serfdom was the common fate of peasants in the east by the middle of the seventeenth century.

The consolidation of serfdom between 1500 and 1650 was accompanied by the growth of estate agriculture, particularly in Poland and eastern Germany. In the sixteenth century European economic expansion and population growth resumed after the great declines of the late Middle Ages. Prices for agricultural commodities also rose sharply as gold and silver flowed in from the New World. Thus, Polish and German lords had powerful economic incentives to increase the production of their estates. And they did.

Lords seized more and more peasant land for their own estates and then demanded and received ever more unpaid serf labor on those enlarged estates. Even when the estates were inefficient and technically backward, as they generally were, the great Polish nobles and middle-rank German lords squeezed sizable, cheap, and thus very profitable surpluses out of their impoverished peasants. These surpluses in wheat and timber were easily sold to big foreign merchants, who exported them to the growing cities of the west. The poor east helped feed the much wealthier west.

The re-emergence of serfdom in eastern Europe in the early modern period was clearly a momentous human development, and historians have advanced a variety of explanations for it. As always, some scholars have stressed the economic interpretation. Agricultural depression and population decline in the fourteenth and fifteenth centuries led to a severe labor shortage, they have argued, and thus eastern landlords naturally tied their precious peasants to the land. With the return of prosperity and the development of export markets in the sixteenth century, the landlords finished the job, grabbing the peasants' land and making them work as unpaid serfs on the enlarged estates. This argument by itself is not very convincing, for almost identical economic developments "caused" the opposite result in the west. Indeed, some historians have maintained that labor shortage and subsequent renewed expansion were key factors in the virtual disappearance of serfdom in western Europe.

PUNISHING SERFS   This seventeenth-century illustration from Olearius's famous Travels to Moscovy *suggests what eastern serfdom really meant. The scene* *is eastern Poland. There, according to Olearius, a common command of the lord was, "Beat him till the skin falls from the flesh." (Photo: Caroline Buckler)*

It seems fairly clear, therefore, that political rather than economic factors were crucial in the simultaneous rise of serfdom in the east and decline of serfdom in the west. Specifically, eastern lords enjoyed much greater political power than their western counterparts. In the late Middle Ages, when much of eastern Europe experienced innumerable wars and general political chaos, the noble landlord class greatly increased its political power at the expense of the ruling monarchs. There were, for example, many disputed royal successions, so that weak kings were forced to grant political favors to win the support of the nobility. Thus while strong "new monarchs" were rising in Spain, France, and England and providing effective central government, kings were generally losing power in the east. Such weak kings could not resist the demands of the lords regarding their peasants.

Moreover, most eastern monarchs did not want to resist even if they could. The typical king was only "first among equals" in the noble class. He too thought mainly in "private" rather than "public" terms. He too wanted to squeeze as much as he could out of *his* peasants and enlarge *his* estates. The western concept and reality of sovereignty, as embodied in a king who protected the interests of all his people, was not well developed in eastern Europe before 1650.

The political power of the peasants was also weaker in eastern Europe, and declined steadily after about 1400. Although there were occasional bloody peasant uprisings against the oppression of the landlords, they never succeeded. Nor did eastern peasants effectively resist day-by-day infringements on their liberties by their landlords. Part of the reason was that the lords, rather than the kings, ran the courts – one of the important concessions nobles extorted from weak monarchs. It has also been suggested that peasant solidarity was weaker in the east, possibly reflecting the lack of long-established village communities on the eastern frontier.

Finally, with the approval of weak kings, the landlords systematically undermined the medieval privileges of the towns and the power of the urban classes. Instead of selling their products to local merchants in the towns, as required in the Middle Ages, the landlords sold directly to big foreign capitalists. For example, Dutch ships sailed up the rivers of Poland and eastern Germany to the loading docks of the great estates, completely short-circuiting the local towns. Moreover, "town air" no longer "made people free," for the eastern towns lost their medieval right of refuge and were compelled to return runaways to their lords. The population of the towns and the importance of the urban middle classes declined greatly. This development both reflected and promoted the supremacy of noble landlords in most of eastern Europe in the sixteenth century.

THE RISE OF AUSTRIA AND PRUSSIA

In spite of the strength of the nobility and the weakness of many monarchs before 1600,

strong kings did begin to emerge in many lands in the course of the seventeenth century. War and the threat of war aided rulers greatly in their attempts to build absolute monarchies. There was an endless struggle for power, as eastern rulers not only fought each other but also battled with hordes of Asiatic invaders. In this atmosphere of continuous wartime emergency, monarchs reduced the political power of the landlord nobility. Cautiously leaving the nobles the unchallenged masters of their peasants, the absolutist monarchs of eastern Europe gradually gained and monopolized political power in three key areas. They imposed and collected permanent taxes without consent. They maintained permanent standing armies, which policed their subjects in addition to fighting abroad. And they conducted relations with other states as they pleased.

As with all general historical developments, there were important variations on the absolutist theme in eastern Europe. The royal absolutism created in Prussia was stronger and more effective than that established in Austria. This advantage gave Prussia a thin edge over Austria in the struggle for power in east-central Europe in the eighteenth century. That edge had enormous long-term political significance, for it was a rising Prussia that unified the German people in the nineteenth century and imposed upon them a fateful Prussian stamp.

AUSTRIA AND THE OTTOMAN TURKS

Like all the peoples and rulers of central Europe, the Habsburgs of Austria emerged from the Thirty Years' War (pages 530–536) impoverished and exhausted. The effort to root out Protestantism in the German lands had failed utterly, and the authority of the Holy Roman Empire and its Habsburg em-

THE OTTOMAN SLAVE TAX *This contemporary drawing shows Ottoman officials rounding up male Christian children in the Balkans. The children became part of a special slave corps, which served the* *sultan for life as soldiers and administrators. The slave tax and the slave corps were of great importance to the Ottoman Turks in the struggle with Austria. (The British Museum)*

perors had declined almost to the vanishing point. Yet defeat in central Europe also opened new vistas. The Habsburg monarchs were forced to turn inward and eastward in the attempt to fuse their diverse holdings into a strong unified state.

An important step in this direction had actually been taken in Bohemia during the Thirty Years' War. Protestantism had been strong among the Czechs of Bohemia, and in 1618 the Czech nobles who controlled the Bohemian Estates – the semiparliamentary body of Bohemia – had risen up against their Habsburg king. Not only was this revolt crushed, but the old Czech nobility was wiped out as well. Those Czech nobles who did not die in 1620 at the battle of the White Mountain (page 533), a momentous turning point in Czech history, had their estates confiscated. The Habsburg king, Ferdinand II (1619–1637), then redistributed the Czech lands to a motley band of aristocratic soldiers of fortune from all over Europe.

In fact, after 1650, 80 to 90 percent of the Bohemian nobility was of recent foreign origin and owed everything to the Habsburgs.

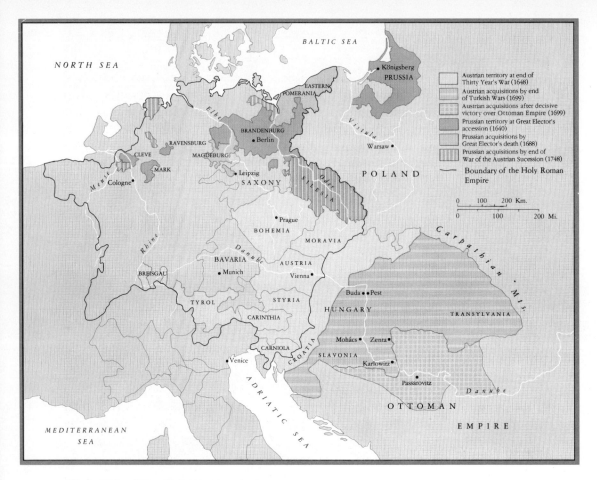

MAP 17.1 THE GROWTH OF AUSTRIA AND BRANDENBURG-PRUSSIA TO 1748 *Austria expanded to the southwest into Hungary and Transylvania at the expense of the Ottoman Empire. But it was unable to hold the rich German province of Silesia, which was conquered by Brandenburg-Prussia.*

With the help of this new nobility, the Habsburgs established strong direct rule over reconquered Bohemia. The condition of the enserfed peasantry worsened: three days per week of unpaid labor – the *robot* – became the norm, and a quarter of the serfs worked for their lords every day but Sundays and religious holidays. Serfs also paid the taxes, which further strengthened the alliance between the Habsburg monarch and the Bohemian nobility. Protestantism was also stamped out, in the course of which a growing unity of religion was brought about. The reorgani-

zation of Bohemia was a giant step toward absolutism.

After the Thirty Years' War, Ferdinand III centralized the government in the old hereditary provinces of Austria proper, the second part of the Habsburg holdings (see Map 17.1). For the first time he created a permanent standing army, which stood ready to put down any internal opposition. The Habsburg monarchy was then ready to turn toward the vast plains of Hungary, which it claimed as the third and largest part of its dominion, in opposition to the Ottoman Turks.

The Ottomans came out of the Anatolia, in present-day Turkey, and they created one of history's greatest military empires. At their peak in the middle of the sixteenth century under Suleiman the Magnificent (1520–1566), they ruled the most powerful empire in the world, bar none. Their possessions stretched from western Persia across North Africa and up into the heart of central Europe. Apostles of Islam, the Ottoman Turks were old and determined foes of the Catholic Habsburgs. Their armies had almost captured Vienna in 1529, and for more than 150 years thereafter they ruled all of the Balkans, almost all of Hungary, and part of southern Russia.

The Ottoman Empire was originally built on a fascinating and very non-European conception of state and society. There was an almost complete absence of private landed property. All the agricultural land of the empire was the personal hereditary property of the sultan, who exploited the land as he saw fit according to Ottoman political theory. There was, therefore, no security of landholding and no hereditary nobility. Everyone was dependent upon the sultan and virtually his slave.

Indeed, the top ranks of the bureaucracy were staffed by the sultan's slave corps. Every year the sultan levied a "tax" of one to three thousand male children upon the conquered Christian populations in the Balkans. These and other slaves were raised in Turkey as Muslims, and trained to fight and to administer. The most talented slaves rose to the top of the bureaucracy; the less fortunate formed the brave and skillful core of the sultan's army, the so-called janissary corps.

As long as the Ottoman Empire expanded, the system worked well. As the sultan won more territory, he could impose his slave tax on larger populations. Moreover, he could amply reward loyal and effective servants by letting them draw a carefully defined income from conquered Christian peasants on a strictly temporary basis. For a long time Christian peasants in eastern Europe were economically exploited less by the Muslim Turks than by Christian nobles, and they were not forced to convert to Islam. After about 1570, however, the powerful, centralized Ottoman system slowly began to disintegrate as the Turks' western advance was stopped. Temporary landholders became hard-to-control permanent oppressors. Weak sultans left the glory of the battlefield for the delights of the harem, and the army lost its dedication and failed to keep up with European military advances.

Yet in the late seventeenth century, under vigorous reforming leadership, the Ottoman Empire succeeded in marshaling its forces for one last mighty blow at Christian Europe. After wresting territory from Poland, fighting a long inconclusive war with Russia, and establishing an alliance with Louis XIV of France, the Turks turned again on Austria. A huge Turkish army surrounded Vienna and laid siege to it in 1683. But after holding out against great odds for two months, the city was relieved by a mixed force of Habsburg, Saxon, Bavarian, and Polish troops, and the Ottomans were forced to retreat. Soon the retreat became a rout. As their Russian and Venetian allies attacked on other fronts, the Habsburgs conquered all of Hungary and Transylvania (part of present-day Rumania) by 1699.

The Turkish wars and this great expansion strengthened the Habsburg army and promoted some sense of unity in the Habsburg lands. The Habsburgs moved to centralize their power and make it as absolute as possible. These efforts to create a fully developed, highly centralized, absolutist state were only partly successful.

The Habsburg state was composed of three separate and distinct territories – the old "hereditary provinces" of Austria, the kingdom of Bohemia, and the kingdom of Hungary. These three parts were tied together primarily by their common ruler – the Habsburg monarch. Each part had its own laws and political life, for the three noble-dominated Estates continued to exist, though with reduced powers. The Habsburgs themselves were well aware of the fragility of the union they had forged. In 1713, Charles VI (1711–1740) proclaimed the so-called Pragmatic Sanction, which stated that the Habsburg possessions were never to be divided and were always to be passed intact to a single heir, who might be female since Charles had no sons. Charles spent much of his reign trying to get this principle accepted by the various branches of the Habsburg family, by the three different Estates of the realm, and by the states of Europe. His fears turned out to be well founded.

The Hungarian nobility, despite its reduced strength, effectively thwarted the full development of Habsburg absolutism. Time and again throughout the seventeenth century, Hungarian nobles – the most numerous in Europe, making up from 5 to 7 percent of the Hungarian population – rose in revolt against the attempts of Vienna to impose absolute rule. They never triumphed decisively, but neither were they ever crushed and replaced as the Czech nobility had been in 1620.

Hungarians resisted because many of them were Protestants, especially in the area long ruled by the more tolerant Turks, and they hated the heavy-handed attempts of the conquering Habsburgs to re-Catholicize everyone. Moreover, the lords of Hungary often found a powerful military ally in Turkey. Finally, the Hungarian nobility, and even part of the peasantry, had become attached to a national ideal long before most of the peoples of Europe. They were determined to maintain as much independence and local control as possible. Thus when the Habsburgs were bogged down in the War of the Spanish Succession (page 570), the Hungarians rose in one last patriotic rebellion under Prince Francis Rakoczy in 1703. Rakoczy and his forces were eventually defeated, but this time the Habsburgs had to accept a definitive compromise. Charles VI restored many of the traditional privileges of the Hungarian aristocracy in return for Hungarian acceptance of hereditary Habsburg rule. Thus Hungary, unlike Austria or Bohemia, never came close to being fully integrated into a centralized, absolute Habsburg state.

PRUSSIA IN THE SEVENTEENTH CENTURY

After 1400, the status of east German peasants declined steadily; their serfdom was formally spelled out in the early seventeenth century. While the local princes lost political power and influence, a revitalized landed nobility became the undisputed ruling class. The Hohenzollern family, which ruled through its senior and junior branches as the electors of Brandenburg and the dukes of Prussia, had little real princely power. The Hohenzollern rulers were nothing more than the "first among equals," the largest landowners in a landlord society.

Nothing suggested that the Hohenzollerns and their territories would ever play an important role in European or even German affairs. The elector of Brandenburg's right to help choose the Holy Roman emperor with six other electors was of little practical value, and the elector had no military strength whatsoever. The territory of his cousin, the duke of Prussia, was actually part of the kingdom of Poland. Moreover, geography conspired against the Hohenzollerns. Brandenburg, their power base, was completely cut off from the sea (see Map 17.1). A tiny part of the vast north European plain that stretches from France to Russia, Brandenburg lacked natural frontiers and lay open to attack from all directions. The land was poor, a combination of sand and swamp. Contemporaries contemptuously called Brandenburg "the sand-box of the Holy Roman Empire."[2]

Brandenburg was a helpless spectator in the Thirty Years' War, its territory alternately ravaged by Swedish and by Habsburg armies. Population fell drastically, and many villages disappeared. The power of the Hohenzollerns reached its lowest point. Yet the devastation of the country prepared the way for Hohenzollern absolutism, because foreign armies dramatically weakened the political power of the Estates – the representative assemblies of the realm. This weakening of the Estates helped the very talented young elector Frederick William (1640–1688), later known as the Great Elector, to ride roughshod over traditional parliamentary liberties and to take a giant step toward royal absolutism. This constitutional struggle, often unjustly neglected by historians, was the most crucial in Prussian history for hundreds of years, until that of the 1860s.

When he came to power in 1640, the twenty-year-old Great Elector was determined to unify his three quite separate provinces and to add to them by diplomacy and war. These provinces were historic Brandenburg, the area around Berlin; Prussia, inherited in 1618 when the junior branch of the Hohenzollern family died out; and completely separate, scattered holdings along the Rhine in western Germany, inherited in 1614 (see Map 17.1). Each of the three provinces was inhabited by Germans; but each had its own Estates, whose power had increased until about 1600 as the power of the rulers declined. Although the Estates had not met regularly during the chaotic Thirty Years' War, they still had the

power of the purse in their respective provinces. Taxes could not be levied without their consent. The Estates of Brandenburg and Prussia were dominated by the nobility and the landowning classes, known as the Junkers. But it must be remembered that this was also true of the English Parliament before and after the Civil War. Had the Estates successfully resisted the absolutist demands of the Great Elector, they too might have evolved toward more broadly based constitutionalism.

The struggle between the Great Elector and the provincial Estates was long, complicated, and intense. After the Thirty Years' War, the representatives of the nobility zealously reasserted the right of the Estates to vote taxes, a right the Swedish armies of occupation had simply ignored. Yet first in Brandenburg in 1653, and then in Prussia between 1661 and 1663, the Great Elector eventually had his way.

To pay for the permanent standing army he first established in 1660, Frederick William forced the Estates to accept the introduction of permanent taxation without consent. Moreover, the soldiers doubled as tax collectors and policemen, becoming the core of the rapidly expanding state bureaucracy. The power of the Estates declined rapidly thereafter, for the Great Elector had both financial independence and superior force. He turned the screws of taxation: the state's total revenue tripled during his reign. The size of the army leaped about tenfold. In 1688, a population of one million was supporting a peacetime standing army of thirty thousand. Many of the soldiers were French Huguenot immigrants, whom the Great Elector welcomed as the talented, hardworking citizens they were.

In accounting for the Great Elector's fateful triumph, two factors appear central. As in the formation of every absolutist state, war was a decisive factor. The ongoing struggle between Sweden and Poland for control of the

Baltic after 1648 and the wars of Louis XIV in western Europe created an atmosphere of permanent crisis. The wild Tartars of southern Russia swept through Prussia in the winter of 1656-1657, killing and carrying off as slaves more than fifty thousand people, according to an old estimate. This invasion softened up the Estates and strengthened the urgency of the elector's demands for more money for more soldiers. It was no accident that, except for commercially minded Holland, constitutionalism won out only in England, the only major country to escape devastating foreign invasions in the seventeenth century.

Second, the nobility had long dominated the government through the Estates, but only for its own narrow self-interest. When the crunch came, the Prussian nobles proved unwilling to join the representatives of the towns in a consistent common front against royal pretensions. The nobility was all too concerned with its own rights and privileges, especially its freedom from taxation and its unlimited control over the peasants. When, therefore, the Great Elector reconfirmed these privileges in 1653 and after, even while reducing the political power of the Estates, the nobility growled but did not bite. It accepted a compromise whereby the bulk of the new taxes fell upon towns, and royal authority stopped at the landlords' gates. The elector could and did use naked force to break the liberties of the towns. The main leader of the urban opposition in the key city of Königsberg, for example, was simply arrested and imprisoned for life without trial.

THE CONSOLIDATION OF PRUSSIAN ABSOLUTISM

By the time of his death in 1688, the Great Elector had created a single state out of scattered principalities. But his new creation was still small and fragile. All the leading states of Europe had many more people – France with 20 million was fully twenty times as populous – and strong monarchy was still a novelty. Moreover, the Great Elector's successor, Elector Frederick III, "the Ostentatious" (1688-1713), was weak of body and mind.

Like so many of the small princes of Germany and Italy at the time, Frederick III imitated Louis XIV in every possible way. He built his own very expensive version of Versailles. He surrounded himself with cultivated artists and musicians and basked in the praise of toadies and sycophants. His only real political accomplishment was to gain the title of king from the Holy Roman emperor, a Habsburg, in return for military aid in the War of the Spanish Succession, and in 1701 he was crowned King Frederick I.

This tendency toward luxury-loving, happy, and harmless petty tyranny was completely reversed by Frederick William I (1713-1740), "the Soldiers' King." A crude, dangerous psychoneurotic, Frederick William I was nevertheless the most talented reformer ever produced by the Hohenzollern family. It was he who truly established Prussian absolutism and gave it its unique character. It was he who created the best army in Europe, for its size, and who infused military values into a whole society. In the words of a leading historian of Prussia:

For a whole generation, the Hohenzollern subjects were victimized by a royal bully, imbued with an obsessive bent for military organization and military scales of value. This left a deep mark upon the institutions of Prussiandom and upon the molding of the "Prussian spirit."[3]

Frederick William's passion for the army and military life was intensely emotional. He had, for example, a bizarre, almost pathological love for tall soldiers, whom he credited

THE "TOBACCO PARLIAMENT" *In absolutist Prussia the informal discussion of politics by the king and his friends over a pipe after dinner was the only parliament. (Historical Picture Service, Chicago)*

with superior strength and endurance. Austere and always faithful to his wife, he confided to the French ambassador: "The most beautiful girl or woman in the world would be a matter of indifference to me, but tall soldiers – they are my weakness." Like some fanatical modern-day basketball coach in search of a championship team, he sent his agents throughout both Prussia and all of Europe, tricking, buying, and kidnapping top recruits. Neighboring princes sent him their giants as gifts to win his gratitude. Prussian mothers told their sons: "Stop growing or the recruiting agents will get you."[4]

Profoundly military in temperament, Frederick William always wore an army uniform, and he lived the highly disciplined life of the professional soldier. He began his work by five or six in the morning; at ten he almost always went to the parade ground to drill or inspect his troops. A man of violent temper, Frederick William personally punished the

MOLDING THE PRUSSIAN SPIRIT   Discipline was strict and punishment brutal in the Prussian army. This scene, intended to instruct school children, shows one soldier being flogged while another is being beaten with canes as he walks between rows of troops. (Photo: Caroline Buckler)

most minor infractions on the spot: a missing button off a soldier's coat quickly provoked a savage beating with his heavy walking stick.

Frederick William's love of the army was also based on a hardheaded conception of the struggle for power and a dog-eat-dog view of international politics. Even before ascending the throne he bitterly criticized his father's ministers: "They say that they will obtain land and power for the king with the pen; but I say it can be done only with the sword." Years later he summed up his life's philoso-

phy in his instructions to his son: "A formidable army and a war chest large enough to make this army mobile in times of need can create great respect for you in the world, so that you can speak a word like the other powers."[5] This unshakable belief that the welfare of king and state depended upon the army above all else reinforced Frederick William's personal passion for playing soldier.

The cult of military power provided the rationale for a great expansion of royal absolutism. As the king himself put it with his characteristic ruthlessness: "I must be served with life and limb, with house and wealth, with honour and conscience, everything must be committed except eternal salvation – that belongs to God, but all else is mine."[6] To make good these extraordinary demands, Frederick William created a strong centralized bureaucracy. More commoners probably rose to top positions in the civil government than at any other time in Prussia's history. The last traces of the parliamentary Estates and local self-government vanished.

The king's grab for power brought him into considerable conflict with the noble landowners, the Junkers. In his early years, he even threatened to destroy them; yet, in the end, the Prussian nobility was not destroyed but enlisted – into the army. Responding to a combination of threats and opportunities, the Junkers became the officer caste. By 1739, all but 5 of 245 officers with the rank of major or above were aristocrats, and most of them were native Prussians. A new compromise had been worked out, whereby the proud nobility imperiously commanded the peasantry in the army as well as on its estates.

Coarse and crude, penny-pinching and hardworking, Frederick William achieved results. Above all, he built a first-rate army on the basis of third-rate resources. The standing army increased from 38,000 to 83,000 during his reign. Prussia, twelfth in Europe in population, had the fourth largest army by 1740. Only the much more populous states of France, Russia, and Austria had larger forces, and even France's army was only twice as large as Prussia's. Moreover, soldier for soldier, the Prussian army became the best in Europe, astonishing foreign observers with its precision, skill, and discipline. For the next two hundred years, Prussia and then Prussianized Germany would almost always win the crucial military battles.

Frederick William and his ministers also built an exceptionally honest and conscientious bureaucracy, which not only administered the country but tried with some success to develop it economically. Finally, like the miser he was, living very frugally off the income of his own landholdings, the king loved his "blue boys" so much that he hated to "spend" them. This most militaristic of kings was, paradoxically, almost always at peace.

Nevertheless, the Prussian people paid a heavy and lasting price for the obsessions of the royal drillmaster. Civil society became rigid and highly disciplined. Prussia became "the Sparta of the North"; unquestioning obedience was the highest virtue. As a Prussian minister later summed it up, "To keep quiet is the first civic duty."[7] Thus, the policies of Frederick William I combined with harsh peasant bondage and Junker tyranny to lay the foundations for what later evolved into probably the most militaristic country of modern times.

Frederick II (1740–1786), also known as Frederick the Great, built masterfully upon his father's work. This was somewhat surprising, for like many children with tyrannical (or kindly) parents, he rebelled against his parents' wishes in his early years. Rejecting the crude life of the barracks, Frederick embraced culture and literature, even writing poetry and fine prose in French, a language his father detested. He threw off his father's dour Calvinism and dabbled with atheism. After trying, unsuccessfully, to run away at age eighteen in 1730, he was virtually imprisoned and even compelled to watch his companion in flight beheaded at his father's command. Yet, like many other rebellious youths, Frederick eventually reached a reconciliation with his father, and by the time he came to the throne ten years later he was determined to follow in his father's footsteps.

When, therefore, the emperor of Austria, Charles VI, also died in 1740 and his young and beautiful daughter, Maria Theresa, became queen of the Habsburg dominions, Frederick suddenly and without warning invaded her rich all-German province of Silesia. This action defied solemn Prussian promises to respect the Pragmatic Sanction, which guaranteed Maria Theresa's succession, but no matter. For Frederick, it was the opportunity of a lifetime to expand the size and power of Prussia. Although Maria Theresa succeeded in dramatically rallying the normally quarrelsome Hungarian nobility, her multinational army was no match for Prussian precision. In 1742, as other greedy powers were falling upon her lands in the general European War of the Austrian Succession (1740–1748), she was forced to cede all of Silesia to Prussia. In one stroke Prussia doubled its population to 6 million people. Now Prussia unquestionably towered above all the other German states and stood as a European Great Power.

Frederick had to spend much of his reign fighting against great odds not only to hold onto his initial gains but to save Prussia from total destruction. In the end he succeeded, worthy heir of "the Soldiers' King" he sought to please. In 1760, at the very height of his struggle against invading armies on all sides, Frederick recounted a dream in which he met his father with his favorite general at the palace. "Have I done well?" he asked. "Very well," Frederick William replied. "That pleases me greatly," said Frederick. "Your approval means more to me than that of the whole world."[8]

THE DEVELOPMENT OF RUSSIA

One of the favorite parlor games of nineteenth-century Russian (and non-Russian) in-

tellectuals was debating whether Russia was a part of western European civilization or was a "nonwestern," "Asiatic" civilization. This question was particularly fascinating because it was unanswerable. A good case could be made for either position. To this day Russia differs fundamentally from the West in some basic ways, though Russian history has paralleled that of the West in other ways. Thus the hypnotic attraction of Russian history.

The differences between Russia and the West were particularly striking before 1700, when Russia's overall development began to draw progressively closer to that of its western neighbors. These early differences and Russia's long isolation from Europe explain why little has so far been said here about Russia. Yet it is impossible to understand how Russia has increasingly influenced and been influenced by western European civilization since roughly the late seventeenth century without looking at the course of early Russian history. Such a brief survey will also help explain how, when absolute monarchy finally and decisively triumphed under the rough guidance of Peter the Great in the early eighteenth century, it was a quite different type of absolute monarchy from that of France or even Prussia.

THE VIKINGS AND THE KIEVAN PRINCIPALITY

In antiquity the Slavs lived as a single people in central Europe. With the start of the mass migrations of the late Roman Empire, the Slavs moved in different directions and split into three groups. Between the fifth and ninth centuries the eastern Slavs, from whom the Ukrainians, the Russians, and the White Russians descend, moved into the vast and practically uninhabited area of present-day European Russia (see Map 17.2).

This enormous area consisted of an immense virgin forest to the north, where most of the eastern Slavs settled, and an endless prairie grassland to the south. Probably organized as tribal communities, the eastern Slavs, like many North American pioneers much later, lived off the great abundance of wild game and a crude "slash and burn" agriculture. After clearing a piece of the forest to build log cabins, they burned the stumps and brush. The ashes left a rich deposit of potash and lime, and the land gave several good crops before it was exhausted. The people then moved on to another untouched area and repeated the process.

In the ninth century the Vikings, those fearless warriors from Scandinavia, appeared in the lands of the eastern Slavs. Called Varangians in the old Russian chronicles, the Vikings were interested primarily in international trade, and the opportunities were good, since the Muslim conquests of the eighth century had greatly reduced Christian trade in the Mediterranean. Moving up and down the rivers, the Vikings soon linked Scandinavia and northern Europe with the Black Sea and the Byzantine Empire with its capital at Constantinople. They built a few strategic forts along the rivers, from which they raided the neighboring Slavic tribes and collected tribute. Slaves were the most important article of tribute, and the word *Slav* even became the word for slave in several European languages.

In order to increase and protect their international commerce, the Vikings declared themselves the rulers of the eastern Slavs. According to tradition, the semilegendary chieftain Ruirik founded the princely dynasty about 860. In any event, the Varangian ruler Oleg (878–912) established his residence at Kiev. He and his successors ruled over a loosely united confederation of Slavic territories – the Kievan state – until 1054. The Viking prince and his clansmen quickly became assimilated into the Slavic population,

taking local wives and emerging as the noble class.

Assimilation and loss of Scandinavian ethnic identity was speeded up by the conversion of the Vikings to Eastern Orthodox Christianity by missionaries from the Byzantine Empire. The written language of these missionaries, Slavic – Church Slavonic – was subsequently used in all religious and nonreligious documents in the Kievan principality. Thus the rapidly Slavified Vikings left two important legacies for the future. They created a loose unification of Slavic territories under a single ruling prince and a single ruling dynasty. And they imposed a basic religious unity by accepting Orthodox Christianity, as opposed to Roman Catholicism, for themselves and the eastern Slavs.

Even at its height under Great Prince Iaroslav the Wise (1019–1054), the unity of the Kievan principality was extremely tenuous. Trade, rather than government, was the main concern of the rulers. Moreover, the Slavified Vikings failed to find a way of peacefully transferring power from one generation to the next. In medieval western Europe this fundamental problem of government was increasingly resolved by resort to the principle of primogeniture: the king's eldest son received the crown as his rightful inheritance when his father died. Civil war was thus averted; order was preserved. In early Kiev, however, there were apparently no fixed rules and much strife accompanied each succession.

Possibly to avoid such chaos, before his death in 1054 Great Prince Iaroslav divided the Kievan principality among his five sons, who in turn divided their properties when they died. Between 1054 and 1237, Kiev disintegrated into more and more competing units, each ruled by a prince claiming to be a descendant of Ruirik. Even when only one prince was claiming to be the great prince, the whole situation was very unsettled.

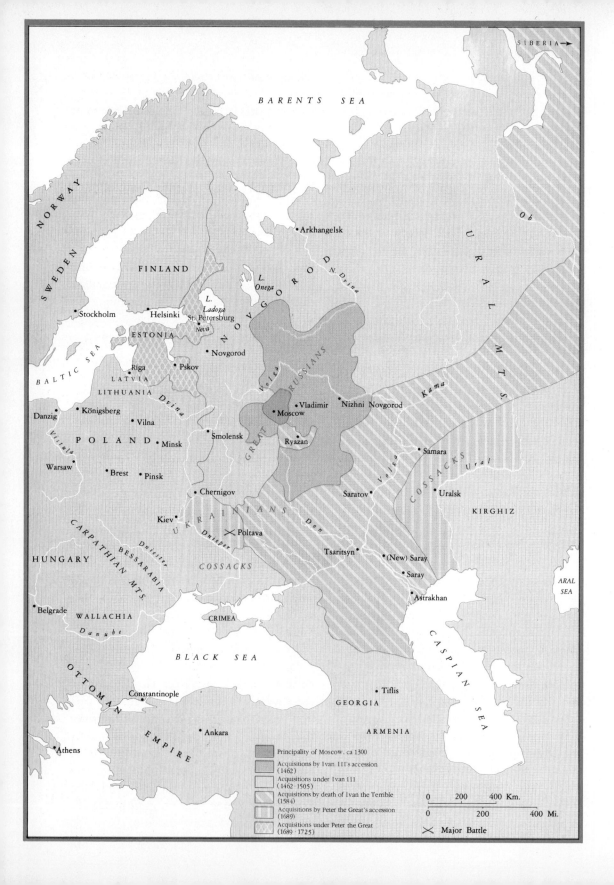

SIBERIA →

BARENTS SEA

NORWAY

SWEDEN

FINLAND

• Stockholm

• Helsinki

• Arkhangelsk

L. Onega

L. Ladoga

St. Petersburg

Neva

ESTONIA

BALTIC SEA

• Riga

LATVIA

• Pskov

• Novgorod

N O V G O R O D

N. Dvina

U R A L

M T S.

Ob

LITHUANIA

Dvina

• Danzig

• Königsberg

• Vilna

POLAND

• Minsk

• Smolensk

• Vladimir

• Moscow

G R E A T

R U S S I A N S

Volga

• Nizhni Novgorod

Kama

• Warsaw

• Brest

• Pinsk

• Ryazan

• Samara

• Chernigov

• Kiev

U K R A I N I A N S

Dnieper

×Poltava

Don

• Saratov

Volga

C O S S A C K S

Ural

• Uralsk

K I R G H I Z

CARPATHIAN MTS.

BESSARABIA

Dniester

C O S S A C K S

• Tsaritsyn

• (New) Saray

• Saray

ARAL SEA

HUNGARY

• Belgrade

WALLACHIA

Danube

CRIMEA

• Astrakhan

C A S P I A N

S E A

OTTOMAN

BLACK SEA

• Constantinople

• Tiflis

GEORGIA

E M P I R E

• Ankara

ARMENIA

• Athens

Principality of Moscow, ca 1300

Acquisitions by Ivan III's accession (1462)

Acquisitions under Ivan III (1462-1505)

Acquisitions by death of Ivan the Terrible (1584)

Acquisitions by Peter the Great's accession (1689)

Acquisitions under Peter the Great (1689-1725)

| 0 | 200 | 400 Km. |

| 0 | 200 | 400 Mi. |

× Major Battle

The princes divided their land like private property because they thought of it as private property. A given prince owned a certain number of farms or landed estates, and had them worked directly by his people, mainly slaves, called *kholops* in Russian. Outside of these estates, which constituted the princely domain, the prince exercised only very limited authority in his principality. Excluding the clergy, two kinds of people lived there: the noble boyars and the commoner peasants.

The boyars were the descendants of the original Viking warriors, and they also held their lands as free and clear private property. And although the boyars normally fought in princely armies, the customary law declared they could serve any prince they wished. The ordinary peasants were also truly free. The peasants could move at will wherever opportunities were greatest. In the touching phrase of the times, theirs was "a clean road, without boundaries."9 In short, fragmented princely power, private property, and personal freedom all went together.

THE MONGOL YOKE AND THE RISE OF MOSCOW

The eastern Slavs, like the Germans and the Italians, might have emerged from the Middle Ages weak and politically divided, had it not been for a development of extraordinary importance – the Mongol conquest of the Kievan state. Wild nomadic tribes from present-day Mongolia, the Mongols were temporarily unified in the thirteenth century by Jenghiz Khan (1162–1227), one of history's greatest

conquerors. In five years his armies subdued all of China. His successors then wheeled westward, smashing everything in their path and reaching the plains of Hungary victoriously before they pulled back in 1242. The Mongol army – the Golden Horde – was savage in the extreme, often slaughtering the entire population of cities before burning them to the ground. On route to Mongolia, Archbishop John of Plano Carpini, the famous papal ambassador to Mongolia, passed through Kiev in southern Russia in 1245-1246 and wrote an unforgettable eyewitness account:

*The Mongols went against Russia and enacted a great massacre in the Russian land. They destroyed towns and fortresses and killed people. They besieged Kiev which had been the capital of Russia, and after a long siege they took it and killed the inhabitants of the city. For this reason, when we passed through that land, we found lying in the field countless heads and bones of dead people; for this city had been extremely large and very populous, whereas now it has been reduced to nothing: barely two hundred houses stand there, and those people are held in the harshest slavery.*10

Having devastated and conquered, the Mongols ruled the eastern Slavs for more than two hundred years. They built their capital of Saray on the lower Volga (see Map 17.2). They forced all the bickering Slavic princes to submit to their rule and to give them tribute and slaves. If the conquered peoples rebelled, the Mongols were quick to punish with death and destruction. Thus, the Mongols unified the eastern Slavs, for the Mongol khan was acknowledged by all as the supreme ruler.

The Mongol unification completely changed the internal political situation. Although the Mongols conquered, they were quite willing to use local princes as their obedient servants and tax collectors. Therefore they did not abolish the title of great prince, bestowing it instead upon the prince who served them best and paid them most handsomely.

Beginning with Alexander Nevsky in 1252, the previously insignificant princes of Moscow became particularly adept at serving the Mongols. They loyally put down popular uprisings and collected the khan's harsh taxes. By way of reward the princes of Moscow emerged as hereditary great princes. Eventually the Muscovite princes were able to destroy their princely rivals and even to replace the khan as supreme ruler. In this complex process, two princes of Moscow after Alexander Nevsky – Ivan I and Ivan III – were especially noteworthy.

Ivan I (1328–1341) was popularly known as Ivan the Moneybag. A bit like Frederick William of Prussia, he was extremely stingy and built up a large personal fortune. This enabled him to buy more property and to increase his influence by loaning money to less frugal princes to pay their Mongol taxes. Ivan's most serious rival was the prince of Tver, whom the Mongols at one point appointed as great prince.

In 1327, the population of Tver revolted against Mongol oppression, and the prince of Tver joined his people. Ivan immediately went to the Mongol capital of Saray, where he was appointed commander of a large Russian-Mongol army, which then laid waste to Tver and its lands. For this proof of devotion, the Mongols made Ivan the general tax collector for all the Slavic lands they had subjugated and named him great prince. Ivan also convinced the metropolitan of Kiev, the leading churchman of all eastern Slavs, to settle in Moscow; Ivan I thus gained greater prestige, while the church gained a powerful advocate before the khan.

In the next hundred-odd years, in the course of innumerable wars and intrigues, the great princes of Moscow significantly in-

creased their holdings. Then, in the reign of Ivan III (1462–1505), the long process was largely completed. After purchasing Rostov, Ivan conquered and annexed other principalities, of which Novgorod with its lands extending as far as the Baltic Sea was most crucial (see Map 17.2). Thus, more than four hundred years after Iaroslav the Wise had divided the embryonic Kievan state, the princes of Moscow defeated all the rival branches of the house of Ruirik and became the unique holder of princely power.

Another dimension to princely power developed. Not only were the princes of Moscow the *unique* rulers, they were the *absolute* rulers, the autocrat, the *tsar* – the Slavic contraction for caesar, with all its connotations. This imperious conception of absolute power is expressed in a famous letter from the aging Ivan III to the Holy Roman emperor Frederick III (1440–1493). Frederick had offered Ivan the title of king in conjunction with the marriage of his daughter to Ivan's nephew. Ivan proudly refused:

We by the grace of God have been sovereigns over our domains from the beginning, from our first forebears, and our right we hold from God, as did our forebears. . . . As in the past we have never needed appointment from anyone, so now do we not desire it.[11]

The Muscovite idea of absolute authority was powerfully reinforced by two developments. First, about 1480 Ivan III stopped acknowledging the khan as his supreme ruler. There is good evidence to suggest that Ivan and his successors saw themselves as khans. Certainly they assimilated the Mongol concept of kingship as the exercise of unrestrained and unpredictable power.

Second, after the fall of Constantinople to the Turks in 1453, the tsars saw themselves as the heirs of both the caesars and Orthodox Christianity, the one true faith. All the other kings of Europe were heretics: only the tsars were rightful and holy rulers. This idea was promoted by Orthodox churchmen, who spoke of "holy Russia" and "the Third Rome." As the metropolitan Zosima stated in 1492: "Two Romes have fallen, the third Rome will be Moscow and a fourth is not to be."[12] Ivan's marriage to Sofia, the daughter of the last Byzantine emperor, further enhanced the aura of an eastern imperial inheritance for Moscow. Worthy successor to the mighty khan and the true Christian emperor, the Muscovite tsar was a king above all others.

TSAR AND PEOPLE TO 1689

By 1505, the great prince of Moscow – the tsar – had emerged as the single hereditary ruler of "all the Russias" – of all the lands of the eastern Slavs – and he was claiming unrestricted power as his God-given right. In effect, the tsar was demanding the same kind of total authority over all his subjects that the princely descendants of Ruirik had long exercised over their slaves on their own landed estates. This was an extremely radical demand.

While peasants had begun losing their freedom of movement in the fifteenth century, so had the noble boyars begun to lose power and influence. Ivan III pioneered in this regard, as in so many others. When Ivan conquered the principality of Novgorod in the 1480s, he confiscated fully 80 percent of the land, executing the previous owners or resettling them nearer Moscow. He then kept more than half of the confiscated land for himself, and distributed the remainder to members of a new emerging service nobility. The boyars had previously held their land as hereditary private property and been free to serve the prince of their choosing. The new service nobility held the tsar's land on the explicit condition that they serve in the tsar's

ST. BASIL'S CATHEDRAL in Moscow, with its steeply sloping roofs and proliferation of multicolored onion-shaped domes, was a striking example of powerful Byzantine influences on Russian culture. According to tradition, an enchanted Ivan the Terrible blinded the cathedral's architects, to insure they would never duplicate their fantastic achievement. (The New York Public Library)

army. Moreover, Ivan III began to require boyars outside of Novgorod to serve him if they wished to retain their lands. Since there were no competing princes left to turn to, the boyars had to yield.

The rise of the new service nobility accelerated under Ivan IV (1533–1584), the famous Ivan the Terrible. Having ascended the throne at age three, Ivan had suffered insults and neglect at the hands of the haughty boyars after his mother mysteriously died, possibly poisoned, when he was just eight. At age sixteen he suddenly pushed aside his hated boyar advisers. In an awe-inspiring ceremony complete with gold coins pouring down upon his head, he majestically crowned himself and officially took the august title of tsar for the first time.

Selecting the beautiful and kind Anastasia of the popular Romanov family for his wife and queen, the young tsar soon declared war on the remnants of Mongol power. He defeated the faltering khanates of Kazan and Astrakhan between 1552 and 1556, adding vast new territories to Russia. In the course of these wars Ivan virtually abolished the old distinction between hereditary boyar private property and land granted temporarily for service. All nobles, old and new, had to serve the tsar in order to hold any land.

The process of transforming the entire nobility into a service nobility was completed in the second part of Ivan the Terrible's reign. In 1557, Ivan turned westward, and for the next twenty-five years Muscovy waged an exhausting, unsuccessful war primarily with the large Polish-Lithuanian state, which controlled not only Poland but much of the Ukraine in the sixteenth century. Quarreling with the boyars over the war and blaming them for the sudden death of his beloved Anastasia in 1560, the increasingly cruel and demented Ivan turned to strike down all who stood in his way.

Above all, he struck down the ancient Muscovite boyars with a reign of terror. Leading boyars, their relatives, and even their peasants and servants were executed en masse by a special corps of unquestioning servants. Dressed in black and riding black horses, they were the forerunners of the modern dictator's secret police. Large estates were confiscated, broken up, and reapportioned to the lower service nobility. The great boyar families were

severely reduced. The newer, poorer, more nearly equal service nobility, which was still less than .5 percent of the total population, was totally dependent upon the autocrat.

Ivan also took giant strides toward making all commoners servants of the tsar. His endless wars and demonic purges left much of central Russia depopulated. It grew increasingly difficult for the lower service nobility to squeeze a living for themselves out of the peasants left on their landholdings. As the service nobles demanded more from the remaining peasants, more and more peasants fled toward the wild, recently conquered territories to the east and south. There they formed free groups and outlaw armies known as Cossacks. The Cossacks maintained a precarious independence beyond the reach of the oppressive landholders and the tsar's hated officials. The solution to this problem was to complete the tying of the peasants to the land, to make them serfs perpetually bound to serve the noble landholders, who were bound in turn to serve the tsar.

In the time of Ivan the Terrible urban traders and artisans were also bound to their towns and jobs, so that the tsar could tax them more heavily. Ivan assumed that the tsar owned Russia's trade and industry, just as he owned all the land. In the course of the sixteenth and seventeenth centuries, the tsars therefore took over the mines and industries and monopolized the country's important commercial activities. The urban classes had no security in their work or property, and even the wealthiest merchants were basically dependent agents of the tsar. If a new commercial activity became profitable, it was often taken over by the tsar and made a royal monopoly. This royal monopolization was in sharp contrast to developments in western Europe, where the capitalist middle classes were gaining strength and security in their private property. The tsar's service obligations checked the growth of the Russian middle classes, just as they led to the decline of the boyars, the rise of the lower nobility, and the final enserfment of the peasants.

Ivan the Terrible's system of autocracy and compulsory service struck foreign observers forcibly. Sigismund Herberstein, a German traveler to Russia, wrote in 1571: "All the people consider themselves to be *kholops,* that is slaves of their Prince." At the same time Jean Bodin, the French thinker who did so much to develop the modern concept of sovereignty, concluded that Russia's political system was fundamentally different from those of all other European monarchies and comparable only to that of the Turkish empire. In both Turkey and Russia, as in other parts of Asia and Africa, "the prince is become lord of the goods and persons of his subjects . . . governing them as a master of a family does his slaves."[13] The Mongol inheritance weighed heavily upon Russia.

As has so often been the case in Russian history, the death of an iron-fisted tyrant – in this case Ivan the Terrible in 1584 – ushered in an era of confusion and violent struggles for power. Events were particularly chaotic after Ivan's son Theodore died in 1598 without an heir. The years from 1598 to 1613 are aptly called the Time of Troubles.

The close relatives of the deceased tsar intrigued against and murdered each other, alternately fighting and welcoming the invading Swedes and Poles, who even occupied Moscow. Most serious for the cause of autocracy, there was a great social upheaval as Cossack bands marched northward, rallying peasants and slaughtering nobles and officials. The mass of Cossacks and peasants called for the "true tsar," who would restore their freedom of movement and allow them to farm for whomever they pleased, who would reduce their heavy taxes and lighten the yoke imposed by the landlords.

This social explosion from below, which combined with a belated surge of patriotic opposition to Polish invaders, brought the nobles, big and small, to their senses. In 1613, they elected Ivan's sixteen-year-old grandnephew, Michael Romanov, the new hereditary tsar. Then they rallied around him in the face of common internal and external threats. Michael's election was a real restoration, and his reign saw the gradual re-establishment of tsarist autocracy. Michael was understandably more kindly disposed toward the supportive nobility than toward the sullen peasants. Thus while peasants were completely enserfed in 1649, Ivan's heavy military obligations upon the nobility were relaxed considerably. In the long reign of Michael's successor, the pious Alexis (1645–1676), this asymmetry of obligations was accentuated. The nobility gained more exemptions from military service, while the peasants were further ground down.

The result was a second round of mass upheaval and protest. In the later seventeenth century the unity of the Russian Orthodox church was torn apart by a great split. The surface question was the religious reforms introduced in 1652 by the patriarch Nikon, a dogmatic purist who wished to bring "corrupted" Russian practices of worship into line with the Greek Orthodox model. The self-serving church hierarchy quickly went along, but the intensely religious common people resisted. They saw Nikon as the anti-Christ, who was stripping them of the only thing they had – the true religion of "holy Russia."

Great numbers left the church and formed illegal communities of Old Believers, who were hunted down and persecuted. As many as twenty thousand people burned themselves alive, singing the "halleluyah" in their chants three times rather than twice as Nikon had demanded and crossing themselves in the old style, with two rather than three fingers, as they went down in flames. After the great split the Russian masses were alienated from the established church, which became totally dependent upon the state for its authority.

Again the Cossacks revolted against the state, which was doggedly trying to catch up with them on the frontiers and reduce them to serfdom. Under Stenka Razin they moved up the Volga River in 1670–1671, attracting a great undisciplined army of peasants, murdering landlords and high church officials, and proclaiming freedom from oppression. This rebellion to overthrow the established order was finally defeated by the government. In response the thoroughly scared upper classes tightened the screws of serfdom even further. Holding down the peasants, and thereby maintaining the tsar, became almost the principal obligation of the nobility until 1689.

THE REFORMS OF PETER THE GREAT

It is now possible to understand the reforms of Peter the Great (1689–1725) and his kind of monarchial absolutism. Contrary to some historians' assertions, Peter was interested primarily in military power and not in some grandiose westernization plan. A gigantic, seven-foot-tall man of enormous energy and will power, Peter was determined to redress the defeats the tsar's armies had occasionally suffered in their wars with Poland and Sweden since the time of Ivan the Terrible.

To be sure, these western foes had never seriously threatened the existence of the tsar's vast kingdom, except perhaps when they had added to the confusion of civil war and domestic social upheaval in the Time of Troubles. Russia had even gained a large mass of the Ukraine from the kingdom of Poland in 1667 (see Map 17.2). And tsarist forces had completed the conquest of the primitive tribes of all Siberia in the seventeenth century. Muscovy, which had been as large as all the rest

of Europe combined in 1600, was three times as large as the rest of Europe in 1689 and by far the largest kingdom on earth. But territorial expansion was the soul of tsardom, and it was natural that Peter would seek further gains. The thirty-six years of his reign knew only one year of peace.

When Peter came to the throne, the heart of his army still consisted of cavalry made up of boyars and service nobility. Foot soldiers played a secondary role, and the whole army served on a part-time basis. The Russian army was lagging behind the professional standing armies being formed in Europe in the seventeenth century. The core of such armies was a highly disciplined infantry – an infantry that fired and refired rifles as it fearlessly advanced, until it charged with bayonets fixed. Such a large permanent army was enormously expensive and could be created only at the cost of great sacrifice. Given the desire to conquer more territory, Peter's military problem was serious.

Peter's solution was, in essence, to tighten up Muscovy's old service system and really make it work. He put the nobility back in harness, with a vengeance. Every nobleman, great or small, was once again required to serve in the army or in the civil administration – for life. Since a more modern army and government required skilled technicians and experts, Peter created schools and even universities. One of his most hated reforms required five years of compulsory education away from home for every young nobleman. Peter established an interlocking military-civilian bureaucracy with fourteen ranks, and he decreed that all must start at the bottom and work toward the top. More people of nonnoble origins rose to high positions in the embryonic meritocracy. Peter searched out talented foreigners – twice in his reign he went abroad to study and observe – and placed them in his service. These measures combined to make the army and government more powerful and more efficient.

Peter also greatly increased the service requirements of the commoners. He established a regular standing army of more than 200,000 soldiers, made up mainly of peasants commanded by officers from the nobility. In addition, special forces of Cossacks and foreigners numbered more than 100,000. The departure of a drafted peasant boy was celebrated by his family and village almost like a funeral, as indeed it was, since the recruit was drafted for life. The peasantry also served with its taxes, which increased threefold during Peter's reign, as people – "souls" – replaced land as the primary unit of taxation. Serfs were also arbitrarily assigned to work in the growing number of factories and mines. Most of these industrial enterprises were directly or indirectly owned by the state, and they were worked almost exclusively for the military. In general, Russian serfdom became more oppressive under the reforming tsar.

The constant warfare of Peter's reign consumed 80 or 85 percent of all revenues but brought only modest territorial expansion. Yet the Great Northern War with Sweden, which lasted from 1700 to 1721, was crowned in the end by Russian victory. After initial losses, Peter's new war machine crushed the smaller army of Sweden's Charles XII in southern Russia at Poltava in 1709, one of the most significant battles in Russian history. Sweden never really regained the offensive, and Russia eventually annexed Estonia and much of present-day Latvia (see Map 17.2), lands that had never before been under Russian rule. Russia became the dominant power on the Baltic Sea and very much a European Great Power. If victory or defeat is the ultimate criterion for historical judgment, Peter's reforms were a success.

REFORMING THE NOBILITY   After a military revolt in 1698 Peter took revenge by decreeing that all nobles adopt Western manners and dress. This contemporary cartoon shows a gigantic Peter personally cutting off the long beard of a noble, thereby humiliating him and symbolically imposing more modern values. (The New York Public Library)

There were other important consequences of Peter's reign. Because of his feverish desire to use modern technology to strengthen the army, many westerners and western ideas flowed into Russia for the first time. A new class of educated Russians began to emerge. At the same time vast numbers of Russians, especially among the poor and weak, hated Peter's massive changes. The split between the enserfed peasantry and the educated nobility thus widened, even though all were caught up in the endless demands of the sovereign.

A new idea of state interest, as distinct from the tsar's personal interests, began to take hold. Peter himself fostered this conception of the public interest by claiming time and again to be serving the common good. For the first time a Russian tsar attached explanations to his decrees in an attempt to gain the confidence and more enthusiastic support of the populace. Yet, as before, the tsar alone decided what the common good was. Here was a source of future tension between tsar and people.

In sum, Peter built on the service obligations of old Muscovy. His monarchial absolutism was truly the culmination of the long development of a unique Russian civilization. Yet the creation of a more modern army and state introduced much that was new and western to that civilization. This development paved the way for Russia to move much closer to the European mainstream in its thought and institutions during the Enlightenment, especially under that famous administrative and sexual lioness, Catherine the Great.

ABSOLUTISM AND THE BAROQUE

The rise of royal absolutism in eastern Europe had many consequences. Nobles served their powerful rulers in new ways while the great inferiority of the urban middle classes and the peasants was reconfirmed. Armies became larger and more professional, while taxes rose and authoritarian traditions were strengthened. Nor was this all. Royal absolutism also interacted with baroque culture and art, baroque music and literature. Inspired in part by Louis XIV of France, the great and not-so-great rulers called upon the artistic talent of the age to glorify their power and magnifi-

cence. This exaltation of despotic rule was particularly striking in architecture, whose lavish masterpieces reflected and reinforced the spirit of absolutism.

BAROQUE ART AND MUSIC

Throughout European history, the cultural tastes of one age have often seemed quite unsatisfactory to the next. So it was with the baroque. The term *baroque* itself may have come from the Portuguese word for an "odd-shaped, imperfect pearl," and was commonly used by late-eighteenth-century art critics as an expression of scorn for what they considered an overblown, unbalanced style. The hostility of these critics, who also scorned the Gothic style of medieval cathedrals in favor of a classicism inspired by antiquity and the Renaissance, has long since passed. Specialists agree that the triumphs of the baroque marked one of the high points in the entire history of Western culture.

The early development of the baroque is complex, but most scholars stress the influence of Rome and the revitalized Catholic church of the later sixteenth century. The papacy and the Jesuits encouraged the growth of an intensely emotional, exuberant art. These patrons wanted artists to go beyond the Renaissance focus on pleasing a small, wealthy cultural elite. They wanted artists to appeal to the senses, and thereby touch the souls and kindle the faith of ordinary churchgoers, while proclaiming the power and confidence of the reformed Catholic church. In addition to this underlying religious emotionalism, the baroque drew its sense of drama, motion, and ceaseless striving from the Catholic Reformation. The interior of the famous Jesuit Church of Jesus in Rome – the Gesù – combined all these characteristics in its lavish, shimmering, wildly active decorations and frescoes.

Taking definite shape in Italy after 1600, the baroque style in the visual arts developed with exceptional vigor in Catholic countries – in Spain and Latin America, Austria, southern Germany, and Poland. Yet baroque art was more than just "Catholic art" in the seventeenth century and the first half of the eighteenth. True, neither Protestant England nor the Netherlands ever came fully under the spell of the baroque, but neither did Catholic France. And Protestants accounted for some of the finest examples of baroque style, especially in music. The baroque style spread partly because its tension and bombast spoke to an agitated age, which was experiencing great violence and controversy in politics and religion.

In painting, the baroque reached maturity early with Peter Paul Rubens (1577–1640), the most outstanding and representative of baroque painters. Studying in his native Flanders and in Italy, where he was influenced by the masters of the High Renaissance such as Michelangelo, Rubens developed his own rich, sensuous, colorful style, which was characterized by animated figures, melodramatic contrasts, and monumental size. Although Rubens excelled in glorifying monarchs, like queen mother Marie de' Medici of France, he was also a devout Catholic. Nearly half of his pictures treat Christian subjects. Yet one of Rubens' trademarks was fleshy, sensual nudes, who populate his canvasses as Roman goddesses, water nymphs, and remarkably voluptuous saints and angels.

Rubens was enormously successful. To meet the demand for his work, he established a large studio and hired many assistants to execute his rough sketches and gigantic murals. Sometimes the master artist added only the finishing touches. Rubens' wealth and position – on occasion he was given special diplomatic assignments by the Habsburgs – attest that distinguished artists continued to enjoy the high social status they had won in the Renaissance.

In music the baroque style reached its culminating point almost a century later in the dynamic, searching, soaring lines of the endlessly inventive Johann Sebastian Bach (1685–1750), one of the greatest composers the Western world has ever produced. Organist and choirmaster of several Lutheran churches across Germany, Bach was equally at home writing secular concertos and sublime religious cantatas. Bach's organ music, the greatest ever written, combined with unsurpassed mastery the baroque spirit of invention, tension, and emotion in an unforgettable striving toward the infinite. Unlike Rubens, Bach was not fully appreciated in his lifetime, but since the early nineteenth century his reputation has grown steadily.

PALACES AND POWER

As soaring Gothic cathedrals expressed the idealized spirit of the High Middle Ages, so dramatic baroque palaces symbolized the age of absolutist power. By 1700, palace building had become a veritable obsession with the rulers of central and eastern Europe. These baroque palaces were clearly intended to overawe the people with the monarch's strength. The great palaces were also visual declarations of equality with Louis XIV, Europe's most awesome ruler, and were therefore modeled after Versailles to a greater or lesser extent. One such palace was Schönbrunn, an enormous Viennese Versailles, begun in 1695 by Emperor Leopold to celebrate Austrian military victories and Habsburg might. Charles XI of Sweden, having reduced the power of the aristocracy, ordered the construction in 1693 of his Royal Palace, which dominates the center of Stockholm to this day. Frederick I of Prussia began his imposing new royal residence in Berlin in 1701, a year after he attained the title of king.

Petty princes also contributed mightily to the palace-building mania. Frederick the Great of Prussia noted that every descendant of a princely family "imagines himself to be something like Louis XIV. He builds his Versailles, has his mistresses, and maintains his army."[14] The not very important elector-archbishop of Mainz, the ruling prince of that city, confessed apologetically that "building is a craze which costs much, but every fool likes his own hat."[15] The archbishop of Mainz's own "hat" was an architectural gem, like that of another churchly ruler, the prince-bishop of Würzburg. So too was the Zwinger palace of Dresden, built by Augustus the Strong of Saxony, who managed to get himself elected king of Poland and unsuccessfully challenged Prussia for leadership among the German states.

In central and eastern Europe the favorite noble servants of royalty became extremely rich and powerful, and they too built grandiose palaces in the capital cities. These palaces were in part an extension of the monarch, for they surpassed the buildings of less favored nobles and showed all with eyes to see the high road to fame and fortune. Take, for example, the palaces of Prince Eugene of Savoy. A French nobleman by birth and education, Prince Eugene entered the service of Leopold I with the relief of besieged Vienna in 1683, and he became Austria's most outstanding military hero. It was he who reorganized the Austrian army, smashed the Turks, fought Louis XIV to a standstill, and generally guided the triumph of absolutism in Austria. Rewarded with great wealth by his grateful royal employer, Eugene called upon the leading architects of the day, J. B. Fischer von Erlach and Johann Lukas von Hildebrandt, to

consecrate his glory in stone and fresco. Fischer built Eugene's Winter (or Town) Palace in Vienna, and he and Hildebrandt collaborated on the prince's Summer Palace on the city's outskirts.

The Summer Palace was actually two enormous buildings, the Lower Belvedere and the Upper Belvedere, completed in 1713 and 1722 respectively, and joined by one of the most exquisite gardens in Europe. The Upper Belvedere, Hildebrandt's masterpiece, stood gracefully, even playfully, behind a great sheet of water. One entered through magnificent iron gates into a fantastic hall where sculptured giants crouched as pillars, and then moved on to a great staircase of dazzling whiteness and luscious ornamentation. Even today the emotional impact of this building is great: here, indeed, art and beauty create a sense of immense power and wealth.

Palaces like the Upper Belvedere were magnificent examples of the baroque style. They expressed the baroque delight in bold, sweeping statements, which were intended to provide a dramatic emotional experience. To create this experience baroque masters dissolved the traditional artistic frontiers: the architect permitted the painter and the artisan to cover his undulating surfaces with wildly colorful paintings, graceful sculptures, and fanciful carvings. Space was used in a highly original way, to blend everything together in a total environment. These techniques shone in all their glory in the churches of southern Germany and in the colossal entrance halls of palaces like that of the prince-bishop of Würzburg. Artistic achievement and political statement reinforced each other.

ROYAL CITIES

Absolute monarchs and baroque architects were not content with fashioning ostentatious

THE WÜRZBURG RESIDENCE   *This palace was a masterpiece of German baroque architecture. Here, in the Hall of the Kaiser, painter, sculptor, and architect have combined to create a dramatic visual experience. (AMA/Adelmann/EPA)*

palaces. They remodeled existing capital cities, or even built new ones, to reflect royal magnificence and the centralization of political power. Karlsruhe, founded in 1715 as the capital city of a small German principality, is only an extreme example. There, broad, straight avenues radiated out from the palace, so that all roads – like all power – were fo-

cused upon the ruler. More typically, the monarch's architects added new urban areas alongside the old city; these areas then became the real heart of the expanding capital.

The distinctive features of these new additions were their broad avenues, their imposing government buildings, and their rigorous mathematical layout. Along these major thoroughfares the nobles built elaborate baroque townhouses; stables and servants' quarters were built on the alleys behind. Wide avenues also facilitated the rapid movement of soldiers through the city to quell any disturbance (the king's planners had the needs of the military constantly in mind). Under the arcades along the avenues appeared smart and very expensive shops, the first department stores, with plateglass windows and fancy displays.

The new avenues brought reckless speed to the European city. Whereas everyone had walked through the narrow, twisting streets of the medieval town, the high and mighty raced down the broad boulevards in their elegant carriages. A social gap opened up between the wealthy riders and the ordinary, gaping, dodging pedestrians. "Mind the carriages!" wrote one eighteenth-century observer in Paris:

Here comes the black-coated physician in his chariot, the dancing master in his coach, the fencing master in his surrey – and the Prince behind six horses at the gallop as if he were in the open country. . . . The threatening wheels of the overbearing rich drive as rapidly as ever over stones stained with the blood of their unhappy victims.[16]

Speeding carriages on broad avenues, an endless parade of power and position: here was the symbol and substance of the baroque city.

THE GROWTH OF ST. PETERSBURG

No city illustrated better than St. Petersburg the close ties among politics, architecture, and urban development in this period. In 1700, when the Great Northern War between Russia and Sweden began, the city did not exist. There was only a small Swedish fortress on one of the water-logged islands at the mouth of the Neva River, where it flows into the Baltic Sea. In 1702, Peter the Great's armies seized this desolate outpost. Within a year the reforming tsar had decided to build a new city there and to make it, rather than ancient Moscow, his capital.

Since the first step was to secure the Baltic coast, military construction was the main concern for the next eight years. A mighty fortress was built on Peter Island, and a port and shipyards were built across the river on the mainland, as a Russian navy came into being. The land was swampy and uninhabited, the climate damp and unpleasant. But Peter cared not at all: for him, the inhospitable northern marshland was a future metropolis, gloriously bearing his name.

After the decisive Russian victory at Poltava in 1709 greatly reduced the threat of Swedish armies, Peter moved into high gear. In one imperious decree after another, he ordered his people to build a city that would equal any in the world. Such a city had to be western and baroque, just as Peter's army had to be western and permanent. From such a new city, his "window on Europe," Peter also believed it would be easier to reform the country militarily and administratively. The hand of tradition would rest lightly on the banks of the Neva.

These general political goals matched Peter's architectural ideas, which had been influenced by his travels in western Europe. First, Peter wanted a comfortable, "modern" city. Modernity meant broad, straight, stone-paved avenues, houses built in a uniform line and not haphazardly set back from the street, large parks, canals for drainage, stone bridges, and street lighting. Second, all building had to conform strictly to detailed architectural regulations set down by the government. Finally, each social group – the nobility, the merchants, the artisans, and so on – was to live in a certain section of town. In short, the city and its population were to conform to a

ST. PETERSBURG, CA 1760 Rastrelli's remodeled Winter Palace is on the left and the Navy Office with its famous spire is on the right. Russia became a naval power and St. Petersburg became a great port. (From G. H. Hamilton, Art and Architecture in Russia, Penguin Books, 1954)

carefully defined urban plan of the baroque type.

Peter used the traditional but reinforced methods of Russian autocracy to build his modern capital. The creation of St. Petersburg was just one of the heavy obligations he dictatorially imposed on all social groups in Russia. The peasants bore the heaviest burdens. Just as the government drafted peasants for the army, it also drafted twenty-five to forty thousand men each summer to labor in St. Petersburg for three months, without pay. Every ten to fifteen peasant households had to furnish one such worker each summer, and then pay a special tax in order to feed that worker in St. Petersburg.

Peasants hated this forced labor in the capital, and each year a fourth to a third of those sent risked brutal punishments and ran away. Many peasant construction workers died each summer from hunger, sickness, and accidents. Many also died because peasant villages tended to elect old men or young boys to labor in St. Petersburg, since strong and able-bodied men were desperately needed on the farm in the busy summer months. Thus beautiful St. Petersburg was built on the shoveling, carting, and paving of a mass of conscripted serfs.

Peter also drafted more privileged groups to his city, but on a permanent basis. Nobles were summarily ordered to build costly stone houses and palaces in St. Petersburg and to live in them most of the year. The more serfs a noble possessed, the bigger his dwelling had to be. Merchants and artisans were also commanded to settle and build in St. Petersburg. These nobles and merchants were then required to pay for the city's avenues, parks, canals, embankments, pilings, and bridges, all of which were very costly in terms of both money and lives because they were built upon a swamp. The building of St. Petersburg was, in truth, an enormous direct tax levied on the wealthy, who in turn forced the peasantry to do most of the work. The only real beneficiaries were the indispensable foreign architects and urban planners, whose often-princely salaries added to the tax burden. No wonder so many Russians hated Peter's new city.

Yet the tsar had his way. By the time of his death in 1725 there were at least six thousand houses and numerous impressive government buildings in St. Petersburg. Under the remarkable women who ruled Russia throughout most of the eighteenth century, St. Petersburg blossomed fully as a majestic and well-organized city, at least in its wealthy showpiece sections. Peter's youngest daughter, the quick-witted, sensual beauty Elizabeth (1741–1762), named as her chief architect Bartolomeo Rastrelli, who had come to Russia from Italy as a boy of fifteen in 1715. Combining Italian and Russian traditions into a unique, wildly colorful St. Petersburg style, Rastrelli built many palaces for the nobility and all the larger government buildings erected during Elizabeth's reign. He also rebuilt the Winter Palace as an enormous, aqua-colored royal residence, now the Hermitage Museum. There Elizabeth established a flashy, luxury-loving, and slightly crude court, which Catherine in turn made truly imperial. All the while St. Petersburg grew rapidly, and its almost 300,000 inhabitants in 1782 made it one of the world's largest cities. Peter and his successors had created out of nothing a magnificent and harmonious royal city, which unmistakably proclaimed the power and grandeur of Russia's rulers.

From about 1400 to 1650 social and economic developments in eastern Europe increasingly diverged from those in western Europe. In the east peasants and townspeople lost precious freedoms, while the nobility increased its power and prestige. It was within this framework of resurgent serfdom and entrenched nobility that Austrian and Prussian monarchs fashioned absolutist states in the seventeenth and early eighteenth centuries. Thus monarchs won absolutist control over standing armies, permanent taxes, and legislative bodies. But they did not question the underlying social and economic relationships. Indeed, they enhanced the privileges of the nobility, which furnished the leading servitors for enlarged armies and growing state bureaucracies.

In Russia the social and economic trends were similar but the timing of political absolutism was different. Mongol conquest and rule was a crucial experience, and a harsh indigenous tsarist autocracy was firmly in place by the reign of Ivan the Terrible in the sixteenth century. More than a century later Peter the Great succeeded in tightening up Russia's traditional absolutism and modernizing it by reforming the army, the bureaucracy, and the defense industry. In Russia and throughout eastern Europe, war and the needs of war weighed heavily in the triumph of absolutism.

Triumphant absolutism interacted spectacularly with the arts. Baroque art, which had grown out of the Catholic Reformation's desire to move the faithful and exalt the true faith, admirably suited the secular aspirations of eastern rulers. They built grandiose baroque palaces, monumental public squares, and even whole cities to glorify their power and majesty. Thus baroque art attained magnificent heights in eastern Europe, symbolizing the ideal and harmonizing with the reality of imperious royal absolutism.

NOTES

1. Quoted by F. L. Carsten, *The Origins of Prussia,* Clarendon Press, Oxford, 1954, p. 152.

2. Ibid., p. 175.

3. H. Rosenberg, *Bureaucracy, Aristocracy, and Autocracy: The Prussian Experience, 1660–1815,* Beacon Press, Boston, 1966, p. 38.

4. Quoted by R. Ergang, *The Potsdam Führer: Frederick William I, Father of Prussian Militarism,* Octagon Books, New York, 1972, pp. 85, 87.

5. Ibid. pp. 6–7, 43.

6. Quoted by R. A. Dorwart, *The Administrative Reforms of Frederick William I of Prussia,* Harvard University Press, Cambridge, Mass., 1953, p. 226.

7. Quoted by Rosenberg, p. 40.

8. Quoted by Ergang, p. 253.

9. Quoted by R. Pipes, *Russia Under the Old Regime,* Charles Scribner's Sons, New York, 1974, p. 48.

10. Quoted by N. V. Riasanovsky, *A History of Russia,* Oxford University Press, New York, 1963, p. 79.

11. Quoted by I. Grey, *Ivan III and the Unification of Russia,* Collier Books, New York, 1967, p. 39.

12. Quoted by R. Mousnier, *Peasant Uprisings in Seventeenth-Century France, Russia, and China,* Harper & Row, New York, 1970, p. 154.

13. Both quoted by Pipes, pp. 65, 85.

14. Quoted by Ergang, p. 13.

15. Quoted by J. Summerson, in *The Eighteenth Century: Europe in the Age of Enlightenment,* ed. A. Cobban, McGraw-Hill, New York, 1969, p. 80.

16. Quoted by L. Mumford, *The Culture of Cities,* Harcourt Brace Jovanovich, New York, 1938, p. 97.

SUGGESTED READING

All of the books cited in the Notes are highly recommended. F. L. Carsten's *The Origins of Prussia* (1954) is the best study on early Prussian history, and H. Rosenberg, *Bureaucracy, Aristocracy, and Autocracy: The Prussian Experience, 1660–1815* (1966), is a masterful analysis of the social context of Prussian absolutism. In addition to R. Ergang's exciting and critical biography of ramrod Frederick William I, *The Potsdam Führer* (1972), there is G. Ritter, *Frederick the Great* (1968), a more sympathetic study of the talented son by one of Germany's leading conservative historians. G. Craig, *The Politics of the Prussian Army, 1640–1945* (1964), expertly traces the great influence of the military on the Prussian state over three hundred years. R. J. Evans, *The Making of the Habsburg Empire, 1550–1770* (1979), and R. A. Kahn, *A History of the Habsburg Empire, 1526–1918* (1974), analyze the development of absolutism in Austria, as does A. Wandruszka, *The House of Habsburg* (1964). J. Stoye, *The Siege of Vienna* (1964), is a fascinating account of the last great Ottoman offensive, which is also treated in the interesting study by P. Coles, *The Ottoman Impact on Europe, 1350–1699* (1968). The Austro-Ottoman conflict is also a theme of L. S. Stavrianos, *The Balkans Since 1453* (1958), and D. McKay's fine biography, *Prince Eugene of Savoy* (1978).

On eastern peasants and serfdom, J. Blum, "The Rise of Serfdom in Eastern Europe," *American His-*

torical Review 62 (July 1957):807–836, is a good point of departure, while R. Mousnier, *Peasant Uprisings in Seventeenth-Century France, Russia, and China* (1970), is an engrossing comparative study. J. Blum, *Lord and Peasant in Russia from the Ninth to the Nineteenth Century* (1961), provides a good look at conditions in rural Russia, and P. Avrich, *Russian Rebels, 1600–1800* (1972), treats some of the violent peasant upheavals those conditions produced. R. Hellie, *Enserfment and Military Change in Muscovy,* (1971), is outstanding, as is Alexander Yanov's provocative *Origins of Autocracy: Ivan the Terrible in Russian History* (1981). In addition to the fine surveys by Pipes and Riasanovsky cited in the Notes, J. Billington, *The Icon and the Axe* (1970), is a stimulating history of early Russian intellectual and cultural developments, such as the great split in the church. M. Raeff, *Origins of the Russian Intelligentsia* (1966), skillfully probes the mind of the

Russian nobility in the eighteenth century. B. H. Sumner, *Peter the Great and the Emergence of Russia* (1962), is a fine brief introduction, which may be compared with the brilliant biography by Russia's greatest prerevolutionary historian, Vasili Klyuchevsky, *Peter the Great* (trans. 1958), and with R. Massie, *Peter the Great* (1980). G. Vernadsky and R. Fisher, eds., *A Source Book for Russian History from Early Times to 1917,* 3 vols. (1972), is an invaluable, highly recommended collection of documents and contemporary writings.

Three good books on art and architecture are E. Hempel, *Baroque Art and Architecture in Central Europe* (1965); G. Hamilton, *The Art and Architecture of Russia* (1954); and N. Pevsner, *An Outline of European Architecture,* 6th ed. (1960). Bach, Handel, and other composers are discussed intelligently by M. Bufkozer, *Music in the Baroque Era* (1947).

CHAPTER 18

TOWARD A NEW WORLD-VIEW

MOST PEOPLE are not philosophers, but nevertheless they have certain ideas and assumptions about the world in which they live. These ideas and assumptions add up to a basic outlook on life, a more or less coherent world-view. At the risk of oversimplification, one may say that the world-view of medieval and early modern Europe was primarily religious and theological. Not only did Christian or Jewish teachings form the core of people's spiritual and philosophical beliefs, but religious teachings also permeated all the rest of human thought and activity. Political theory relied on the divine right of kings, for example, and activities ranging from marriage and divorce to eating habits and hours of business were regulated by churches and religious doctrines.

In the course of the eighteenth century, this religious and theological world-view of the educated classes of western Europe underwent a fundamental transformation. Many educated people came to see the world primarily in secular and scientific terms. And while few abandoned religious beliefs altogether, many became openly hostile to established Christianity. The role of churches and religious thinking in earthly affairs and in the pursuit of knowledge was substantially reduced. Among many in the upper and middle classes a new critical, scientific, and very "modern" world-view took shape. Why did this momentous change occur? How did this new outlook on life affect society and politics? This chapter seeks to answer these questions.

THE SCIENTIFIC REVOLUTION

The foremost cause of the change in world-view was the scientific revolution. Modern science – precise knowledge of the physical world based upon the union of experimental observations with sophisticated mathematics – crystallized in the seventeenth century. Whereas science had been secondary and subordinate in medieval intellectual life, it became independent and even primary for many educated people.

The emergence of modern science was a development of tremendous long-term significance. A noted historian has even said that the scientific revolution of the late sixteenth and seventeenth centuries "outshines everything since the rise of Christianity and reduces the Renaissance and Reformation to the rank of mere episodes, mere internal displacements, within the system of medieval Christendom." The scientific revolution was "the real origin both of the modern world and the modern mentality."[1] This statement is an exaggeration, but not much of one. Of all the great civilizations, only that of the West developed modern science. It was with the scientific revolution that Western society began to acquire its most distinctive traits.

Although historians agree that the scientific revolution was enormously important, they approach it in quite different ways. Some scholars believe that the history of scientific achievement in this period had its own basic "internal" logic and that "nonscientific" factors had quite limited significance. These scholars write brilliant, often highly technical, intellectual studies, but they neglect the broader historical context. Other historians stress "external" economic, social, and religious factors, brushing over the scientific developments themselves. Historians of science now realize that these two approaches need to be brought together, but they are only beginning to do so. It is best, therefore, to examine the milestones on the fateful march toward modern science first and then to search for nonscientific influences along the route.

ARISTOTLE'S UNIVERSE In this late medieval woodcut the great Greek mathematician Archimedes stands on the motionless earth, surrounded by the other three elements — water, air, and fire. Beyond fire is the perfect celestial world of the sun, the planets, and the stars. (Royal Astronomical Society/Ann Ronan Picture Library)

SCIENTIFIC THOUGHT IN 1500

Since developments in astronomy and physics were at the heart of the scientific revolution, one must begin with the traditional European conception of the universe and movement in it. In the early 1500s, traditional European ideas about the universe were still based primarily upon the ideas of Aristotle, the great Greek philosopher of the fourth century B.C. These ideas had gradually been recovered during the Middle Ages and then brought into harmony with Christian doctrines by medieval theologians. According to this revised Aristotelian view, a motionless earth was fixed at the center of the universe. Around it moved ten separate, transparent, crystal spheres. In the first eight spheres were embedded, in turn, the moon, the sun, the five known planets, and the fixed stars. Then followed two spheres added during the Middle Ages to account for slight changes in the positions of the stars over the centuries. Beyond the tenth sphere was heaven, with the throne of God and the souls of the saved. Angels kept the spheres moving in perfect circles.

Aristotle's views, suitably revised by medieval philosophers, also dominated thinking about physics and motion on earth. Aristotle had distinguished sharply between the world of the celestial spheres and that of the earth – the sublunar world. The spheres consisted of a perfect, incorruptible "quintessence," or fifth essence. The sublunar world, however, was made up of four imperfect, changeable elements. The "light" elements – air and fire – naturally moved upward, while the "heavy" elements – water and earth – naturally moved downward. The natural directions of motion did not always prevail, however, for elements were often mixed together, and could be affected by an outside force such as a human being. Aristotle and his followers also believed that a uniform force moved an object at a constant speed and that the object would stop as soon as that force was removed.

Aristotle's ideas about astronomy and physics were accepted with minor revisions for two thousand years, and with good reason. First, they offered an understandable common-sense explanation for what the eye actually saw. Second, Aristotle's science, as interpreted by Christian theologians, fit neatly with Christian doctrines. It established a home for God and a place for Christian souls. It put human beings at the center of the universe, and made them the critical link in a "great chain of being" that stretched from the throne of God to the most lowly insect on earth. Thus science was primarily a branch of theology, and it reinforced religious thought. At the same time, medieval "scientists" were already providing closely reasoned explanations of the universe, explanations they felt were worthy of God's perfect creation.

THE COPERNICAN HYPOTHESIS

The desire to explain and thereby glorify God's handiwork led to the first great departure from the medieval system. This departure was the work of the Polish clergyman and as-

tronomer Nicolaus Copernicus (1473–1543). As a young man Copernicus studied church law and astronomy in various European universities. He saw how professional astronomers were still dependent for their most accurate calculations on the work of Ptolemy, the last great ancient astronomer, who had lived in Alexandria in the second century A.D. Ptolemy's achievement had been to work out complicated rules to explain the minor irregularities in the movement of the planets. These rules enabled stargazers and astrologers to track the planets with greater precision. Many people then (and now) believed that the changing relationships between planets and stars influenced and even determined an individual's future.

The young Copernicus was uninterested in astrology, and felt that Ptolemy's cumbersome and occasionally inaccurate rules detracted from the majesty of a perfect Creator. He hit upon an old Greek idea being discussed in Renaissance Italy: the idea that the sun rather than the earth was at the center of the universe. Finishing his university studies and returning to a church position in east Prussia, Copernicus worked on his hypothesis from 1506 to 1530. Never questioning the Aristotelian belief in crystal spheres or the idea that circular motion was most perfect and divine, Copernicus theorized that the stars and planets, including the earth, revolve around a fixed sun. Yet Copernicus was a cautious man. Fearing the ridicule of other astronomers, he did not publish his *On the Revolutions of the Heavenly Spheres* until 1543, the year of his death.

Copernicus's theory had enormous scientific and religious implications, many of which the conservative Copernicus was unaware of. First, it put the stars at rest, their apparent nightly movement simply a result of the earth's rotation. Thus it destroyed the main reason for believing in crystal spheres capable of moving the stars around the earth. Second, Copernicus's theory suggested a universe of staggering size. If in the course of a year the earth moved around the sun and yet the stars appeared to remain in the same place, then the universe was unthinkably large or even infinite. Finally, by characterizing the earth as just another planet, Copernicus destroyed the basic idea of Aristotelian physics – the idea that the earthly world was quite different from the heavenly one. Where, then, was the realm of perfection? Where was heaven and the throne of God?

The Copernican theory quickly brought sharp attacks from religious leaders, especially Protestant leaders. Hearing of Copernicus's work even before it was published, Martin Luther spoke of Copernicus as "the new astrologer who wants to prove that the earth moves and goes round. . . . The fool wants to turn the whole art of astronomy upside down." Luther did, however, note that "as the Holy Scripture tells us, so did Joshua bid the sun stand still and not the earth." Calvin also condemned Copernicus, citing as evidence the first verse of Psalm 93: "The world also is established that it cannot be moved." "Who," asked Calvin, "will venture to place the authority of Copernicus above that of the Holy Spirit?"[2] Catholic reaction was milder at first. The Catholic church had never been hypnotized by literal interpretations of the Bible, and not until 1616 did it officially declare the Copernican theory false.

This slow reaction also reflected the slow progress of Copernicus's theory for many years. Other events were almost as influential in creating doubts about traditional astronomical ideas. In 1572, a new star appeared and shone very brightly for almost two years. The new star, which was actually a distant exploding star, made an enormous impression

upon people. It seemed to contradict the idea that the heavenly spheres were unchanging and therefore perfect. In 1577, a new comet suddenly moved through the sky, cutting a straight path across the supposedly impenetrable crystal spheres. It was time, as a typical scientific writer put it, for "the radical renovation of astronomy."[3]

FROM TYCHO BRAHE TO GALILEO

One astronomer who agreed was Tycho Brahe (1546–1601). Born into a leading Danish noble family and earmarked for a career in government, Brahe was at an early age tremendously impressed by a partial eclipse of the sun. It seemed to him "something divine that men could know the motions of the stars so accurately that they were able a long time beforehand to predict their places and relative positions."[4] Completing his studies abroad and returning to Denmark, Brahe established himself as Europe's leading astronomer with his detailed observations of the new star of 1572. Aided by generous grants from the king of Denmark, which made him one of the richest men in the country, Brahe built the most sophisticated observatory of his day. For twenty years he meticulously observed the stars and planets with the naked eye. An imposing man who had lost a piece of his nose in a duel and replaced it with a special bridge of gold and silver alloy, a noble who exploited his peasants arrogantly and approached the heavens humbly, Brahe's great contribution was his mass of data. His limited understanding of mathematics prevented him, however, from making much sense out of his data. Part Ptolemaic, part Copernican, he believed that all the planets revolved around the sun and that the entire group of sun and planets revolved in turn around the earth-moon system.

EFFIGIES TYCHONIS BRAHE O.F.
ÆDIFICII ET INSTRUMENTORUM
ASTRONOMICORUM STRUCTORIS.
Æ NOMINE 1587. ÆTATIS SUÆ 40.

TYCHO BRAHE'S MAIN OBSERVATORY   Lavishly financed by the king of Denmark, Brahe built his magnificent observatory at Uraniborg between 1576 and 1580. For twenty years he studied the heavens and accumulated a mass of precise but undigested data. (The British Library)

It was left to Brahe's brilliant young assistant, Johannes Kepler (1571–1630), to go much farther. Kepler was a medieval figure in many ways. Coming from a minor German noble family and trained for the Lutheran ministry, he long believed that the universe was built on mystical mathematical relationships and a musical harmony of the heavenly bodies. Working and reworking Brahe's

mountain of observations in a staggering sustained effort after the Dane's death, this brilliant mathematician eventually went beyond mystical intuitions.

Kepler formulated three famous laws of planetary motion. First, building upon Copernican theory, he demonstrated in 1609 that the orbits of the planets around the sun are elliptical rather than circular. Second, he demonstrated that the planets do not move at a uniform speed in their orbits. Third, in 1619 he showed that the time a planet takes to make its complete orbit is precisely related to its distance from the sun. Kepler's contribution was monumental. Whereas Copernicus had speculated, Kepler proved mathematically the precise relations of a sun-centered (solar) system. His work demolished the old system of Aristotle and Ptolemy, and in his third law he came close to formulating the idea of universal gravitation.

While Kepler was unraveling planetary motion, a young Florentine name Galileo Galilei (1564–1642) was challenging all the old ideas about motion. Like so many early scientists, Galileo was a poor nobleman first marked for a religious career. However, he soon became fascinated by mathematics. A brilliant student, Galileo became a professor of mathematics in 1589 at age twenty-five. He proceeded to examine motion and mechanics in a new way. Indeed, his great achievement was the elaboration and consolidation of the modern experimental method. Rather than speculate about what might or should happen, Galileo conducted controlled experiments to find out what actually *did* happen.

In his famous "acceleration experiment," he showed that a uniform force – in this case gravity – produced a uniform acceleration. Here is how Galileo described his pathbreaking method and conclusion in his *Two New Sciences:*

A piece of wooden moulding ... was taken; on its edge was cut a channel a little more than one finger in breadth. Having made this groove very straight, smooth and polished, and having lined it with parchment, also as smooth and polished as possible, we rolled along it a hard, smooth and very round bronze ball.... Noting ... the time required to make the descent ... we now rolled the ball only one-quarter the length of the channel; and having measured the time of its descent, we found it precisely one-half of the former.... In such experiments [over many distances], repeated a full hundred times, we always found that the spaces traversed were to each other as the squares of the times, and that this was true for all inclinations of the plane.[5]

With this and other experiments, Galileo also formulated the law of inertia. That is, rather than "rest" being the natural state of objects, an object continues in motion forever unless stopped by some external force. Aristotelian physics was in a shambles.

In the tradition of Brahe, Galileo also applied the experimental method to astronomy. His astronomical discoveries had a very great impact on scientific development. On hearing that the telescope had just been invented in Holland, Galileo made one for himself and trained it on the heavens. He quickly discovered the first four moons of Jupiter, which clearly suggested that Jupiter could not possibly be embedded in any impenetrable crystal sphere. This discovery provided new evidence for the Copernican theory, in which Galileo already believed.

Galileo then pointed his telescope at the moon. He wrote in 1610 in *Siderus Nuncius:*

I feel sure that the moon is not perfectly smooth, free from inequalities, and exactly spherical, as a large school of philosophers considers with regard to the moon and the other heavenly bodies. On the contrary, it is full of inequalities, uneven, full of hollows and protuberances, just like the surface of the earth itself, which is varied everywhere by lofty mountains and deep valleys.... The next object which I have observed is the essence or substance of the Milky Way. By the aid of a telescope anyone may behold this in a manner which so distinctly appeals to the senses that all the disputes which have tormented philosophers through so many ages are exploded by the irrefutable evidence of our eyes, and we are freed from wordy disputes upon the subject. For the galaxy is nothing else but a mass of innumerable stars planted together in clusters. Upon whatever part of it you direct the telescope straightway a vast crowd of stars presents itself to view; many of them are tolerably large and extremely bright, but the number of small ones is quite beyond determination.[6]

Reading these famous lines, one feels that a crucial corner in Western civilization is being turned. The traditional religious and theological world-view, which rested on determining and then accepting the proper established authority, is beginning to give way in certain fields to a critical, "scientific" method. This new method of learning and investigating was the greatest accomplishment of the entire scientific revolution, for it has proved capable of enormous extension. A historian critically investigating the documents of the past, for example, is not much different from a Galileo investigating stars and rolling balls.

Galileo was employed in Florence by the Medici grand dukes of Tuscany, and his work eventually aroused the ire of some theologians. The issue was presented in 1624 to Pope Urban VII, who permitted Galileo to write about different possible systems of the world, as long as he did not presume to judge which one actually existed. After the publication in Italian of his widely read *Dialogue on the Two Chief Systems of the World* in 1632, which too openly lampooned the traditional views of Aristotle and Ptolemy and defended those of Copernicus, Galileo was tried for heresy by the papal Inquisition. Imprisoned and threatened with torture, the aging Galileo recanted, "renouncing and cursing" his Copernican errors. Of minor importance in the development of science, Galileo's trial later became for some writers the perfect symbol of the inevitable conflict between religious belief and scientific knowledge.

NEWTON'S SYNTHESIS

The accomplishments of Kepler, Galileo, and other scientists had had their effect by about 1640. The old astronomy and physics were in ruins, and several fundamental breakthroughs had been made. The new findings had not, however, been fused together in a new synthesis, a synthesis that would provide a single set of explanations for motion both on earth and in the skies. That synthesis, which prevailed until the twentieth century, was the work of Isaac Newton (1642-1727).

Newton was born into the lower English gentry, and attended Cambridge University. He was a very complex individual. A great genius who spectacularly united the experimental and theoretical-mathematical sides of modern science, Newton was also fascinated by alchemy. He sought the elixir of life and a way to change base metals into gold and silver. Not without reason did the twentieth-century economist John Maynard Keynes call Newton "the last of the magicians." Newton was intensely religious. He had a highly suspicious nature, lacked all interest in women and sex, and in 1693 had a nervous breakdown from which he later recovered. He was far from being the perfect rationalist so endlessly eulogized by writers in the eighteenth and nineteenth centuries.

Of his intellectual genius and incredible powers of concentration there can be no doubt, however. Arriving at some of his most basic ideas about physics in 1666 at age twenty-four, but unable to prove these theories mathematically, he attained a professorship and studied optics for many years. In 1684, Newton returned to physics for eighteen extraordinarily intensive months. For weeks on end he seldom left his room except to read his lectures. His meals were sent up but he usually forgot to eat them, his mind fastened like a vise on the laws of the universe. Thus did Newton open the third book of his immortal *Mathematical Principles of Natural Philosophy,* published in Latin in 1687 and generally known as the *Principia,* with these lines:

In the preceding books I have laid down the principles of philosophy [that is, science]. . . . These principles are the laws of certain motions, and powers or forces, which chiefly have respect to philosophy. . . . It remains that from the same principles I now demonstrate the frame of the System of the World.

Newton made good his grandiose claim. His towering accomplishment was to integrate in a single explanatory system the astronomy of Copernicus, as corrected by Kepler's laws, with the physics of Galileo and his predecessors. Newton did this by means of a set of mathematical laws that explain motion and mechanics. These laws of dynamics are complex, and it took scientists and engineers two hundred years to work out all their implications. Nevertheless, the key feature of the Newtonian synthesis was the law of universal gravitation. According to this law, every body in the universe attracts every other body in the universe in a precise mathematical relationship, whereby the force of attraction is proportional to the quantity of matter of the

science and applied technology, which we take for granted today, simply did not exist before the nineteenth century. Thus, the scientific revolution of the seventeenth century was first and foremost an intellectual revolution. It is not surprising that for more than a hundred years its greatest impact was on how people thought and believed.

THE ENLIGHTENMENT

The scientific revolution was the single most important factor in the creation of the new world-view of the eighteenth-century Enlightenment. This world-view, which has played a very large role in shaping the modern mind, was made up of a rich mix of ideas, sometimes conflicting, for intellectuals delight in playing with ideas as athletes delight in playing games. In this rich diversity, three central concepts stand out.

The most important and original idea of the Enlightenment was that the methods of natural science could and should be used to examine and understand all aspects of life. This was what intellectuals meant by *reason,* a favorite word of Enlightenment thinkers. Nothing was to be accepted on faith. Everything was to be submitted to the rational, critical, "scientific" way of thinking. This approach brought the Enlightenment into a head-on conflict with the established churches, which rested their beliefs on the special authority of the Bible and Christian theology. A second important Enlightenment concept was that the scientific method was capable of discovering the laws of human society as well as those of nature. Thus was "social science" born. Its birth led to the third key idea, the idea of progress. Armed with the proper method of discovering the laws of human existence, Enlightenment thinkers believed it was at least possible to create better societies and better people. Their belief was strengthened by some genuine improvements in economic and social life during the eighteenth century, as we shall see in the next two chapters.

The Enlightenment was, therefore, profoundly secular. It revived and expanded the Renaissance concentration on worldly explanations. In the course of the eighteenth century, the Enlightenment had a profound impact on the thought and culture of the urban middle and upper classes. It did not have much appeal for the poor and the peasants.

THE EMERGENCE OF THE ENLIGHTENMENT

The Enlightenment reached its maturity about 1750, when a brilliant band of French thinkers known as the philosophes effectively propagandized the new world-view across Europe. Yet it was the generation that came of age between the publication of Newton's masterpiece in 1687 and the death of Louis XIV in 1715 that tied the crucial knot between the scientific revolution and a new outlook on life.

Talented writers of that generation popularized the hard-to-understand scientific achievements for the educated elite. The most famous and influential popularizer was a very versatile French man of letters, Bernard de Fontenelle (1657-1757). Fontenelle practically invented the technique of making highly complicated scientific findings understandable to a broad nonscientific audience. He set out to make science witty and entertaining, as easy to read as a novel. This was a tall order, but Fontenelle largely succeeded.

His most famous work, *Conversations on the Plurality of Worlds* of 1686, begins with two elegant figures walking in the gathering shadows of a large park. One is a woman, a so-

POPULARIZING SCIENCE *The frontpiece illustration of Fontenelle's* Conversations on the Plurality of Worlds *invites the reader to share the pleasures of astronomy with an elegant lady and an entertaining teacher. (Photo: Caroline Buckler)*

There came on the scene a certain German, one Copernicus, who made short work of all those various circles, all those solid skies, which the ancients had pictured to themselves. The former he abolished; the latter he broke in pieces. Fired with the noble zeal of a true astronomer, he took the earth and spun it very far away from the center of the universe, where it had been installed, and in that center he put the sun, which had a far better title to the honor.[9]

Rather than tremble in despair in the face of these revelations, Fontenelle's lady rejoices in the advance of knowledge. Fontenelle thus went beyond entertainment to instruction, suggesting that the human mind was capable of making great progress.

This idea of progress was essentially a new idea of the later seventeenth century. Medieval and Reformation thinkers had been concerned primarily with sin and salvation. The humanists of the Renaissance had emphasized worldly matters, but they had been backward-looking. They had believed it might be possible to equal the magnificent accomplishments of the ancients, but they did not ask for more. Fontenelle and like-minded writers had come to believe that, at least in science and mathematics, their era had gone far *beyond* antiquity. Progress, at least intellectual progress, was clearly possible. During the eighteenth century, this idea would sink deeply into the consciousness of the European elite.

Fontenelle and other literary figures of his generation were also instrumental in bringing science into conflict with religion. Contrary to what is often assumed, many seventeenth-century scientists, both Catholic and Protestant, believed that their work exalted God. They did not draw antireligious implications from their scientific findings. The greatest scientist of them all, Isaac Newton, was a devout if unorthodox Christian who saw all of his studies as directed toward explaining God's

phisticated aristocrat, and the other is her friend, perhaps even her lover. They gaze at the stars, and their talk turns to a passionate discussion of . . . astronomy! He confides that "each star may well be a different world." She is intrigued by his novel idea: "Teach me about these stars of yours." And he does, gently but persistently stressing how error is giving way to truth. At one point he explains:

message. Newton devoted far more of his time to angels and biblical prophecies than to universal gravitation, and he was convinced that all of his inquiries were equally "scientific."

Fontenelle, on the other hand, was skeptical about absolute truth and cynical about the claims of organized religion. Since such views could not be stated openly in Louis XIV's France, Fontenelle made his point through subtle editorializing about science. His depiction of the cautious Copernicus as a self-conscious revolutionary was typical. In his *Eulogies of Scientists* Fontenelle exploited with endless variations the basic theme of rational, progressive scientists versus prejudiced, reactionary priests. Time and time again Fontenelle's fledgling scientists attended church and studied theology; then, at some crucial moment, each was converted from the obscurity of religion to the clarity of science.

The progressive and antireligious implications that writers like Fontenelle drew from the scientific revolution reflected a very real crisis in European thought at the end of the seventeenth century. This crisis had its roots in several intellectual uncertainties and dissatisfactions, of which the demolition of Aristotelian-medieval science was only one.

A second uncertainty involved the whole question of religious truth. The destructive wars of religion had been fought, in part, because religious freedom was an intolerable idea in the early seventeenth century. Both Catholics and Protestants had believed that religious truth was absolute and therefore worth fighting and dying for. It was also generally believed that a strong state required unity in religious faith. Yet the disastrous results of the many attempts to impose such religious unity, such as Louis XIV's expulsion of the French Protestants in 1685, led some people to ask if ideological conformity in re-

ligious matters was really necessary. Others skeptically asked if religious truth could ever be known with absolute certainty, and concluded that it could not.

The most famous of these skeptics was Pierre Bayle (1647–1706), a French Huguenot who took refuge in Holland. A teacher by profession and a crusading journalist by inclination, Bayle critically examined the religious beliefs and persecutions of the past in his *Historical and Critical Dictionary,* published in 1697. Demonstrating that human beliefs had been extremely varied and very often mistaken, Bayle concluded that nothing can ever be known beyond all doubt. In religion as in philosophy, humanity's best hope was open-minded toleration. Bayle's skeptical views were very influential. Many eighteenth-century writers mined his inexhaustible vein of critical skepticism for ammunition for their attacks on superstition and Christian theology. Bayle's four-volume *Dictionary* was more frequently found in the private libraries of eighteenth-century France than any other book.

The rapidly growing travel literature on non-European lands and cultures was a third cause of uncertainty. In the wake of the great discoveries, Europeans were learning that the peoples of China, India, Africa and the Americas all had their own very different beliefs and customs. Europeans shaved their faces and let their hair grow. The Turks shaved their heads and let their beards grow. In Europe a man bowed before a woman to show respect. In Siam a man turned his back on a woman when he met her, because it was disrespectful to look directly at her. Countless similar examples discussed in the travel accounts helped change the perspective of educated Europeans. They began to look at truth and morality in relative rather than absolute terms. Anything was possible, and who could say what was right or wrong? As one Frenchman wrote: "There is nothing that opinion, prejudice, custom, hope, and a sense of honor cannot do." Another wrote disapprovingly of religious skeptics who were corrupted "by extensive travel and lose whatever shreds of religion that remained with them. Every day they see a new religion, new customs, new rites."[10]

A fourth cause and manifestation of European intellectual turmoil was John Locke's epoch-making *Essay Concerning Human Understanding*. Published in 1690 – the same year Locke published his famous *Second Treatise on Civil Government* – Locke's essay brilliantly set forth a new theory about how human beings learn and form their ideas. In doing so he rejected the prevailing view of Descartes, who had held that all people are born with certain basic ideas and ways of thinking. Locke insisted that all ideas are derived from experience. The human mind is like a blank tablet at birth, a tablet on which environment writes the individual's understanding and beliefs. Human development is, therefore, determined by education and social institutions, for good or for evil. Locke's *Essay Concerning Human Understanding* passed through many editions and translations. It was, along with Newton's *Principia,* one of the dominant intellectual inspirations of the Enlightenment.

THE PHILOSOPHES AND THEIR IDEAS

By the death of Louis XIV in 1715, many of the ideas that would soon coalesce into the new world-view had been assembled. Yet Christian Europe was still strongly attached to its traditional beliefs, as witnessed by the powerful revival of religious orthodoxy in the first half of the eighteenth century. By the outbreak of the American Revolution in 1775, however, a large portion of western Europe's educated elite had embraced many of the new

ideas. This acceptance was the work of one of history's most influential groups of intellectuals, the philosophes. It was the philosophes who proudly and effectively proclaimed that they, at long last, were bringing the light of knowledge to their ignorant fellow creatures in a great Age of Enlightenment.

Philosophe is the French word for philosopher, and it was in France that the Enlightenment reached its highest development. The French philosophes were indeed philosophers. They asked fundamental philosophical questions about the meaning of life, about God, human nature, good and evil, and cause and effect. But, in the tradition of Bayle and Fontenelle, they were not content with abstract arguments or ivory-tower speculations among a tiny minority of scholars and professors. They wanted to influence and convince a broad audience.

The philosophes were intensely committed to reforming society and humanity, yet they were not free to write as they wished, since it was illegal in France to criticize openly either church or state. Their most radical works had to circulate in France in manuscript form, very much as critical works are passed from hand to hand in unpublished form in dictatorships today. Knowing that direct attacks would probably be banned or burned, the philosophes wrote novels and plays, histories and philosophies, dictionaries and encyclopedias, all filled with satire and double meanings to spread the message.

One of the greatest philosophes, the baron de Montesquieu (1689-1755), brilliantly pioneered this approach in *The Persian Letters,* an extremely influential social satire published in 1721. Montesquieu's work consisted of amusing letters supposedly written by Persian travelers, who see European customs in "strange ways" and thereby cleverly criticize existing practices and beliefs. Having shown wit to be a powerful weapon against the cruelty and superstition he despised, Montesquieu turned to political theory and as we shall see in Chapter 21, contributed greatly to the development of liberalism.

The most famous and in many ways most representative philosophe was François Marie Arouet, who was known by the pen name of Voltaire (1694–1778). In his long career this son of a comfortable middle-class family wrote over seventy witty volumes, hobnobbed with kings and queens, and died a millionaire because of shrewd business speculations. His early career, however, was turbulent. In 1717, Voltaire was imprisoned for eleven months in the Bastille in Paris for insulting the regent of France. In 1726, a barb from his sharp tongue led a great French nobleman to have him beaten and arrested. This experience made a deep impression upon Voltaire. All his life he struggled against legal injustice and class inequalities before the law.

Released from prison after promising to leave the country, Voltaire lived in England for three years. He then wrote various works praising English institutions and popularizing English scientific progress. Newton, he wrote, was history's greatest man, for he had used his genius for the benefit of humanity. "It is," wrote Voltaire, "the man who sways our minds by the prevalence of reason and the native force of truth, not they who reduce mankind to a state of slavery by force and downright violence . . . that claims our reverence and admiration."[11] In the true style of the Enlightenment, Voltaire mixed the glorification of science and reason with an appeal for better people and institutions.

Yet, like almost all of the philosophes, Voltaire was a reformer and not a revolutionary in social and political matters. Returning to France, he was eventually appointed royal historian in 1743, and his *Age of Louis XIV* portrayed Louis as the dignified leader of his age. Voltaire also began a long correspon-

VOLTAIRE was a prodigious worker. This painting shows him dictating from the very moment he hops out of bed. (Bulloz)

dence with Frederick the Great, and he accepted Frederick's flattering invitation to come brighten up the Prussian court in Berlin. The two men later quarreled, but Voltaire always admired Frederick as a freethinker and an enlightened monarch.

Voltaire pessimistically concluded that the best one could hope for in the way of government was an enlightened monarch, since human beings "are very rarely worthy to govern themselves." Nor did he believe in social equality in human affairs. The idea of making servants equal to their masters was "absurd and impossible." The only realizable equality Voltaire thought was that "by which the citizen only depends on the laws which protect the freedom of the feeble against the ambitions of the strong."[12]

Voltaire's philosophical and religious positions were much more radical. In the tradition of Bayle, his voluminous writings challenged – often indirectly – the Catholic church and Christian theology at almost every point. Although he was considered by many devout Christians to be a shallow blasphemer, Voltaire's religious views were influential and quite typical of the mature Enlightenment. The essay on religion from his widely read *Philosophical Dictionary* sums up many of his criticisms and beliefs:

I meditated last night; I was absorbed in the contemplation of nature; I admired the immensity, the course, the harmony of these infinite globes which the vulgar do not know how to admire.

I admired still more the intelligence which directs these vast forces. I said to myself: "One must be blind not to be dazzled by this spectacle; one must be stupid not to recognize its author; one must be mad not to worship the Supreme Being."

I was deep in these ideas when one of those genii who fill the intermundane spaces came down to me . . . and transported me into a desert all covered with piles of bones. . . . He began with the first pile. "These," he said, "are the twenty-three thousand Jews who danced before a calf, with the twenty-four thousand who were killed while lying with Midianitish women. The number of those massacred for such errors and offences amounts to nearly three hundred thousand.

"In the other piles are the bones of the Christians slaughtered by each other because of metaphysical disputes. . . ."

"What!" I cried, "brothers have treated their brothers like this, and I have the misfortune to be of this brotherhood! . . . Why assemble here all these abominable monuments to barbarism and fanaticism?"

"To instruct you. . . . Follow me now." . . .

I saw a man with a gentle, simple face, who seemed to me to be about thirty-five years old. From afar he looked with compassion upon those piles of whitened bones, through which I had been led to reach the sage's dwelling place. I was astonished to find his feet swollen and bleeding, his hands likewise, his side pierced, and his ribs laid bare by the cut of the lash. "Good God!" I said to him, "is it possible for a just man, a sage, to be in this state? . . . Was it . . . by priests and judges that you were so cruelly assassinated?"

With great courtesy he answered, "Yes."

"And who were these monsters?"

"They were hypocrites."

"Ah! that says everything; I understand by that one word that they would have condemned you to the cruelest punishment. Had you then proved to them, as Socrates did, that the Moon was not a goddess, and that Mercury was not a god?"

"No, it was not a question of planets. My countrymen did not even know what a planet was; they were all arrant ignoramuses. Their superstitions were quite different from those of the Greeks."

"Then you wanted to teach them a new religion?"

"Not at all; I told them simply: 'Love God with all your heart and your neighbor as yourself, for that is the whole of mankind's duty.' Judge yourself if this precept is not as old as the universe; judge yourself if I brought them a new religion." . . .

"Did you not say once that you were come not to bring peace, but a sword?"

"It was a scribe's error; I told them that I brought peace and not a sword. I never wrote anything; what I said can have been changed without evil intention."

"You did not then contribute in any way by your teaching, either badly reported or badly interpreted, to those frightful piles of bones which I saw on my way to consult with you?"

"I have only looked with horror upon those who have made themselves guilty of all these murders."

. . . [Finally] I asked him to tell me in what true religion consisted.

"Have I not already told you? Love God and your neighbor as yourself."

"What! Can we love God and still eat meat on Friday?"

"I always ate what was given me; for I was too poor to give dinner to anyone."

"Must I take sides for either the Greek or the Latin church?"

"When I was in the world I never made any distinction between the Jew and the Samaritan."

"Well, if that is so, I take you for my only master." Then he made me a sign with his head which filled me with consolation. The vision disappeared, and a clear conscience stayed with me.[13]

This passage requires careful study, for it suggests many Enlightenment themes of religion and philosophy. As the opening paragraphs show, Voltaire clearly believed in a God. But the God of Voltaire and most philosophes was a distant, deistic God, a great Clockmaker who built an orderly universe and then stepped aside and let it run. Finally, the philosophes hated all forms of religious intolerance. They believed that people had to be wary of dogmatic certainty and religious disputes, which often led to fanaticism and savage, inhuman action. Simple piety and human kindness – the love of God and the golden rule – were religion enough, even Christianity enough, as Voltaire's interpretation of Christ suggests.

The ultimate strength of the philosophes lay, however, in their numbers, dedication, and organization. The philosophes felt keenly that they were engaged in a common undertaking that transcended individuals. Their greatest and most representative intellectual achievement was, quite fittingly, a group effort – the seventeen-volume *Encyclopedia: The Rational Dictionary of the Sciences, the Arts, and the Crafts,* edited by Denis Diderot (1713–1774) and Jean le Rond d'Alembert (1717–1783). Diderot and d'Alembert made a curious pair. Diderot began his career as a hack writer, first attracting attention with a skeptical tract on religion that was quickly burned by the judges of Paris. D'Alembert was one of Europe's leading scientists and mathematicians, the orphaned and illegitimate son of celebrated aristocrats. Moving in different circles and with different interests, the two men set out to find coauthors who would examine the whole of rapidly expanding human knowledge. Even more fundamentally, they set out to teach people how to think critically and objectively about all matters. As Diderot said, he wanted the *Encyclopedia* to "change the general way of thinking."[14]

The editors of the *Encyclopedia* had to conquer innumerable obstacles. After the appearance in 1751 of the first volume, which dealt with such controversial subjects as atheism, the soul, and blind people – all words beginning with *a* in French – the government temporarily banned publication. The pope later placed it on the Index and pronounced excommunication on all who read or bought it. The timid publisher mutilated some of the articles in the last ten volumes without the editors' consent in an attempt to appease the authorities. Yet Diderot's unwavering belief in the importance of his mission held the encyclopedists together for fifteen years, and the enormous work was completed in 1765. Hundreds of thousands of articles by leading scientists and famous writers, skilled workers and progressive priests, treated every aspect of life and knowledge.

Not every article was daring or original, but the overall effect was little short of revolutionary. Science and the industrial arts were exalted, religion and immortality questioned. Intolerance, legal injustice, and out-of-date social institutions were openly criticized. More generally, the writers of the *Encyclopedia* showed that human beings could use the proc-

CANAL WITH LOCKS *The articles on science and the industrial arts in the* Encyclopedia *carried lavish explanatory illustrations. This typical engraving from the section on water and its uses shows advances in canal building and reflects the encyclopedists' faith in technical progress. (Photo: Caroline Buckler)*

ess of reasoning to expand human knowledge. Encyclopedists were convinced that greater knowledge would result in greater human happiness, for knowledge was useful and made possible economic, social, and political progress. The *Encyclopedia* was extremely influential in France and throughout western Europe as well. It summed up the new world-view of the Enlightenment.

THE LATER ENLIGHTENMENT

After about 1770, the harmonious unity of the philosophes and their thought began to break down. As the new world-view became increasingly accepted by the educated public, some thinkers sought originality by exaggerating certain ideas of the Enlightenment to the exclusion of others. These latter-day philosophes built rigid, dogmatic systems.

In his *System of Nature* (1770) and other works, the aristocratic Baron Paul d'Holbach (1723–1789) argued that human beings were machines completely determined by outside forces. Free will, God, and immortality of the soul were foolish myths. D'Holbach's rabid atheism and determinism, which were coupled with extreme hostility toward Christianity and all other religions, dealt the Enlightenment movement a severe blow. Deists like Voltaire, who believed in God but not in established churches, found d'Holbach's inflexible atheism repulsive. They saw in him the same dogmatic intolerance they had been fighting all their lives.

Another aristocrat, the marquis Marie-Jean

de Condorcet (1743–1794), transformed the Enlightenment belief in gradual, hard-won progress into fanciful utopianism. In his *Progress of the Human Mind,* written in 1793 during the French Revolution, Condorcet traced the nine stages of human progress that had already occurred and predicted that the tenth would bring perfection. Ironically, Condorcet wrote this work while fleeing for his life. Caught and condemned by revolutionary extremists, he preferred death by his own hand to the blade of the guillotine.

Other thinkers and writers after about 1770 began to attack the Enlightenment's faith in reason, progress, and moderation. The most famous of these was the Swiss Jean-Jacques Rousseau (1712–1778), a brilliant but difficult thinker, an appealing but neurotic individual. Born into a poor family of watchmakers in Geneva, Rousseau went to Paris and was greatly influenced by Diderot and Voltaire. Always extraordinarily sensitive and suspicious, Rousseau came to believe his philosophe friends were plotting against him. In the mid-1750s he broke with them personally and intellectually, living thereafter as a lonely outsider with his uneducated common-law wife and going in his own highly original direction.

Like other Enlightenment thinkers, Rousseau was passionately committed to individual freedom. Unlike them, however, he attacked rationalism and civilization as destroying rather than liberating the individual. Warm, spontaneous feeling had to complement and correct the cold intellect. Moreover, the individual's basic goodness had to be protected from the cruel refinements of civilization. As we shall see in Chapter 23, these ideas greatly influenced the early romantic movement, which rebelled against the culture of the Enlightenment in the late eighteenth century.

Applying his heartfelt ideas to children, Rousseau had a powerful impact upon the development of modern education. In his famous novel *Emile* (1762) he argued that education must shield the naturally unspoiled child from the corrupting influences of civilization and too many books. According to Rousseau, children must develop naturally and spontaneously, at their own speed and in their own way. It is eloquent testimony to Rousseau's troubled life and complicated personality that he placed all five of his own children in orphanages.

Rousseau also made an important contribution to political theory in the *Social Contract* (1762). His fundamental ideas were the general will and popular sovereignty. According to Rousseau, the general will is sacred and absolute, reflecting the common interests of the people, who have displaced the monarch as the holder of the sovereign power. The general will is not necessarily the will of the majority, however, although minorities have to subordinate themselves to it without question. Little noticed before the French Revolution, Rousseau's dogmatic concept of the general will appealed greatly to democrats and nationalists after 1789. The concept has also been used since 1789 by many dictators, who have claimed that they, rather than some momentary majority of the voters, represent the general will and thus the true interests of the sovereign masses.

THE SOCIAL SETTING OF THE ENLIGHTENMENT

The philosophes were splendid talkers as well as effective writers. Indeed, sparkling conversation in private homes spread Enlightenment ideas to Europe's upper middle class and aristocracy. Paris set the example, and other French cities and European capitals followed. In Paris a number of talented and often rich women presided over regular social gatherings of the great and near-great in their elegant drawing rooms, or salons. There, a d'Alembert and a Fontenelle could exchange witty, uncensored observations on literature, science, and philosophy with great aristocrats, wealthy middle-class financiers, high-ranking officials, and noteworthy foreigners. These intellectual salons practiced the equality the philosophes preached. They were open to all men and women with good manners, provided only that they were famous or talented, rich or important. More generally, the philosophes championed greater rights and expanded education for women, arguing that the subordination of females was an unreasonable prejudice and the sign of a barbaric society.

One of the most famous salons was that of Madame Geoffrin, the unofficial godmother of the *Encyclopedia.* Having lost her parents at an early age, the future Madame Geoffrin was married at fifteen by her well-meaning grandmother to a rich and boring businessman of forty-eight. It was the classic marriage of convenience – the poor young girl and the rich old man – and neither side ever pretended that love was a consideration. After dutifully raising her children, Madame Geoffrin sought to break out of her gilded cage as she entered middle age. The very proper businessman's wife became friendly with a neighbor, the marquise de Tencin. In her youth the marquise had been rather infamous as the mistress of the regent of France, but she had settled down to run a salon that counted Fontenelle and the philosopher Montesquieu among its regular guests.

When the marquise died in 1749, Madame Geoffrin tactfully transferred these luminaries to her spacious mansion for regular dinners. At first Madame Geoffrin's husband loudly protested the arrival of this horde of "para-sites." But his wife's will was much stronger than his, and he soon opened his purse and even appeared at the twice-weekly dinners. "Who was that old man at the end of the table who never said anything?" an innocent newcomer asked one evening. "That," replied Madame Geoffrin without the slightest emotion, "was my husband. He's dead."[15]

When M. Geoffrin's death became official, Madame Geoffrin put the large fortune and spacious mansion she inherited to good use. She welcomed the encyclopedists – Diderot, d'Alembert, Fontenelle, and a host of others. She gave them generous financial aid and helped to save their enterprise from collapse, especially after the first eight volumes were burned by the authorities in 1759. She also corresponded with the king of Sweden and Catherine the Great of Russia. Madame Geoffrin was, however, her own woman. She remained a practicing Christian, and would not tolerate attacks on the church in her house. It was said that distinguished foreigners felt they had not seen Paris unless they had been invited to one of her dinners. The plain and long-neglected Madame Geoffrin managed to become the most renowned hostess of the eighteenth century.

There were many other hostesses, but Madame Geoffrin's greatest rival, Madame du Deffand, was one of the most interesting. While Madame Geoffrin was middle-class, pious, and chaste, Madame du Deffand was a skeptic from the nobility who lived fast and easy, at least in her early years. Another difference was that women – mostly highly intelligent, worldly members of the nobility – were fully the equal of men in Madame du Deffand's intellectual salon. Forever pursuing fulfillment in love and life, Madame du Deffand was an accomplished and liberated woman. An exceptionally fine letter writer, she carried on a vast correspondence with

MADAME GEOFFRIN'S SALON   In this stylized group portrait a famous actor reads to a gathering of leading philosophes and aristocrats in 1755. Third from the right presiding over her gathering, is Ma-dame Geoffrin, next to the sleepy ninety-eight-year-old Bernard de Fontenelle. (Malmaison Chateau/ Giraudon)

leading men and women all across Europe. Voltaire was her most enduring friend.

Madame du Deffand's closest female friend was Julie de Lespinasse, a beautiful, talented young woman whom she befriended and made her protégée. The never-acknowledged illegitimate daughter of noble parents, Julie de Lespinasse had a hard youth, but she flowered in Madame du Deffand's drawing room — so much so that she was eventually dismissed by her jealous patroness.

Once again Julie de Lespinasse triumphed.

Her friends gave her money so that she could form her own salon. Her highly informal gatherings — she was not rich enough to supply more than tea and cake — attracted the keenest minds in France and Europe. As one philosophe marveled, "Nowhere was the conversation more brilliant nor better supervised. . . . She could toss out an idea for debate, make her contribution with clarity and sometimes with eloquence, and direct the conversation with the skill of a fairy." Another philosophe wrote:

She could unite the different types, even the most antagonistic, sustaining the conversation by a well-aimed phrase, animating and guiding it at will. . . . Politics, religion, philosophy, news: nothing was excluded. Her circle met daily from five to nine. There one found men of all ranks in the State, the Church, and the Court, soldiers and foreigners, and the leading writers of the day.[16]

Thus in France the ideas of the Enlightenment thrived in a social setting that graciously united members of the intellectual, economic, and social elites. Never before and never again would social and intellectual life be so closely and so pleasantly joined. In such an atmosphere the philosophes and the French nobility and upper middle class increasingly influenced one another. Critical thinking became fashionable, and flourished alongside hopes for human progress through greater knowledge.

ENLIGHTENED ABSOLUTISM

How did the Enlightenment influence political developments? To this important question there is no easy answer. On the one hand, the philosophes were primarily interested in converting people to critical "scientific" thinking and were not particularly concerned with politics. On the other hand, such thinking naturally led to political criticism and interest in political reform. Educated people, who belonged mainly to the nobility and middle class, came to regard political change as both possible and desirable.

Until the American Revolution, however, most Enlightenment thinkers believed that political change should come from above – from the ruler – rather than from below, especially in central and eastern Europe. There were several reasons for this essentially moderate belief. First, royal absolutism was a fact

of life, and the kings and queens of Europe's leading states clearly had no intention of giving up their great powers. Second, the philosophes generally believed that a benevolent absolutism offered the best opportunities for improving society. Critical thinking was turning the art of good government into an exact science. Therefore, it was necessary only to educate and "enlighten" the monarch, who could then swiftly and successfully make good laws and promote human happiness. Third, the philosophes turned toward the rulers because the rulers seemed to be listening. Just as the philosophes and the increasingly receptive upper middle class and nobility influenced one another, so did the philosophes and the "enlightened monarchs" come to form a mutual admiration society. Finally, although the philosophes did not dwell on this fact, they distrusted the masses. Known simply as "the people" in the eighteenth century, the peasant masses and the urban poor were, according to the philosophes, still enchained by the superstitions of the priests. Moreover, violent passions rather than logical thinking guided the people's actions. No doubt the people were maturing, but they were still children in need of firm parental guidance.

Encouraged and instructed by the philosophes, several absolutist rulers of the later eighteenth century tried, to the best of their abilities, to govern in an enlightened manner. The actual programs of these rulers varied greatly. Let us, therefore, examine these monarchs at close range before trying to form any overall judgment regarding the success or failure of enlightened absolutism.

THE "GREATS": FREDERICK OF PRUSSIA AND CATHERINE OF RUSSIA

Just as the French absolutism of Louis XIV had been the model for European rulers in the late seventeenth century, the enlightened absolutism of the French philosophes inspired European monarchs in the second half of the eighteenth century. French was the international language of the educated classes, and the education of future kings and queens across Europe lay in the hands of French tutors espousing Enlightenment ideas. France's cultural leadership was reinforced by the fact that it was still the wealthiest and most populous country in Europe. Thus, absolutist monarchs in several west German and Italian states, as well as in Spain and Portugal, proclaimed themselves more enlightened. By far the most influential of the new-style monarchs were Frederick II of Prussia and Catherine II of Russia, both styled "the Great."

FREDERICK THE GREAT Frederick II, as we have seen (pages 605–606), carried on most of the stern military traditions he inherited from his father. His unprovoked attack on Maria Theresa's Austria in 1740 in order to seize Silesia helped contribute to a generation of warfare and almost resulted in the destruction of Prussia in the Seven Years' War (1756–1763). Yet in spite of his aggression and the philosophes' hatred of war, Frederick II was universally acknowledged as an "enlightened" absolute monarch, for two basic reasons.

First of all, Frederick adopted the cultural outlook of the Enlightenment. He wrote verse in French, delighted in witty conversation, and openly made fun of Christian doctrines. Yet he tolerantly allowed his subjects to believe as they wished in religious and philosophical matters. He also promoted the advancement of knowledge, improving his country's schools and universities.

Second, Frederick tried to improve the lives of his subjects. As he wrote his friend Voltaire: "I must enlighten my people, cultivate their manners and morals, and make them as happy as human beings can be, or as happy as the means at my disposal permit." The legal

system and the bureaucracy were Frederick's primary tools. Prussia's laws were simplified, and judges decided cases quickly and impartially. Prussian officials became famous for their hard work and honesty. After the Seven Years' War ended in 1763, Frederick's government also energetically promoted the reconstruction of agriculture and industry in his war-torn country. In all this Frederick set a good example. He worked hard and lived modestly, claiming that he was "only the first servant of the state." Thus, Frederick justified monarchy in terms of practical results and said nothing of the divine right of kings.

Frederick's dedication to high-minded principles went only so far, however. He never tried to change Prussia's existing social structure. True, he condemned serfdom in the abstract, but he accepted it in practice and did not even free the serfs on his own estates. He accepted the old privileges of the nobility and extended new ones as well. It became practically impossible for a middle-class person to gain a top position in the government. The Junker nobility remained the backbone of the army and the entire Prussian state.

CATHERINE THE GREAT Catherine the Great of Russia (1762–1796) was one of the most remarkable rulers who ever lived, and the philosophes adored her. Catherine was a German princess from Anhalt-Zerbst, a totally insignificant principality sandwiched between Prussia and Saxony. Her father commanded a regiment of the Prussian army, but her mother was related to the Romanovs of Russia, and that proved to be her chance.

Peter the Great had abolished the hereditary succession of tsars so that he could name his successor and thus preserve his policies. This move opened a period of palace intrigue and a rapid turnover of rulers until Peter's youngest daughter Elizabeth came to the Russian throne in 1741. A crude, shrewd woman noted for her hard drinking and hard loving – one of her official lovers was an illiterate shepherd boy – Elizabeth named her nephew Peter heir to the throne and chose Catherine to be his wife in 1744. It was a mismatch from the beginning. The fifteen-year-old Catherine was intelligent and attractive; her husband was stupid and ugly, his face badly scarred by smallpox. Ignored by her childish husband, Catherine carefully studied Russian, endlessly read writers like Bayle and Voltaire, and made friends at court. Soon she knew what she wanted. "I did not care about Peter," she wrote in her *Memoirs,* "but I did care about the crown."[17]

As the old empress Elizabeth approached death, Catherine plotted against her unpopular husband. A dynamic, sensuous woman, Catherine used her powerful sexual desire to good political advantage. She selected as her new lover a tall, dashing young officer named Gregory Orlov, who with his four officer brothers commanded considerable support among the soldiers stationed in St. Petersburg. When Peter came to the throne in 1762, his first act was to withdraw Russian troops from the coalition against the hard-pressed Frederick of Prussia, whom he greatly admired. This decision saved Prussia from certain destruction, but it further alienated the army. Nor did Peter III's attempt to gain support from the Russian nobility by freeing it from compulsory state service succeed. At the end of six months Catherine and the military conspirators deposed Peter III in a palace revolution. Then the Orlov brothers murdered him. The German princess became empress of Russia.

Catherine had drunk deeply at the Enlightenment well. Never questioning the common assumption that absolute monarchy was the best form of government, she set out to rule in an enlightened manner. One of her most enduring goals was to bring the sophisticated culture of western Europe to backward Russia. To do so, she imported Western architects, sculptors, musicians, and intellectuals. She bought masterpieces of Western art in wholesale lots and created one of the best collections in all Europe. Throughout her reign Catherine patronized the philosophes. An enthusiastic letter writer, she corresponded extensively with Voltaire and praised him as "the champion of the human race." When the French government banned the *Encyclopedia,* she offered to publish it in St. Petersburg. She discussed reform with Diderot in St. Petersburg; and when Diderot needed money, she purchased his library for a small fortune but allowed him to keep it during his lifetime. With these and countless similar actions, Catherine skillfully won a good press for herself and for her country in the West. Moreover, this intellectual ruler, who wrote plays and articles and loved good talk, set the tone for the entire Russian nobility. Peter the Great westernized Russian armies, but it was Cahterine who westernized the thinking of the Russian nobility.

Catherine's second goal was domestic reform, and she began her reign with sincere and ambitious projects. Better laws were a major concern. In 1767, she drew up enlightened instructions for the special legislative commission she appointed to prepare a new law code. No new unified code was ever produced, but Catherine did restrict the practice of torture and allowed limited religious toleration. She also tried to improve education and strengthen local government. The philosophes applauded these measures and hoped more would follow.

Such was not the case. In 1773, a simple Cossack soldier named Emelian Pugachev sparked a gigantic uprising of serfs, very much as Stenka Razin had done a century earlier (page 614). Proclaiming himself the true tsar, Pugachev issued "decrees" abolishing serfdom, taxes, and army service. Thousands joined his cause, slaughtering landlords and officials over a vast area of southwestern Russia. Pugachev's hordes eventually proved no match for Catherine's noble-led regular army. Betrayed by his own men, Pugachev was captured and savagely executed.

Pugachev's rebellion was a decisive turning point in Catherine's domestic policy. On coming to the throne she had condemned serfdom in theory, but she was smart enough to realize that any changes would have to be very gradual or else she would quickly follow her departed husband. Pugachev's rebellion put an end to any illusions she might have had about reforming serfdom. The peasants were clearly dangerous, and her empire rested on the support of the nobility. After 1775, Catherine gave the nobles absolute control of their serfs. She extended serfdom into new areas, such as the Ukraine. In 1785, she formalized the nobility's privileged position, freeing them forever from taxes and state service. She also confiscated the lands of the Russian Orthodox church and gave them to favorite officials. Under Catherine the Russian nobility attained its most exalted position, and serfdom entered its most oppressive phase.

Catherine's third goal was territorial expansion, and in this respect she was extremely successful. Her armies subjugated the last descendants of the Mongols, the Crimean Tartars, and began the conquest of the Caucasus.

Her greatest coup by far was the partitioning of Poland. Poland had failed to build a strong absolutist state. For decades all important decisions had required the unanimous agreement of every Polish noble, which meant that nothing could ever be done. When be-

CATHERINE THE GREAT *Intelligent, pleasure-loving, and vain, Catherine succeeded in bringing Russia closer to western Europe than ever before. (John R. Freeman)*

tween 1768 and 1772 Catherine's armies scored unprecedented victories against the Turks and thereby threatened to disturb the balance of power between Russia and Austria in eastern Europe, Frederick of Prussia obligingly came forward with a deal. He proposed that Turkey be let off easily, and that Prussia, Austria, and Russia each "compensate" itself by taking a gigantic slice of Polish territory. Catherine jumped at the chance. The first partition of Poland took place in 1772. Two more partitions, in 1793 and 1795, gave all three powers more Polish territory, and the kingdom of Poland simply vanished from the map (see Map 18.1).

Expansion helped Catherine keep the nobility happy, for it provided her vast new lands to give to her faithful servants. Expansion also helped Catherine reward her lovers, of whom twenty-one have been definitely identified. Upon all these royal favorites she lavished large estates with many serfs, as if to make sure there were no hard feelings when her interest cooled. Until the end this remarkably talented woman – who always believed that, in spite of her domestic setbacks, she was slowly civilizing Russia – kept her zest for life. Fascinated by a new twenty-two-year-old flame when she was a roly-poly grandmother in her sixties, she happily reported her good fortune to a favorite former lover: "I have come back to life like a frozen fly; I am gay and well."[18]

ABSOLUTISM IN FRANCE AND AUSTRIA

LOUIS XV OF FRANCE   In building French absolutism, Louis XIV successfully drew on the middle class to curb the powers of the nobility. As long as the Grand Monarch lived, the nobility could only grumble and, like the duke of Saint-Simon in his *Memoirs,* scornfully lament the rise of "the vile bourgeoisie." But

when Louis XIV finally died in 1715, to be succeeded by his five-year-old great-grandson Louis XV (1715–1774), the nobility staged a rapid comeback. The duke of Orléans, who governed as regent until 1723, favored the high nobility.

The duke restored to the high court of Paris – the Parlement – the right to "register" and thereby approve the king's decrees. This was a fateful step. By the eighteenth century, the judges of the Parlement of Paris were mostly nobles. Moreover, they actually owned their seats on the bench and passed them as private property from father to son. They could not be replaced by the king. By establishing the right of this intensely aristocratic group to register the king's laws, the duke of Orléans practically destroyed French absolutism.

This result became clear when the heavy expenses of the War of the Austrian Succession (page 606) plunged France into a financial crisis. In 1748, Louis XV appointed a finance minister who decreed a 5 percent income tax on every individual regardless of social status. Exemption from taxation had been one of the most hallowed privileges of the nobility. The nobility immediately exploded in angry indignation, and the Parlement of Paris refused to ratify the new tax. All the other groups that had over time bought or extracted special privileges in taxation – the clergy, the large towns, certain wealthy bourgeoisie – added their voices to the protest. The monarchy retreated; the new tax was dropped. Following the disastrously expensive Seven Years' War the same drama was re-enacted. The government tried to maintain emergency taxes after the war ended. The nobility, effectively led by the Parlement of Paris, protested violently. The government caved in and withdrew the wartime measures in 1764.

Indolent and sensual by nature, more inter-

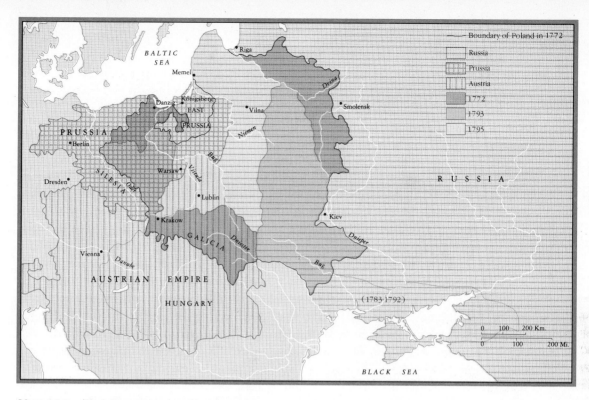

MAP 18.1 THE PARTITION OF POLAND AND
RUSSIA'S EXPANSION, 1772–1795 *Although all
three of the great eastern absolutist states profited from
the division of large but weak Poland, Catherine's
Russia gained the most.*

ested in his many mistresses than in affairs of state, Louis XV finally roused himself for a determined attempt to salvage his absolutist inheritance. "The magistrates," he angrily told the Parlement of Paris in a famous face-to-face confrontation, "are my officers. . . . In my person only does the sovereign power rest."[19] In 1768, Louis appointed a tough career official named René de Maupeou as chancellor and ordered him to end the usurpations of the Paris judges.

Maupeou abolished the Parlement of Paris and exiled its members. He created a new and docile parlement of royal officials and began once again to tax the privileged groups. Most of the philosophes applauded these measures: the sovereign was using his power to introduce badly needed reforms for the common good. And in spite of the predictable cries from the nobility and their privileged allies, Louis XV might have prevailed – if he had lived to a very ripe old age.

But Louis XV died in 1774. The new king, Louis XVI (1774–1792), was a shy twenty-year-old with good intentions. Taking the throne, he is reported to have said: "What I should like most is to be loved."[20] The eager-to-please monarch immediately collapsed before the noble-led opposition, dismissing Maupeou and repudiating the great minister's work. The old Parlement of Paris was reinstated and the old ways were once again embraced. Royal absolutism, enlightened or otherwise, no longer existed in France. The country was drifting toward renewed financial crisis and political upheaval.

JOSEPH II OF AUSTRIA In some ways Joseph II (1780–1790) of Austria was the most spectacular enlightened absolutist of all. Named co-regent with his mother, the empress Maria Theresa, in 1765 but able to exercise little influence on her policies of gradual reform, Joseph sought to make up for lost time after her death. Determined to improve the life of the people, he saw the nobility and the clergy as the chief obstacles to this goal.

In a series of revolutionary decrees Joseph attacked the privileged groups head-on. He abolished serfdom and gave the peasants secure tenure of their land. He taxed all groups equally. Establishing complete religious toleration even for atheists, Joseph took education out of the hands of the Catholic church. He granted equal civil rights to Protestants and Jews. To accomplish this revolution from above, Joseph strengthened the central state and tried to erase the old provincial differences. Although guided to a considerable extent by very personal beliefs, Joseph demonstrated that Enlightenment ideas had revolutionary social and political implications if pushed to their logical extreme.

Joseph II was a heroic but colossal failure. He encountered opposition from all the privileged groups. His top officials and local bureaucrats, who were of necessity drawn largely from the nobility since the middle class was small and weak, subverted his program at every turn. Hungary and other parts of the empire rose up in open revolt. Joseph died prematurely at forty-nine, a broken and disillusioned man. His brother Leopold (1790–1792) came to the throne and was forced to cancel almost all of Joseph's revolutionary edicts in order to re-establish order. The nobles won back most of their traditional privileges, and the peasants lost most of their gains. Once again peasants were required to do forced labor for their lords. After Leopold's death in 1792, the reaction born of the French Revolution swept away the rest of Joseph's progressive measures.

AN OVERALL EVALUATION

In spite of their differences, the leading monarchs of the later eighteenth century all clearly believed that they were acting on the principles of the Enlightenment. The philosophes generally agreed with this assessment and cheered them onward. It is now possible to evaluate the enlightened absolutists and understand what they did and did not do.

The enlightened monarchs, especially Catherine and Frederick, encouraged and spread the cultural values of the Enlightenment. Perhaps this was their greatest achievement. Skeptical in religion and intensely secular in basic orientation, they unabashedly accepted the here-and-now and sought their happiness in the enjoyment of it. At the same time they were proud of their intellectual accomplishments and good taste, and they supported knowledge, education, and the arts. No wonder the philosophes felt the monarchs were kindred spirits.

The enlightened absolutists also tried to make life better for their subjects by enacting needed reforms. They had some successes, notably in Prussia and in the general area of the law and religious toleration. Yet cautious Frederick, ambitious Catherine, lazy Louis XV, and radical Joseph II all ended up with modest results. The life of the masses remained very hard in the eighteenth century. Everywhere the gap between the privileged nobility and the heavily burdened people remained as great as ever.

Some historians have concluded that the enlightened absolutists were not really sincere in their reform efforts. This interpretation, however, fits only in some instances. It probably applies to Catherine after Pugachev's rebellion, but it does not explain the failure of the fanatically committed Joseph II. It ignores Frederick's genuine concern for his subjects. It overlooks Louis XV's all-out effort to curb the Parlement of Paris and tax the nobility during Maupeou's administration. For a better explanation of the limited accomplishments of enlightened absolutism, one must look beyond motives to the structure of political and social power.

Chapters 16 and 17 have described how European monarchs dramatically strengthened their authority in the later seventeenth and early eighteenth centuries. With the striking exceptions of England, Holland, and Poland, European rulers created absolutist states. Arbitrarily and without consent, they raised standing armies, waged war, and imposed new taxes. In doing so, absolutist monarchs like Louis XIV and the Great Elector of Prussia reduced some of the power of the nobility, the only group besides themselves that really mattered politically.

Yet royal absolutism went only so far. It never touched the social and economic privileges of the nobility in any fundamental way. Indeed, nobles in eastern Europe often succeeded in working out very advantageous compromises: in return for accepting the monarch's greater control over the state, they won greater control over their peasants and the towns. The power of even the most absolute monarch was still balanced and restrained by the social and economic power of the nobles. Thus, the social and economic reforms of enlightened absolutists were of necessity limited and superficial: powerful nobilities simply would not permit radical measures to succeed.

More fundamentally, monarchs as a group were partners with the nobility and could not seriously support antinoble reforms for very long. Monarchy and nobility were like the husband and wife in an old-fashioned marriage. They loved and quarreled, cooperated

ENLIGHTENMENT CULTURE *was elegant, intellectual, and international. This painting shows the seven-year-old Austrian child prodigy, Wolfgang Amadeus Mozart (1756–1791), playing his own composition while his older sister sings and his father plays the violin. The elder Mozart displayed his children in the houses of leading aristocrats all across Europe. (Musée Condé de Chantilly/Giraudon)*

and changed; but they always knew they were joined together forever for better or worse. European monarchs and nobles were privileged groups in a society that used hierarchy and inequality as its basic organizing principles. Both appealed primarily to tradition to justify their inherited position, and the great privileges of one could hardly be secure without those of the other. No wonder that when monarchs built their absolutist states they normally turned to nobles to lead their armies and expanded bureaucracies. And if Louis XIV quite exceptionally preferred middle-class officials, Louis XV and Louis XVI did not: between 1714 and 1789, all but three of France's ministers were titled nobles.

The great eighteenth-century philosophe and aristocrat Montesquieu summed it all up in one famous line: "No monarchy, no nobility; no nobility, no monarchy."[21] Montesquieu was right: for centuries monarchy and nobility flourished together in Europe, and together they later declined and have almost disappeared.

———◆———

This chapter has focused on the complex development of a new world-view in Western civilization. This new view of the world was essentially critical and secular, drawing its inspiration from the Scientific Revolution and crystallizing in the Enlightenment.

The decisive breakthroughs in astronomy and physics in the seventeenth century, which demolished the imposing medieval synthesis of Aristotelian philosophy and Christian theology, had only limited practical consequences despite the expectations of scientific enthusiasts like Bacon. Yet the impact of new scientific knowledge on intellectual life became great. Interpreting scientific findings and Newtonian laws in an antitraditional, antireligious manner, the French philosophes of the Enlightenment extolled the superiority of rational, critical thinking. This new method, they believed, promised not just increased knowledge but even the discovery of the fundamental laws of human society, which could then be implemented by enlightened rulers for the general good. Although social and political realities frustrated these fond hopes, the philosophes succeeded in spreading their radically new world-view. That was a momentous accomplishment.

NOTES

1. H. Butterfield, *The Origins of Modern Science,* Macmillan, New York, 1951, p. viii.

2. Quoted by A. G. R. Smith, *Science and Society in the Sixteenth and Seventeenth Centuries,* Harcourt Brace Jovanovich, New York, 1972, p. 97.

3. Quoted by Butterfield, p. 47.

4. Quoted by Smith, p. 100.

5. Ibid. pp. 115–116.

6. Ibid. p. 120.

7. A. R. Hall, *From Galileo to Newton, 1630–1720,* Harper & Row, New York, 1963, p. 290.

8. Quoted by R. K. Merton, *Science, Technology and Society in Seventeenth-Century England,* rev. ed., Harper & Row, New York, 1970, p. 164.

9. Quoted by P. Hazard, *The European Mind, 1680–1715,* Meridian Books, Cleveland, 1963, pp. 304–305.

10. Ibid., pp. 11–12.

11. Quoted by L. M. Marsak, ed., *The Enlightenment,* John Wiley & Sons, New York, 1972, p. 56.

12. Quoted by G. L. Mosse et al., eds., *Europe in Review,* Rand McNally, Chicago, 1964, p. 156.

13. M. F. Arouet de Voltaire, *Oeuvres complètes,* Firmin-Didot Frères, Fils et Cie, Paris, 1875, VIII, 188–90.

14. Quoted by P. Gay, "The Unity of the Enlightenment," *History* 3 (1960):25.

15. Quoted by G. P. Gooch, *Catherine the Great and Other Studies,* Archon Books, Hamden, Conn., 1966, p. 112.

16. Ibid., p. 149.

17. Ibid., p. 15.

18. Ibid., p. 53.

19. Quoted by R. R. Palmer, *The Age of Democratic Revolution,* Princeton University Press, Princeton, 1959, 1.95–96.

20. Quoted by G. Wright, *France in Modern Times,* Rand McNally, Chicago, 1960, p. 42.

21. Quoted by P. Anderson, *Lineages of the Absolutist State,* LLB, London, 1974, p. 298.

SUGGESTED READING

The first three authors cited in the Notes – H. Butterfield (rev. ed. 1966), A. G. R. Smith, and A. R. Hall – have written excellent general interpretations of the scientific revolution. Another good study is M. Boas, *The Scientific Renaissance, 1450–1630* (1966), which is especially insightful on the influence of magic on science and on Galileo's trial. T. Kuhn, *The Copernican Revolution* (1957), is the best treatment of the subject; his *The Structure of Scientific Revolutions* (1962) is a challenging, much-discussed attempt to understand major breakthroughs in scientific thought over time. Two stimulating books on the ties between science and society in history are B. Merton, *Science, Technology and Society in Seventeenth-Century England,* rev. ed. (1970), and J. Ben-David, *The Scientist's Role in Society* (1971). E. Andrade, *Sir Isaac Newton* (1958), is a good, short biography, which may be compared with F. Manuel, *The Religion of Isaac Newton* (1974).

P. Hazard, *The European Mind, 1680–1715* (1963), is a classic study of the formative years of Enlightenment thought, and his *European Thought in the Eighteenth Century* (1954) is also recommended. A famous, controversial interpretation of the Enlightenment is that of C. Becker, *The Heavenly City of the Eighteenth Century Philosophes* (1932), which maintains that the world-view of medieval Christianity continued to influence the philosophes greatly. Becker's ideas are discussed interestingly in R. O. Rockwood, ed., *Carl Becker's Heavenly City Revisited* (1958). P. Gay has written several major studies on the Enlightenment: *Voltaire's Politics* (1959) and *The Party of Humanity* (1971) are two of the best. I. Wade, *The Structure and Form of the French Enlightenment* (1977), is a recent major synthesis. F. Baumer's *Religion and the Rise of Skepticism* (1969), H. Payne's *The Philosophes and the People* (1976), K. Rogers's *Feminism in Eighteenth-Century England* (1982), and J. B. Bury's old but still exciting *The Idea of Progress* (1932) are stimulating studies of important aspects of Enlightenment thought. Above all, one should read some of the philosophes and let them speak for themselves. Two good anthologies are C. Brinton, ed., *The Portable Age of Reason* (1956), and F. Manuel, ed., *The Enlightenment* (1951). Voltaire's most famous and very amusing novel, *Candide,* is highly recommended, as are S. Gendzier, ed., *Denis Diderot: The Encyclopedia: Selections* (1967) and A. Wilson's biography, *Diderot* (1972).

In addition to the works mentioned in the Suggested Reading for Chapters 16 and 17, the monarchies of Europe are carefully analyzed in Charles Tilly, ed., *The Formation of National States in Western Europe* (1975), and ably discussed in J. Gagliardo, *Enlightened Despotism* (1967), both of which have useful bibliographies. Other recommended studies on the struggle for power and reform in different countries are: F. Ford, *Robe and Sword* (1953), which traces the resurgence of the French nobility after the death of Louis XIV; R. Herr, *The Eighteenth-Century Revolution in Spain* (1958), on the impact of Enlightenment thought in Spain; and P. Bernard, *Joseph II* (1968). In addition to I. de Madariaga's masterful *Russia in the Age of Catherine the Great* (1981) and D. Ransel's solid *Politics of Catherinean Russia* (1975), the ambitious reader should look at A. N. Radishchev, *A Journey From St. Petersburg to Moscow* (trans. 1958), a famous 1790 attack on Russian serfdom and an appeal to Catherine the Great to free the serfs, for which Radishchev was exiled to Serbia.

The culture of the time may be approached through A. Cobban, ed., *The Eighteenth Century,* (1969), a richly illustrated work with excellent essays, and C. B. Behrens, *The Ancien Régime* (1967). C. Rosen, *The Classical Style: Haydn, Mozart, Beethoven* (1972), brilliantly synthesizes music and society, as did Mozart himself in his great opera *The Marriage of Figaro,* where the count is the buffoon and his servant the hero.

CHAPTER 19

THE EXPANSION OF EUROPE IN THE

EIGHTEENTH CENTURY

THE WORLD OF ABSOLUTISM and aristocracy, a combination of raw power and elegant refinement, was a world apart from that of ordinary men and women. For the overwhelming majority of the population in the eighteenth century, life remained a struggle with poverty and uncertainty, with the landlord and the tax collector. In 1700, peasants on the land and artisans in their shops lived little better than had their ancestors in the Middle Ages. Only in science and thought, and there only among a few intellectual leaders, had Western society succeeded in going beyond the great achievements of the High Middle Ages, achievements that in turn owed so much to Greece and Rome.

Everyday life was a struggle because the men and women of European societies, despite their best efforts, still could not produce very much by modern standards. Ordinary people might work like their beasts in the fields, and they often did, but there was seldom enough good food, warm clothing, and decent housing. Life went on; history went on. The wars of religion ravaged Germany in the seventeenth century; Russia rose to become a Great Power; the kingdom of Poland simply disappeared; monarchs and nobles continuously jockeyed for power and wealth. In 1700 or even 1750, the idea of progress – the idea that the lives of great numbers of people could improve substantially here on earth – was still only the dream of a small elite in their fashionable salons.

Yet the economic basis of European life was beginning to change. In the course of the eighteenth century, the European economy emerged from the long crisis of the seventeenth century, responded to challenges, and began to expand once again. Some areas were more fortunate than others. The rising Atlantic powers – Holland, France, and above all England – and their colonies led the way.

Agriculture and industry, trade and population, began a surge comparable to that of the eleventh- and twelfth-century springtime of European civilization. Only this time development was not cut short. This time the response to new challenges led toward one of the most influential developments in human history, the Industrial Revolution, which we shall consider in Chapter 22. What were the causes of this renewed surge? Why were the fundamental economic underpinnings of European society beginning to change, and what were the dimensions of those changes? How did these changes affect people and their work? These are the questions this chapter will try to answer.

AGRICULTURE AND THE LAND

At the end of the seventeenth century the economy of Europe was agrarian, as it had been for several hundred years. With the possible exception of Holland, at least 80 percent of the people of all western European countries drew their livelihoods from agriculture. In eastern Europe the percentage was considerably higher.

Men and women lavished their attention on the land, plowing fields and sowing seed, reaping harvests and storing grain. The land repaid these efforts, year after year yielding up the food and most of the raw materials for industry that made life possible. Yet the land was stingy. Even in a rich agricultural region like the Po valley in northern Italy, every bushel of wheat sown yielded on average only five or six bushels of grain at harvest during the seventeenth century. The average French yield in the same period was somewhat less. Such yields were barely more than those attained in fertile, well-watered areas in the

FARMING THE LAND   Agricultural methods in Europe changed very slowly from the Middle Ages to the early eighteenth century. This realistic picture from Diderot's Encyclopedia *has striking similarities with agricultural scenes found in medieval manuscripts. (Photo: Caroline Buckler)*

thirteenth century or in ancient Greece. By modern standards output was distressingly low. (For each bushel of wheat seed sown today on fertile land with good rainfall, an American or French farmer can expect roughly forty bushels of produce.) In 1700, European agriculture was much more ancient and medieval than modern.

If the land was stingy, it was also capricious. In most regions of Europe in the six-teenth and seventeenth centuries, harvests were poor, or even failed completely, every eight or nine years. The vast majority of the population who lived off the land might survive a single bad harvest by eating less and drawing on their reserves of grain. But when the land combined with persistent bad weather – too much rain rotting the seed, or drought withering the young stalks – the result was catastrophic. Meager grain reserves were soon exhausted, and the price of grain soared. Provisions from other areas with better harvests were hard to obtain.

In such crisis years, which periodically stalked Europe in the seventeenth and even into the eighteenth century, a terrible tightening knot in the belly forced people to tragic substitutes – the "famine foods" of a desperate population. People gathered chestnuts and stripped bark in the forests; they cut dandelions and grass; and they ate these substitutes to escape starvation. In one community in Norway in the early 1740s people were forced to wash dung from the straw in old manure piles in order to bake a pathetic substitute for bread. Even cannibalism occurred in the seventeenth century.

Such unbalanced and inadequate food in famine years made people weak and extremely susceptible to illness and epidemics. The eating of rough material like bark or grass – really unfit for human consumption – resulted in dysentery and intestinal ailments of every kind. Influenza and smallpox preyed with particular savagery upon populations weakened by famine. In famine years the number of deaths soared far above normal. A third of a village's population might disappear in a year or two. The 1690s were as dismal as many of the worst periods of earlier times. One county in Finland, which was probably typical of the entire country, lost fully 28 percent of its inhabitants in 1696 and 1697. Certain well-studied villages in the Beauvais region of northern France suffered a similar fate. In preindustrial Europe the harvest was the real king, and the king was seldom generous and often cruel.

To understand why Europeans produced barely enough food in good years and occasionally agonized through years of famine throughout the later seventeenth century, one must follow the plowman, his wife, and his children into the fields to observe their battle for food and life. There the ingenious pattern of farming that Europe had developed in the Middle Ages, a pattern that allowed fairly large numbers of people to survive but could never produce material abundance, was still dominant.

THE OPEN-FIELD SYSTEM

The greatest accomplishment of medieval agriculture was the open-field system of village agriculture developed by European peasants (page 321). That system divided the land to be cultivated by the peasants into a few large fields, which were in turn cut up into long narrow strips. The fields were open and the strips were not enclosed into small plots by fences or hedges. An individual peasant family – if it were fortunate – held a number of strips scattered throughout the various large fields. The land of those who owned but did not till, primarily the nobility, the clergy, and wealthy townsmen, was also in scattered strips. The peasant community farmed each large field as a community, with each family following the same pattern of plowing, sowing, and harvesting in accordance with tradition and the village leaders.

The ever-present problem was exhaustion of soil. If the community planted wheat year after year in a field, the nitrogen in the soil was soon depleted and crop failure was certain. Since the supply of manure for fertilizer was limited, the only way for the land to recover its life-giving fertility was for a field to lie fallow for a period of time. In the early Middle Ages a year of fallow was alternated with a year of cropping, so that half the land stood idle in a given year. With time three-year rotations were introduced, especially on more fertile lands. This system permitted a year of wheat or rye to be followed by a year

of oats or beans, and only then by a year of fallow. Even so, only awareness of the tragic consequences of continuous cropping forced undernourished populations to let a third (or a half) of their land lie constantly idle, especially when the fallow had to be plowed two or three times a year to keep down the weeds.

Traditional rights reinforced the traditional pattern of farming. In addition to rotating the field crops in a uniform way, villages maintained open meadows for hay and natural pasture. These lands were "common" lands, set aside primarily for the draft horses and oxen so necessary in the fields, but open to the cows and pigs of the village community as well. After the harvest, the people of the village also pastured their animals on the wheat or rye stubble. In many places such pasturing followed a brief period, also established by tradition, for the gleaning of grain. Poor women would go through the fields picking up the few single grains that had fallen to the ground in the course of the harvest. The subject of a great nineteenth-century painting, *The Gleaners* by Jean François Millet, this backbreaking work by hardworking but impoverished women meant quite literally the slender margin of survival for some people in the winter months.

In the age of absolutism and nobility, state and landlord continued to levy heavy taxes and high rents as a matter of course. In so doing they stripped the peasants of much of their meager earnings. The level of exploitation varied. Conditions for the rural population were very different in different areas.

Generally speaking, the peasants of eastern Europe were worst off. As we have seen in Chapter 17, they were still serfs, bound to their lords in hereditary service. Though serfdom in eastern Europe in the eighteenth century had much in common with medieval serfdom in central and western Europe, it was, if anything, harsher and more oppressive. In much of eastern Europe there were no real limitations on the amount of forced labor the lord could require, and five or six days of unpaid work per week on the lord's land was not uncommon. Well into the nineteenth century individual Russian serfs and serf families were regularly sold with and without land. Serfdom was often very close to slavery. The only compensating factor in much of eastern Europe was that, as with slavery, differences in well-being among serfs were slight. In Russia, for example, the land available to the serfs for their own crops was divided among them almost equally.

Social conditions were considerably better in western Europe. Peasants were generally free from serfdom. In France and western Germany they owned land and could pass it on to their children. Yet life in the village was unquestionably hard, and poverty was the great reality for most people. For the Beauvais region of France at the beginning of the eighteenth century, it has been carefully estimated that in good years and bad only a tenth of the peasants could live satisfactorily off the fruits of their landholdings. Owning less than half of the land, the peasants had to pay heavy royal taxes, the church's tithe, and dues to the lord, as well as set aside seed for the next season. Left with only half of their crop for their own use, they had to toil and till for others and seek work far afield in a constant scramble for a meager living. And this was in a country where peasants were comparatively well off. The privileges of the ruling elites weighed heavily upon the people of the land.

AGRICULTURAL REVOLUTION

The social conditions of the countryside were well entrenched. The great need was for new farming methods that would enable Europeans to produce more and eat more. The idle fields were the heart of the matter. If peasants could replace the fallow with crops, they could increase the land under cultivation by 50 percent. So remarkable were the possibilities and the results that historians have often spoken of the progressive elimination of the fallow, which occurred slowly throughout Europe from the late seventeenth century onward, as an Agricultural Revolution.

This agricultural revolution, which took longer than historians used to believe, was a great milestone in human development. The famous French scholar Marc Bloch, who gave his life in the resistance to the Nazis in World War Two, summed it up well: "The history of the conquest of the fallow by new crops, a fresh triumph of man over the earth that is just as moving as the great land clearing of the Middle Ages, [is] one of the noblest stories that can be told."[1]

Because grain crops exhaust the soil and make fallowing necessary, the secret to eliminating the fallow lies in alternating grain with certain nitrogen-storing crops. Such crops not only rejuvenate the soil even better than fallowing, but give more produce as well. The most important of these land-reviving crops are peas and beans, root crops such as turnips and potatoes, and clovers and grasses. In the eighteenth century, peas and beans were old standbys; turnips, potatoes, and clover were newcomers to the fields. As time went on, the number of crops that were systematically rotated grew, and farmers developed increasingly sophisticated patterns of rotation to suit different kinds of soils. For example, farmers in French Flanders near Lille in the late eighteenth century used a ten-year rotation, alternating a number of grain, root, and hay crops on a ten-year schedule. Continuous experimentation resulted in more scientific farming.

Improvements in farming had multiple effects. The new crops made ideal feed for animals. Because peasants and larger farmers had more fodder – hay and root crops – for the winter months, they could build up their small herds of cattle and sheep. More animals meant more meat and better diets for the people. More animals also meant more manure for fertilizer, and therefore more grain for bread and porridge. The vicious cycle in which few animals meant inadequate manure, which meant little grain and less fodder, which led to fewer animals, and so on, could be broken. The cycle became positive: more animals meant more manure, which meant more grain and more fodder, which meant more animals.

Technical progress had its price, though. The new rotations were scarcely possible within the traditional framework of open fields and common rights. A farmer who wanted to experiment with new methods would have to control the village's pattern of rotation. To wait for the entire village to

agree might mean waiting forever. The improving, innovating agriculturalist needed to enclose and consolidate his scattered holdings into a compact fenced-in field. In doing so, he would also seek to enclose his share of the natural pasture, the "common." Yet the common rights were precious to many rural people. Thus when the small landholders and the poor could effectively oppose the enclosure of the open fields, they did so. Only powerful social and political pressures could overcome the traditionalism of rural communities.

The old system of unenclosed open fields and the new system of continuous rotation coexisted in Europe for a very long time. In large parts of central Russia, for example, the old system did not disappear until after the Communist Revolution in 1917. It could also be found in much of France and Germany in the early years of the nineteenth century. Indeed, until the end of the eighteenth century the promise of the new system was extensively realized only in the Low Countries – present-day Holland, Belgium, and French Flanders – and in England.

THE LEADERSHIP OF THE LOW COUNTRIES AND ENGLAND

The new methods of the agricultural revolution originated in the Low Countries. The vibrant, dynamic middle-class society of seventeenth-century republican Holland was the most advanced in Europe in many areas of human endeavor. In shipbuilding and navigation, in commerce and banking, in drainage and agriculture, the people of the Low Countries, especially the Dutch, provided models the jealous English and French sought to copy or to cripple.

By the middle of the seventeenth century, intensive farming was well established throughout much of the Low Countries. Enclosed fields, continuous rotation, heavy manuring, and a wide variety of crops: all these innovations were present. Agriculture was highly specialized and commercialized. The same skills that grew turnips produced flax to be spun into linen for clothes and tulip bulbs to lighten the heart with their beauty. The fat cattle of Holland, so beloved by Dutch painters, gave the most milk in Europe. Dutch cheeses were already world-renowned.

The reasons for early Dutch leadership in farming were basically threefold. In the first place, since the end of the Middle Ages the Low Countries had been one of the most densely populated areas in Europe. Thus, in order to feed themselves and provide employment, the Dutch were forced at an early date to seek maximum yields from their land, and to increase it through the steady draining of marshes and swamps. Even so, they had to import wheat from Poland and eastern Germany.

The pressure of population was connected with the second cause, the growth of towns and cities in the Low Countries. Stimulated by commerce and overseas trade, Amsterdam grew from 30,000 to 200,000 in its golden seventeenth century. The growth of urban population provided Dutch peasants with good markets for all they could produce and allowed each region to specialize efficiently in what it did best.

Finally, there was the quality of the people. Oppressed neither by grasping nobles nor warminded monarchs, the Dutch could develop their potential in a free and capitalistic society. The Low Countries became "the Mecca of foreign agricultural experts who came . . . to see Flemish agriculture with their own eyes, to write about it and to propagate its methods in their home lands."[2]

The English were the best students. Indeed,

they were such good students that it is often forgotten that they had teachers at all. Drainage and water control was one subject in which they received instruction. Large parts of seventeenth-century Holland had once been sea and sea marsh, and the efforts of centuries had made the Dutch the world's leaders in the skills of drainage. In the first half of the seventeenth century, Dutch experts made a great contribution to draining the extensive marshes, or fens, of wet and rainy England.

The most famous of these Dutch engineers, Cornelius Vermuyden, directed one large drainage project in Yorkshire and another in Cambridgeshire. The project in Yorkshire was supported by Charles I and financed by a group of Dutch capitalists, who were to receive one-third of all land reclaimed in return for their investment. Despite local opposition, Vermuyden drained the land by means of a large canal – his so-called Dutch river – and settlers cultivated the new fields in the Dutch fashion. In the Cambridge fens, Vermuyden and his Dutch workers eventually reclaimed forty thousand acres, which were then farmed intensively in the Dutch manner. Although all these efforts were disrupted in the turbulent 1640s by the English Civil War, Vermuyden and his countrymen largely succeeded. A swampy wilderness was converted into thousands of acres of some of the best land in England. On such new land, where traditions and common rights were not established, farmers introduced new crops and new rotations fairly easily.

Dutch experience was also important to Viscount Charles Townsend (1674-1738), one of the pioneers of English agricultural improvement. This lord from the upper reaches of the English aristocracy learned about turnips and clover while serving as English ambassador to Holland. In the 1710s, he was using these crops in the sandy soil of his large

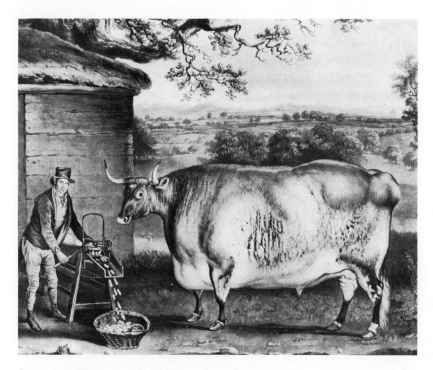

SELECTIVE BREEDING meant bigger livestock and more meat on English tables. This gigantic champion, one of the new improved shorthorn breed, was known as the Newbus Ox. Such great fat beasts were pictured in the press and praised by poets. (Institute of Agricultural History and Museum of English Rural Life, University of Reading)

estates in Norfolk in eastern England, already one of the most innovative agricultural areas in the country. When Lord Charles retired from politics in 1730 and returned to Norfolk, it was said that he spoke of turnips, turnips, and nothing but turnips. This led some wit to nickname his lordship "Turnip" Townsend. But Townsend had the last laugh. Draining extensively, manuring heavily, and sowing crops in regular rotation without fallowing, the farmers who leased Townsend's lands produced larger crops. They and he earned higher incomes. Those who had scoffed reconsidered. By 1740, agricultural improvement in various forms had become something of a craze among the English aristocracy.

Jethro Tull (1674–1741), part crank and part genius, was another important English innovator. A true son of the early Enlightenment, Tull constantly tested accepted ideas about farming in an effort to develop better methods through empirical research. He was especially enthusiastic about horses, in preference to slower-moving oxen. He also advocated sowing seed with drilling equipment, rather than scattering it by hand. Drilling distributed seed evenly and at the proper depth. There were also improvements in livestock, inspired in part by the earlier successes of English country gentlemen in breeding ever-faster horses for the races and fox hunts that were their passions. Selective breeding of ordinary livestock was a marked improvement over the old pattern, which has been graphically described as little more than "the haphazard union of nobody's son with everybody's daughter."

By the mid-eighteenth century, English agriculture was in the process of a radical and desirable transformation. The eventual result was that by 1870 English farmers produced 300 percent more food than they had produced in 1700, although the number of people working the land had increased by only 14 percent. This great surge of agricultural production provided food for England's rapidly growing urban population. It was a tremendous achievement.

THE DEBATE OVER ENCLOSURE

To what extent was technical progress a product of social injustice? There are sharp differences of opinion among historians. The oldest and still widely accepted view is that the powerful ruling class, the English landowning aristocracy, enclosed the open fields and divided up the common pasture in such a way that poor people lost their small landholdings and were pushed off the land. The large landowners controlled Parliament, which made the laws. They had Parliament pass hundreds of "enclosure acts," each of which authorized the fencing of open fields in a given district and abolished common rights there. Small farmers who had little land and cottagers who had only common rights could no longer make a living. They lost position and security and had to work for a large landowner for wages or else move to town in search of work. This view, popularized by Karl Marx in

the nineteenth century, has remained dear to many historians to this day.

There is some validity to this idea, but more recent studies have shown that the harmful consequences of enclosure in the eighteenth century have often been exaggerated. In the first place, as much as half of English farmland was already enclosed by 1750. A great wave of enclosure of English open fields into sheep pastures had already occurred in the sixteenth and early seventeenth centuries, in order to produce wool for the thriving textile industry. In the later seventeenth and early eighteenth centuries, many open fields were enclosed fairly harmoniously by mutual agreement among all classes of landowners in English villages. Thus, parliamentary enclosure, the great bulk of which occurred after 1760 and particularly during the Napoleonic wars early in the nineteenth century, only completed a process that was in full swing. Nor did an army of landless farm laborers appear only in the last years of the eighteenth century. Much earlier, and certainly by 1700, there were perhaps two landless agricultural workers in England for every self-sufficient farmer. In 1830, after the enclosures were complete, the proportion of landless laborers on the land was not much greater.

Indeed, by 1700 a highly distinctive pattern of landownership existed in England. At one extreme were a few large landowners, at the other a large mass of laborers who held little land and worked for wages. In between stood two other groups: small self-sufficient farmers who owned their own land, and substantial tenant farmers who rented land from the big landowners and hired wage laborers. Yet the small independent English farmers were already declining in number by 1700, and they continued to do so in the eighteenth century.

They could not compete with the profit-minded, market-oriented tenant farmers.

The tenant farmers, many of whom had formerly been independent owners, were the key to mastering the new methods of farming. Well financed by the large landowners, the tenant farmers fenced fields, built drains, and improved the soil with fertilizers. Such improvements actually increased employment opportunities for wage workers in the countryside. So did new methods of farming, for land was farmed more intensively without the fallow, and new crops like turnips required more care and effort. Thus, enclosure did not force people off the land by eliminating jobs. By the early nineteenth century, rural poverty was often greatest in those areas of England where the new farming techniques had not been adopted.

THE BEGINNING OF THE POPULATION EXPLOSION

There was another factor that affected the existing order of life and forced economic changes in the eighteenth century. This was the remarkable growth of European population, the beginning of the "population explosion." This population explosion continued in Europe until the twentieth century, by which time it was affecting non-Western areas of the globe. What caused the growth of population, and what did the challenge of more mouths to feed and more hands to employ do to the European economy?

LIMITATIONS ON POPULATION GROWTH

Many commonly held ideas about population in the past are wrong. One such mistaken idea

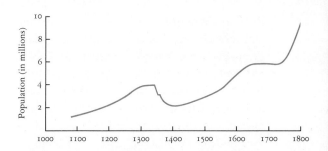

FIGURE 19.1 THE GROWTH OF POPULATION IN ENGLAND 1000–1800. *England is a good example of both the uneven increase of European population before 1700 and the third great surge of growth, which began in the eighteenth century. (Source: E. A. Wrigley,* Population and History, *McGraw-Hill, New York, 1969)*

is that people always married young and had large families. A related error is the belief that past societies were so ignorant that they could do nothing to control their numbers and that population was always growing too fast. On the contrary, until 1700 the total population of Europe grew slowly much of the time, and by no means constantly (see Figure 19.1). There were very few occurrences of the frightening increases so common in many poor countries today.

In seventeenth-century Europe, births and deaths, fertility and mortality, were in a crude but effective balance. The birthrate – annual births as a proportion of the population – was fairly high, but far lower than it would have been if all women between ages fifteen and forty-five had been having as many children as biologically possible. The death rate in normal years was also high, though somewhat lower than the birthrate. As a result, the population grew modestly in normal years at a rate of perhaps .5 to 1 percent, or enough to double the population in 70 to 140 years. This is, of course, a generalization encompassing many different patterns. In areas like Russia and colonial New England, where there was a great deal of frontier to be settled, the annual rate of increase might well exceed 1 percent. In a country like France, where the land had long been densely settled, the rate of increase might be less than .5 percent.

Although population growth of even 1 percent per year is fairly modest by the standards of many African and Latin American countries today – some of which are growing at about 3 percent annually – it will produce a very large increase over a long period. An annual increase of even 1 percent will result in sixteen times as many people in three hundred years. Such gigantic increases simply did not occur in agrarian Europe before the eighteenth century. In certain abnormal years and tragic periods, many more people died than were born. Total population fell sharply, even catastrophically. A number of years of modest growth would then be necessary to make up for those who had died in such an abnormal year. Such savage increases in deaths helped check total numbers and kept the population from growing rapidly for long periods.

The grim reapers of demographic crisis were famine, epidemic disease, and war. Famine, the inevitable result of poor farming methods and periodic crop failures, was particularly murderous because it was accompanied by disease. With a brutal one-two punch, famine stunned and weakened a population and disease finished it off. Disease could also ravage independently, even in years of adequate harvests. Bubonic plague returned again and again to Europe for more than three hundred years after the ravages of the Black Death in the fourteenth century. Not until the late 1500s did most countries have as many people as in the early 1300s. Epidemics of dysentery and smallpox also operated independently of famine.

War was another scourge. The indirect effects were more harmful than the organized killing. War spread disease. Soldiers and camp followers passed venereal disease through the countryside to scar and kill. Armies requisitioned scarce food supplies for their own use and disrupted the agricultural cycle. The Thirty Years' War (pages 530–536) witnessed all possible combinations of distress. In the German states, the number of inhabitants declined by more than *two-thirds* in some large areas and by at least one-third almost everywhere. The Thirty Years' War reduced total German population by no less than 40 percent. But numbers inadequately convey the dimensions of such human tragedy. One needs the vision of the artist. The great sixteenth-century artist, Albrecht Dürer, captured the horror of demographic crisis in his chilling woodcut *The Four Horsemen of the Apocalypse*. Death, accompanied by his trusty companions War, Famine, and Disease, takes his merciless ride of destruction. The narrow victory of life over death that prevails in normal times is being undone.

THE NEW PATTERN OF THE EIGHTEENTH CENTURY

In the eighteenth century, the population of Europe began to grow markedly. This increase in numbers occurred in all areas of Europe – western and eastern, northern and southern, dynamic and stagnant. Growth was especially dramatic after about 1750, as Figure 19.2 shows.

Although it is certain that Europe's population grew greatly, it is less clear why. Recent painstaking and innovative research in population history has shown that, because population grew everywhere, it is best to look for general factors and not those limited to individual countries or areas. What, then, caused fewer people to die or, possibly, more babies to be born? In some kinds of families women may have had more babies than before. Yet the basic cause was a decline in mortality – fewer deaths.

The bubonic plague mysteriously disappeared. Following the Black Death in the fourteenth century, plagues remained a part of the European experience, striking again and again with savage force, particularly in towns. As a German writer of the early sixteenth century noted, "It is remarkable and astonishing that the plague should never wholly cease, but it should appear every year here and there, making its way from one place to another. Having subsided at one time, it returns within a few years by a circuitous route."3

As late as 1720, a ship from Syria and the Levant, where plague was ever-present, brought the monstrous disease to Marseilles. In a few weeks, forty thousand of the city's ninety thousand inhabitants died. The epidemic swept southern France, killing a third, a half, even three-fourths of those in the larger towns. Once again an awful fear swept across Europe. But the epidemic passed, and that was the last time plague fell upon western and central Europe. The final disappearance of plague was due in part to stricter measures of quarantine in Mediterranean ports and along the Austrian border with Turkey. Human carriers of plague were carefully isolated. Chance and plain good luck were more important, however.

It is now understood that bubonic plague is, above all, a disease of rats. The epidemic spreads among humans only after they are bitten by fleas that have fed on diseased rats. More precisely, it is the black rat that spreads major epidemics, for the black rat's flea is the principal carrier of the plague bacillus. After 1600, for reasons unknown, a new rat of Asiatic origin – the brown, or wander, rat –

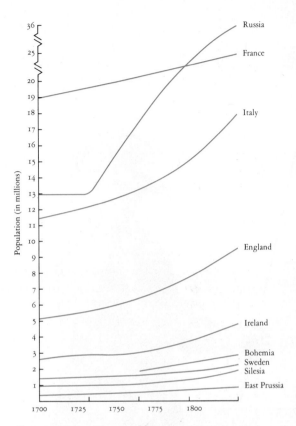

FIGURE 19.2   THE INCREASE OF POPULATION IN EUROPE IN THE EIGHTEENTH CENTURY   *The number of people grew substantially all across Europe. France's large population continued to support French political and intellectual leadership, but Russia emerged as Europe's most populous state.*

began to drive out and eventually eliminate its black competitor. In the words of a noted authority, "This revolution in the animal kingdom must have gone far to break the lethal link between rat and man."4 Although the brown rat also contracts the plague, another kind of flea is its main parasite. That flea carries the plague poorly and, for good measure, has little taste for human blood.

Advances in medical knowledge did not contribute much to reducing the death rate in the eighteenth century. The most important advance in preventive medicine in this period was inoculation against smallpox. Yet this great improvement was long confined mainly to England and probably did little to reduce deaths throughout Europe until the later part of the century. Improvements in the water supply and sewerage promoted somewhat better public health and helped reduce such diseases as typhoid and typhus in some urban areas of western Europe. Yet those early public-health measures had only limited general significance. In fact, changes in the rat population helped millions of human beings in their struggle against untimely death much more than did doctors and medical science in the eighteenth century.

Human beings were more successful in their efforts to safeguard the supply of food and protect against famine. The eighteenth century was a time of considerable canal and road building in western Europe. These advances in transportation, which were among the more positive aspects of enlightened absolutism, lessened the impact of local crop failure and famine. Emergency supplies could be brought in. The age-old spectacle of localized starvation became less frequent. Wars became more gentlemanly and less destructive than in the seventeenth century and spread fewer epidemics. New foods, particularly the potato, were introduced. Potatoes served as an important alternative source of vitamins A and C for the poor, especially when the grain crops were skimpy or failed. In short, population grew in the eighteenth century primarily because years of abnormal death rates were less catastrophic. Famines, epidemics, and wars continued to occur, but their severity moderated.

DOCTOR IN PROTECTIVE CLOTHING *Most doctors believed, incorrectly, that poisonous smells carried the plague. This doctor has placed strong-smelling salts in his "beak" to protect himself against deadly plague vapors. (Germanisches Nationalmuseum, Nuremberg)*

The growth of population in the eighteenth century cannot be interpreted as a sign of human progress. Plague faded from memory, transport improved, people learned to eat potatoes; yet for the common people life was still a great struggle. Indeed, for many it was more of a struggle than ever, for in many areas increasing numbers led to overpopulation. A serious imbalance between the number of people and the economic opportunities available to them developed. There was only so much land available, and tradition slowed the adoption of better farming methods. Therefore, agriculture could not provide enough work for the rapidly growing labor force. Everyone might work steadily during planting and harvesting, when many hands were needed, but at other times rural people were often unemployed or underemployed.

Growing numbers increased the challenge of poverty, especially the severe poverty of the rural poor. People in the countryside had to look for new ways to make a living. Even if work outside of farming paid poorly, small wages were better than none. Thus, in the eighteenth century growing numbers of people and acute poverty were even more influential than new farming methods as forces for profound changes in agrarian Europe.

THE GROWTH OF COTTAGE INDUSTRY

The growth of population contributed to the development of industry in rural areas. The poor in the countryside were eager to supplement their earnings from agriculture with other types of work, and capitalists from the city were eager to employ them, often at lower wages than urban workers commanded.

Manufacturing with hand tools in peasant cottages grew markedly in the eighteenth century. Rural industry became a crucial feature of the European economy.

To be sure, peasant communities had always made some clothing, processed some food, and constructed some housing for their own use. But in the High Middle Ages peasants did not produce manufactured goods on a large scale for sale in a market; they were not handicraft workers as well as farmers and field laborers. Industry in the Middle Ages was dominated and organized by urban craft guilds and urban merchants, who jealously regulated handicraft production and sought to maintain it as an urban monopoly. By the eighteenth century, however, the pressures of rural poverty and the need for employment in the countryside had proved too great, and a new system was expanding lustily. The new system had many names. Sometimes referred to as cottage industry or domestic industry, it has often been called "the putting-out system."

THE PUTTING-OUT SYSTEM

The two main participants in the putting-out system were the merchant-capitalist and the rural worker. The merchant lent or put out raw materials – raw wool, for example – to several cottage workers. Those workers processed the raw material in their own homes, spinning and weaving the wool into cloth in this case, and returned the cloth to the merchant. The merchant paid the outworkers for their work by the piece and proceeded to sell the finished product. There were endless variations on this basic relationship. Sometimes rural workers would buy their own materials and work as independent producers before they sold to the merchant. The relative im-

RURAL INDUSTRY IN ACTION *This French engraving suggests just how many things could be made in the countryside with simple hand tools. These men are making inexpensive but long-lasting wooden shoes, which were widely worn by the poor. (Photo: Caroline Buckler)*

portance of earnings from the land and from industry varied greatly for handicraft workers. In all cases, however, the putting-out system was a kind of capitalism. Merchants needed large amounts of capital, which they held in the form of goods being worked up and sold in distant markets. They sought to make profits and increase their capital in their businesses.

The putting-out system was not perfect, but it had definite advantages. It increased employment in the countryside and provided the poor with additional income. Since pro-

duction in the countryside was unregulated, workers and merchants could change procedures and experiment as they saw fit. Because they did not need to meet rigid guild standards, which maintained quality but discouraged the development of new methods, cottage industry became capable of producing many kinds of goods. Textiles, all manner of knives, forks, and housewares, buttons and gloves, clocks and musical instruments could be produced quite satisfactorily in the countryside. Luxury goods for the rich, such as exquisite tapestries and fine porcelain, de-

manded special training, close supervision, and centralized workshops. Yet such goods were as exceptional as those who used them. The skills of rural industry were sufficient for everyday articles.

Rural manufacturing did not spread across Europe at an even rate. It appeared first in England and developed most successfully there, particularly for the spinning and weaving of woolen cloth. By 1500, half of England's textiles were being produced in the countryside. By 1700, English industry was generally more rural than urban and heavily reliant on the putting-out system. Continental countries developed rural industry more slowly.

In France at the time of Louis XIV, Colbert had revived the urban guilds and used them as a means to control the cities and collect taxes (page 565). But the pressure of rural poverty proved too great. In 1762 the special privileges of urban manufacturing were abolished in France, and the already-developing rural industries were given free rein from then on. The royal government in France had come to believe that the best way to help the poor

THE WOOLEN INDUSTRY   *Many steps went into the production of woolen cloth. This illustration suggests schematically how cottage workers combed out the fleece of the sheep and made raw wool ready for spinning.*

peasants was to encourage the growth of cottage manufacturing. Thus in France, as in Germany and other areas, the later part of the eighteenth century witnessed a remarkable expansion of rural industry in certain densely populated regions. The pattern established in England was spreading to the Continent.

THE TEXTILE INDUSTRY

Throughout most of history, until at least the nineteenth century, the industry that has always employed the most people has been textiles. The making of linen, woolen, and eventually cotton cloth was the typical activity of cottage workers engaged in the putting-out system. A look inside the cottage of the English rural textile worker illustrates a way of life as well as an economic system.

The rural worker lived in a small cottage, with tiny windows and little space. Indeed, the worker's cottage was often a single room that served as workshop, kitchen, and bedroom. There were only a few pieces of furni-

ture, of which the weaver's loom was by far the largest and most important. That loom had changed somewhat in the early eighteenth century, when John Kay's invention of the flying shuttle enabled the weaver to throw the shuttle back and forth between the threads with one hand. Aside from that improvement, however, the loom was as it had been for much of history. In the cottage there were also spinning wheels, tubs for dyeing cloth and washing raw wool, and carding pieces to comb and prepare the raw material.

These different pieces of equipment were necessary because cottage industry was first and foremost a family enterprise. All the members of the family helped in the work, so that "every person from seven to eighty (who retained their sight and who could move their hands) could earn their bread," as one eighteenth-century English observer put it.[5] While the women and children prepared the raw material and spun the thread, the man of the house wove the cloth. There was work for everyone, even the youngest. After the dirt was beaten out of the raw cotton, it had to be thoroughly cleaned with strong soap in a tub, where tiny feet took the place of the agitator in a washing machine. George Crompton, the son of Samuel Crompton, who in 1784 invented the mule for cotton spinning, recalled that "soon after I was able to walk I was employed in the cotton manufacture.... My mother tucked up my petticoats about my waist, and put me into the tub to tread upon the cotton at the bottom."[6] Slightly older children and aged relatives carded and combed the cotton or wool, so the woman and the older daughter she had taught could spin it into thread. Each member had a task. The very young and very old worked in the family unit as a matter of course.

There was always a serious imbalance in this family enterprise: the work of four or five spinners was needed to keep one weaver steadily employed. Therefore, the wife and the husband had constantly to try to find more thread and more spinners. Widows and unmarried women – those "spinsters" who spun for their living – were recruited by the wife. Or perhaps the weaver's son went off on horseback to seek thread. The need for more thread might even lead the weaver and his wife to become small capitalist employers. At the end of the week, when they received the raw wool or cotton from the merchant-manufacturer, they would put out some of this raw material to other cottages. The following week they would return to pick up the thread and pay for the spinning – spinning that would help keep the weaver busy for a week until the merchant came for the finished cloth.

Relations between workers and employers were not always harmonious. In fact, there was continuous conflict. An English popular song written about 1700, called "The Cloth-ier's Delight, or the Rich Men's Joy and The Poor Men's Sorrow," has the merchant boasting of his countless tricks used to "beat down wages":

We heapeth up riches and treasure great store
Which we get by griping and grinding the poor.
And this is a way for to fill up our purse
Although we do get it with many a curse.[7]

There were constant disputes over weights of materials and the quality of the cloth. Merchants accused workers of stealing raw materials, and weavers complained that merchants delivered underweight bales. Both were right; each tried to cheat the other, even if only in self-defense.

There was another problem, at least from the merchant-capitalist's point of view. Rural labor was cheap, scattered, and poorly organized. For these reasons it was hard to control. Cottage workers tended to work in spurts. After they got paid on Saturday afternoon, the men in particular tended to drink and carouse for two or three days. Indeed, Monday was called "holy Monday" because inactivity was so religiously observed. By the end of the week the weaver was probably working feverishly to make his quota. But if he did not succeed, there was little the merchant could do. When times were good and the merchant could easily sell everything produced, the weaver and his family did fairly well and were particularly inclined to loaf, to the dismay of the capitalist. Thus, in spite of its virtues, the putting-out system in the textile industry had definite shortcomings. There was an imbalance between spinning and weaving. Labor relations were often poor, and the merchant was unable to control the quality of the cloth or the schedule of the workers. The merchant-capitalist's search for new methods of production became intense.

BUILDING THE ATLANTIC ECONOMY

In addition to agricultural improvement, population pressure, and expanding cottage industry, the expansion of Europe in the eighteenth century was characterized by the growth of world trade. Spain and Portugal revitalized their empires and began drawing more wealth from renewed development. Yet, once again, the countries of northwestern Europe – the Netherlands, France, and above all Great Britain – benefited most. Great Britain (formed in 1707 by the union of England and Scotland in a single kingdom), became the leading maritime power. In the eighteenth century, British ships and merchants succeeded in dominating long-distance trade, particularly the fast-growing intercontinental trade across the Atlantic Ocean. The British played the critical role in building a fairly unified Atlantic economy, which offered remarkable opportunities for them and their colonists.

MERCANTILISM AND COLONIAL WARS

Britain's commercial leadership in the eighteenth century had its origins in the mercantilism of the seventeenth century (page 565). European mercantilism was a system of economic regulations aimed at increasing the power of the state. As practiced by a leading advocate like Colbert under Louis XIV, mercantilism aimed particularly at creating a favorable balance of foreign trade in order to increase a country's stock of gold. A country's gold holdings served as an all-important treasure chest, to be opened periodically to pay for war in a violent age.

Early English mercantilists shared these views. As Thomas Mun, a leading merchant and early mercantilist, wrote in *England's Treasure by Foreign Trade* (1630, published 1664): "The ordinary means therefore to increase our wealth and treasure is by foreign trade wherein we must observe this rule; to sell more to strangers yearly than we consume of theirs in value." What distinguished English mercantilism was the unusual idea that governmental economic regulations could and should serve the private interests of individuals and groups as well as the public needs of the state. As Josiah Child, a very wealthy brewer and director of the East India Company, put it, in the ideal economy "Profit and Power ought jointly to be considered."[8]

In France and other continental countries, by contrast, seventeenth-century mercantilists generally put the needs of the state far above those of businessmen and workers. And they seldom saw a possible harmony of public and private interests for a common good.

The result of the English desire to increase both its military power and private wealth was the mercantile system of the Navigation Acts. Oliver Cromwell established the first of these laws in 1651, and the restored monarchy of Charles II extended them further in 1660 and 1663; the Navigation Acts of the seventeenth century were not seriously modified until 1786. The acts required that most goods imported from Europe into England and Scotland be carried on British-owned ships with British crews, or on ships of the country producing the article. Moreover, these laws gave British merchants and shipowners a virtual monopoly on trade with the colonies. The colonists were required to ship their products – sugar, tobacco, and cotton – on British ships, and to buy almost all of their European goods from the mother country. It was believed that these economic regulations would provide British merchants and workers with profits and employment, and colonial

THE PORT OF DIEPPE IN 1754 This painting by Joseph Vernet (1714–1789) was one of fourteen in a famous series of port scenes commissioned by Louis XV. Vernet's work admirably captures the spirit and excitement of French maritime expansion. (Louvre. Photo: Bulloz)

plantation owners and farmers with a guaranteed market for their products. And the state would develop a shipping industry with a large number of tough, experienced deepwater seamen, who could be drafted when necessary into the Royal Navy to protect the island nation.

The Navigation Acts were a form of economic warfare. Their initial target was the Dutch, who were far ahead of the English in shipping and foreign trade in the mid-seventeenth century. The Navigation Acts, in conjunction with three Anglo-Dutch wars between 1652 and 1674, did seriously damage Dutch shipping and commerce. The thriving Dutch colony of New Amsterdam was seized

in 1664 and rechristened New York. By the later seventeenth century, when the Dutch and the English became allies to stop the expansion of France's Louis XIV, the Netherlands was falling behind England in shipping, trade, and colonies.

As the Netherlands followed Spain into relative decline, France emerged as a far more serious rival. Rich in natural resources and endowed with a population three or four times that of England, France too was intent upon building a powerful fleet and a worldwide system of rigidly monopolized colonial trade. And France, aware that Great Britain coveted large parts of Spain's American empire, was determined to revitalize its Spanish ally. Thus, from 1701 to 1763, Britain and France were locked in a series of wars to decide, in part, which nation would become the leading maritime power and claim a lion's share of the profits of Europe's overseas expansion (see Map 19.1).

The first round was the War of the Spanish Succession (page 570), which started when Louis XIV declared his willingness to accept the Spanish crown willed to his grandson. Besides upsetting the continental balance of power, a union of France and Spain threatened to destroy the British colonies in North America. The thin ribbon of British settlements along the Atlantic seaboard from Massachusetts to the Carolinas would be surrounded by a great arc of Franco-Spanish power stretching south and west from French Canada to Florida and the Gulf of Mexico (see Map 19.1). Defeated by a great coalition of states after twelve years of fighting, Louis XIV was forced in the Peace of Utrecht (1713) to cede Newfoundland and Nova Scotia to Britain. Spain was compelled to give Britain control of the lucrative West African slave trade – the so-called *asiento* – and to let Britain send one ship of merchandise into the Spanish colonies annually, through Porto Bello on the Isthmus of Panama.

France was still a mighty competitor. The War of the Austrian Succession (1740–1748), which started when Frederick the Great of Prussia seized Silesia from Austria's Maria Theresa, became a world war, including Anglo-French conflicts in India and North America. Indeed, it was the seizure of French territory in Canada by New England colonists that forced France to sue for peace in 1748, and to accept gladly a return to the territorial situation existing in North America at the beginning of the war. France's Bourbon ally, Spain, defended itself surprisingly well and Spain's empire remained intact.

MAP 19.1 *THE ECONOMY OF THE ATLANTIC BASIN IN 1701* *The growth of trade encouraged both economic development and military conflict in the Atlantic Basin.*

This inclusive stand-off helped set the stage for the Seven Years' War (1756–1763). In central Europe, Austria's Maria Theresa sought to win back Silesia and crush Prussia, thereby re-establishing the Habsburgs' traditional leadership in German affairs. She almost succeeded, skillfully winning France – the Habsburgs' long-standing enemy – and Russia to her cause. Yet the Prussian state survived, saved by its army and the sudden decision of the newly crowned Peter III of Russia to withdraw from the war in 1762.

Outside of Europe, the Seven Years' War was the decisive round in the Franco-British competition for colonial empire. Led by William Pitt (1708–1788), whose grandfather had made a fortune as a trader in India, the British concentrated on using superior sea power to destroy the French fleet and choke off French commerce around the world. Capturing Quebec in 1759 and winning a great naval victory at Quiberon Bay, the British also strangled France's valuable sugar trade with its Caribbean islands and smashed French forts in India. After Spain entered the war on France's side in 1761, the surging British temporarily occupied Havana in Cuba, and Manila in the Philippines. With the Treaty of Paris (1763), France lost all its possessions on the mainland of North America. French Canada as well as French territory east of the Mississippi River passed to Britain, and France ceded Louisiana to Spain as compensation for Spain's loss of Florida to Britain. France also gave up most of its holdings in India, opening the way to British dominance on the subcontinent. By 1763, British naval power, built in large part upon the rapid growth of the British shipping

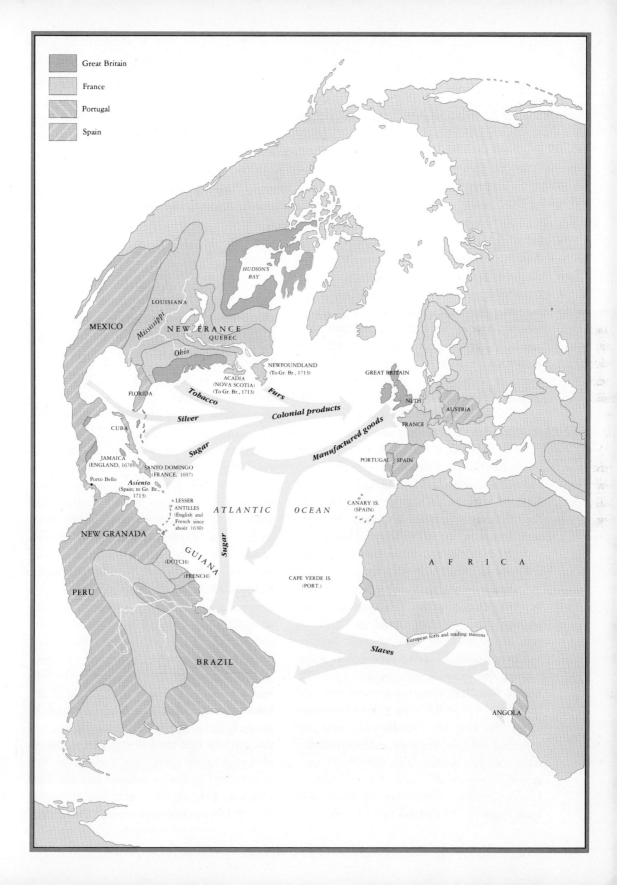

Great Britain

France

Portugal

Spain

HUDSON'S
BAY

LOUISIANA

MEXICO

NEW FRANCE

QUEBEC

Mississippi

Ohio

NEWFOUNDLAND
(To Gr. Br., 1713)

GREAT BRITAIN

ACADIA
(NOVA SCOTIA)
(To Gr. Br., 1713)

Furs

NETH.

FLORIDA

Tobacco

FRANCE

Silver

Colonial products

Manufactured goods

CUBA

Sugar

JAMAICA
(ENGLAND, 1670)

SANTO DOMINGO
(FRANCE, 1697)

PORTUGAL   SPAIN

Porto Bello

Asiento
(Spain; to Gr. Br.,
1713)

AUSTRIA

LESSER
ANTILLES
(English and
French since
about 1630)

ATLANTIC   OCEAN

CANARY IS.
(SPAIN)

NEW GRANADA

GUIANA

(DUTCH)

(FRENCH)

Sugar

AFRICA

PERU

CAPE VERDE IS.
(PORT.)

BRAZIL

European forts and trading stations

Slaves

ANGOLA

industry after the passage of the Navigation Acts, had triumphed decisively. Britain had realized its goal of monopolizing a vast trading and colonial empire for its exclusive benefit.

LAND AND WEALTH IN NORTH AMERICA

Of all Britain's colonies, those on the North American mainland proved most valuable in the long run. The settlements along the Atlantic coast provided an important outlet for surplus population, so that migration abroad limited poverty in England, Scotland, and northern Ireland. The settlers also benefited. In the mainland colonies, they had privileged access to virtually free and unlimited land. The availability of farms was a precious asset in preindustrial Europe, where agriculture was the main source of income and prestige.

The possibility of having one's own farm was particularly attractive to ordinary men and women from the British Isles. Land in England was already highly concentrated in the hands of the nobility and gentry in 1700, and became more so with agricultural improvement in the eighteenth century. White settlers who came to the colonies as free men and women, or as indentured servants pledged to work seven years for their passage, or as prisoners and convicts, could obtain their own farms on easy terms as soon as they had their personal freedom. Many poor white farmers also came to the mainland from the British West Indies, crowded out of those islands by the growth of big sugar plantations using black slave labor. To be sure, life in the mainland colonies was hard and rough, especially on the frontier. Yet the settlers succeeded in paying little or no rent to grasping landlords, and taxes were very low. Unlike the great majority of European peasants, who had

to accept high rents and taxes as part of the order of things, American farmers could keep most of what they managed to produce.

The availability of land made labor expensive in the colonies. This basic fact, rather than any repressive aspects of the Navigation Acts, limited the growth of industry in the colonies. As the Governor of New York put it in 1767:

The price of labor is so great in this part of the world that it will always prove the greatest obstacle to any manufacturers attempting to set up here, and the genius of the people in a country where everyone can have land to work upon leads them so naturally into agriculture that it prevails over every other occupation.[9]

The advantage for colonists was in farming, and farm they did.

Cheap land and scarce labor were also critical factors in the growth of slavery in the southern colonies. By 1700 British indentured servants were carefully avoiding the Virginia lowlands, where black slavery was spreading, and by 1730 the large plantations there had gone over completely to black slaves. Slave labor permitted an astonishing tenfold increase in tobacco production between 1700 and 1774, and created a wealthy aristocratic planter class in Maryland and Virginia.

In the course of the eighteenth century, the farmers of New England and, particularly, the middle colonies of Pennsylvania and New Jersey began to produce more food than they needed. They exported ever more food stuffs, primarily to the West Indies. There the owners of the sugar plantations came to depend on the mainland colonies for grain and dried fish to feed their slaves. The plantation owners, whether they grew tobacco in Virginia and Maryland or sugar in the West Indies, had the exclusive privilege of supplying the British Isles with their products. Eng-

1651–1663	British Navigation Acts create the mercantile system, which is not seriously modified until 1786
1652–1674	Three Anglo-Dutch wars damage Dutch shipping and commerce
1664	New Amsterdam is seized and renamed New York
1701–1714	War of the Spanish Succession
1713	Peace of Utrecht: Britain wins parts of Canada from France and control of the west African slave trade from Spain
1740–1748	War of the Austrian Succession, resulting in no change in territorial holdings in North America
1756–1763	Seven Years' War (known in North America as the French and Indian War), a decisive victory for Britain
1763	Treaty of Paris: Britain receives all French territory on the North American mainland and achieves dominance in India

lishmen could not buy cheaper sugar from Brazil, nor were they allowed to grow tobacco in the home islands. Thus the colonists too had their place in the protective mercantile system of the Navigation Acts. The American shipping industry grew rapidly in the eighteenth century, for example, because colonial shippers enjoyed the same advantages as their fellow British citizens in the mother country.

The abundance of almost free land resulted in a rapid increase in the colonial population in the eighteenth century. In a mere three-quarters of a century after 1700, the white population of the mainland colonies multiplied a staggering ten times as immigrants arrived and colonial couples raised large families. In 1774, 2.2 million whites and 330,000 blacks inhabited what would soon become the independent United States.

Rapid population growth did not reduce

the settlers to poverty. On the contrary, agricultural development resulted in fairly high standards of living for mainland colonists, in eighteenth-century terms. There was also an unusual degree of economic equality, by the standards of Europe. Few people were extremely rich and few were extremely poor. Most remarkable of all, on the eve of the American Revolution, the *average* white man or woman in the mainland British colonies probably had the highest income and standard of living in the world. It has been estimated that between 1715 and 1775 the real income of the average American was increasing about 1 percent per year per person, almost two-thirds as fast as it increased with massive industrialization between 1840 and 1959. When one considers that between 1775 and 1840 Americans experienced no improvement in their standard of living, it is clear just how

TOBACCO *was a key commodity in the Atlantic trade.* *This engraving from 1775 shows a merchant and his* *slaves preparing a cargo for sail. (The British Mu-* *seum)*

much the colonists benefited from hard work and the mercantile system created by the Navigation Acts.[10]

THE GROWTH OF FOREIGN TRADE

England also profited greatly from the mercantile system. Above all, the rapidly growing and increasingly wealthy agricultural populations of the mainland colonies provided an expanding market for English manufactured goods. This situation was extremely fortunate, for England in the eighteenth century was gradually losing, or only slowly expanding, its sales to many of its traditional European markets. However, rising demand for manufactured goods from North America, as well as from the West Indies, Africa, and Latin America, allowed English cottage industry to continue to grow and diversify. Merchant-capitalists and manufacturers found

new and exciting opportunities for profit and wealth.

Since the late Middle Ages, England had relied very heavily on the sale of woolen cloth in foreign markets. Indeed, as late as 1700 woolen cloth was the only important manufactured good exported from England, and fully 90 percent of it was sold to Europeans. In the course of the eighteenth century, the states of continental Europe were trying to develop their own cottage textile industries in an effort to deal with rural poverty and overpopulation. Like England earlier, these states adopted protectionist, mercantilist policies. They tried by means of tariffs and other measures to exclude competing goods from abroad, whether English woolens or the cheap but beautiful cotton calicos the English East India Company brought from India and sold in Europe.

France had already closed its markets to the

English in the seventeenth century. In the eighteenth century, German states purchased much less woolen cloth from England and encouraged cottage production of coarse, cheap linens, which became a feared competitor in all of central and southern Europe. By 1773, England was selling only about two-thirds as much woolen cloth to northern and western Europe as it had in 1700. The decline of sales to the Continent meant that the English economy badly needed new markets and new products in order to develop and prosper.

Protected colonial markets came to the rescue. More than offsetting stagnating trade with Europe, they provided a great stimulus for many branches of English manufacturing. The markets of the Atlantic economy led the way, as may be seen in Figure 19.3. English exports of manufactured goods to continental Europe increased very modestly, from roughly £2.9 million in 1700 to only £3.3 million in 1773. Meanwhile, sales of manufactured products to the Atlantic economy – primarily the mainland colonies of North America and the West Indian sugar islands, with an important assist from West Africa and Latin America – soared from £500,000 to £3.9 million. Sales to other "colonies" – Ireland and India – also rose substantially in the eighteenth century.

English exports became much more balanced and diversified. To America and Africa went large quantities of metal items – axes to frontiersmen, firearms, chains for slaveowners. There were also clocks and coaches, buttons and saddles, china and furniture, musical instruments and scientific equipment, and a host of other things. By 1750, half the nails made in England were going to the colonies. Foreign trade became the bread-and-butter of some industries.

Thus, the mercantile system formed in the seventeenth century to attack the Dutch and

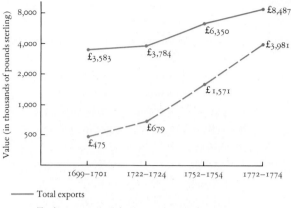

— Total exports

– – – Total exports to the Atlantic economy: North America, West Indies, Spanish America, and West Africa

Note: Data exclude English re-exports.

FIGURE 19.3 EXPORTS OF ENGLISH MANUFACTURED GOODS 1700–1774 *While trade with Europe stagnated after 1700, English exports to Africa and the Americas boomed and greatly stimulated English economic development. (Source: R. Davis, "English Foreign Trade, 1700–1774," Economic History Review, 2d series, 15 (1962); 302–303)*

win power and profit for England continued to shape trade in the eighteenth century. The English concentrated in their hands much of the demand for manufactured goods from the growing Atlantic economy. The pressure of demand from three continents upon the cottage industry of one medium-sized country heightened the efforts of English merchant-capitalists to find new and improved ways to produce more goods. By the 1770s, England stood on the threshold of radical industrial change, as we shall see in Chapter 22.

REVIVAL IN COLONIAL LATIN AMERICA

When the last Spanish Habsburg, the feeble-minded Charles II, died in 1700 (page 570), Spain was "little less cadaverous than its defunct master."[11] Its vast empire lay before

Europe awaiting dismemberment. Yet, in one of those striking reversals with which history is replete, Spain revived. The empire held together and even prospered, while a European-oriented landowning aristocracy enhanced its position in colonial society.

Spain recovered in part because of better leadership. Louis XIV's grandson, who took the throne as Philip V (1700–1746), brought new men and fresh ideas with him from France, and rallied the Spanish people to his Bourbon dynasty in the long War of the Spanish Succession. When peace was restored, a series of reforming ministers reasserted royal authority, overhauling state finances and strengthening defense. To protect the colonies, they restored Spain's navy to a respectable third place in Europe behind Great Britain and France. Philip's ministers also promoted the economy with vigorous measures that included a gradual relaxation of the state monopoly on colonial trade. The able Charles III (1759–1788), a truly enlightened monarch, further extended economic and administrative reform.

Revitalization in Madrid had positive results in the colonies. The colonies succeeded in defending themselves from numerous British attacks and even increased in size. Spain received Louisiana from France in 1763, and missionaries and ranchers extended Spanish influence all the way to northern California.

Political success was matched by economic improvement. After declining markedly in the seventeenth century, silver mining recovered in Mexico and Peru. Output quadrupled between 1700 and 1800, when Spanish America accounted for half of world silver production. Ever a risky long shot at sudden riches, silver mining encouraged a gambler's attitude toward wealth and work. The big profits of the lucky usually went into land. Silver mining also encouraged food production for large mining camps and gave the creoles – people of Spanish blood born in the Americas – the means to purchase more and more European luxuries and manufactured goods. A class of wealthy merchants arose to handle this flourishing trade, which often relied on smuggled goods from Great Britain. As in British North America, industry remained weak, although workshops employing forced Indian labor made Mexican and Peruvian wool into coarse fabrics for the Latin American masses. Spain's colonies were an important part of the Atlantic economy.

Economic development strengthened the creole elite, which came to rival the top government officials dispatched from Spain. As in most preindustrial societies, land was the main source of wealth. In contrast to British America but like Spain and eastern Europe, creole estate owners controlled much of the land. Small independent farmers were rare.

The Spanish crown had given large holdings to the conquering pioneers and their followers, and beginning in the late sixteenth century many big tracts of state land were sold to favored settlers. Thus, although the Crown decreed that Indian communities were to retain the use of their tribal lands, a class of big landholders grew up in sparsely settled regions and in the midst of the defeated Indian populations.

The Spanish settlers strove to become a genuine European aristocracy, and they largely succeeded. As good aristocrats, they believed that work in the fields was the proper occupation of a depressed, impoverished peasantry. The defenseless Indians suited their needs. As the Indian population recovered in numbers, slavery and periodic forced labor gave way to widespread debt peonage from 1600 onward. Under this system, a planter or rancher would keep his Christianized, increasingly Hispanicized Indians in perpetual debt bondage by periodically advancing food, shelter, and a little money. Debt peonage subjugated the Indians and was a form of agricultural serfdom.

The landowning class practiced primogeniture, passing everything from eldest son to eldest son to prevent fragmentation of land and influence. Also like European nobles, wealthy creoles built ornate townhouses, contributing to the development of a lavish colonial baroque style that may still be seen in Lima, Peru, and Mexico City. The creole elite followed European cultural and intellectual trends. Enlightenment ideas spread to colonial salons and universities, encouraging a questioning attitude and preparing the way for the creoles' rise to political power with the independence movements of the early nineteenth century.

There were also creoles of modest means, especially in the cities, since estate agriculture discouraged small white farmers. (Chile was an exception: since it had few docile Indians to exploit, white settlers had to work their small farms to survive.) The large middle group in Spanish colonies consisted of racially mixed *mestizos,* the offspring of Spanish men and Indian women. The most talented mestizos realistically aspired to join the creoles, for enough wealth and power could make one white. This ambition siphoned off the most energetic mestizos and lessened the build-up of any lower-class discontent. Thus, by the end of the colonial era roughly 20 percent of the population was classified as white and about 30 percent as mestizo. Pure-blooded Indians accounted for most of the remainder, for only on the sugar plantations of Cuba and Puerto Rico did black slavery ever take firm root in Spanish America.

The situation was quite the opposite in Portuguese Brazil. As in the West Indies, enormous numbers of blacks were brought in chains to work the sugar plantations. About half the population of Brazil was of African origin in the early nineteenth century. Even more than in the Spanish territories, the people of Brazil intermingled sexually and culturally. In contrast to North America, where racial lines were hard and fast, at least in theory, colonial Brazil made a virtue of miscegenation and the population grew to include every color in the racial rainbow.

───◆───

While some European intellectual elites were developing a new view of the world in the eighteenth century, Europe as a whole was experiencing a gradual but far-reaching expansion. As agriculture showed signs of modest improvement across the continent, first the Low Countries and then England succeeded in launching the epoch-making Agricultural Revolution. Plague disappeared and the populations of all countries grew significantly, encouraging the progress of cottage industry and merchant capitalism.

Europeans also continued their overseas expansion, fighting for empire and profit and consolidating their hold on the Americas in particular. A revived Spain and its Latin American colonies participated fully in this expansion. As in agriculture and cottage industry, however, England and its empire proved most successful. The English concentrated much of the growing Atlantic trade in their hands, which challenged and enriched English industry and intensified the search for new methods of production. Thus, by the 1770s, England was on the verge of an economic breakthrough fully as significant as the great political upheaval destined to develop shortly in neighboring France.

NOTES

1. M. Bloch, *Les caractères originaux de l'histoire rurale française,* Librarie Armand Colin, Paris 1960, 1.244–245.

2. B. H. Slicher van Bath, *The Agrarian History of Western Europe, A.D. 500–1850,* St. Martin's Press, New York, 1963, p. 240.

3. Quoted in E. E. Rich and C. H. Wilson, eds., *Cambridge Economic History of Europe,* Cambridge University Press, Cambridge, England, 4.74.

4. Ibid., p. 85.

5. Quoted by I. Pinchbeck, *Women Workers and the Industrial Revolution, 1750–1850,* F. S. Crofts, New York, 1930, p. 113.

6. Quoted by S. Chapman, *The Lancashire Cotton Industry,* Manchester University Press, Manchester, 1903, p. 13.

7. Quoted by P. Mantoux, *The Industrial Revolution in the Eighteenth Century,* Harper & Row, New York, 1961, p. 75.

8. Quoted by C. Wilson, *England's Apprenticeship, 1603–1763,* Longmans, Green, London, 1965, p. 169.

9. Quoted by D. Dillard, *Economic Development of the North Atlantic Community,* Prentice-Hall, Englewood Cliffs, N.J., 1967, p. 192.

10. G. Taylor, "America's Growth Before 1840," *Journal of Economic History* 24 (December 1970):427–444.

11. J. Rippy, *Latin America: A Modern History,* rev. ed., University of Michigan Press, Ann Arbor, 1968, p. 97.

SUGGESTED READING

B. H. Slicher van Bath, *The Agrarian History of Western Europe, A.D. 500–1850* (1963), is a wide-ranging general introduction to the gradual transformation of European agriculture, as is M. Bloch's great classic, cited in the Notes, which has been translated as *French Rural History* (1966). J. Blum, *The End of the Old Order in Rural Europe* (1978), is an impressive comparative study. J. de Vries, *The Dutch Rural Economy in the Golden Age, 1500–1700* (1974), skillfully examines the causes of early Dutch leadership in farming, and E. L. Jones, *Agriculture and Economic Growth in England, 1650–1815* (1967), shows the importance of the agricultural revolution for England. Two recommended and complementary studies on landowning nobilities are R. Forster, *The Nobility of Toulouse in the Eighteenth Century* (1960), and G. E. Mingay, *English Landed Society in the Eighteenth Century* (1963). A. Goodwin, ed., *The European Nobility in the Eighteenth Century* (1967), is an exciting group of essays on aristocrats in different countries. R. and E. Forster, eds., *European Society in the Eighteenth Century* (1969), assembles a rich collection of contemporary writing on a variety of economic and social topics. E. L. Ladurie, *The Peasants of Languedoc* (1976), a brilliant and challenging study of rural life in southern France for several centuries, complements J. Goody et al., eds., *Family and Inheritance: Rural Society in Western Europe, 1200–1800* (1976). Life in small-town preindustrial France comes alive in P. Higonnet, *Pont-de-Montvert: Social Structure and Politics in a French Village, 1700–1914* (1971), while O. Hufton deals vividly and sympathetically with rural migration, work, women, and much more in *The Poor in Eighteenth-Century France* (1974). P. Mantoux, *The Industrial Revolution in the Eighteenth Century* (1928), and D. Landes, *The Unbound Prometheus* (1969), provide excellent discussions of the development of cottage industry.

Two excellent multivolume series, *The Cambridge Economic History of Europe,* and C. Cipolla, ed., *The Fontana Economic History of Europe,* cover the sweep of economic developments from the Middle Ages to the present and have extensive bibliographies. In the area of trade and colonial competition, V. Barbour, *Capitalism in Amsterdam* (1963), and C. R. Boxer, *The Dutch Seaborne Empire* (1970), are very interesting on Holland. C. Wilson, *Profit and Power: A Study of England and the Dutch Wars* (1957), is exciting scholarship, as are W. Dorn, *The*

Competition for Empire, 1740–1763 (1963), D. K. Fieldhouse, *The Colonial Empires* (1971), and R. Davies, *The Rise of Atlantic Economies* (1973). R. Pares, *Yankees and Creoles* (1956), is a short, lively work on trade between the mainland colonies and the West Indies. E. Williams, *Capitalism and Slavery* (1966), provocatively argues that slavery provided the wealth necessary for England's industrial development. Another exciting work is J. Nef, *War and Human Progress* (1968), which examines the impact of war on economic and industrial development in European history between about 1500 and 1800 and may be compared with M. Gutmann, *War and Rural Life in the Early Modern Low Countries* (1980). J. Fagg's *Latin America* (1969) provides a good introduction to the colonial period and has a useful bibliography, while C. Haring, *The Spanish in America* (1947), is a fundamental modern study.

Three very fine books on the growth of population are C. Cipolla's short and lively *The Economic History of World Population* (1962); E. A. Wrigley's more demanding *Population and History* (1969); and T. McKeown's scholarly *The Modern Rise of Population* (1977). In addition to works on England cited in the Suggested Reading for Chapter 22, D. George, *England in Transition* (1953), and C. Wilson, *England's Apprenticeship, 1603–1763* (1965), are highly recommended. The greatest novel of eighteenth-century English society is Henry Fielding's unforgettable *Tom Jones,* although Jane Austen's novels about country society, *Emma* and *Pride and Prejudice* are not far behind.

CHAPTER 20

THE LIFE OF THE PEOPLE

THE DISCUSSION OF AGRICULTURE and industry in the last chapter showed the ordinary man and woman at work, straining to make ends meet and earn a living. Yet work is only part of human experience. What about the rest? What about such basic things as marriage and childhood, food and drink, diet and medicine? How, in short, did "the people" – the peasant masses and the urban poor – really live in western Europe before the age of revolution began at the end of the eighteenth century? This is the simple but profound question that the economic and social developments naturally raise.

MARRIAGE AND THE FAMILY

The basic unit of social organization is the family. It is within the structure of the family that human beings love, mate, and reproduce themselves. It is primarily the family that teaches the child, imparting values and customs that condition an individual's behavior for a lifetime. The family is also an institution woven into the web of history. It evolves and changes, and it has taken different forms in different times and places.

EXTENDED AND NUCLEAR FAMILIES

In many traditional Asian and African societies, the typical family has often been an extended family. A newly married couple, instead of establishing their own home, will go to live with either the bride's or the groom's family. The couple raises their children while living under the same roof with their own brothers and sisters, who may also be married. The family is a big three- or four-generation clan, headed by a patriarch or perhaps a matriarch, and encompassing everyone from the youngest infant to the oldest grandparent.

Extended families, it is often said, provide security for adults and children in traditional agrarian peasant economies. Everyone has a place within the extended family, from cradle to grave. Sociologists frequently assume that the extended family gives way to the conjugal, or "nuclear," family with the advent of industrialization and urbanization. Couples establish their own households and their own family identities when they marry. They live with the children they raise, apart from their parents. Something like this is indeed happening in much of Asia and Africa today. And since Europe was once agrarian and preindustrial, it has often been believed that the extended family must also have prevailed in Europe before it was destroyed by the Industrial Revolution.

In fact, the situation was quite different in western and central European societies. By 1700, the extended three-generational family was a great rarity in western and central Europe. Indeed, the extended family may never have been common in Europe, although it is hard to know about the Middle Ages because there are fewer records for the historian to study. When young European couples married, they normally established their own households and lived apart from their parents. When a three-generation household came into existence, it was usually a parent who moved in with a married child, rather than a newly married couple moving in with either set of parents. The married couple, and the children that were sure to follow, were on their own from the beginning.

Perhaps because European couples set up separate households when they married, people did not marry young in the seventeenth and early eighteenth centuries. By the standards of today the average person, who was neither rich nor aristocratic, married suprisingly late, many years after reaching adulthood and many more after beginning to work. In one well-studied typical English village, both men and women married for the first time at an average age of twenty-seven or older in the seventeenth and eighteenth centuries. For one long period, the average age for women at first marriage was thirty years. In early eighteenth-century France the average man and woman marrying for the first time were in their late twenties. Moreover, a substantial portion of men and women never married at all.

Between two-fifths and three-fifths of European women capable of bearing children — that is, women between fifteen and forty-four — were unmarried at any given time. The contrast with traditional non-Western societies is once again striking. In those societies the pattern has very often been almost universal and very early marriage. The union of a teenage bride and her teenage groom has been the general rule.

The custom of late marriage and nuclear family was a distinctive characteristic of European society. The consequences have been tremendous, though still only partially explored. It seems likely that the dynamism and creativity that have characterized European society were due in large part to the pattern of marriage and family. This pattern fostered and required self-reliance and independence. In preindustrial western Europe in the sixteenth through eighteenth centuries, marriage normally joined a mature man and a mature woman — two adults who had already experienced a great deal of life and could transmit self-reliance and real skills to the next generation.

Why was marriage delayed? The main reason was that couples normally could not marry until they could support themselves economically. The land was the main source of income. The peasant son often needed to wait until his father's death to inherit the family farm and marry his sweetheart. Similarly, the peasant daughter and her family needed to accumulate a small dowry to help her boy friend buy land or build a house.

There were also laws and regulations to temper impetuous love and physical attraction. In some areas couples needed the legal permission or tacit approval of the local lord or landowner in order to marry. In Austria and Germany there were legal restrictions on marriage, and well into the nineteenth century poor couples had particular difficulty securing the approval of local officials. These officials believed that freedom to marry for the lower classes would mean more paupers, more abandoned children, and more money for welfare. Thus prudence, custom, and law combined to postpone the march to the altar. This pattern helped society maintain some kind of balance between the number of people and the available economic resources.

WORK AWAY FROM HOME

Many young people worked within their families until they could start their own households. Boys plowed and wove; girls spun and tended the cows. Many others left home to work elsewhere. In the towns a lad might be apprenticed to a craftsman for seven or fourteen years to learn a trade. During that time he would not be permitted to marry. In most trades he earned little and worked hard, but if he were lucky he might eventually be admitted to a guild and establish his economic independence. More often, the young man would drift from one tough job to another: hired hand for a small farmer, laborer on a new road, carrier of water in a nearby town. He was always subject to economic fluctua-

THE CHIMNEY SWEEP *Some boys and girls found work as chimney sweeps, especially if they were small. Climbing up into chimneys was dirty, dangerous work. Hot stones could set the sweep's clothing on fire. (Photo: Caroline Buckler)*

tions, and unemployment was a constant threat.

Girls also left their families to work, at an early age and in large numbers. The range of opportunities open to them was more limited, however. Service in another family's household was by far the most common job. Even middle-class families often sent their daughters into service (as they sent their sons to workshops and counting houses) and hired others as servants in return. Thus, a few years

away from home as a servant was a normal part of growing up. If all went well, the girl (or boy) would work hard and save some money for parents and marriage. At the least, there would be one less mouth to feed at home.

The legions of young servant girls worked hard but had little real independence. Sometimes the employer paid the girl's wages directly to her parents. Constantly under the eye of her mistress, her tasks were many – cleaning, shopping, cooking, caring for the baby – and often endless, for there were no laws to limit her exploitation. Few girls were so brutalized that they snapped under the strain, like the Russian servant girl Varka in Chekhov's chilling story, "Sleepy," who, driven beyond exhaustion, finally quieted her mistress's screaming child by strangling it in its cradle. But court records are full of complaints by servant girls of physical mistreatment by their mistresses. There were many others like the fifteen-year-old English girl in the early eighteenth century who told the judge that her mistress had not only called her "very opprobrious names, as Bitch, Whore and the like," but also "beat her without provocation and beyond measure."[1]

There was also the pressure of seducers and sexual attack. In theory, domestic service offered protection and security for a young girl leaving home. The girl had food, lodging, and a new family. She did not drift in a strange and often dangerous environment. But in practice, she was often the easy prey of a lecherous master, or his sons, or his friends. Indeed, "the evidence suggests that in all European countries, from Britain to Russia, the upper classes felt perfectly free to exploit sexually girls who were at their mercy."[2] If the girl became pregnant, she was quickly fired and thrown out in disgrace to make her own way. Prostitution and petty thievery were often the harsh alternatives that lay ahead. "What are we?" exclaimed a bitter Paris prostitute during the French Revolution. "Most of us are unfortunate women, without origins, without education, servants and maids for the most part."[3]

PREMARITAL SEX AND BIRTH-CONTROL PRACTICES

Did the plight of some ex-servant girls mean that late marriage in preindustrial Europe went hand in hand with premarital sex and many illegitimate children? For most of western and central Europe, until at least 1750, the answer seems to be no. English parish registers, in which the clergy recorded the births and deaths of the population, seldom list more than one bastard out of every twenty children baptized. Some French parishes in the seventeenth century had extraordinarily low rates of illegitimacy, with less than one percent of the babies born out of wedlock. Illegitimate babies were apparently a rarity, at least as far as the official church records are concerned.

At the same time premarital sex was clearly commonplace. In one well-studied English village one-third of all first children were conceived before the couple was married, and many were born within three months of the marriage ceremony. No doubt many of these couples were already betrothed, or at least "going steady," before they entered into an intimate relationship. But the very low rates of illegitimate birth also reflect the powerful social controls of the traditional village, particularly the open-field village with its pattern of cooperation and common action. Irate parents and village elders, indignant priests and authoritative landlords, all combined to pressure any young people who wavered about marriage in the face of unexpected pregnancy. These controls meant that premarital sex was not entered into lightly. In the countryside it was generally limited to those contemplating marriage.

Once a woman was married, she generally had several children. This does not mean that birth control within marriage was unknown in western and central Europe before the nineteenth century. But it was primitive and quite undependable. The most common method was coitus interruptus – withdrawal by the male before ejaculation. The French, who were apparently early leaders in contraception, were using this method extensively to limit family size by the end of the eighteenth century. The same technique was apparently used in some English communities and no doubt elsewhere, since awareness of this way to prevent conception was widespread. Withdrawal as a method of birth control was in keeping with the European pattern of nuclear family, in which the father bore the direct responsibility of supporting his children. Withdrawal – a male technique – was one way to meet that responsibility.

Mechanical and other means of contraception were not unknown in the eighteenth century, but they appear to have been used mainly by certain sectors of the urban population. The "fast set" of London used the "sheath" regularly, although primarily to protect against venereal disease, not pregnancy. Prostitutes used various contraceptive techniques to prevent pregnancy, and such information was probably available to anyone who really sought it. The second part of an indictment for adultery against a late-sixteenth-century English vicar charged that the wayward minister was "also an instructor of young folks [in] how to commit the sin of adultery or fornication and not to beget or bring forth children."[4]

In the second half of the eighteenth century, the pattern of late marriage and few illegitimate children began to break down. It is hard to say why. Certainly, changes in the economy had a gradual but profound impact. The growth of cottage industry created new opportunities for earning a living, opportunities not tied to limited and hard-to-get land. Because a scrap of ground for a garden and a cottage for the loom and spinning wheel could be quite enough for a modest living, young people had greater independence and did not need to wait for a good-sized farm. A contemporary observer of an area of rapidly growing cottage industry in Switzerland at the end of the eighteenth century described these changes: "The increased and sure income offered by the combination of cottage manufacture with farming hastened and multiplied marriages and encouraged the division of landholdings, while enhancing their value; it also promoted the expansion and embellishment of houses and villages."[5]

As a result cottage workers not only married earlier, but for different reasons. Nothing could be so businesslike, so calculating, as a peasant marriage, which was often dictated by the needs of the couple's families. After 1750, however, courtship became more extensive and freer as cottage industry grew. It was easier to yield to the attraction of the opposite sex and fall in love. The older generation was often shocked by the lack of responsibility they saw in the early marriages of the poor, the union of "people with only two spinning wheels and not even a bed." But the laws and regulations they imposed, especially in Ger-

many, were often disregarded. Unions based on love rather than economic considerations were increasingly the pattern for cottage workers. Factory workers, numbers of whom first began to appear in England after about 1780, followed the path blazed by cottage workers.

Changes in the timing and motivation of marriage went hand in hand with a rapid increase in illegitimate births between about 1750 and 1850. Some historians even speak of an "illegitimacy explosion," a phrase that is no exaggeration in many instances. In Frankfurt, Germany, for example, only about 2 percent of all births were illegitimate in the early 1700s. This figure rose to 5 percent in about 1760, to about 10 percent in 1800, and peaked at about 25 percent around 1850. In Bordeaux, France, illegitimate births rose steadily until by 1840 fully one out of every three babies was born out of wedlock. Small towns and villages less frequently experienced such startlingly high illegitimacy rates, but increases from a range of 1 to 3 percent initially to 10 to 20 percent between 1750 and 1850 were commonplace. A profound sexual and cultural transformation was taking place. Fewer girls were abstaining from premarital intercourse, and fewer boys were marrying the girls they got pregnant.

It is hard to know exactly why this change occurred and what it meant. The old idea of a safe, late, economically secure marriage did not reflect economic and social realities. The growing freedom of thought in the turbulent years beginning with the French Revolution in 1789 influenced sexual and marital behavior. And illegitimate births, particularly in Germany, were also the result of open rebellion against class laws limiting the right of the poor to marry. Unable to show a solid financial position and thereby obtain a marriage license, couples asserted their independence and lived together anyway. Children were the natural and desired result of "true love" and greater freedom. Eventually, when the stuffy old-fashioned propertied classes gave in and repealed their laws against "imprudent marriage," poor couples once again went to the altar, often accompanied by their children, and the number of illegitimate children declined.

More fundamentally, the need to seek work outside farming and the village made young people more mobile. Mobility in turn encouraged new sexual and marital relationships, which were less subject to parental pressure and village tradition. As in the case of young servant girls who became pregnant and were then forced to fend for themselves, some of these relationships promoted loose living or prostitution. This resulted in more illegitimate births and strengthened an urban subculture of habitual illegitimacy.

EARLY SEXUAL EMANCIPATION?

It has been suggested that the increase in illegitimate births represented a stage in the emancipation of women. According to this view, new economic opportunities outside the home, in the city and later in the factory, revolutionized women's attitudes about themselves. Young working women became individualistic and rebelled against old restrictions like late marriage. They sought fulfillment in the pleasure of sexuality. Since there was little birth control, freer sex for single women meant more illegitimate babies.

No doubt single working women in towns and cities were of necessity more independent and self-reliant. Yet, until at least the late nineteenth century, it seems unlikely that such young women were motivated primarily by visions of emancipation and sexual liberation. Most women were servants or textile workers. These jobs paid poorly, and the possibility of a truly independent "liberated" life was correspondingly limited. Most women in the city probably looked to marriage and family life as an escape from hard, poorly paid work and as the foundation of a satisfying life.

Hopes and promises of marriage from men of the working girl's own class led naturally enough to sex.[6] In one medium-sized French city in 1787–1788 the great majority of unwed mothers stated that sexual intimacy had followed promises of marriage. Many soldiers, day laborers, and male servants were no doubt sincere in their proposals. But their lives were insecure, and many hesitated to take on the heavy economic burdens of wife and child. Nor were their backbones any longer stiffened by the traditional pressures of the village.

In a growing number of cases, therefore, the intended marriage did not take place. The romantic yet practical dreams and aspirations of many young working women and men were frustrated by low wages, inequality, and changing economic and social conditions. Old patterns of marriage and family were breaking down among the common people. Only in the late nineteenth century would more stable patterns reappear.

WOMEN AND CHILDREN

In the traditional framework of preindustrial Europe women married late, but then began bearing children rapidly. If a woman married before she was thirty, and if both she and her husband lived to forty-five, the chances were roughly one in two that she would give birth to six or more children. The newborn child entered a dangerous world. Infant mortality – the number of babies who would die

creases the likelihood of pregnancy for the average woman by delaying the resumption of ovulation. Although women may have been only vaguely aware of the link between nursing and not getting pregnant, they were spacing their children – from two and a half to three or more years apart in many communities – and limiting their fertility by nursing their babies. If a newborn baby died, nursing stopped and a new life could be created. Nursing also saved lives: the breast-fed infant was more likely to survive on its mother's milk than on any artificial foods. In many areas of Russia, where common practice was to give a new child a sweetened (and germ-ladened) rag to suck on for its subsistence, half the babies did not survive for the first year.

In contrast to the laboring poor, the women of the aristocracy and upper middle class seldom nursed their own children. The upper-class woman felt that breast-feeding was crude and common, and well beneath her dignity. Instead she hired a wet nurse – a nursing mother from the poor – to suckle her child. The mother of more modest means – the wife of a shopkeeper or artisan – also commonly used a wet nurse, sending her baby to some poor woman in the country as soon as possible.

Wet-nursing was a very widespread and flourishing business in the eighteenth century, a dismal business within the framework of the putting-out system. The traffic was in babies rather than in wool and cloth, and two or three years often passed before the wet-nurse worker finished her task. The great French historian Jules Michelet described with compassion the plight of the wet nurse, who was still going to the homes of the rich in the early nineteenth century in France:

People do not know how much these poor women are exploited and abused, first by the vehicles

before their first birthday – was high. One in five was sure to die, and one in three was quite likely to in the poorer areas. Newborn children are very likely to catch infectious diseases of the stomach and chest. Not until the late nineteenth century were these diseases and their treatment understood. Thus little could be done for an ailing child, even in rich families. Childhood itself was dangerous. Parents in preindustrial Europe could count themselves fortunate if half their children lived to adulthood.

CHILD CARE AND NURSING

Women of the lower classes generally breast-fed their infants, and for much longer periods than is customary today. Breast-feeding de-

which transport them (often barely out of their confinement), and afterward by the employment offices which place them. Taken as nurses on the spot, they must send their own child away, and consequently it often dies. They have no contact with the family that hires them, and they may be dismissed at the first caprice of the mother or doctor. If the change of air and place should dry up their milk, they are discharged without any compensation. If they stay there [in the city] they pick up the habits of the easy life, and they suffer enormously when they are forced to return to their life of [rural] poverty. A good number become servants in order to stay in the town. They never rejoin their husbands, and the family is broken.[7]

Other observers noted the flaws of wet nurses. It was a common belief that a nurse passed her bad traits to the baby with her milk. When a child turned out poorly, it was assumed that "the nurse changed it." Many observers charged that nurses were often negligent and greedy. They claimed that there were large numbers of "killing nurses" with whom no child ever survived. The nurse let the child die quickly, so that she could take another child and another fee. No matter how the adults fared in the wet-nurse business, the child was a certain loser.

FOUNDLINGS AND INFANTICIDE

In the ancient world and in Asian societies it was not uncommon to allow or force newborn babies, particularly girl babies, to die when there were too many mouths to feed. To its great and eternal credit the early medieval church, strongly influenced by Jewish law, denounced infanticide as a pagan practice and insisted that every human life was sacred. The willful destruction of newborn children became a crime punishable by death. And yet, as the reference to "killing nurses" suggests, direct and indirect methods of eliminating unwanted babies did not disappear. There were, for example, many cases of "overlaying" – parents rolling over and suffocating the child placed between them in their bed. Such parents claimed they were drunk and had acted unintentionally. In Austria in 1784, suspicious authorities made it illegal for parents to take children under five into bed with them. Severe poverty on the one hand, and increasing illegitimacy on the other, conspired to force the very poor to thin their own ranks.

The young girl – very likely a servant – who could not provide for her child had few choices. If she would not stoop to abortion or the services of a killing nurse, she could bundle up her baby and leave it on the doorstep of a church. In the late seventeenth century Saint Vincent de Paul was so distressed by the number of babies brought to the steps of Notre Dame in Paris that he established a home for foundlings. Others followed his example. In England the government acted on a petition calling for a foundling hospital "to prevent the frequent murders of poor, miserable infants at birth" and "to suppress the inhuman custom of exposing newborn children to perish in the streets."

In much of Europe in the eighteenth century, foundling homes became a favorite charity of the rich and powerful. Great sums were spent on them. The foundling home in St. Petersburg, perhaps the most elaborate and lavish of its kind, occupied the former palaces of two members of the high nobility. In the early nineteenth century it had 25,000 children in its care and was receiving 5,000 new babies a year. At their best, the foundling homes of the eighteenth century were a good example of Christian charity and social concern in an age of great poverty and inequality.

Yet the foundling home was no panacea. By the 1770s, one-third of all babies born in

ABANDONED CHILDREN   At this Italian found-lings' home a frightened, secretive mother could dis-creetly deposit her baby. (Bettmann Archive)

Paris were immediately abandoned to the foundling home by their mothers. Fully a third of all those foundlings were abandoned by married couples, a powerful commentary on the standard of living among the working poor, for whom an additional mouth to feed often meant tragedy. In London competition for space in the foundling home soon became so great that it led "to the disgraceful scene of women scrambling and fighting to get to the door, that they might be of the fortunate few to reap the benefit of the Asylum."[8]

Furthermore, great numbers of babies entered, but few left. Even in the best of these homes half the babies normally died within a year. In the worst, fully 90 percent did not survive! They succumbed to long journeys over rough roads, the intentional and unintentional neglect of their wet nurses, and the customary childhood illnesses. So great was the carnage that some contemporaries called the foundling hospitals "legalized infanticide."

Certainly, some parents and officials looked upon the hospitals as a dump for unwanted babies. In the early 1760s, when the London Foundling Hospital was obliged to accept all babies offered, it was deluged with babies from the countryside. Many parish officers placed with the foundling home the abandoned children in their care, just as others apprenticed five-year-old children to work in factories. Both practices reduced the cost of welfare at the local level. Throughout the eighteenth century, millions of children of the poor continued to exit after the briefest of appearances upon the earthly stage. True, they died after being properly baptized, an important consideration in still-Christian Europe. Yet those people who would dream of an idyllic past should do well to ponder the foundling's fate.

What were the more typical circumstances of children's lives? Did the treatment of foundlings reflect the attitudes of normal parents? Harsh as it may sound, the young child was very often of little concern to its parents and to society in the eighteenth century. This indifference toward children was found in all classes; rich children were by no means exempt. The practice of using wet nurses, who were casually selected and often negligent, is one example of how even the rich and the prosperous put the child out of sight and out of mind. One French moralist, writing in 1756 about how to improve humanity, observed that "one blushes to think of loving one's children." It has been said that the English gentleman of the period "had more interest in the diseases of his horses than of his children."[9]

Parents believed that the world of the child was an uninteresting one. When parents did stop to notice their offspring, they often treated them as dolls or playthings – little puppies to fondle and cuddle in a moment of relaxation. The psychological distance between parent and child remained vast.

Much of the indifference was due to the terrible frequency, the terrible banality, of death among children of all classes. Parents simply could not afford to become too emotionally involved with their children, who were so unlikely to survive. The great eighteenth-century English historian Edward Gibbon (1737–1794) wrote that "the death of a new born child before that of its parents may seem unnatural but it is a strictly probable event, since of any given number the greater part are extinguished before the ninth year, before they possess the faculties of the mind and the body." Gibbon's father named all his boys Edward, hoping that at least one of them would survive to carry his name. His prudence was not misplaced. Edward the future historian and eldest survived. Five brothers and sisters who followed him all died in infancy.

Doctors were seldom interested in the care of children. One contemporary observer quoted a famous doctor as saying that "he never wished to be called to a young child because he was really at a loss to know what to offer for it." There were "physicians of note who make no scruple to assert that there is nothing to be done for children when they are ill." Children were caught in a vicious circle: they were neglected because they were very likely to die, and they were likely to die because they were neglected.

Indifference toward children often shaded off into brutality. When parents and other adults did turn toward children, it was normally to discipline and control them. The novelist Daniel Defoe (1660?–1731), always delighted when he saw very young children working hard in cottage industry, coined the axiom "Spare the rod and spoil the child." He meant it. So did Susannah Wesley, mother of John Wesley (1703–1791), the founder of Methodism. According to her, the first task of a parent toward her children was "to conquer the will, and bring them to an obedient temper." She reported that her babies were "taught to fear the rod, and to cry softly; by which means they escaped the abundance of correction they might otherwise have had, and that most odious noise of the crying of children was rarely heard in the house, but the family lived in as much quietness as if there had not been a child among them."[10]

It was hardly surprising – indeed, it was quite predictable – that when English parish officials dumped their paupers into the first

THE FIVE SENSES *Published in 1774, J. B. Base-*
dow's Elementary Reader *helped spread new atti-*
tudes toward child development and education.
Drawing heavily upon the theories of Locke and
Rousseau, the German educator advocated nature
study and contact with everyday life. In this illustra-
tion for Basedow's reader, gentle teachers allow un-
corrupted children to learn about the five senses
through direct experience. (Photo: Caroline Buckler)

factories late in the eighteenth century, the
children were beaten and brutalized, as we
shall see. That was part of the childrearing
pattern – widespread indifference on the one
hand and strict physical discipline on the
other – that prevailed through most of the
eighteenth century.

Late in the century this pattern came under
attack. Critics like Jean-Jacques Rousseau
called for greater love, tenderness, and understanding toward children. In addition to supporting foundling homes to discourage
infanticide and urging wealthy women to

nurse their own babies, these new voices ridiculed the practice of swaddling. Wrapping
youngsters in tight-fitting clothes and blankets
was generally believed to form babies properly
by "straightening them out." By the end of
the century small children were often dressed
in simpler, more comfortable clothing, allowing much greater freedom of movement.
More parents expressed a delight in the love
and intimacy of the child and found real pleasure in raising their offspring. These changes
were part of the general growth of humani-
tarianism and optimism about human poten-

tial that characterized the eighteenth-century Enlightenment.

SCHOOLS AND EDUCATION

The role of formal education outside the home, in those special institutions called schools, was growing more important. The aristocracy and the rich had led the way in the sixteenth century with special colleges, often run by the Jesuits. But "little schools," charged with elementary education of the children of the masses, did not appear until the seventeenth century. Unlike medieval schools, which mingled all age groups, the little schools specialized in boys and girls from seven to twelve, who were instructed in basic literacy and religion.

Although large numbers of common people got no education at all in the eighteenth century, the beginnings of popular education were recognizable. France made a start in 1682 with the establishment of Christian schools, which taught the catechism and prayers as well as reading and writing. The Church of England and the dissenting congregations established "charity schools" to instruct the children of the poor. As early as 1717, Prussia made attendance at elementary schools compulsory. Inspired by the old Protestant idea that every believer should be able to read and study the Bible in the quest for personal salvation, and by the new idea of a population capable of effectively serving the state, Prussia led the way in the development of universal education. Religious motives were also extremely important elsewhere. From the middle of the seventeenth century, Presbyterian Scotland was convinced that the path to salvation lay in careful study of the Scriptures, and this belief led to an effective network of parish schools for rich and poor alike. The Enlightenment commitment to greater knowledge through critical thinking reinforced interest in education in the eighteenth century.

The result of these efforts was a remarkable growth of basic literacy between 1600 and 1800, especially after 1700. Whereas in 1600 only one male in six was barely literate in France and Scotland, and one in four in England, by 1800 almost 90 percent of the Scottish male population was literate. At the same time two out of three males were literate in France, and in advanced areas such as Normandy literacy approached 90 percent. More than half of English males were literate by 1800. In all three countries the bulk of the jump occurred in the eighteenth century. Women were also increasingly literate, although they probably lagged behind men somewhat in most countries. (For example, in England in 1840 – the first date for which there is complete census evidence – two-thirds of newly married men and half of newly married women were literate.) Some elementary education was becoming a reality for European peoples, and schools were of growing significance in everyday life.

THE EUROPEAN'S FOOD

Plague, starvation, and economic crisis, which recurred often in the seventeenth century, gradually disappeared in the eighteenth century. This phenomenon probably accounts in large part for the rapid growth in the total number of Europeans and for their longer lives. The increase in the average life span, allowing for regional variations, was remarkable. In 1700, the average European could expect at birth to live only twenty-five years. A century later, a newborn European could expect to live fully ten years longer, to age thirty-five. The doubling of the adult life span meant that there was more time to produce and create, and more reason for parents to stress learning and preparation for adulthood.

People also lived longer because ordinary years were progressively less deadly. People ate better and somewhat more wisely. Doctors and hospitals probably saved a few more lives than they had in the past. How and why did health and life expectancy improve, and how much did they improve? And what were the differences between rich and poor? To answer these questions, it is necessary first to follow the eighteenth-century family to the table, and then to see what contribution doctors made.

DIETS AND NUTRITION

Although the accomplishments of doctors and hospitals are constantly in the limelight today, the greater if less spectacular part of medicine is preventive medicine. The great breakthrough of the second half of the nineteenth century was the development of public health techniques – proper sanitation and mass vaccinations – to prevent outbreaks of communicable diseases. Even before the nineteenth century, when medical knowledge was slight and doctors were of limited value, prevention was the key to longer life. Good clothing, warm dry housing, and plentiful food make for healthier populations, much more capable of battling off disease. Clothing and housing for the masses probably improved only modestly in the eighteenth century, but the new agricultural methods and increased agricultural output had a beneficial effect. The average European ate more and better food and was healthier as a result in 1800 than in 1700. This pattern is apparent if we look at the fare of the laboring poor.

At the beginning of the eighteenth century,

ordinary men and women depended on grain as fully as they had in the past. Bread was quite literally the staff of life. Peasants in the Beauvais region of France ate two pounds of bread a day, washing it down with water, green wine, beer, or (if they were lucky) a little skimmed milk. Their dark bread was made from a mixture of rough-ground wheat and rye – the standard flour of the poor. The poor also ate grains in soup and gruel. In rocky northern Scotland, for example, people depended on oatmeal, which they often ate half-cooked so it would swell in their stomachs and make them feel full. No wonder, then, that the supply of grain and the price of bread were always critical questions for most of the population.

The poor, rural and urban, also ate a fair quantity of vegetables. Indeed, vegetables were considered "poor people's food." Peas and beans were probably the most common; grown as field crops in much of Europe since the Middle Ages, they were eaten fresh in late spring and summer. Dried, they became the basic ingredients in the soups and stews of the long winter months. In most regions other vegetables appeared on the tables of the poor in season, primarily cabbages, carrots, and wild greens. Fruit was uncommon and limited to the summer months.

The European poor loved meat and eggs, but even in England – the wealthiest country in Europe in 1700 – they seldom ate their fill. Meat was too expensive. When the poor did eat meat – on a religious holiday or at a wedding or other special occasion – it was most likely lamb or mutton. Sheep could survive on rocky soils and did not compete directly with humans for the slender resources of grain.

Milk was rarely drunk. It was widely believed that milk caused sore eyes, headaches, and a variety of ills, except among the very young and very old. Milk was used primarily to make cheese and butter, which the poor liked but could afford only occasionally. Medical and popular opinion considered whey, the watery liquid left after milk was churned, "an excellent temperate drink."

The diet of the rich – aristocrats, officials, and the comfortable bourgeoisie – was traditionally quite different from that of the poor. The men and women of the upper classes were rapacious carnivores, gorging on meat, meat, and more meat. To a large extent a person's standard of living and economic well-being was judged by the amount of meat eaten. A truly elegant dinner among the great and the powerful consisted of one rich meat after another – a chicken pie, a leg of lamb, a grilled steak, for example. Three separate meat courses might be followed by three fish courses, laced with piquant sauces and complemented with sweets, cheeses, and nuts of all kinds. Fruits and vegetables were not often found on the tables of the rich. The long-standing dominance of meat and fish in the diet of the upper classes continued throughout the eighteenth century. There was extravagant living, and undoubtedly great over-eating and gluttony, not only among the aristocracy but among the prosperous business and professional classes as well.

There was also an enormous amount of drunkenness and overdrinking among the rich. The English squire, for example, who loved to ride with his hounds, loved drink with a similar passion. He became famous as the "four-bottle man." With his dinner he drank red wine from France or white wine from the Rhineland, and with his dessert he took sweet but strong port or Madeira from Portugal. Sometimes he ended the evening under the table in a drunken stupor, but very often he did not. The wine and the meat were consumed together in long hours of sustained excess, permitting the "gentleman" and his guests to drink enormous quantities.

The diet of small traders, master craftsmen, minor bureaucrats – the people of the towns and cities – was probably less monotonous than that of the peasantry. The markets, stocked by market gardens in the outskirts, provided a substantial variety of meats, vegetables, and fruits, although bread and beans still formed the bulk of the poor family's diet.

There were also regional dietary differences in 1700. Generally speaking, northern, Atlantic Europe ate better than southern Mediterranean Europe. The poor of England probably ate best of all. Contemporaries on both sides of the Channel often contrasted the English-man's consumption of meat with the French peasant's greater dependence on bread and vegetables. The Dutch were also considerably better fed than the average European, in large part because of their advanced agriculture and diversified gardens.

The Impact of Diet on Health

How were the poor and the rich served by their quite different diets? Good nutrition depends on a balanced supply of food, as well as on an adequate number of calories. Modern research has shown that the chief determinant of nutritional balance is the relationship between carbohydrates (sugar and starch) and proteins. A diet consisting primarily of carbohydrates is seriously incomplete.

At first glance the diet of the laboring poor, relying as it did on carbohydrates, seems unsatisfactory. Even when a peasant got his daily two or three pounds of bread, his supply of protein and essential vitamins would seem too low. A closer look reveals a brighter picture. Most bread was "brown" or "black," made from wheat or rye. Flour was quite different from that used in the mushy white bread of an American supermarket. The flour of the eighteenth century was a whole-meal flour, produced by stone grinding. It contained most of the bran – the ground-up husk – and the all-important wheat germ. The bran and germ contain higher proportions of some minerals, vitamins, and good-quality proteins than does the rest of the grain. Only when they are removed does bread become a foodstuff providing relatively more starch and less of the essential nutrients.

In addition, the field peas and beans eaten by poor people since Carolingian days contained protein that complemented the proteins in whole-meal bread. The proteins in whey, cheese, and eggs, which the poor ate at least occasionally, also supplemented the value of the protein in the bread and vegetables. Indeed, a leading authority concludes that if a pint of milk and some cheese and whey were eaten each day, the balance of the poor people's diet "was excellent, far better indeed than in many of our modern diets."[11]

The basic bread-and-vegetables diet of the poor *in normal times* was satisfactory. It protected effectively against most of the disorders associated with a deficiency of the vitamin-B complex, for example. The lack of sugar meant that teeth were not so plagued by cavities. Constipation was almost unknown to peasants and laborers living on coarse cereal breads, which provided the roughage modern diets lack. The common diet of the poor also generally warded off anemia, although anemia among infants was not uncommon.

The key dietary problem was probably getting enough green vegetables (or milk), particularly in the late winter and early spring, to insure adequate supplies of vitamins A and C. A severe deficiency of vitamin C produces scurvy, an awful disease that leads to loose

teeth and rotting, stinking gums, swelling of the limbs, and great weakness. Before the season's first vegetables, many people had used up their bodily reserves of vitamin C and were suffering from mild cases of scurvy. Sailors on long voyages suffered most. By the end of the sixteenth century the exceptional antiscurvy properties of lemons and limes led to the practice of supplying some crews with a daily ration of lemon juice, which had highly beneficial effects. English sailors came to be known as "limeys" because of their habit of sucking on limes. "Scurvy grass" – a kind of watercress – also guarded against scurvy, and this disease was increasingly controlled on even the longest voyages.

The practice of gorging on meat, sweets, and spirits caused the rich their own nutritional problems. They too were very often deficient in vitamins A and C, because of their great disdain for fresh vegetables. Gout was a common affliction of the overfed and underexercised rich. No wonder they were often caricatured dragging their flabby limbs and bulging bellies to the table, to stuff their swollen cheeks and poison their livers. People of moderate means, who could afford some meat and dairy products with fair regularity but who had not abandoned the bread and vegetables of the poor, were probably best off from a nutritional standpoint.

NEW FOODS AND NEW KNOWLEDGE

In nutrition and food consumption, Europe in the early eighteenth century had not gone

beyond its medieval accomplishments. This situation began to change markedly as the century progressed. Although the introduction of new methods of farming was confined largely to the Low Countries and England, a new food – the potato – came to the aid of the poor everywhere.

Introduced into Europe from the Americas, along with corn, squash, tomatoes, chocolate, and many other useful plants, the humble potato is an excellent food. It contains a good supply of carbohydrates and calories. More important, it is rich in vitamins A and C, especially if the skin is eaten and it is not overcooked. The lack of green vegetables that could lead to scurvy was one of the biggest deficiencies in the poor person's winter and early spring diet. The potato, which gave a much higher caloric yield than grain for a given piece of land, provided the needed vitamins and supplemented the bread-based diet. Doctors, increasingly aware of the dietary benefits of potatoes, prescribed them for the general public and in institutions such as schools and prisons.

For some poor people, especially desperately poor peasants who needed to get every possible calorie from a tiny plot of land, the potato replaced grain as the primary food in the eighteenth century. This happened first in Ireland, where in the seventeenth century Irish rebellion had led to English repression and the perfection of a system of exploitation worthy of the most savage Eastern tyrant. The foreign (and Protestant) English landlords took the best land, forcing large numbers of poor (and Catholic) peasants to live off tiny scraps of rented ground. By 1700, the poor in Ireland lived almost exclusively on the bountiful fruits of the potato plot. And since intensive cultivation gave so much good food from so little land, ever more people were able to eke out a meager existence.

Elsewhere in Europe the potato took hold more slowly. Potatoes were first fed to pigs and livestock, and there was considerable debate over whether they were fit for humans. In Germany the severe famines caused by the Seven Years' War (page 651) settled the matter: potatoes were edible and no "famine food." By the end of the century the potato was an important dietary supplement in much of Europe.

There was also a general growth of market gardening and a greater variety of vegetables in towns and cities. Potatoes, cabbages, peas, beans, radishes, spinach, asparagus, lettuce, parsnips, carrots, and other vegetables were much more common. They were sold in central markets and streets, from "moveable shops that run upon wheels, attended by ill looking fellows," according to one London observer. In the course of the eighteenth century the large towns and cities of maritime Europe began to receive semitropical fruit, such as oranges, lemons, and limes, from Portugal and the West Indies, although they were not cheap.

The growing variety of food was matched by some improvement in knowledge about diet and nutrition. For the poor, such improvement was limited primarily to the insight that the potato and other root crops improved health in the winter and helped to prevent scurvy. The rich began to be aware of the harmful effects of their meat-ladened, wine-drowned meals.

The waning influence of Galen's medical teachings was another aspect of progress. Galen's Roman synthesis of ancient medical doctrines held that the four basic elements – air, fire, water, and earth – combine to produce in each person a complexion and a corresponding temperament. Foods were grouped into four categories appropriate for each complexion. Galen's notions dominated the dietary thinking of the seventeenth-century medical profession: "Galen said that the flesh of a hare preventeth fatness, causeth sleep and cleanseth the blood," and so on for a thousand things.

Conventional wisdom had also held, quite erroneously, that vegetables and fruits caused poor health. Vegetables were seen as "windy" and tending to cause fevers, and fruits were considered dangerous except in very small amounts. Similarly, butter, an excellent food rich in vitamin A, which the poor used on bread whenever they could, was regarded with great suspicion by the rich and the medical profession. It was believed bad for children because, according to typical opinion, it choked the "glands and capillaries" and made children "weakly, corpulent, big-belly'd, very subject to breakings-out, and to breed lice."

The growth of scientific experimentation in the seventeenth century led to a generally beneficial questioning of the old views. Haphazardly, by trial and error, and influenced by advances in chemistry, saner ideas developed. Experiments with salts led to the belief that foods were by nature either acid (all fruits and most vegetables) or alkaline (all meats). Doctors and early nutritionists came to believe that one key to good health was a *balance* of the two types.

An English doctor writing at the end of the century as the "Soldier's Friend" on "the means of preserving the health of military men" stated categorically that "ripe fruits, in moderate quantity, are wholesome; and, contrary to the vulgar prejudice, tend rather to prevent than to induce bowel complaints."[12] Excessive consumption of meat was identified by some medical men as a dangerous practice. Gout, the class hazard of the rich, was linked with overeating and lack of exercise. Thus, the eighteenth century saw increased understanding of the importance of a balanced diet

for proper health. Such awareness – and the potato – were no doubt important factors in the rise in life expectancy and the growth of Europe's population.

Not all changes in the eighteenth century were for the better. Bread began to change, most noticeably in England. Rising incomes and new tastes led to a shift from whole-meal black or brown bread to white bread made from finely ground and sifted flour. On the Continent such white bread was generally limited to the well-to-do. To the extent that the preferred wheaten flour was stone-ground and sifted for coarse particles only, white bread remained satisfactory. But the desire for "bread as white as snow" was already leading to a decline in nutritional value.

The coarser bran, which is necessary for roughage, and at least some of the germ, which darkened the bread but contained the grain's nutrients, were already being sifted out to some extent. Bakers in English cities added the chemical alum to their white loaves to make them smoother, whiter, and larger. In the nineteenth century, "improvements" in milling were to lead to the removal of almost all the bran and germ from the flour, leaving it perfectly white and perfectly reduced in nutritional value. The only saving grace in the sad deterioration of bread was that people began to eat less of it and therefore depended on it less.

Another sign of nutritional decline was the growing consumption of sweets in general and sugar in particular. Initially a luxury, sugar dropped rapidly in price, as slave-based production increased in the Americas, and it was much more widely used in the eighteenth century. This development probably led to an increase in cavities and to other ailments as well. Overconsumption of refined sugar can produce, paradoxically, low blood sugar (hypoglycemia) and, for some individuals at least, a variety of physical and mental ailments. Of course the greater or lesser poverty of the laboring poor saved most of them from the problems of the rich and well-to-do.

MEDICAL SCIENCE AND THE SICK

Advances in medical science played a very small part in improving the health and lengthening the lives of people in the eighteenth century. Such seventeenth-century advances as William Harvey's discovery of the circulation of blood were not soon translated into better treatment. The sick had to await the medical revolution of the later nineteenth century for much help from doctors.

Yet developments in medicine reflected the general thrust of the Enlightenment. The prevailing focus on discovering the laws of nature and on human problems, rather than on God and the heavens, gave rise to a great deal of research and experimentation. The century saw a remarkable rise in the number of doctors, and a high value was placed on their services. Thus when the great breakthroughs in knowledge came in the nineteenth century, they could be rapidly diffused and applied. Eighteenth-century medicine, in short, gave promise of a better human existence, but most of the realization lay far in the future.

THE MEDICAL PROFESSIONALS

Care of the sick was the domain of several competing groups – faith healers, apothecaries, surgeons, and physicians. Since the great majority of common ailments have a tendency to cure themselves, each group could point to successes and win adherents. When the doctor's treatment made the patient worse, as it often did, the original medical problem could always be blamed.

Faith healers, who had been one of the most important kinds of physicians in medieval Europe, remained active. They and their patients believed that demons and evil spirits caused disease by lodging in people and that the proper treatment was to exorcise or drive out the offending devil. Good Christians became exorcists: had not Jesus himself cured by casting out devils? The men and women who cast out devils had to be careful to keep their mouths closed, for the devil could jump from the patient's mouth into their own. By the eighteenth century, this demonic view of disease was still common among the poor, especially in the countryside, as was faith in the healing power of religious relics, prayer, and the laying on of hands. Faith healing was particularly effective in the treatment of mental disorders like hysteria and depression, where the link between attitude and illness is most direct.

Apothecaries, or pharmacists, sold a vast number of herbs, drugs, and patent medicines for every conceivable "temperament and distemper." Early pharmacists were seldom regulated, and they frequently diagnosed as freely as the doctors whose prescriptions they filled. Their prescriptions were incredibly complex – a hundred or more drugs might be included in a single prescription – and often very expensive. Some of the drugs undoubtedly worked: strong laxatives were given to the rich for their constipated bowels. The apothecary regularly and profitably administered enemas for the same purpose. Indeed, the medical profession continued to believe that regular "purging" of the bowels was essential for good health and the treatment of illness. Much purging was harmful, however, and only bloodletting for the treatment of disease was more effective in speeding patients to their graves.

Drugs were prescribed and concocted in a helter-skelter way. With so many different drugs being combined, it was impossible to isolate cause and effect. Nor was there any standardization. A complicated prescription filled by ten different pharmacists would result in ten different preparations with different medical properties.

Surgeons competed vigorously with barbers and "bone benders," the forerunners of chiropractors. The eighteenth-century surgeon (and patient) labored in the face of incredible difficulties. Almost all operations were performed without any pain killer, for anesthesia was believed too dangerous. The terrible screams of people whose limbs were being sawed off shattered hospitals and battlefields. Such operations were common, because a surgeon faced with an extensive wound sought to obtain a plain surface that he could cauterize with fire. Thus, if a person broke an arm or a leg and the bone stuck out, off came the limb. Many patients died from the agony and shock of such operations.

Surgery was also performed in the midst of filth and dirt. There simply was no knowledge of bacteriology and the nature of infection. The simplest wound treated by a surgeon festered, often fatally. In fact, surgeons encouraged wounds to fester in the belief — a remnant of Galen's theory — that the pus was beneficially removing the base portions of the body.

Physicians, the fourth major group, were trained like surgeons. They were apprenticed in their teens to a practicing physician for several years of on-the-job training. This training was then rounded out with hospital work or some university courses. To their credit, physicians in the eighteenth century

KNIVES FOR BLOODLETTING   In the eighteenth century doctors continued to use these diabolical instruments to treat almost every illness, with disastrous results. (Courtesy, World Heritage Museum. Photo: Caroline Buckler)

were increasingly willing to experiment with new methods, but the hand of Galen lay heavily upon them. Bloodletting was still considered a medical cure-all. It was the way "bad blood," the cause of illness, was removed and the balance of humors necessary for good health restored.

According to a physician practicing medicine in Philadelphia in 1799, "No operation of surgery is so frequently necessary as bleeding.... But though practiced by midwives, gardeners, blacksmiths, etc., very few know when it is proper." The good doctor went on to explain that bleeding was proper at the onset of all inflammatory fevers, in all inflammations, and for "asthma, sciatic pains, coughs, head-aches, rheumatisms, the apoplexy, epilepsy, and bloody fluxes." It was also necessary after all falls, blows, and bruises. The doctor warned against bleeding children with leeches, the common practice. With leeches, it was impossible to know the quantity of blood taken, and "the bleeding is often very difficult to stop, and the wounds are not easily healed."[13] With a little care, he advised, a child could be bled with a knife as easily as an adult.

Physicians, like apothecaries, laid great stress on purging. They also generally believed that disease was caused by bad odors, and for this reason they carried canes whose heads contained ammonia salts. As they made their rounds in the filthy, stinking hospitals, physicians held their canes to their noses to protect themselves from illness.

While ordinary physicians were bleeding, apothecaries purging, surgeons sawing, and faith healters praying, the leading medical thinkers were attempting to pull together and assimilate all the information and misinformation they had been accumulating. The attempt was ambitious: to systematize medicine around simple, basic principles, as Newton had done in physics. But the schools of thought resulting from such speculation and theorizing did little to improve medical care. Proponents of animism explained life and disease in terms of *anima,* the "sensitive soul," which they believed was present throughout the body and prevented its decay and self-destruction. Another school, vitalism, stressed "the vital principle," which inhabited all parts of the body. Vitalists tried to classify diseases systematically.

More interesting was the homeopathic system of Samuel Hahnemann of Leipzig. Hahnemann believed that very small doses of drugs that produce certain symptoms in a healthy person will cure a sick person with those symptoms. This theory was probably preferable to most eighteenth-century treatments, in that it was a harmless alternative to the extravagant and often fatal practices of bleeding, purging, drug taking, and induced vomiting. The patient gained confidence, and the body had at least a fighting chance of recovering. Hahnemann engaged in bitter debate with the apothecaries, whom he accused of incompetence and greed with their expensive treatments.

HOSPITALS

Hospitals were terrible throughout most of the eighteenth century. There was no isolation of patients. Operations were performed in the patient's bed. The nurses were old, ignorant, greedy, and often drunk women. Fresh air was considered harmful, and infections of every kind were rampant. Diderot's article in the *Encyclopedia* on the Hôtel-Dieu in Paris, the "richest and most terrifying of all French hospitals," vividly describes normal conditions of the 1770s:

Imagine a long series of communicating wards filled with sufferers of every kind of disease who are sometimes packed three, four, five or even six into a bed, the living alongside the dead and dying, the air polluted by this mass of unhealthy bodies, passing pestilential germs of their afflictions from one to the other, and the spectacle of suffering and agony on every hand. That is the Hôtel-Dieu.

The result is that many of these poor wretches come out with diseases they did not have when they went in, and often pass them on to the people they go back to live with. Others are half-cured and

spend the rest of their days in an invalidism as hard to bear as the illness itself; and the rest perish, except for the fortunate few whose strong constitutions enable them to survive.[14]

No wonder the poor of Paris hated hospitals and often saw confinement there as a plot to kill paupers.

In the last years of the century, the humanitarian concern already reflected in Diderot's description of the Hôtel-Dieu led to a movement for hospital reform through western Europe. Efforts were made to improve ventilation and eliminate filth, on the grounds that bad air caused disease. The theory was wrong, but the results were beneficial, since the spread of infection was somewhat reduced.

MENTAL ILLNESS

Mental hospitals too were incredibly savage institutions. The customary treatment for mental illness was bleeding and cold water, administered more to maintain discipline than to effect a cure. Violent persons were chained to the wall and forgotten. A breakthrough of sorts occurred in the 1790s, when William Tuke founded the first humane sanatorium in

England. In Paris an innovative warden, Philippe Pinel, took the chains off the mentally disturbed in 1793 and tried to treat them as patients rather than prisoners.

In the eighteenth century, there were all sorts of wildly erroneous ideas about mental illness. One was that moonlight caused madness, a belief reflected in the word *lunatic* – someone harmed by lunar light. Another mid-eighteenth-century theory, which lasted until at least 1914, was that masturbation caused madness, not to mention acne, epilepsy, and premature ejaculation.

The initial form of this theory was the work of a Swiss doctor, Samuel Tissot. In 1758, Tissot argued that semen was

the Essential Oil of the animal liquors . . . the dissipation whereof leaves the other humors weak. . . . The seminal liquor has so great an influence upon the corporeal powers that . . . the physicians of all ages have been unanimously of the opinion that the loss of an ounce of this humor would weaken more than that of forty ounces of blood.[15]

This being the case, parents, religious institutions, and schools waged relentless war on masturbation by males, although they were curiously uninterested in female masturbation. In the nineteenth century this misguided idea was to reach its greatest height, resulting in increasingly drastic medical treatment. Doctors ordered their "patients" to wear mittens, fitted them with wooden braces between the knees, or simply tied them up in straitjackets.

MEDICAL EXPERIMENTS AND RESEARCH

In the second half of the eighteenth century, medicine in general turned in a more practical and experimental direction. Some of the experimentation was creative quackery involving the recently discovered phenomenon of electricity. One magnificent quack, James Graham of London, opened a great hall filled with the walking sticks, crutches, eyeglasses, and ear trumpets of supposedly cured patients, which he kept as symbols of his victory over disease. Great glass globes, mysterious sphinxes, and the rich perfumes of burning incense awaited all who entered. Graham's principal treatment involved his Celestial Bed, which stood on forty pillars of rich glass and was decorated with magnets and electrical devices. Graham claimed that by sleeping in it youths would keep their good looks, their elders would be rejuvenated, and couples would have beautiful, healthy children. The fee for a single night in the Medico-Magnetico-Musico-Electrical Bed was £100 – a great sum of money.

The rich could buy expensive treatments, but the prevalence of quacks and the general lack of knowledge meant they often got little for their money. Because so many treatments were harmful, the poor were probably much less deprived by their almost total lack of access to medical care than one might think.

Renewed experimentation and the intensified search for solutions to human problems also led to some real advances in medicine after 1750, although most were still modest compared to the advances of the nineteenth and twentieth centuries. The eighteenth century's greatest medical triumph was the conquest of smallpox.

With the progressive decline of bubonic plague, smallpox became the most terrible of the infectious diseases. In the words of the historian Thomas Macaulay, "smallpox was always present, filling the churchyard with corpses, tormenting with constant fears all whom it had not stricken." In the seventeenth century, one in every four deaths in the British Isles was due to smallpox, and it is estimated that 60 million Europeans died of it in

the eighteenth century. Fully 80 percent of the population was stricken at some point in life, and 25 percent of the total population was left permanently scarred. If ever a human problem cried out for a humane solution, it was small-pox.

The first step in the conquest of this killer came in the early eighteenth century. An Eng-lish aristocrat whose great beauty had been marred by the pox, Lady Mary Wortley Mon-tague, learned about the practice of inocula-tion in the Ottoman Empire while her husband was serving as British ambassador

there. She had her own son successfully inoc-ulated in Constantinople, and was instrumen-tal in spreading the practice in England after her return in 1722.

Inoculation against smallpox had long been practiced in the Middle East. The skin was deliberately broken, and a small amount of matter taken from the pustule of a smallpox victim was applied. The person thus con-tracted a mild case of smallpox that gave last-ing protection against further attack. Inoculation was risky. Some of the very first to undergo it in England were felons sentenced to death, who were granted a pardon in return for inoculation. All these unsung heroes recovered and escaped hanging. Generally, about one person in fifty died from inoculation. Soon it was discovered that people who had been inoculated were just as infectious as those who had caught the disease by chance. Inoculated people thus spread the disease, and the practice of inoculation against smallpox was widely condemned in the 1730s.

Success in overcoming this problem in British colonies led the British College of Physicians in 1754 to strongly advocate inoculation. The procedure became complicated, however, involving elaborate and expensive preparatory treatment with bleeding, purging, blisters, and so on. Doctors reaped fine fees and large fortunes, and only people of substantial means could afford inoculation.

A successful search for cheaper methods led to something approaching mass inoculation in England in the 1760s. One specialist treated seventeen thousand patients and only five died. Both the danger and the cost had been reduced, and deadly smallpox struck all classes less frequently. On the Continent, the well-to-do were also inoculated, beginning with royal families like those of Maria Theresa and Catherine the Great. The practice then spread to the middle classes. Smallpox inoculation played some part in the decline of the death rate at the end of the century and the increase in population.

The final breakthrough against smallpox came at the end of the century. Edward Jenner (1749–1823), a talented country doctor, noted that in the English countryside there was a longstanding belief that dairy maids who had contracted cowpox did not get smallpox. Cowpox produces sores on the cow's udder and on the hands of the milker. The sores resemble those of smallpox, but the disease is mild and not contagious.

For eighteen years Jenner practiced a kind of Baconian science, carefully collecting data on protection against smallpox by cowpox. Finally, in 1796, he performed his first vaccination on a young boy, using matter taken from a milkmaid with cowpox. Two months later he inoculated the boy with smallpox pus, but the disease did not take. In the next two years twenty-three successful vaccinations were performed, and in 1798 Jenner published his findings. There was some skepticism and hostility, but after Austrian medical authorities replicated Jenner's results, the new method of treatment spread rapidly. Smallpox soon declined to the point of disappearance in Europe and then throughout the world. Jenner eventually received prizes of £30,000 from the British government for his great discovery, a fitting recompense for a man who gave an enormous gift to humanity and helped lay the foundation for the rise of the science of immunology in the nineteenth century. The struggle against fate and death, against the unknown but not unknowable, had won a great victory.

———————

In recent years imaginative research has greatly increased the specialist's understanding of ordinary life and social patterns in the past. The human experience, as recounted by historians, has become richer and more meaningful, and many mistaken ideas have fallen. This has been particularly true of eighteenth-century, preindustrial Europe. The intimacies of family life, the contours of women's history and of childhood, and vital problems of medicine and nutrition are emerging from obscurity. Nor is this all. A deeper, truer understanding of the life of common people can shed light on the great economic and political developments of longstanding concern, as we shall see in the next chapter.

1. Quoted by J. M. Beattie, "The Criminality of Women in Eighteenth-Century England," *Journal of Social History* 8 (Summer 1975):86.

2. W. L. Langer, "Infanticide: A Historical Survey," *History of Childhood Quarterly* 1 (Winter 1974):357.

3. Quoted by R. Cobb, *The Police and the People: French Popular Protest, 1789–1820,* Clarendon Press, Oxford, 1970, p. 238.

4. Quoted by E. A. Wrigley, *Population and History,* McGraw-Hill, New York, 1969, p. 127.

5. Quoted in D. S. Landes, ed., *The Rise of Capitalism,* Macmillan, New York, 1966, pp. 56–57.

6. See L. A. Tilly, J. W. Scott, and M. Cohen, "Women's Work and European Fertility Patterns," *Journal of Interdisciplinary History* 6 (Winter 1976):447–476.

7. J. Michelet, *The People,* trans. with an introduction by J. P. McKay, University of Illinois Press, Urbana, 1973 (original publication, 1846), pp. 38–39.

8. J. Brownlow, *The History and Design of the Foundling Hospital,* London, 1868, p. 7.

9. Quoted by B. W. Lorence, "Parents and Children in Eighteenth-Century Europe," *History of Childhood Quarterly* 2 (Summer 1974):1–2.

10. Ibid., pp. 13, 16.

11. J. C. Drummond and A. Wilbraham, *The Englishman's Food: A History of Five Centuries of English Diet,* 2nd ed., Jonathan Cape, London, 1958, p. 75.

12. Ibid., p. 235.

13. Quoted by L. S. King, *The Medical World of the Eighteenth Century,* University of Chicago Press, Chicago, 1958, p. 320.

14. Quoted by R. Sand, *The Advance to Social Medicine,* Staples Press, London, 1952, pp. 86–87.

15. Quoted by R. P. Neuman, "Masturbation, Madness, and the Modern Concepts of Childhood and Adolescence," *Journal of Social History* 8 (Spring 1975):2.

Although often ignored in many general histories of the Western world, social topics of the kind considered in this chapter flourish in specialized journals today. The articles cited in the Notes are typical of the exciting work being done, and the reader is strongly advised to take time to look through recent volumes of some leading journals: *Journal of Social History, Past and Present, History of Childhood Quarterly,* and *Journal of Interdisciplinary History.* In addition, the number of book-length studies has begun to expand rapidly.

Among general introductions to the history of the family, women, and children, E. A. Wrigley, *Population and History* (1969), is excellent. P. Laslett, *The World We Have Lost* (1965), is an exciting pioneering investigation of England before the Industrial Revolution, though some of his conclusions have been weakened by further research. Lawrence Stone, *The Family, Sex and Marriage in England, 1500–1800* (1977), is a brilliant general interpretation, and L. Tilly and J. Scott, *Women, Work and Family* (1978), is excellent. P. Ariès, *Centuries of Childhood: A Social History of Family Life* (1962), is another stimulating study. E. Shorter, *The Making of the Modern Family* (1975), is an all-too-lively and rather controversial interpretation. All four works are highly recommended. T. Rabb and R. I. Rothberg, eds., *The Family in History* (1973), is a good collection of articles dealing with both Europe and the United States. A. MacFarlane, *The Family Life of Ralph Josselin* (1970), is a brilliant re-creation of the intimate family circle of a seventeenth-century English clergyman who kept a detailed diary; MacFarlane's *Origins of English Individualism: The Family, Property and Social Transition* (1978) is a major work. I. Pinchbeck and M. Hewitt, *Children in English Society* (1973), is a good introduction. E. Flexner has written a fine biography on the early feminist Mary Wollstonecraft (1972). Various aspects of sexual relationships are treated imaginatively by M. Foucault, *The History of Sexuality* (1981), and R. Wheaton and T. Hareven, eds., *Family and Sexuality in French History* (1980).

J. Burnett, *A History of the Cost of Living* (1969), has a great deal of interesting information about what people spent their money on in the past and complements the fascinating work of J. C. Drummond and A. Wilbraham, *The Englishman's Food: A History of Five Centuries of English Diet* (1958). J. Knyveton, *Diary of a Surgeon in the Year 1751–1752* (1937), gives a contemporary's unforgettable picture of both eighteenth-century medicine and social customs. Good introductions to the evolution of medical practices are B. Ingles, *History of Medicine* (1965); O. Bettmann, *A Pictorial History of Medicine* (1956); and H. Haggard's old but interesting *Devils, Drugs, and Doctors* (1929). W. Boyd, *History of Western Education* (1966), is a standard survey, which may be usefully supplemented by an important article by L. Stone, "Literacy and Education in England, 1640–1900," *Past and Present* 42 (February 1969):69–139. M. D. George, *London Life in the Eighteenth Century* (1965), is a delightfully written book, while L. Chevalier, *Labouring Classes and Dangerous Classes* (1973), is a keen analysis of the poor people of Paris in a slightly later period. G. Rudé, *The Crowd in History, 1730–1848* (1964), is an innovative effort to see politics and popular protest from below. An important series edited by Robert Forster and Orest Ranuum considers neglected social questions such as diet, abandoned children, and deviants, as does Peter Burke's excellent study, *Popular Culture in Early Modern Europe* (1978). Finally, J. Howard, *State of the Prisons,* first published in 1777 and reissued in 1929, takes one on an exhaustive tour of European jails in the eighteenth century and shows the beginning of concern for humanitarian reform of unbelievably harsh penal conditions.

CHAPTER 21

THE REVOLUTION IN POLITICS,

1775–1814

THE LAST YEARS of the eighteenth century were a time of great upheaval. A series of revolutions and revolutionary wars challenged the old order of kings and aristocrats. The ideas of freedom and equality, ideas that have not stopped shaping the world since that era, flourished and spread. The revolution began in North America in 1775. Then in 1789 France, the largest and most influential country in Europe, became the leading revolutionary nation. It established first a constitutional monarchy, then a radical republic, and finally a new empire under Napoleon. The armies of France also joined forces with patriots and radicals abroad in an effort to establish new governments based on new principles throughout much of Europe. The world of modern domestic and international politics was born.

What caused this era of revolution? What were the ideas and objectives of the men and women who rose up violently to undo the established system? What were the gains and losses for privileged groups and for ordinary people in a generation of war and upheaval? These are the questions this chapter will seek to answer in an examination of the French and American revolutions.

LIBERTY AND EQUALITY

Two ideas fueled the revolutionary period in both America and Europe: liberty and equality. What did eighteenth-century politicians and other people mean by liberty and equality, and why were those ideas so radical and revolutionary in their day?

The call for liberty was first of all a call for individual human rights. Even the most enlightened monarchs customarily claimed that it was their duty to regulate what people wrote and believed. Liberals of the revolutionary era protested such controls from on high. They demanded freedom to worship according to the dictates of their consciences instead of according to the politics of their prince. They demanded the end of censorship and the right to express their beliefs freely in print and at public meetings. They demanded freedom from arbitrary laws and from judges who simply obeyed orders from the government.

These demands for basic personal freedoms, which were incorporated into the American Bill of Rights and other liberal constitutions, were very far-reaching. Indeed, eighteenth-century revolutionaries demanded more freedom than most governments today believe it is desirable to grant. The Declaration of the Rights of Man, issued at the beginning of the French Revolution, proclaimed, "Liberty consists in being able to do anything that does not harm another person." A citizen's rights had, therefore, "no limits except those which assure to the other members of society the enjoyment of these same rights." Liberals called for the freedom of the individual to develop and to create to the fullest possible extent. In the context of aristocratic and monarchial forms of government that then dominated Europe, this was a truly radical idea.

The call for liberty was also a call for a new kind of government. The revolutionary liberals believed that the people were sovereign — that is, that the people alone had the authority to make laws limiting the individual's freedom of action. In practice, this system of government meant choosing legislators who represented the people and who were accountable to them. Moreover, liberals of the revolutionary era believed that every people —

every ethnic group – had this right of self-determination, and thus the right to form a free nation.

By equality, eighteenth-century liberals meant that all citizens were to have identical rights and civil liberties. Above all, the nobility had no right to special privileges based on the accident of birth.

Liberals did not define equality as meaning that everyone should be equal economically. Quite the contrary. As Thomas Jefferson wrote in an early draft of the American Declaration of Independence, before changing "property" to the more noble-sounding "happiness," everyone was equal in "the pursuit of property." Jefferson and other liberals certainly did not expect equal success in that pursuit. Great differences in wealth and income between rich and poor were perfectly acceptable to liberals. The essential point was that everyone should legally have an equal chance. French liberals and revolutionaries said they wanted "careers opened to talent." They wanted employment in government, in business, and in the professions to be based on ability, not on family background or legal status.

Equality of opportunity was a very revolutionary idea in eighteenth-century Europe. Legal inequality between classes and groups was the rule, not the exception. Society was still legally divided into groups with special privileges, such as the nobility and the clergy, and groups with special burdens, like the peasantry. In many countries, various middle-class groups – professionals, businessmen, townspeople, and craftsmen – enjoyed privileges that allowed them to monopolize all sorts of economic activity. It was this kind of economic inequality, an inequality based on artificial legal distinctions, against which liberals protested.

The ideas of liberty and equality – the central ideas of classical liberalism – have deep roots in Western history. The ancient Greeks and the Judeo-Christian tradition had affirmed for hundreds of years the sanctity and value of the individual human being. The Judeo-Christian tradition, reinforced by the Reformation, had long stressed personal responsibility on the part of both common folk and exalted rulers, thereby promoting the self-discipline without which liberty becomes anarchy. The hounded and persecuted Protestant radicals of the later sixteenth century had died for the revolutionary idea that individuals were entitled to their own religious beliefs.

Although the liberal creed had roots deep in the Western tradition, classical liberalism first crystallized at the end of the seventeenth century and during the Enlightenment of the eighteenth century.

Liberal ideas reflected the Enlightenment's stress on human dignity and human happiness on earth. They shared the Enlightenment's general faith in science, rationality, and progress: the adoption of liberal principles meant better government and a better society for all. Almost all the writers of the Enlightenment were passionately committed to greater personal liberty. They preached religious toleration, freedom of press and speech, and fair and equal treatment before the law. Yet many of the French philosophers – Voltaire was typical – believed that these liberties could be realized through the enlightened absolutism of a wise king or queen. A minority of eighteenth-century thinkers thought otherwise. It was these thinkers who were mainly responsible for wedding the liberal concept of self-government to the Enlightenment's concern with personal freedom and legal equality.

Almost all the great proponents of the liberal theory of self-government came from England and France. Two of them were particularly influential. John Locke, who was so influential in giving the Enlightenment new ideas about how human beings learn (page 641), turned to English history as a basis for his political theory. England's long political tradition rested, according to Locke, on "the rights of Englishmen" and on representative government through Parliament. Thus in the controversy over excluding the strong-minded James, Duke of York, from the English throne, Locke argued for strict limitations on monarchy in order to preserve liberty. An admirer of the great Whig noblemen who subsequently made the bloodless revolution of 1688 (pages 582–583), Locke maintained that a government that oversteps its proper function – protecting the natural rights of life, liberty, and private property – becomes a tyranny. In such extreme cases the people have the natural right of rebellion. Locke thought such drastic action could usually be avoided, if the government respected the rights of its citizens and the people were zealous in the defense of their liberty. Thus Locke helped to revive the powerful idea, inherited from ancient Greece and Rome (page 131), that there are natural or universal rights that are equally valid for all peoples and societies.

It is important to note that Locke's strong defense of economic liberty and private property was linked to his love of political freedom. Locke prophetically saw that there was a close relationship between economic freedom and political freedom. If a significant number of citizens, such as the large English landowners, were not economically independent, there would be no basis for independent political opposition. Locke's ideas, as well as those of other English thinkers who lauded liberty and denounced the danger of tyranny, were particularly popular in colonial America.

Few of the French philosophes were particularly interested in political theorizing, but the baron de Montesquieu (1689–1755) was a towering exception. Having made his name as a social satirist, he turned to liberal political philosophy in the course of the eighteenth century. Montesquieu was a great noble, and he was dismayed by the triumph of absolute government in France under Louis XIV. Inspired by the example of the physical sciences, Montesquieu set out to apply the critical method to the problem of government in *The Spirit of Laws* (1748). The result was a comparative study of republics, monarchies, and despotisms – a great pioneering inquiry in the emerging social sciences.

Fearful of the tyrannical possibility of an unrestrained state, as was Locke, Montesquieu developed the idea that despotism would be avoided if political power were divided – among legislative, executive, and judicial branches of government. Each branch would check the tendency of the other to usurp power and curtail liberty. Montesquieu especially admired England and the English balance of power among the king, the Parliament, and the independent courts. Montesquieu's theory of separation of powers had great impact: the constitutions of the young United States in 1789 and of France in 1791 were based in large part on this theory.

THE ATTRACTION OF LIBERALISM

Locke and Montesquieu were spokesmen for liberal ideals. Were they also, as is often said, spokesmen for "a rising middle class," a class impatient with the pretensions of monarchy and the privileges of aristocracy? To some extent, they were. Equality before the law and equality of opportunity were ideals particularly dear to ambitious and educated bourgeois. Yet liberal ideas about individual rights and political freedom also appealed to much of the aristocracy, at least in western Europe and as formulated by Montesquieu. Representative government did not mean democracy, which liberal thinkers tended to equate with mob rule. Rather, they envisioned voting for representatives as being restricted to those who owned property, those with "a stake in society." England had shown the way. After 1688, it had combined a parliamentary system and considerable individual liberty with a restricted franchise and unquestionable aristocratic pre-eminence.

Eighteenth-century liberalism, then, appealed not only to the middle class, but also to some aristocrats. It found broad support among the educated elite and the substantial classes in western Europe. What it lacked from the beginning was strong mass support. For comfortable liberals, the really important questions were theoretical and political. They had no need to worry about their stomachs and the price of bread. For the much more numerous laboring poor, the great questions were immediate and economic. Getting enough to eat was the crucial challenge. These differences in outlook and well-being were to lead to many misunderstandings and disappointments for both groups in the revolutionary era.

THE AMERICAN REVOLUTION, 1775–1789

The era of liberal revolution began in the New World. The thirteen mainland colonies of British North America revolted against

their mother country and then succeeded in establishing a new unified government.

Americans have long debated the meaning of their revolution. Some have even questioned whether or not it was a real revolution, as opposed to a war for independence. According to some scholars, the revolution was conservative and defensive in that its demands were for the traditional liberties of Englishmen; Americans were united against the British, but otherwise they were a satisfied people and not torn by internal conflict. Other scholars have argued that, on the contrary, the American Revolution was quite radical. It split families between patriots and Loyalists and divided the country. It achieved goals that were fully as advanced as those obtained by the French in their great revolution a few years later.

How does one reconcile these positions? Both contain large elements of truth. The American revolutionaries did believe they were demanding only the traditional rights of English men and women. But those traditional rights were liberal rights, and in the American context they had very strong democratic and popular overtones. Thus, the American Revolution was fought in the name of established ideals that were still quite radical in the context of the times. And in founding a government firmly based on liberal principles, the Americans set an example that had a forceful impact on Europe and speeded up political development there.

THE ORIGINS OF THE REVOLUTION

The American Revolution had its immediate origins in a squabble over increased taxes. The British government had fought and decisively won the Seven Years' War (page 682) on the strength of its professional army and navy.

THE BOSTON TEA PARTY *In this 1789 engraving men disguised as Indians dump East India Company tea into the harbor. The large crowd on shore indicates widespread support. (Library of Congress)*

The American colonists had furnished little real aid. The high cost of the war to the British, however, had led to a doubling of the British national debt. Anticipating further expense defending its recently conquered western lands from Indian uprisings like that of Pontiac, the British government in London set about reorganizing the empire with a series of bold, largely unprecedented measures. Breaking with tradition, the British decided to maintain a large army in North America after peace was restored in 1763. Moreover, they sought to exercise strict control over their newly conquered western lands and to tax the colonies directly. In 1765, the government pushed through Parliament the Stamp Act, which levied taxes on a long list of commercial and legal documents, diplomas, pamphlets, newspapers, almanacs, dice, and playing cards. A stamp glued to each article indicated the tax had been paid.

The effort to increase taxes as part of tightening up the empire seemed perfectly reasonable to the British. Heavier stamp taxes had been collected in Great Britain for two generations, and Americans were being asked only to pay a share of their own defense. Moreover, Americans had been paying only very low local taxes. The Stamp Act would have doubled taxes to about two shillings per person. No other people in the world (except the Poles) paid so little. The British, meanwhile, paid the world's highest taxes in about 1765 – twenty-six shillings per person. It is not surprising that taxes per person in the newly independent American nation were much higher in 1785 than in 1765, when the British no longer subsidized American defense. The colonists protested the Stamp Act vigorously and violently, however, and after rioting and boycotts against British goods, Parliament reluctantly repealed the new tax.

As the fury of the Stamp Act controversy revealed, much more was involved than taxes. The key question was political. To what extent could the home government refashion the empire and reassert its power while limiting the authority of colonial legislatures and their elected representatives? Accordingly, who should represent the colonies, and who had the right to make laws for Americans? While a troubled majority of Americans searched hard for a compromise, some radicals began to proclaim that "taxation without representation is tyranny." The British government replied that Americans were represented in Parliament, albeit indirectly (like most Englishmen themselves), and that the absolute supremacy of Parliament throughout the empire could not be questioned. Many Americans felt otherwise. As John Adams put it, "A Parliament of Great Britain can have no more rights to tax the colonies than a Parliament of Paris." Thus imperial reorganization and Parliamentary supremacy came to appear as grave threats to Americans' existing liberties and time-honored institutions.

Americans had long exercised a great deal of independence and gone their own way. In British North America, unlike England and Europe, there was no powerful established church, and personal freedom in questions of religion was taken for granted. The colonial assemblies made the important laws, which were seldom overturned by the home govern-

ment. The right to vote was much more widespread than in England. In many parts of colonial Massachusetts, for example, as many as 95 percent of the adult males could vote.

Moreover, greater political equality was matched by greater social and economic equality. Neither a hereditary nobility nor a hereditary serf population existed, although the slavery of the Americas consigned blacks to a legally oppressed caste. Independent farmers were the largest group in the country and set much of its tone. In short, the colonial experience had slowly formed a people who felt themselves separate and distinct from the home country. The controversies over taxation intensified those feelings of distinctiveness and separation and brought them to the fore.

In 1773, the dispute over taxes and representation flared up again. The British government had permitted the financially hard-pressed East India Company to ship its tea from China directly to its agents in the colonies, rather than through London middlemen who then sold to independent merchants in the colonies. Thus, the company secured a virtual monopoly on the tea trade, and colonial merchants were suddenly excluded from a highly profitable business. The colonists were quick to protest.

In Boston, men disguised as Indians had a rowdy "tea party," and threw the company's tea into the harbor. This led to extreme measures. The so-called Coercive Acts closed the port of Boston, curtailed local elections and town meetings, and greatly expanded the royal governor's power. County conventions in Massachusetts protested vehemently and urged that the acts be "rejected as the attempts of a wicked administration to enslave America." Other colonial assemblies joined in the denunciations. In September 1774, the First Continental Congress met in Philadelphia, where the more radical members argued successfully against concessions to the Crown. Compromise was also rejected by the British Parliament and in April 1775 fighting began at Lexington and Concord.

INDEPENDENCE

The fighting spread, and the colonists moved slowly but inevitably toward open rebellion and a declaration of independence. The uncompromising attitude of the British government and its use of German mercenaries went a long way toward dissolving long-standing loyalties to the home country and rivalries among the separate colonies. *Common Sense* (1775), a brilliant attack by the recently arrived English radical Thomas Paine, also mobilized public opinion in favor of independence. A runaway best seller with sales of 120,000 copies in a few months, Paine's tract ridiculed the idea of a small island ruling a great continent. In his call for freedom and republican government, Paine expressed Americans' growing sense of separateness and moral superiority.

On July 4, 1776, the Second Continental Congress adopted the Declaration of Independence. Written by Thomas Jefferson, the Declaration of Independence boldly listed the tyrannical acts committed by George III (1760–1820) and confidently proclaimed the natural rights of man and the sovereignty of the American states. Sometimes called the world's greatest political editorial, the Declaration of Independence in effect universalized the traditional rights of Englishmen and made them the rights of all mankind. It stated that "all men are created equal ... they are endowed by their Creator with certain unalienable rights . . . among these are life, liberty, and the pursuit of happiness." No other American political document has ever caused

THE DECLARATION OF INDEPENDENCE The famous document, principally authored by Thomas Jefferson, bears many well-known signatures. (National Archives, Washington, D.C.)

such excitement, both at home and abroad.

Many American families remained loyal to Britain; many others divided bitterly. After the Declaration of Independence, the conflict often took the form of a civil war pitting patriot against Loyalist. The Loyalists tended to be wealthy and politically moderate. Many patriots too were wealthy – individuals such as John Hancock and George Washington – but willingly allied themselves with farmers and artisans in a broad coalition. This coalition harassed the Loyalists and confiscated their property to help pay for the American war effort. The broad social base of the revolutionaries tended to make the liberal revolution democratic. State governments extended the right to vote to many more people in the course of the war and re-established themselves as republics.

On the international scene, the French were sympathetic to the rebels from the beginning. They wanted revenge for the humiliating defeats of the Seven Years' War. Officially neutral until 1776, they supplied the great bulk of guns and gunpowder used by the American revolutionaries, very much as neutral Great Powers supply weapons for "wars of national liberation" today. In 1778, the French offered the Americans a formal alliance, and in 1779 and 1780 the Spanish and Dutch declared war on Britain. Catherine the Great of Russia helped organize a League of Armed Neutrality in order to protect neutral shipping rights, which Britain refused to recognize.

Thus by 1780, Great Britain was engaged in an imperial war against most of Europe as well as the thirteen colonies. In these circum-

IN CONGRESS. JULY 4, 1776.

The unanimous Declaration of the thirteen united States of America,

When in the Course of human events, it becomes necessary for one people to dissolve the political bands which have connected them with another, and to assume among the powers of the earth, the separate and equal station to which the Laws of Nature and of Nature's God entitle them, a decent respect to the opinions of mankind requires that they should declare the causes which impel them to the separation.

We hold these truths to be self-evident, that all men are created equal, that they are endowed by their Creator with certain unalienable Rights, that among these are Life, Liberty and the pursuit of Happiness.— That to secure these rights, Governments are instituted among Men, deriving their just powers from the consent of the governed,— That whenever any Form of Government becomes destructive of these ends, it is the Right of the People to alter or to abolish it, and to institute new Government, laying its foundation on such principles and organizing its powers in such form, as to them shall seem most likely to effect their Safety and Happiness. Prudence, indeed, will dictate that Governments long established should not be changed for light and transient causes; and accordingly all experience hath shewn, that mankind are more disposed to suffer, while evils are sufferable, than to right themselves by abolishing the forms to which they are accustomed. But when a long train of abuses and usurpations, pursuing invariably the same Object evinces a design to reduce them under absolute Despotism, it is their right, it is their duty, to throw off such Government, and to provide new Guards for their future security.— Such has been the patient sufferance of these Colonies; and such is now the necessity which constrains them to alter their former Systems of Government. The history of the present King of Great Britain is a history of repeated injuries and usurpations, all having in direct object the establishment of an absolute Tyranny over these States. To prove this, let Facts be submitted to a candid world.

He has refused his Assent to Laws, the most wholesome and necessary for the public good.
He has forbidden his Governors to pass Laws of immediate and pressing importance, unless suspended in their operation till his Assent should be obtained; and when so suspended, he has utterly neglected to attend to them.
He has refused to pass other Laws for the accommodation of large districts of people, unless those people would relinquish the right of Representation in the Legislature, a right inestimable to them and formidable to tyrants only.
He has called together legislative bodies at places unusual, uncomfortable, and distant from the depository of their public Records, for the sole purpose of fatiguing them into compliance with his measures.
He has dissolved Representative Houses repeatedly, for opposing with manly firmness his invasions on the rights of the people.
He has refused for a long time, after such dissolutions, to cause others to be elected; whereby the Legislative powers, incapable of Annihilation, have returned to the People at large for their exercise; the State remaining in the mean time exposed to all the dangers of invasion from without, and convulsions within.
He has endeavoured to prevent the population of these States; for that purpose obstructing the Laws for Naturalization of Foreigners; refusing to pass others to encourage their migrations hither, and raising the conditions of new Appropriations of Lands.
He has obstructed the Administration of Justice, by refusing his Assent to Laws for establishing Judiciary powers.
He has made Judges dependent on his Will alone, for the tenure of their offices, and the amount and payment of their salaries.
He has erected a multitude of New Offices, and sent hither swarms of Officers to harrass our people, and eat out their substance.
He has kept among us, in times of peace, Standing Armies without the Consent of our legislatures.
He has affected to render the Military independent of and superior to the Civil power.
He has combined with others to subject us to a jurisdiction foreign to our constitution, and unacknowledged by our laws; giving his Assent to their Acts of pretended Legislation:
For Quartering large bodies of armed troops among us: — For protecting them, by a mock Trial, from punishment for any Murders which they should commit on the Inhabitants of these States: — For cutting off our Trade with all parts of the world: — For imposing Taxes on us without our Consent: — For depriving us in many cases, of the benefits of Trial by Jury: — For transporting us beyond Seas to be tried for pretended offences — For abolishing the free System of English Laws in a neighbouring Province, establishing therein an Arbitrary government, and enlarging its Boundaries so as to render it at once an example and fit instrument for introducing the same absolute rule into these Colonies: — For taking away our Charters, abolishing our most valuable Laws, and altering fundamentally the Forms of our Governments: — For suspending our own Legislatures, and declaring themselves invested with power to legislate for us in all cases whatsoever.
He has abdicated Government here, by declaring us out of his Protection and waging War against us.
He has plundered our seas, ravaged our Coasts, burnt our towns, and destroyed the lives of our people.
He is at this time transporting large Armies of foreign Mercenaries to compleat the works of death, desolation and tyranny, already begun with circumstances of Cruelty & perfidy scarcely paralleled in the most barbarous ages, and totally unworthy the Head of a civilized nation.
He has constrained our fellow Citizens taken Captive on the high Seas to bear Arms against their Country, to become the executioners of their friends and Brethren, or to fall themselves by their Hands.
He has excited domestic insurrections amongst us, and has endeavoured to bring on the inhabitants of our frontiers, the merciless Indian Savages, whose known rule of warfare, is an undistinguished destruction of all ages, sexes and conditions.
In every stage of these Oppressions We have Petitioned for Redress in the most humble terms: Our repeated Petitions have been answered only by repeated injury. A Prince, whose character is thus marked by every act which may define a Tyrant, is unfit to be the ruler of a free people. Nor have We been wanting in attentions to our British brethren. We have warned them from time to time of attempts by their legislature to extend an unwarrantable jurisdiction over us. We have reminded them of the circumstances of our emigration and settlement here. We have appealed to their native justice and magnanimity, and we have conjured them by the ties of our common kindred to disavow these usurpations, which, would inevitably interrupt our connections and correspondence. They too have been deaf to the voice of justice and of consanguinity. We must, therefore, acquiesce in the necessity, which denounces our Separation, and hold them, as we hold the rest of mankind, Enemies in War, in Peace Friends.

We, therefore, the Representatives of the united States of America, in General Congress, Assembled, appealing to the Supreme Judge of the world for the rectitude of our intentions, do, in the Name, and by Authority of the good People of these Colonies, solemnly publish and declare, That these United Colonies are, and of Right ought to be Free and Independent States; that they are Absolved from all Allegiance to the British Crown, and that all political connection between them and the State of Great Britain, is and ought to be totally dissolved; and that as Free and Independent States, they have full Power to levy War, conclude Peace, contract Alliances, establish Commerce, and to do all other Acts and Things which Independent States may of right do.— And for the support of this Declaration, with a firm reliance on the Protection of Divine Providence, we mutually pledge to each other our Lives, our Fortunes and our sacred Honor.

Button Gwinnett
Lyman Hall
Geo Walton.

Wm Hooper
Joseph Hewes,
John Penn

Edward Rutledge.

Thos Heyward Junr.
Thomas Lynch Junr.
Arthur Middleton

John Hancock

Samuel Chase
Wm Paca
Thos Stone
Charles Carroll of Carrollton

George Wythe
Richard Henry Lee
Th Jefferson
Benj Harrison
Thos Nelson jr.
Francis Lightfoot Lee
Carter Braxton

Robt Morris
Benjamin Rush
Benj. Franklin
John Morton
Geo Clymer
Jas. Smith
Geo. Taylor
James Wilson
Geo. Ross
Caesar Rodney
Geo Read
Tho M:Kean

Wm Floyd
Phil. Livingston
Frans. Lewis
Lewis Morris

Richd Stockton
Jno Witherspoon
Fras Hopkinson
John Hart
Abra Clark

Josiah Bartlett
Wm Whipple
Saml Adams
John Adams
Robt Treat Paine
Elbridge Gerry
Step Hopkins
William Ellery
Roger Sherman
Sam Huntington
Wm Williams
Oliver Wolcott
Matthew Thornton

stances, and in the face of severe reverses in India, the West Indies, and at Yorktown in Virginia, a new British government decided to cut its losses. American negotiators in Paris were receptive. They feared that France wanted a treaty that would bottle up the new United States east of the Alleghenies and give British holdings west of the Alleghenies to France's ally, Spain. Thus the American negotiators ditched the French and accepted the extraordinarily favorable terms Britain offered.

By the Treaty of Paris of 1783, Britain ceded all its territory between the Appalachians and the Mississippi River to the Americans and recognized the independence of the thirteen colonies. Out of the no-win rivalries of the Old World, the Americans snatched dominion over half a continent.

FRAMING THE CONSTITUTION

The liberal program of the American Revolution was consolidated by the federal Constitution, the Bill of Rights and the creation of a national republic. Assembling in Philadelphia in the summer of 1787, the delegates to the Constitutional Convention were determined to end the period of economic depression, social uncertainty, and very weak central government that had followed independence. The delegates decided, therefore, to grant the federal, or central, government important powers: regulation of domestic and foreign trade, the right to levy taxes, and the means to enforce its laws.

Strong rule was placed squarely in the context of representative self-government. Senators and congressmen would be the lawmaking delegates of the voters, and the president of the republic would be an elected official. The central government was to operate in a Lockean framework of checks and balances. The executive, legislative, and judicial branches would systematically balance each other. The power of the federal government would in turn be checked by the powers of the individual states.

When the results of the secret deliberation of the Constitutional Convention were presented to the states for ratification, a great public debate began. The opponents of the proposed constitution – the Anti-Federalists – charged that the framers of the new document had taken too much power from the individual states and made the federal government too strong. Moreover, many Anti-Federalists feared for the personal liberties and individual freedoms for which they had just fought. In order to overcome these objections, the Federalists solemnly promised to spell out these basic freedoms as soon as the new constitution was adopted. The result was the first ten amendments to the Constitution, which the first Congress passed shortly after it met in New York in March 1789. These amendments formed an effective bill of rights to safeguard the individual. Most of them – trial by jury, due process of law, right to assembly, freedom from unreasonable search – had their origins in English law and the English Bill of Rights of 1689. Others – the freedoms of speech, the press, and religion – reflected natural-law theory and the American experience.

The American Constitution and the Bill of Rights exemplified the great strengths and the limits of what came to be called classical liberalism. Liberty meant individual freedoms and political safeguards. Liberty also meant representative government, but did not necessarily mean democracy with its principle of the one man, one vote.

Equality – slaves excepted – meant equality

before the law, not equality of political participation or economic well-being. Indeed, economic inequality was resolutely defended by the elite who framed the Constitution. The right to own property was guaranteed by the Fifth Amendment, and if the government took private property the owner was to receive "just compensation." The radicalism of liberal revolution in America was primarily legal and political, not economic or social.

THE REVOLUTION'S IMPACT ON EUROPE

Hundreds of books, pamphlets, and articles analyzed and romanticized the American upheaval. Thoughtful Europeans noted, first of all, its enormous long-term implications for international politics. A secret report by the Venetian ambassador to Paris in 1783 stated what many felt: "If only the union of the Provinces is preserved, it is reasonable to expect that, with the favorable effects of time, and of European arts and sciences, it will become the most formidable power in the world."[1] More generally, American independence fired the imaginations of those few aristocrats who were uneasy with their privileges and of those commoners who yearned for greater equality. Many Europeans believed that the world was moving now and that America was leading the way. As one French writer put it in 1789: "This vast continent which the seas surround will soon change Europe and the universe."

Europeans who dreamed of a new era were fascinated by the political lessons of the American Revolution. The Americans had begun with a revolutionary defense against tyrannical oppression, and they had been victorious. They had then shown how rational beings could assemble together to consolidate their gains in a permanent written constitu-

tion – a new social contract. All this gave greater reality to the concepts of individual liberty and representative government. It reinforced one of the primary ideas of the Enlightenment, the idea that a better world here on earth was possible.

THE FRENCH REVOLUTION, 1789–1791

No country felt the consequences of the American Revolution more directly than France. Hundreds of French officers served in America and were inspired by the experience. The most famous of these, the young and impressionable Marquis de Lafayette (1757–1834), left home wanting only to fight France's traditional foe, England. He returned with a love of liberty and firm republican convictions. French intellectuals and publicists engaged in passionate analysis of the federal Constitution, as well as the constitutions of the various states of the new United States. The American Revolution undeniably hastened upheaval in France.

Yet the French Revolution did not mirror the American example. It was more violent and more complex, more influential and more controversial, more loved and more hated. For Europeans and most of the rest of the world, it was *the* great revolution of the eighteenth century, the revolution that opened the modern era in politics.

THE CRISIS OF THE OLD ORDER

Like the American Revolution, the French Revolution had its immediate origins in the financial difficulties of the government. War with England had greatly increased France's

*LOUIS XVI Louis was a handsome, well-meaning
youth when he came to the throne in 1774. This stunning portrait by Duplessis idealizes him as a majestic,
self-confident ruler, worthy heir of Louis XIV and
French absolutism. Actually, Louis XVI was shy, indecisive, and somewhat stupid. (Chateau de Ver-
sailles/Giraudon)*

national debt; bankruptcy or a sharp rise in
taxes became inevitable. The government's
yearly income from taxation and other sources
was, quite simply, less than it spent. For a
long time the government had been living
with the problem by means of haphazard def-
icit financing, borrowing ever more money
from bankers and the well-to-do. By 1788,
fully half of France's annual budget went for
ever-increasing interest payments on the ever-
increasing debt. Another quarter went to
maintain the military, while 6 percent was absorbed by the costly and extravagant king and
his court at Versailles. Less than one-fifth of

the entire national budget was available for the productive functions of the state, such as transportation and general administration. It was an impossible financial situation.

One way out would have been for the government to declare partial bankruptcy, forcing its creditors to accept greatly reduced payments on the debt. Following widespread medieval practice, the powerful Spanish monarchy had regularly repudiated large portions of its debt in the late sixteenth and seventeenth centuries. France had done likewise in the early eighteenth century, after an attempt by John Law, a Scottish adventurer, to establish a French national bank ended in financial disaster in 1720. Yet by the 1780s the French debt was held by an army of aristocratic and bourgeois creditors, and the French monarchy, though absolute in theory, had become far too weak for such a drastic and unpopular action.

Nor could the king and his ministers, unlike modern governments, print money and create inflation to cover their deficits. Unlike England and Holland, which had far larger national debts relative to their populations, France after John Law's unsuccessful experiment had no central bank, no paper currency, and no means of creating credit. French money was good gold coin. Even in times of severe economic crisis the government could not create credit and paper money. It could only beg, unsuccessfully, for new gold loans from its frightened and hard-pressed population. Bound up in the straitjacket of a primitive banking system, the monarchy had no alternative but to try to increase taxes.

TAXES AND PRIVILEGES

France's system of taxation was unfair and out of date. Increased taxes were possible only in conjunction with developing new sources of revenue, and such tax reform opened a Pandora's box of social and political demands. Taxes were based on the inequality of a society still legally divided into the medieval orders or "estates" – the clergy, the nobility, and everyone else – and were apportioned among the estates very unequally.

Constituting only about 100,000 of France's 24 million inhabitants, the clergy had important privileges. It owned about 10 percent of the land in France and was lightly taxed. Moreover, it levied on the crops of the peasantry an oppressive tax (the tithe) that averaged somewhat less than 10 percent. The clergy's top jobs, soft and overpaid, were jealously monopolized by nobles, to the intense dissatisfaction of the poor parish priests of lower-class origin.

The second estate consisted of some 400,000 noblemen and noblewomen, whose privileges were not only great but growing. Fully in keeping with the general European compromise of bureaucratic absolutism, the French nobility in the late eighteenth century had come to hold almost all the top positions in the government. The nobles also owned fully 25 percent of all the land in the country and were very lightly taxed by the government. Like the clergy, they taxed the peasantry for their own profit. This was done by means of exclusive rights to hunt and fish, village monopolies on baking bread and pressing grapes for wine, fees for justice, and a host of other privileges. Thus in France, as in most of Europe, the wealthiest group in the country – the nobility – systematically exploited the poorest – the peasantry. Long accustomed to a sumptuous banquet of privilege, the appetite of the French nobility had only increased with eating. Ironically, in view of all that followed, it was the pretensions of the nobility that turned a financial crisis into a revolution.

Everyone else was a commoner, a member of the third estate. A few commoners were extremely rich businessmen or highly successful doctors and lawyers. Many more were urban artisans and unskilled day laborers. The vast majority of the third estate consisted of the peasants and agricultural workers in the countryside. Thus, the third estate was a conglomeration of vastly different social groups, united only by their shared legal status as distinct from the privileged nobility and clergy.

FORMATION OF THE NATIONAL ASSEMBLY

The Revolution was under way by 1787, though no one could have realized what was to follow. That year Louis XVI's minister of finance dusted off old proposals to impose a general tax on all landed property, and he convinced the king to call an Assembly of Notables to gain support for the idea. The assembled notables, who were mainly important noblemen and high-ranking clergy of noble birth, were not in favor of it. In return for their support they demanded control over all government spending and decision making through provincial assemblies, which they expected to control. Denouncing arbitrary taxation by the king, the nobility sought in the name of liberty to assure its own domination of the state. The king tried to reassert his authority. A great wave of protest swept the country. Finlly, in July 1788, a beaten Louis XVI called for a spring session of the Estates General, the old representative body of all three estates that had not met since 1614. Absolute monarchy was falling.

What would replace it? Throughout the winter of 1788–1789, that question excited France. The Estates General of 1614 had sat as three separate houses – clergy, nobility, and commoners. Any action had required the agreement of all three branches, a requirement that had guaranteed control by the privileged orders. The nobility expected that history would repeat itself. The noble judges of the Parlement of Paris – a kind of supreme court in the eighteenth century – did their part. Accustomed to thundering against the rule of despotism, they ruled that the Estates should sit separately.

This ruling infuriated middle-class intellectuals. They wanted the three estates to meet as a single house, so that commoners from the third estate would have the dominant voice and be able to prevent aristocratic control. This issue and many others were thoroughly discussed in pamphlets and in the drafting of grievance petitions at the local level. There was great popular participation. Almost all male commoners twenty-five years or older had the right to vote for their representatives to the Estates General. However, the voting for the representatives required two, three, or even four stages, which meant that most of the representatives finally selected by the third estate were well-educated and prosperous members of the middle class. Most of them were not businessmen, but lawyers and government officials. Social status and prestige were matters of great concern to this economic elite. There were hardly any representatives from the great mass of laboring poor – the peasants, the artisans, and the day laborers.

In May 1789, the twelve hundred delegates of the three estates paraded in medieval pageantry through the streets of Versailles to an opening session clothed in feudal magnificence. The estates were almost immediately deadlocked. Delegates of the third estate refused to transact any business until the king ordered the privileged orders to sit with them in a single body. Finally, after a six-week war of nerves, a few parish priests began to go over to the third estate, which on June 17 voted to call itself the National Assembly. On June 20, excluded from their hall because of "repairs," they moved to a large indoor tennis court. There they swore the famous Oath of the Tennis Court, pledging never to disband until they had written a new constitution.

The king's actions were then somewhat contradictory. On June 23 he made a conciliatory speech to a joint session, urging reforms, and then ordered the three estates to meet together. At the same time he apparently followed the advice of the nobles, who saw things working out quite differently than they had expected and urged the king to dissolve the Estates General. The king called an army of eighteen thousand troops toward Versailles, and on July 11 he dismissed his finance minister and his more liberal ministers. Faced first with aristocratic and then with bourgeois revolt, Louis XVI had resigned himself to bankruptcy. Now he sought again to reassert his divine and historic right to rule. The middle-class delegates had done their best, but they were resigned to being disbanded at the point of bayonets. One third-estate delegate reassured a worried colleague: "You won't hang – you'll only have to go back home."[2]

THE REVOLT OF THE POOR AND THE OPPRESSED

While the third estate struggled at Versailles for symbolic equality with the nobility and clergy in a single legislative body, economic hardship gripped the masses of France in a tightening vise. Grain was the basis of the diet of ordinary people, and in 1788 the harvest had been extremely poor. The price of

bread, which had been rising gradually since 1785, began to soar. By July 1789, the price of bread in the provinces climbed as high as eight sous per pound. In Paris, where bread was subsidized by the government in an attempt to prevent popular unrest, the price rose to four sous. The poor could scarcely afford to pay two sous per pound, for even at that price a laborer with a wife and three children had to spend half of his wages to buy the family's bread.

Harvest failure and high bread prices unleashed a classic economic depression of the preindustrial age. With food so expensive and with so much uncertainty, the demand for manufactured goods collapsed. Thousands of artisans and small traders were thrown out of work. By the end of 1789, almost half of the French people would be in need of relief. One person in eight was a pauper, living in extreme want. In Paris, the situation was desperate in July 1789: perhaps 150,000 of the city's 600,000 people were without work.

Against this background of dire poverty and desperation, the people of Paris entered decisively onto the revolutionary stage. They believed in a general though ill-defined way that their economic distress had human causes. They believed that they should have steady work and enough bread to survive. Specifically, they feared that the dismissal of the king's moderate finance minister would throw them at the mercy of aristocratic landowners and grain speculators. Stories, like that quoting the wealthy financier Joseph François Foulon as saying that the poor "should eat grass, like my horses," and rumors that the king's troops would sack the city, began to fill the air. Angry crowds formed and passionate voices urged action. On July 13, the people began to seize arms for the defense of the city, and on July 14, several

STORMING THE BASTILLE *This contemporary drawing conveys the fury and determination of the revolutionary crowd on July 14, 1789. This successful popular action had enormous symbolic significance, and July 14 has long been France's most important national holiday. (Photo: Flammarion)*

hundred of the most determined people marched to the Bastille to search for gunpowder.

An old medieval fortress with walls ten feet thick and eight great towers each a hundred feet high, the Bastille had long been used as a prison. It was guarded by eighty retired soldiers and thirty Swiss guards. The governor of the fortress-prison refused to hand over the powder, panicked, and ordered his men to fire, killing ninety-eight people attempting to enter. Cannon were brought to batter the

main gate, and fighting continued until the governor of the prison surrendered. While he was being taken under guard to city hall, a band of men broke through and hacked him to death. His head and that of the mayor of Paris, who had been slow to give the crowd arms, were stuck on pikes and paraded through the streets. The next day a committee of citizens appointed Lafayette commander of the city's armed forces. Paris was lost to the king, who was forced to recall the finance minister and to disperse his troops. The uprising of the masses of Paris had saved the National Assembly.

As the delegates resumed their long-winded and inconclusive debates at Versailles, the people in the countryside sent them a radical and unmistakable message. All across France peasants began to rise in spontaneous, violent, and effective insurrection against their lords. Neither middle-class landowners, who often owned manors and village monopolies, nor the larger, more prosperous farmers, were spared. In some areas the nobles and bourgeoisie combined forces and organized patrols to protect their property. Yet the peasant insurrection went on. Recent enclosures were undone; old common lands were reoccupied; and the forests were seized. Taxes went unpaid. Fear of vagabonds and outlaws – the so-called Great Fear – seized the countryside and fanned the flames of rebellion. The long-suffering peasants were doing their best to free themselves from aristocratic privilege and exploitation.

Faced with chaos and fearful of calling on the king to restore order, the more liberal aristocrats and bourgeois at Versailles responded to peasant demands with a surprise maneuver on the night of August 4, 1789. The duke of Aiguillon, one of the greatest landowners in France, declared that

in several provinces the whole people forms a kind of league for the destruction of the manor houses, the ravaging of the lands, and especially for the seizure of the archives where the title deeds to feudal properties are kept. It seeks to throw off at last a yoke that has for many centuries weighted it down.[3]

He urged equality in taxation and the elimination of feudal dues. In the end, all the old exactions were abolished, generally without compensation: serfdom where it still existed, exclusive hunting rights for nobles, fees for

justice, village monopolies, the right to make peasants work on the roads, and a host of others. The church's tithe was also abolished. Thus the French peasantry, which already owned about 30 percent of all the land, quickly achieved a great and unprecedented victory. Henceforth, the French peasants would seek mainly to consolidate their triumph. As the Great Fear subsided, they became a force for order and stability.

A LIMITED MONARCHY

The National Assembly moved forward. On August 27, 1789, it issued the Declaration of the Rights of Man. This great liberal document had a very American flavor, and Lafayette even discussed his draft in detail with the American ambassador in Paris, Thomas Jefferson, the author of the American Declaration of Independence. According to the French declaration, "men are born and remain free and equal in rights." Mankind's natural rights are "liberty, property, security, and resistance to oppression." Also, "every man is presumed innocent until he is proven guilty." As for law, "it is an expression of the general will; all citizens have the right to concur personally or through their representatives in its formation.... Free expression of thoughts and opinions is one of the most precious rights of mankind: every citizen may therefore speak, write, and publish freely." In short, this clarion call of the liberal revolutionary ideal guaranteed equality before the law, representative government for a sovereign people, and individual freedom. This revolutionary credo, only two pages long, was propagandized throughout France and Europe and around the world.

Moving beyond general principles to draft a constitution proved difficult. The questions of how much power the king should retain

à Versailles à Versailles du 5 Octobre 1789.

*"To Versailles"   This print is one of many com-
memorating the women's march on Versailles. Notice
on the left that the fashionable lady from the well-to-
do is a most reluctant revolutionary. (Photo: Flammarion)*

and whether he could permanently veto legislation led to another deadlock. Once again the
decisive answer came from the poor, in this
instance the poor women of Paris.

To understand what happened one must
remember that the work and wages of women
and children were essential in the family
economy of the laboring poor. In Paris great
numbers of women worked, particularly
within the putting-out system in the garment
industry – making lace, fancy dresses, em-
broidery, ribbons, bonnets, corsets, and so on.
Most of these goods were beautiful luxury
items, destined for an aristocratic and international clientele.[4] Immediately after the fall of
the Bastille, many of France's greatest nobles

began to leave for foreign courts, so that demand for luxuries began to plummet. International markets also declined, and the church
was no longer able to give its traditional
grants of food and money to the poor. Unemployment and hunger increased further,
and the result was another popular explosion.

On October 5, some seven thousand desperate women marched the twelve miles from
Paris to Versailles to demand action. A middle-class deputy looking out from the assembly saw "multitudes arriving from Paris
including fishwives and bullies from the market, and these people wanted nothing but
bread." This great crowd invaded the assembly, "armed with scythes, sticks and pikes."

One coarse, tough old woman directing a large group of younger women defiantly shouted into the debate: "Who's that talking down there? Make the chatterbox shut up. That's not the point: the point is that we want bread."[5] Hers was the genuine voice of the people, without which any understanding of the French Revolution is hopelessly incomplete.

The women invaded the royal apartments, slaughtered some of the royal bodyguards, and furiously searched for the despised queen, Marie Antoinette. "We are going to cut off her head, tear out her heart, fry her liver, and that won't be the end of it," they shouted, surging through the palace in a frenzy. It seems likely that only the intervention of Lafayette and the National Guard saved the royal family. But the only way to calm the disorder was for the king to go and live in Paris, as the crowd demanded.

The next day the king, the queen, and their son left for Paris in the midst of a strange procession. The heads of two aristocrats, stuck on pikes, led the way. They were followed by the remaining members of the royal bodyguard, unarmed and surrounded and mocked by fierce men holding sabers and pikes. A mixed and victorious multitude surrounded the king's carriage, hurling crude insults at the queen. There was drinking and eating among the women. "We are bringing the baker, Mrs. Baker, and the baker's boy," they joyfully sang. The National Assembly followed the king to Paris. Reflecting the more radical environment, it adopted a constitution that gave the virtually imprisoned "baker" only a temporary veto in the lawmaking process. And, for a time, he and the government made sure that the masses of Paris did not lack bread.

The next two years until September 1791 saw the consolidation of the constructive phase of the Revolution. The National Assembly established a constitutional monarchy, which Louis XVI reluctantly accepted in July 1790. The king remained the head of state, but all lawmaking power was placed in the hands of the National Assembly, elected by the economic upper half of French males. Counties or departments of approximately equal size replaced the complicated old patchwork of provinces with their many historic differences. The jumble of weights and measures that varied from province to province was abolished and replaced by the simple, rational metric system. The National Assembly promoted economic freedom. Monopolies and guilds were prohibited, and barriers to trade within France were abolished in the name of economic liberty. Thus, the National Assembly applied the critical spirit of the Enlightenment to reform France's laws and institutions completely.

The assembly also seized the property of nobles who had left France, and it nationalized the property of the church. The government used former church property as collateral to guarantee a new paper currency, the so-called assignats, and then sold these properties in an attempt to put the state's finances on a solid footing. Although the church's land was sold in large blocks, a procedure that favored nimble speculators and the rich, peasants eventually purchased much of it as it was subdivided. These purchases strengthened their attachment to the revolutionary state.

The most unfortunate aspect of the reorganization of France was that it brought the new government into conflict with the Catholic church. Many middle-class delegates to the National Assembly, imbued with the rationalism and skepticism of the eighteenth-century philosophes, harbored a deep distrust of "superstitious religion." They were interested in the church only to the extent they could seize its land and use the church to strengthen the new state. In the Civil Constitution of the Clergy of 1790 they established a national church. In the face of resistance, the National Assembly required the clergy to take a loyalty oath to the new government. The clergy became just so many more employees of the state. The pope formally condemned this attempt to subjugate the church. Against such a backdrop, it is not surprising that only half the priests of France took the oath of allegiance. The result was a deep division within the country on the religious question, and confusion and hostility among French Catholics were pervasive. The attempted reorganization and subjugation of the Catholic church was the revolutionary government's first great failure.

WORLD WAR AND REPUBLICAN FRANCE, 1791–1799

When Louis XVI accepted the final version of the completed constitution in September 1791, a young and still obscure provincial lawyer and member of the National Assembly named Maximilien Robespierre (1758–1794) evaluated the work of two years and concluded "The Revolution is over." Robespierre was both right and wrong. He was right in the sense that most of the constructive and lasting reforms were in place. Nothing substantial in the way of liberty and equality would be added in the next generation, though much would be lost. He was wrong in the sense that the most tormented and most radical stages lay ahead. New heroes and new myths were to emerge in revolutionary wars and international conflict.

THE BEGINNING OF WAR

The outbreak and progress of revolution in France produced great excitement and a sharp division of opinion in Europe and the United States. Liberals and radicals such as the English scientist Joseph Priestley (1733–1804) and the American patriot Tom Paine (1739–1809) saw a mighty triumph of liberty over despotism. Conservative spirits like Edmund Burke (1729–1797) were deeply troubled. In 1790, Burke published *Reflections on the Revolution in France,* one of the great intellectual defenses of European conservatism. He defended inherited privileges in general and those of the English monarchy and aristocracy in particular. He predicted that unlimited reform would lead only to chaos and renewed tyranny. By 1791, fear was growing outside France that the great hopes raised by the revolution might be tragically dashed. The moderate German writer Friederich von Gentz was apprehensive that if moderate and intelligent revolution failed in France, all the old evils would be ten times worse: "It would be felt that men could be happy only as slaves, and every tyrant, great or small, would use this confession to seek revenge for the fright that the awakening of the French nation had given him."[6]

The kings and nobles of Europe, who had at first welcomed the revolution in France as weakening a competing power, began to feel threatened themselves. At their courts they listened to the French aristocrats who had fled France and were urging intervention in France's affairs. When Louis XVI and Marie Antoinette were arrested and returned to Paris after trying unsuccessfully to slip out of France in June 1791, the kings of Austria and Prussia issued the Declaration of Pillnitz. This carefully worded statement declared their willingness to intervene in France, but only with the unanimous agreement of all the Great Powers, which they did not expect to receive. Austria and Prussia expected their threat to have a sobering effect on revolutionary France without causing war.

The crowned heads of Europe misjudged the revolutionary spirit in France. When the National Assembly had disbanded, it had sought popular support by decreeing that none of its members would be eligible for election to the new Legislative Assembly. This meant that when the new representative body was duly elected and convened in October 1791, it had a different character. The great majority were still prosperous, well-educated, and middle class, but they were younger and more reckless than their predecessors. Loosely allied as Jacobins, so named after their political club, the new representatives were passionately committed to liberal revolution.

The Jacobins were full of hatred toward aristocrats and despotic monarchs, and easily whipped themselves into a patriotic fury with bombastic oratory. So the courts of Europe were attempting to incite a war of kings against France; well then, "we will incite a war of people against kings. . . . Ten million Frenchmen, kindled by the fire of liberty, armed with the sword, with reason, with eloquence would be able to change the face of the world and make the tyrants tremble on their thrones."[7] Only Robespierre and a very few others argued that people do not welcome liberation at the point of a gun. Such warnings were brushed aside. France would "rise to the full height of her mission," as one deputy urged. In April 1792, France declared war on the king of Austria.

France's crusade against tyranny went poorly at first. Prussia joined Austria in the Austrian Netherlands (present-day Belgium),

and French forces broke and fled at their first encounter with armies of this First Coalition. The road to Paris lay open, and it is possible that only conflict between the eastern monarchs over the division of Poland saved France from defeat.

Military reversals and Austro-Prussian threats caused a wave of patriotic fervor to sweep France. The Legislative Assembly declared the country in danger.· Volunteer armies from the provinces streamed through Paris, fraternizing with the people and singing patriotic songs like the stirring *Marseillaise,* later the French national anthem.

In this supercharged wartime atmosphere, rumors of treason by the king and queen spread in Paris. Once again, as in the storming of the Bastille, the common people of Paris acted decisively. On August 10, 1792, a revolutionary mob attacked the royal palace at the Tuileries, capturing it after heavy fighting with the Swiss Guards. The king and his family fled for their lives to the nearby Legislative Assembly, which suspended the king from all his functions, imprisoned him, and called for a new National Convention to be elected by universal male suffrage. Monarchy in France was on its deathbed, mortally wounded by war and popular revolt.

THE SECOND REVOLUTION

The fall of the monarchy marked a rapid radicalization of the Revolution, which historians often call "the second revolution." Louis's imprisonment was followed by the September Massacres, which disgraced the Revolution in the eyes of most of its remaining foreign supporters. Wild stories seized the city that imprisoned counter-revolutionary aristocrats and priests were plotting with the allied invaders. As a result, frenzied crowds invaded the pris-

THE END OF LOUIS XVI   *Some cheered and others wept at the sight of Louis's severed head. The execution of the king was a victory for the radicals, but it horrified Europe's monarchs and conservatives. (Photo: Flammarion)*

ons of Paris and summarily slaughtered half the men and women they found. In late September 1792, the new, popularly elected National Convention proclaimed France a republic. The republic adopted a new revolutionary calendar, and citizens were expected to address each other with the friendly "thou" of the people, rather than with the formal "you" of the rich and powerful.

All of the members of the National Convention were Jacobins and republicans, and the great majority continued to come from the well-educated middle class. But the convention was increasingly divided into two well-defined, bitterly competitive groups –

the Girondists and the Mountain, so called because its members, led by Danton and Robespierre, sat on the uppermost left-hand rows of the assembly hall. Many indecisive members seated in "the Plain" below floated back and forth between the rival factions.

The division was clearly apparent after the National Convention overwhelmingly convicted Louis XVI of treason. By a single vote, 361 of the 720 members of the convention then unconditionally sentenced him to death in January 1793. Louis died with tranquil dignity on the newly invented guillotine. One of his last sentences was, "I am innocent and shall die without fear. I would that my death might bring happiness to the French, and ward off the dangers which I foresee."[8]

Both the Girondists and the Mountain were determined to continue the "war against tyranny." The Prussians had been stopped at the indecisive battle of Valmy on September 20, 1792, one day before the republic was proclaimed. Republican armies then successfully invaded Savoy and captured Nice. A second army corps invaded the German Rhineland and took the city of Frankfurt. To the north the revolutionary armies won their first major battle at Jemappes and occupied the entire Austrian Netherlands by November 1792. Everywhere they went, French armies of occupation chased the princes, "abolished feudalism," and found support among some peasants and middle-class people.

But the French armies also lived off the land, requisitioning food and supplies and plundering local treasures. The liberators looked increasingly like foreign invaders. International tensions mounted. In February 1793 the National Convention, at war with Austria and Prussia, declared war on Britain, Holland, and Spain as well. Republican France was now at war with almost all of Europe, a great war that would last almost without interruption until 1815.

As the forces of the First Coalition drove the French from the Austrian Netherlands, peasants in western France revolted against being drafted into the army. They were supported and encouraged by devout Catholics, royalists, and foreign agents.

In Paris, the quarrelsome convention found itself locked in a life-and-death political struggle between the Girondists and the Mountain. The two groups were in general agreement on questions of policy. Sincere republicans, they hated privilege and wanted to temper economic liberalism with social concern. Yet personal hatreds ran deep. The Girondists feared a bloody dictatorship by the Mountain, and the Mountain was no less convinced that the more moderate Girondists would turn to conservatives and even royalists in order to retain power. With the middle-class delegates so bitterly divided, the laboring poor of Paris emerged as the decisive political factor.

The great mass of the Parisian laboring poor always constituted – along with the peasantry in the summer of 1789 – the elemental force that drove the Revolution forward. It was the artisans, shopkeepers, and day laborers who had stormed the Bastille, marched on Versailles, driven the king from the Tuileries, and carried out the September Massacres. The laboring poor were often known as the *sans-culottes,* "without breeches," because they wore trousers instead of the knee breeches of the aristocracy and the solid middle class. The immediate interests of the sans-culottes were mainly economic, and in the spring of 1793 the economic situation was as bad as the military situation. Rapid inflation, unemployment, and food shortages were again weighing heavily on the poor.

Moreover, by the spring of 1793 the sans-culottes were keenly interested in politics. Encouraged by the so-called "angry men," such as the passionate young ex-priest and journalist Jacques Roux, the sans-culottes were demanding radical political action to guarantee them their daily bread. At first the Mountain joined the Girondists in violently rejecting these demands. But in the face of military defeat, peasant revolt, and hatred of the Girondists, the Mountain and especially Robespierre became more sympathetic. The Mountain joined with sans-culottes activists in the city government to engineer a popular uprising, which forced the convention to arrest thirty-one Girondist deputies for treason on June 2. All power passed to the Mountain.

THE FRENCH REVOLUTION

May 5, 1789	Estates General convene at Versailles
June 17, 1789	Third Estate declares itself the National Assembly
June 20, 1789	Oath of the Tennis Court
July 14, 1789	Storming of the Bastille
July–August 1789	The Great Fear in the countryside
August 4, 1789	National Assembly abolishes feudal privileges
August 27, 1789	National Assembly issues Declaration of the Rights of Man
October 5, 1789	Parisian women march on Versailles and force royal family to return to Paris
November 1789	National Assembly confiscates church lands
July 1790	Civil Constitution of the Clergy establishes a national church
	Louis XVI reluctantly agrees to accept a constitutional monarchy
June 1791	Arrest of the royal family while attempting to flee France
August 1791	Declaration of Pillnitz by Austria and Prussia
April 1792	France declares war on Austria
August 1792	Parisian mob attacks palace and takes Louis XVI prisoner
September 1792	September Massacres
	National Convention declares France a republic and abolishes monarchy

Robespierre and others from the Mountain joined the recently formed Committee of Public Safety, to which the Convention had given dictatorial power to deal with the national emergency. These developments in Paris triggered revolt in leading provincial cities, such as Lyons and Marseilles, where moderates denounced Paris and demanded a decentralized government. The peasant revolt spread and the republic's armies were driven back on all fronts. By July 1793, only the areas around Paris and on the eastern frontier were firmly controlled by the central government. Defeat appeared imminent.

TOTAL WAR AND THE TERROR

A year later, in July 1794, the Austrian Netherlands and the Rhineland were once again in the hands of conquering French armies, and the First Coalition was falling apart. This remarkable change of fortune was due to the revolutionary government's success in harnessing, for perhaps the first time in history, the explosive forces of a planned economy, revolutionary terror, and modern nationalism in a total war effort.

Robespierre and the Committee of Public Safety advanced with implacable resolution on

The French Revolution (continued)

January 1793	Execution of Louis XVI
February 1793	France declares war on Britain, Holland, and Spain
	Revolts in provincial cities
March 1793	Bitter struggle in the National Convention between Girondists and the Mountain
April–June 1793	Robespierre and the Mountain organize the Committee of Public Safety and arrest Girondist leaders
September 1793	Price controls to aid the sans-culottes and mobilize war effort
1793–1794	Reign of Terror in Paris and the provinces
Spring 1794	French armies victorious on all fronts
July 1794	Execution of Robespierre
	Thermidorean Reaction begins
1795–1799	The Directory
1795	End of economic controls and suppresion of the sans-culottes
1797	Napoleon defeats Austrian armies in Italy and returns triumphant to Paris
1798	Austria, Great Britain, and Russia form the Second Coalition against France
1799	Napoleon overthrows the Directory and seizes power

several fronts in 1793–1794. In an effort to save revolutionary France, they collaborated with the fiercely patriotic and democratic sans-culottes. They established, as best they could, a planned economy with egalitarian social overtones. Rather than let prices be determined by supply and demand, the government decreed the maximum allowable prices, fixed in paper assignats, for a host of key products. Although the state was too weak to enforce all its price regulations, it did fix the price of bread in Paris at levels the poor could afford. Rationing and ration cards were introduced to make sure that the limited supplies of bread

were shared fairly. Quality was also controlled. Bakers were permitted to make only the "bread of equality" – a brown bread made of a mixture of all available flours. White bread and pastries were outlawed as frivolous luxuries. The poor of Paris may not have eaten well, but they ate.

They also worked, mainly to produce arms and munitions for the war effort. Craftsmen and small manufacturers were told what to produce and when to deliver. The government nationalized many small workshops and requisitioned raw materials and grain from the peasants. Sometimes planning and control did

THE REIGN OF TERROR *A man, woman, and child accused of political crimes are brought before a special revolutionary committee for trial. The Terror's iron dictatorship crushed individual rights as well as treason and opposition. (Photo: Flammarion)*

not go beyond orders to meet the latest emergency: "Ten thousand soldiers lack shoes. You will take the shoes of all the aristocrats in Strasbourg and deliver them ready for transport to headquarters at 10 A.M. tomorrow." Failures to control and coordinate were failures of means and not of desire: seldom if ever before had a government attempted to manage an economy so thoroughly. The second revolution and the ascendancy of the sans-culottes had produced an embryonic emergency socialism, which was to have great influence on the subsequent development of socialist ideology.

While radical economic measures supplied the poor with bread and the armies with weapons, a Reign of Terror (1793–1794) was solidifying the home front. Special revolutionary courts, responsible only to Robespierre's Committee of Public Safety, tried rebels and "enemies of the nation" for political crimes. Drawing on popular, sans-culottes support centered in the local Jacobin clubs, these local courts ignored normal legal procedures and judged severely. Forty thousand French men and women were executed. Another 300,000 suspects crowded the prisons and often brushed close to death in a revolutionary court.

Robespierre's Reign of Terror was one of the most controversial phases of the French Revolution. Most historians now believe that the Terror was not directed against any single class. Rather, it was a political weapon directed impartially against all who might oppose the revolutionary government. For many Europeans of the time, however, the Reign of Terror represented a terrible perversion of the generous ideals of 1789. It strengthened the belief that France had foolishly replaced a weak king with a bloody dictatorship.

The third and perhaps decisive element in the French republic's victory over the First Coalition was its ability to continue drawing on the explosive power of patriotic dedication to a national state and a national mission. This is the essence of modern nationalism. With a common language and a common tradition, newly reinforced by the idea of popular sovereignty, the French people were stirred by a common loyalty. The shared danger of foreign foes and internal rebels unified all classes in a heroic defense of the nation.

In such circumstances war was no longer the gentlemanly game of the eighteenth century, but a life-and-death struggle between good and evil. Everyone had to participate in the national effort. According to a famous decree of August 1793:

The young men shall go to battle and the married men shall forge arms. The women shall make tents and clothes, and shall serve in the hospitals; children shall tear rags into lint. The old men will be guided to the public places of the cities to kindle the courage of the young warriors and to preach the unity of the Republic and the hatred of kings.

Like the wars of religion, war in 1793 was a crusade; this war, though, was fought for a secular rather than a religious ideology.

As all unmarried young men were subject to the draft, the French armed forces swelled to 1 million men in fourteen armies. A force of this size was unprecedented in the history of European warfare. The soldiers were led by young, impetuous generals, who had often risen rapidly from the ranks and personified the opportunities the Revolution seemed to offer gifted sons of the people. These generals used mass attacks at bayonet point by their highly motivated forces to overwhelm the enemy. By the spring of 1794, French armies were victorious on all fronts. The republic was saved.

THE THERMIDORIAN REACTION AND THE DIRECTORY, 1794–1799

The success of the French armies led Robespierre and the Committee of Public Safety to relax the emergency economic controls, but they extended the political Reign of Terror. Their lofty goal was increasingly an ideal democratic republic, where justice would reign and there would be neither rich nor poor. Their lowly means were unrestrained despotism and the guillotine, which struck down any who might seriously question the new order. In March 1794, to the horror of many sans-culottes, Robespierre's Terror wiped out many of the "angry men," led by the radical social democrat Jacques Hébert. Two weeks later, several of Robespierre's long-standing collaborators, led by the famous orator Danton, marched up the steps to the guillotine. Knowing that they might be next, a strange assortment of radicals and moderates in the convention organized a conspiracy. They howled down Robespierre when he tried to speak to the convention on 9 Thermidor (July 27, 1794). On the following day it was Robespierre's turn to be shaved by the revolutionary razor.

As Robespierre's closest supporters followed their leader, France unexpectedly experienced a thorough reaction to the despotism of the Reign of Terror. In a general way this "Thermidorian reaction" recalled the early days of the Revolution. The respectable middle-class lawyers and professionals who had led the liberal Revolution of 1789 reasserted their authority. Drawing support from their own class, the provincial cities, and the better-off peasants, the convention abolished many economic controls, printed more paper currency, and let prices rise sharply. It severely restricted the local political organizations where the sans-culottes had their strength. And all the while, the wealthy bankers and new-rich speculators celebrated the sudden end of the Terror with an orgy of self-indulgence and ostentatious luxury.

The collapse of economic controls coupled with runaway inflation hit the working poor very hard. The gaudy extravagance of the rich wounded their pride. The sans-culottes accepted private property, but they believed passionately in small business and the right of all to earn a decent living. Increasingly disorganized after Robespierre purged their radical spokesmen, the common people of Paris finally revolted against the emerging new order in early 1795. The convention quickly used the army to suppress these insurrections. For the first time since the fall of the Bastille, bread riots and uprisings by Parisians living on the edge of starvation were effectively put down by a government that made no concessions to the poor.

In the face of all these catastrophes the revolutionary fervor of the laboring poor finally subsided. As far as politics was concerned, their interest and influence would remain very limited until 1830. There arose, especially from the women, a great cry for peace and a turning toward religion. As the government looked the other way, the women brought back the Catholic church and the worship of God. In one French town women fought with each other over which of their children should be baptized first. After six tumultuous years the women of the poor concluded that the Revolution was a failure.

As for the middle-class members of the convention, they wrote yet another constitution, which they believed would guarantee their political supremacy. The mass of the population could vote only for "electors," who would be men of means. The electors then elected the members of a reorganized assembly, as well as important officials throughout France. The assembly also chose the five-man executive – the Directory.

The men of the Directory continued to support French military expansion abroad. War was no longer so much a crusade as a means to meet the ever-present, ever-unsolved economic problem. Large, victorious French armies reduced unemployment at home, and they were able to live off the territories they conquered and plundered.

The unprincipled action of the Directory reinforced widespread disgust with war and starvation. This general dissatisfaction revealed itself clearly in the national elections of 1797, which returned a large number of conservative and even monarchial deputies who favored peace at almost any price. Fearing for their skins, the members of the Directory used the army to nullify the elections and began to govern dictatorially. Two years later, Napoleon Bonaparte ended the Directory in a coup d'état and substituted a strong dictatorship for a weak one. The Revolution was over.

THE NAPOLEONIC ERA, 1799–1814

For almost fifteen years, from 1799 to 1814, France was in the hands of a keen-minded military dictator masquerading first as a Roman consul and then as an emperor. Napoleon Bonaparte was clever enough to end the civil strife in France, in order to consolidate his rule. Had he stopped there, his achievement would have been considerable. But he did not, for the military dictator was also a military adventurer. Peace was boring; the dream of universal empire was irresistible. Napoleon pushed onward with wars of aggression, steadfastly rejecting compromises with his foes until, at last, he destroyed himself.

NAPOLEON'S RULE OF FRANCE

In 1799, when he seized power, young General Napoleon was a national hero. Born in Corsica into an impoverished noble family in 1769, Napoleon left home to become a lieutenant in the French artillery in 1785. Ever the opportunist, he went back to Corsica to fight for the island's independence in 1789. When that adventure failed miserably after about four years, he returned to France as a French patriot and a dedicated revolutionary. Rising rapidly in the new army, Napoleon was placed in command of French forces in Italy and won brilliant victories there in 1796 and 1797. His next campaign, in Egypt, was a failure, but Napoleon succeeded in abandoning his army and returning to France before the fiasco was generally known.

Napoleon soon learned that some prominent members of the assembly were plotting against the Directory. The dissatisfaction of these plotters stemmed not so much from the fact that the Directory was a dictatorship, but that it was a weak dictatorship. Ten years of upheaval and gore had made firm rule much more appealing than liberty and popular politics to these disillusioned revolutionaries. The abbé Sieyès personified this evolution in thinking. In 1789 he had written in his famous pamphlet *What Is the Third Estate?* that the nobility was useless and that the entire people should rule the French nation.

"EMPEROR NAPOLEON" Napoleon soon minted new gold coins like this one. In doing so, he ended a decade of financial upheaval and gained support from the middle class. (Courtesy of the American Numismatic Society, New York)

Now Sieyès' motto was "confidence from below, authority from above."

Like the other members of his group, Sieyès wanted a strong military ruler. The flamboyant thirty-year-old Napoleon was ideal. Thus the conspirators and Napoleon organized a takeover. On November 9, 1799, soldiers disbanded the assembly at bayonet point. Napoleon was named first consul of the republic, and a new constitution consolidating his position was overwhelmingly approved in a plebiscite in December 1799. Republican appearances were maintained for the moment, but Napoleon was the virtual dictator of France.

The essence of Napoleon's domestic policy was to use dictatorial powers to maintain order and put an end to civil strife. He did so by working out unwritten agreements with powerful groups in France, whereby these groups received favors in return for obedient service. Napoleon's bargain with the solid middle class was codified in the famous civil code of 1800, which reasserted two of the fundamental principles of this class and of their moderate revolution of 1789: equality of all citizens before the law, and absolute security of wealth and private property. Napoleon and the leading bankers of Paris established a privately owned Bank of France, which loyally served the interests of both the state and the financial oligarchy. Napoleon's devotion to the economic status quo also appealed to the peasants, who had bought some of the lands confiscated from the church and nobility. Thus, Napoleon accepted the gains of the peasantry and reassured the middle class, which had lost its revolutionary illusions in the face of social upheaval.

At the same time Napoleon accepted and strengthened the position of the French bureaucracy. France became a thoroughly centralized state. A network of prefects, subprefects, and centrally appointed mayors depended on Napoleon and served him well. Nor were members of the old nobility slighted. In 1800 and again in 1802 Napoleon granted amnesty to a hundred thousand émigrés on the condition that they return to France and take a loyalty oath. Members of this returning elite soon ably occupied many high posts in the expanding centralized state. Only a thousand diehard monarchists were exempted and remained abroad. Napoleon also created a new, ostentatious imperial nobility in order to reward his most talented generals and officials.

Napoleon's policy of buying off important groups in return for their support is illustrated by his treatment of the Catholic church in France. In 1800, the French clergy was still divided into two groups: those who had taken an oath of allegiance to the revolutionary government, and those in exile or hiding who had refused to do so. Personally uninterested in religion, Napoleon wanted to heal the religious division so that a united Catholic church in France could serve as one of the pillars of his regime. After long and arduous negotiations, Napoleon and Pope Pius VII (1800–1823) signed the Concordat of 1801. The pope gained for French Catholics the precious right to practice their religion freely, but Napoleon gained the most politically. His government now nominated bishops, paid the clergy, and exerted great influence over the church in France. Thus was Napoleon successful in using religion to strengthen his rule.

Napoleon's autocratic and supposedly efficient reorganization of France's church, bureaucracy, laws, and finances has led some historians to call him "the last of the enlightened despots." This discription is flattering, for it neglects Napoleon's endless foreign aggression and insatiable power drive, which might better earn him the epithet "the first of the modern madmen." Be that as it may, the characterization of Napoleon as an enlightened despot is at least half accurate: he was thoroughly despotic. Free speech and freedom of the press – fundamental rights of the liberal revolution, enshrined in the Declaration of the Rights of Man – were constantly and cynically violated. Shortly after seizing power, Napoleon reduced the number of newspapers in Paris from seventy-three to thirteen. By 1811, only four were left, and they were rigorously censored – little more than organs of government propaganda.

In 1802, Napoleon tried and failed to restore the black slavery the Revolution had abolished in France's former colony of Haiti; on the French islands of Martinique and Gua-

The Napoleonic Era

November 1799	Napoleon overthrows the Directory
December 1799	French voters overwhelmingly approve Napoleon's new constitution
1800	Napoleon founds the Bank of France
1801	France defeats Austria and acquires Italian and German territories in the Treaty of Lunéville
	Napoleon signs a concordat with the pope
1802	Treaty of Amiens with Britain
March 1804	Execution of the Duke of Engheim
December 1804	Napoleon crowns himself emperor
October 1805	Battle of Trafalgar: Britain defeats the French and Spanish fleets
December 1805	Battle of Austerlitz: Napoleon defeats Austria and Prussia
1807	Treaties of Tilsit: Napoleon redraws the map of Europe
1810	Height of the Grand Empire
June 1812	Napoleon invades Russia with 600,000 men
Winter 1812	Disastrous retreat from Russia
March 1814	Russia, Prussia, Austria, and Britain form the Quadruple Alliance to defeat France
April 1814	Napoleon abdicates and is exiled to Elba

deloupe, he succeeded. Here as elsewhere, the military dictator betrayed the revolutionary ideals of freedom and liberty.

Napoleon could honestly boast that his government was based on three forces: "My policemen, my officials, and my priests." The occasional elections were a farce. Later laws prescribed harsh penalties for political offenses. Whereas the Revolution had established that a person was presumed innocent until proven guilty, Napoleon's penal code placed the burden of proving one's innocence upon the defendant.

These changes in the law were part of the creation of a police state in France. Since Napoleon was usually busy making war, this task was largely left to Joseph Fouché, an unscrupulous opportunist who had earned a reputation for brutality during the Reign of Terror. As minister of police – a kind of super police chief at the national level – Fouché organized a ruthlessly efficient spy system, which kept thousands of citizens under continuous police surveillance. People even suspected of subversive thoughts were arbitrarily detained, placed under house arrest, or – shades of modern totalitarian states – consigned to insane asylums. After 1810 political suspects were held in state prisons, as they had been during the Terror. There were about 2,500 such political prisoners in 1814.

NAPOLEON'S WARS AND FOREIGN POLICY

Napoleon was above all a military man, and a great one. After coming to power in 1799, he sent peace feelers to Austria and Great Britain, the two remaining members of the Second Coalition, which had been formed against France in 1798. When these overtures were rejected, French armies led by Napoleon decisively defeated the Austrians. In the Treaty of Lunéville (1801) Austria accepted the loss of its Italian possessions, and German territory on the west bank of the Rhine was incorporated into France. Once more, as in 1797, the British were alone, and war-weary, like the French.

Still seeking to consolidate his regime domestically, Napoleon concluded the Treaty of Amiens with Great Britain in 1802. Britain agreed to return Trinidad and the Caribbean islands, which it had seized from France since 1792. The treaty said very little about Europe, though. France remained in control of Holland, the Austrian Netherlands, the west bank of the Rhine, and most of the Italian peninsula. Napoleon was free to reshape the German states as he wished. To the dismay of British businessmen, the Treaty of Amiens did not provide for expansion of the commerce between Britain and the Continent. It was clearly a diplomatic triumph for Napoleon, and peace with honor and profit increased his popularity at home.

In 1802, Napoleon was secure but unsatisfied. Always more of a romantic gambler than an enlightened administrator, he could not contain his power drive. Aggressively redraw-

ing the map of Germany so as to weaken Austria and attract the secondary states of southwestern Germany toward France, Napoleon was also almost entirely responsible for renewed war with Great Britain. Regarding war with Britain as inevitable, he threatened British interests in the eastern Mediterranean and tried to restrict British trade with all of Europe. Britain had technically violated the Treaty of Amiens by failing to evacuate the island of Malta, but it was Napoleon's decision to renew war. Like Hitler in 1940, he concentrated his armies in the French ports on the Channel in the fall of 1803 and began making preparations to invade England. Yet Great Britain remained mistress of the seas. When Napoleon tried to bring his Mediterranean fleet around Gibraltar to northern France, a combined French and Spanish fleet was, after a series of mishaps, virtually annihilated by Lord Nelson at the battle of Trafalgar on October 21, 1805. Invasion of England was henceforth impossible.

Renewed fighting had its advantages, however, for the cunning first consul used the wartime atmosphere to have himself proclaimed emperor. He secretly supplied money to French royalists in England, who were organizing a conspiracy to restore the Bourbons, and then fell upon the émigrés caught in his trap when they got to France in early 1804. Unable to find any clear tie between the captured émigrés and any of the Bourbons, Napoleon nonetheless seized a Bourbon prince, the duke of Enghein, in the neutral German state of Baden in March 1804. Subsequently, aware that his widely publicized charges against the duke of Enghein were in fact false, Napoleon nevertheless had the duke executed immediately after his arrival in Paris. On the basis of these plots and lies, Napoleon then asked the people to make him emperor. He needed more power to save the nation

WAR IN SPAIN This drawing from Goya's Disasters of War *shows French soldiers about to kill Spanish guerrillas. The patriotic Goya has captured the savagery of the struggle in Spain after 1808. (Courtesy of the Hispanic Society of America)*

from the Bourbons! It worked, and France accepted a restored monarchy.

Austria, Russia, and Sweden joined with Britain to form the Third Coalition against France shortly before the battle of Trafalgar. Actions like the execution of the duke of Enghein and Napoleon's decision to make himself king of Italy had convinced both Alexander I of Russia and Francis II of Austria that Napoleon had to be checked. Yet the Austrians and the Russians were no match for Napoleon, who scored a brilliant victory over them at the battle of Austerlitz in December 1805. Alexander I decided to pull back, and Austria accepted large territorial losses in return for peace as the Third Coalition collapsed.

Victorious at Austerlitz, Napoleon proceeded to reorganize the German states to his liking. In 1806, he abolished many of the tiny German states as well as the ancient Holy Roman Empire, whose emperor had traditionally been the king of Austria. Napoleon established by decree a German Confederation of the Rhine, a union of fifteen German states minus Austria, Prussia, and Saxony. Naming himself "protector" of the confederation, Napoleon controlled western Germany with an iron hand. In 1806, for example, a Nuremberg bookseller named Johann Philipp Palm distributed a short work entitled *Germany in Her Deepest Humiliation.* Palm's pamphlet appealed to the kings of Saxony and Prussia to free the German people from Napoleon's destruction. Napoleon ordered Palm executed for this relatively minor offense.

Napoleon's actions in Germany alarmed the Prussians, who had been at peace with France for more than a decade. Expecting help from his ally Russia, Frederick William III of Prussia mobilized his armies. Napoleon attacked and won two more brilliant victories in October 1806 at Jena and Auerstadt, where the Prussians were outnumbered two to one. The war with Prussia and Russia continued into the following spring, and after Napoleon's larger armies won another victory Alexander decided to seek peace.

For several days in June 1807, the young tsar and the French emperor negotiated face-to-face on a raft anchored in the middle of the Niemen River. All the while, the helpless Frederick William rode back and forth on the shore, anxiously awaiting the results. As the German poet Heinrich Heine said later, Napoleon had but to whistle and Prussia would have ceased to exist. In the subsequent treaties of Tilsit, Prussia lost half of its population, while Russia accepted Napoleon's reorganization of western and central Europe, and Napoleon promised Alexander help against the Turks. A secret clause called upon Alexander I to declare war on Britain if Napoleon could not make peace on favorable terms with his island enemy.

After the victory of Austerlitz and even

MAP 21.1   NAPOLEONIC EUROPE IN 1810

more after the treaties of Tilsit, Napoleon saw himself as the emperor of Europe and not just of France. The so-called Grand Empire he built had three parts. The core was an ever-expanding France, which by 1810 included Belgium, Holland, parts of northern Italy, and much German territory on the east bank of the Rhine. Beyond French borders Napoleon established a number of dependent satellite kingdoms, upon the thrones of which he placed (and replaced) the members of his large family. Third, there were the independent but allied states of Austria, Prussia, and Russia. Both satellites and allies were expected after 1806 to support Napoleon's continental system, and thus to cease all trade with Britain.

The impact of the Grand Empire on the peoples of Europe was considerable. In the areas incorporated into France and in the satellites (see Map 21.1) Napoleon introduced many French laws, abolishing feudal dues and serfdom where French revolutionary armies had not already done so. Some of the peasants and middle-class benefited from these reforms. These benefits were purchased, however, at the price of heavy taxes in money and men for Napoleon's armies. Napoleon came to be regarded much more as a conquering tyrant than an enlightened liberator.

The first great revolt occurred in Spain. In 1808 a coalition of Catholics, monarchists, and patriots rebelled against Napoleon's attempts to make Spain a French satellite with a Bonaparte as its king. French armies occupied Madrid, but the foes of Napoleon fled to the hills and waged uncompromising guerrilla warfare. Spain was a clear warning. It was time to stop.

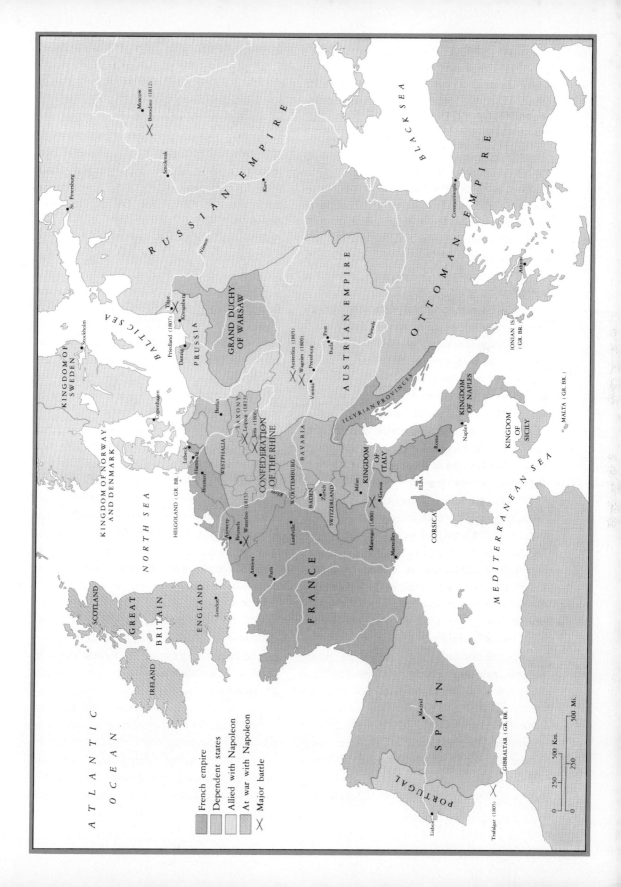

ATLANTIC OCEAN

RUSSIAN EMPIRE

Moscow
Borodino (1812)

Smolensk

St. Petersburg

Kiev

BLACK SEA

OTTOMAN EMPIRE

Constantinople

BALTIC SEA

KINGDOM OF SWEDEN

Stockholm

Tilsit
Königsberg
Friedland (1807)
Danzig

PRUSSIA

GRAND DUCHY OF WARSAW

AUSTRIAN EMPIRE

Austerlitz (1805)
Wagram (1809)
Pest
Buda
Pressburg
Vienna

Danube

IONIAN IS. (GR. BR.)

KINGDOM OF NORWAY AND DENMARK

Copenhagen

HELGOLAND (GR. BR.)

NORTH SEA

Berlin

Lübeck
Hamburg
Bremen

WESTPHALIA

SAXONY
Leipzig (1813)
Jena (1806)

CONFEDERATION OF THE RHINE

BAVARIA

ILLYRIAN PROVINCES

Athens

MALTA (GR. BR.)

KINGDOM OF NAPLES

Rome

Naples

KINGDOM OF SICILY

Antwerp
Brussels
Waterloo (1815)

Amiens
Paris

Lunéville

Rhine

WÜRTTEMBURG
BADEN
Zürich
SWITZERLAND

Milan

KINGDOM OF ITALY

Genoa

Marengo (1800)

Marseilles

ELBA

CORSICA

MEDITERRANEAN SEA

FRANCE

GREAT BRITAIN
SCOTLAND
ENGLAND
London
IRELAND

SPAIN

Madrid

GIBRALTAR (GR. BR.)

PORTUGAL

Lisbon

Trafalgar (1805)

French empire
Dependent states
Allied with Napoleon
At war with Napoleon
X Major battle

500 Km.
500 Mi.
250
250
0   0

Yet Napoleon would not, could not. In 1810, when the Grand Empire was at its height, Britain still remained at war with France, helping the guerrillas in Spain and Portugal (see Map 21.1). The continental system, organized to exclude British goods from the Continent and force that "nation of shopkeepers" to its knees, was a failure. Instead, it was France that suffered from Britain's counterblockade, which created hard times for Napoleon's strongest supporters – the French middle class. Perhaps looking for a scapegoat, Napoleon turned upon Alexander I of Russia, who had been fully supporting Napoleon's war of prohibitions against British goods.

Napoleon's invasion of Russia began in June 1812 with a force that eventually numbered 600,000, probably the largest force yet assembled in a single army. Only one-third of this force was French, however; nationals of all the satellites and allies were drafted into the operation. Originally planning to winter in the Russian city of Smolensk if Alexander did not sue for peace, Napoleon reached Smolensk and recklessly pressed on. The great battle of Borodino that followed was a draw, and the Russians retreated in good order. Alexander ordered the evacuation of Moscow, which then burned, and he refused to negotiate. Finally, after five weeks in the burned-out city, Napoleon ordered a retreat. That retreat was one of the great military disasters in history. The Russian army and the Russian winter cut Napoleon's army to pieces. Only 100,000 men returned to their homelands.

As before in Egypt, Napoleon deserted his troops and fled to Paris to raise yet another army. He might still have had peace and saved his throne if he had been willing to accept a France reduced to its historic size. This was what Austria's foreign minister Metternich proposed. But Napoleon refused. Austria and Prussia deserted Napoleon and joined Russia and Great Britain in the Fourth Coalition. All across Europe patriots called for a "war of liberation" against Napoleon's oppression, and the well-disciplined regular armies of Napoleon's enemies closed in for the kill. This time the coalition held together, cemented by the Treaty of Chaumont, which created a Quadruple Alliance to last for twenty years. Less than a month later, on April 4, 1814, a defeated, abandoned Napoleon abdicated his throne. An era had ended. Peace in Europe was possible.

❖

The revolution that began in America and spread to France was a liberal revolution. Inspired by English history, especially the Glorious Revolution, and some of the teachings of the Enlightenment, revolutionaries on both sides of the Atlantic sought to establish civil liberties and equality before the law within the framework of representative government. Success in America was subsequently matched by success in France, thanks to the decisive action of the poor and the oppressed – the sans-culottes and the peasants. The government and society established by the Declaration of the Rights of Man and the French constitution of 1791 were remarkably similar to those created in America by the federal Constitution and the Bill of Rights. All classes except the nobility benefited from this great step forward in human history, though the prosperous middle class may have profited most.

Yet the revolution in France did not end with the liberal victory of 1789-1791. As Robespierre led the determined French people in a total effort against foreign foes, it became more democratic, radical, and violent. This effort succeeded, but at the price of dictatorship, first by Robespierre himself and then by the Directory and Napoleon. Some historians blame the excesses of the French revolutionaries for the emergence of dictatorship, while others hold the conservative monarchs of Europe responsible. In any case, historians have often concluded that the French Revolution ended in failure.

This conclusion is highly debatable, though. After the fall of Robespierre the solid middle class with its liberal philosophy and Enlightenment world-view reasserted itself. Under the Directory it salvaged a good portion of the social and political gains that it and the peasantry had made between 1789 and 1791. In so doing, the middle-class leaders repudiated the radical social and economic measures associated with Robespierre, but they never reestablished the old order of privileged nobility and absolute monarchs. And although napoleon drastically curtailed thought and speech, his dictatorship used rather than weakened the middle class nd the peasantry. Careers were open to talent, and private wealth remained secure. In spite of a generation of war and upheaval, a very substantial part of the liberal triumph of 1789-1791 survived in France in 1814. Old Europe would never be the same.

NOTES

1. Quoted by R. R. Palmer, *The Age of Democratic Revolution,* Princeton University Press, Princeton, N.J., 1959, 1.239.

2. G. Lefebvre, *The Coming of the French Revolution,* Vintage Books, New York, 1947, p. 81.

3. P. H. Beck, ed., *The French Revolution,* Walker, New York, 1970, p. 89.

4. O. Hufton, "Women in Revolution," *Past and Present* 53 (November 1971): 91-95.

5. G. Pernoud and S. Flaisser, eds., *The French Revolution,* Fawcett Publications, Greenwich, Conn., 1960, p. 61.

6. L. Gershoy, *The Era of the French Revolution, 1789-1799,* Van Nostrand, New York, 1957, p. 135.

7. Ibid., p. 150.

8. Pernoud and Flaisser, pp. 193-194.

SUGGESTED READING

In addition to the fascinating eyewitness reports on the French Revolution in P. Beck, *The French Revolution,* and G. Pernoud and S. Flaisser, eds., *The French Revolution* (1960), A. Young's *Travels in France During the Years 1787, 1788 and 1789* (1969) offers an engrossing contemporary description of France and Paris on the eve of revolution. Edmund Burke, *Reflections on the Revolution in France,* first published in 1790, is the classic conservative indictment. The intense passions the French Revolution has generated may be seen in the nineteenth-century French historians, notably the enthusiastic Jules Michelet, *History of the French Revolution;* the hostile Hippolyte Taine; and the judicious Alexis de Tocqueville, whose masterpiece, *The Old Regime and the French Revolution,* was first published in 1856. Important recent general studies on the entire period are R. R. Palmer, *The Age of Democratic Revolution* (1959, 1964), which paints a comparative international picture; E. J. Hobsbawm, *The Age of Revolution, 1789-1848* (1962); C. Breunig, *The Age of Revolution and Reaction, 1789-1850* (1970); O. Connelly, *French Revolution – Napoleonic Era* (1979); and L. Dehio, *The Precarious Balance: Four Centuries of the European Power Struggle* (1962). C. Brinton's older but delightfully written *A Decade of Revolution, 1789-1799* (1934) complements his stimulating *Anatomy of Revolution* (1938), an ambitious comparative approach to revolution in England, America, France, and Russia. A. Cobban, *The Social Interpretation of the French Revolution* (1964), is an exciting reassessment of many well-worn ideas, to be compared with W. Doyle, *Origins of the French Revolution* (1981); G. Lefebvre, *The Coming of the French Revolution* (1947); and N. Hampson, *A Social History of the French Revolution* (1963). G. Rudé makes the men and women of the great days of upheaval come alive in his *The Crowd in the French Revolution* (1959). R. R. Palmer studies sympathetically the leaders of the Terror in *Twelve Who Ruled* (1941). Two other particularly interesting detailed works are C. L. R. James, *The Black Jacobins* (1938), on black slave revolt in Haiti, and J. C. Herold, *Mistress to an Age* (1955), on the remarkable Madame de Staël. On revolution in America, E. Morgan, *The Birth of the Republic, 1763–89,* and B. Bailyn, *The Ideological Origins of the American Revolution* (1967), are noteworthy. Three important recent studies on aspects of revolutionary France are D. Jourdan's vivid *The King's Trial: Louis XVI vs. the French Revolution* (1979); W. Sewell, Jr.'s imaginative *Work and Revolution in France: The Language of Labor from the Old Regime to 1848* (1980); and R. Phillips' *Family Breakdown in Late Eighteenth-Century France: Divorces in Rouen, 1792–1803* (1980).

P. Geyl, *Napoleon, For and Against* (1949), is a delightful discussion of changing historical interpretations of Napoleon. Good biographies are J. M. Thompson, *Napoleon Bonaparte: His Rise and Fall* (1952); F. H. M. Markham, *Napoleon* (1964); and E. Ludwig's popular novel *Napoleon* (1915). Other wonderful novels inspired by this period are Raphael Sabatini, *Scaramouche,* a swashbuckler of revolutionary intrigue with accurate historical details; Charles Dickens's classic *Tale of Two Cities;* and Leo Tolstoy's monumental saga of Napoleon's invasion of Russia (and much more), *War and Peace.*

NOTES ON THE ILLUSTRATIONS

Page 391 St. Sebastian Interceding for the Plague-Stricken by Josse Lieferinxe, in the Walters Art Gallery, Baltimore, Maryland.

Page 392 From MS. of Gilles le Msisis, *Annales,* Bibliothèque Royale 13076/7, fol. 16v, in the Bibliothèque Royale Albert I, Brussels.

Page 399 Episode from the battle of Crècy from Froissart's *Chronicle,* as reproduced in *Larousse Ancient and Medieval History,* p. 363.

Page 405 Florentine school, sixteenth century (c. 1530). Allegorical portrait of Dante on wood, 50 by 47¼ inches.

Page 412 From Froissart's *Chronicles,* MS. Fr. 2643, fol. 125, in Bibliothèque Nationale, Paris.

Page 416 Miniature from *Roman de Fauvel,* MS. Fr. 146, fol. 34, in Bibliothèque Nationale, Paris.

Page 418 *The Four Horsemen of the Apocalypse,* woodcut c. 1498, by Albrecht Dürer, German painter and engraver (1471-1528) regarded as leader of the German Renaissance school of painting.

Page 423 Sixteenth-century woodcut.

Page 425 Banquet scene from Boccaccio's *Decameron* by Sandro Botticelli, Italian painter (1444?-1510).

Page 430 The original painting can be found in the Uffizi Gallery, Florence.

Page 432 Hans Memling (real name Mimmelinghe, also spelled Memline and Hemmelinck), active c. 1465-d. 1494. Tomasso Portinari (c. 1432-1501), tempera and oil on wood, 17⅜ inches high by 13¼ wide. Maria Portinari (b. 1456), tempera and oil on wood, 17⅜ inches high by 13⅜ wide.

Page 434 Terracotta, School of Luca della Robbia, late fifteenth century. Della Robbia's invention of the process of making polychrome glazed terracottas led contemporaries to consider him one of the great artistic innovators. The warm humanity of this roundel (circular panel) is characteristic of della Robbia's art.

Page 438 Engraving by Johannes Stradanus (J. van der Straet), Belgian painter (1523-1605).

Page 441 Tiziano Vecellio, Italian painter, 1477-1576.

Page 442 *The Adoration,* 1507, by Hans Baldung (also called Hans Grien or Grün), German painter, engraver, and designer of woodcuts and glass painting (1476?-1545).

Page 450 Hieronymus Bosch (Hieronymus van Aeken), Dutch painter (c. 1450-1516).

Page 454 Paolo Uccello, Florentine painter (1397-1475).

Page 456 Fifteenth-century miniature from *Ethique d'Aristotle,* MS. I.2, fol. 145, in Bibliothèque Municipale, Rouen, France.

Page 472 *The Small Crucifixion,* c. 1510, by Matthias Grünewald, German painter (c. 1465-1528). Wood.

Page 493 *Sir Thomas More* (1478-1535), painted in 1527 by Hans Holbein the Younger, German painter (1497?-1543) and court painter to Henry VIII.

Page 509 World chart by Vesconte Maggiolo, 1511, showing North America as a promontory of Asia.

Page 521 Long the site of a royal residence and hunting lodge, Fontainebleau was expanded and transformed by Francis I in 1530-1540. Il Rosso (Giovanni Battista de'Rossi, 1494-1540), Florentine painter; Francesco Primaticcio, Italian painter and architect (1504-1570); and Sebastiano Serlio, Italian architect and writer on art (1475-1554) were called by Francis I from Italy to build and decorate the palace. The gallery of Francis I set a fashion in decoration imitated throughout Europe.

Page 527 *Iconoclasts in The Netherlands,* 1583.

Page 539 *Mars and Venus United by Love,* c. 1580, by Paolo Veronese, Italian painter (1528-1588).

Page 547 From George Turberville, *The Noble Art of Venery* (1575).

Page 548 *Portrait of Juan de Paraja,* c. 1650, by Diego Rodriguez de Silva y Velasquez, Spanish painter (1599-1660). Oil.

Page 562 On the left side of the palace are the Parterres du Nord, on the right the Parterres du Midi (South of France). In the middle distance are the water gardens and Fountain de Latone, and in the foreground, the beginning of the Green Carpet. The Orangérie (hot house) extends to the lower right of the palace. Construction of Versailles was begun in the mid-seventeenth century under the direction of the French architect Louis Le Vau (1612-

1670); after his death, Jules Hardouin-Mansart (1646–1708), Louis XIV's building superintendent and architect, completed the palace. Charles Le Brun (1619–1690), first painter to the king, worked for eighteen years on decoration of the palace. André Le Nôtre (1613–1700), French landscape architect and director of royal gardens, designed the famous gardens.

Page 569 *The Rape of the Sabine Women,* c. 1636–1637, by Nicolas Poussin, French painter (1594–1665). Oil on canvas.

Page 573 *Las Menimas* (The Maids of Honor), 1656, by Diego Rodriguez de Silva y Velasquez (1599–1660), leading painter of the Spanish school.

Page 577 Title page of *The Lamentable Complaints of Nick Froth the Tapster and Rulerost the Cooke,* 1641, in The British Library.

Page 581 Second Great Seal of the Commonwealth, 1651.

Page 587 *A Woman Weighing Gold,* by Jan Vermeer, Dutch genre, landscape, and portrait painter (1632–1675). Canvas.

Page 597 From A. Thevet, *Cosmographie universelle,* 1575.

Page 611 Feast of the Trinity at St. Basil's, Moscow.

Page 619 The episcopal residence, built 1720–1744, was designed by the German architect Balthasar Neumann (1687–1753), master of the German Baroque school. The Venetian Giovanni Battista Tiepolo (1696–1770) came to Würzburg to paint the ceilings in 1750, accompanied by his sons, Giovanni Domenico (1727–1804) and Lorenzo (1736–1776). Damaged by bombing in World War II, the palace was restored in the 1950s.

Page 621 The Winter Palace *(left),* designed for Peter the Great by Domenico Trezzini and refurbished for Elizabeth by Bartolomeo Rastrelli (1700–1771), and *(right)* the Old Admiralty, St. Petersburg, from an engraving by M. I. Makhaev, 1761.

Page 629 Illustration of the four Greek elements – earth, air, water, and fire – surrounded by the dome of the fixed stars. It also shows Thales' concept of a flat earth floating on water. The central figure represents Archimedes. From Archimedes' *Tetragonismus . . . ,* Venice, 1503.

Page 632 Engraving by Joannes Blaeu from his *Atlas Major,* 1662, in the Map Library at The British Library.

Page 637 Louis XIV and Colbert visiting the Académie des Sciences, from C. Perrault's *Mémoires pour servir à l'histoire naturelle des animaux,* 1671.

Page 643 Painting by Huber, in the Musée Carnavalet, Paris.

Page 649 *Une Soirée chez Madame Geoffrin* by A. Ch. G. Lemonnier, French painter (1793–1824).

Page 653 Engraving after Borovikovsky, in the British Museum.

Page 657 *Mozart enfant, son père et sa soeur,* 1764, by Louis Carmontelle (Louis Carrogis), French painter, engraver, and writer (1717–1806).

Page 665 *Les Glaneuses* by Jean François Millet (1814–1875), French genre and landscape painter of the Barbizon school. The original can be seen in the Louvre.

Page 674 Colored engraving, 1746.

Page 686 Frontispiece from a map of "the most Inhabited part of Virginia containing the whole province of Maryland with part of Pensilvania, New Jersey and North Carolina drawn by Joshua Fry and Peter Jefferson in 1775," in Thomas Jeffrey's *American Atlas,* 1776, in The British Library.

Page 700 *Peasant Family* by Giacomo Ceruti, Italian painter active c. 1750.

Page 702 After an engraving by R. Lehman of the foundlings' home called La Rota.

Page 709 *Famille de paysans,* c. 1640, by Louis Le Nain, French painter (1593–1648). The original can be seen in the Louvre.

Page 715 Engraving, 1746.

Page 717 "The Remarkable Effects of Vaccination," an anonymous nineteenth-century Russian cartoon in the Clements C. Fry Collection of Medical Prints and Drawings, Yale Medical Library.

Page 734 This portrait of Louis XVI by Joseph-Siffrein Duplessis, French portrait painter (1725–1802), hangs in the Marie Antoinette Gallery at Versailles.

Page 738 This drawing by Persin de Prieur, "Premier assaut contre La Bastille," can be seen in the Musée Carnavalet, Paris.

Page 744 "Fin Tragique de Louis XVI," drawn from life by Fious; engraving by Sarcifu. Louis XVI was executed on 21 January 1793 in the Place de Louis XV, renamed the Place de la Révolution, and now called the Place de la Concorde.

Page 748 "Un Comité révolutionnaire sous la Terreur," after Alexandre Évariste Fragonard, French historical painter (1780–1850).

Page 755 "Con razón o sin ella," by Francisco José de Goya y Lucientes (1746–1828), Plate 2 in *Los desastres de la guerra,* 1863. Etching. A Spanish painter, etcher, and lithographer, Goya was the chief master of the Spanish school in the eighteenth century.

INDEX

Ariosto, 519
Aristocracy: conflict with monarchies, 451–462; Spanish, 574. *See also* Nobility
Aristotle, ideas on universe, 629–630
Armada, Spanish, 530
Armagnacs, 450
Arouet, François Marie, *see* Voltaire
Arras, Treaty of, 480
Art: vernacular literature, 404–406; Renaissance, 426, 429–433; 450; Renaissance, to France, 520–522; French classicism, 567–568; Dutch, 586–587 (illus.); baroque, 616–622
Arthur, prince of England, 458, 491
Artillery, 399, 516
Artists, *see* Art
Asia, spice trade, 518
Astrakhan, 612
Astrolabe, 517
Astrology, 630
Astronomy: Aristotelian, 629–630; Copernicus theory, 630–631; Tycho Brahe's observations, 631; Kepler's laws, 632; Galileo's work, 632–634; Newton's law, 634–635
Auerstadt, battle of, 756
Augsburg, Confession of, 476
Augsburg, Peace of, 484, 530, 531
Augustine, bishop of Hippo Regius, *see* St. Augustine
Augustus the Strong of Saxony, 618
Austerlitz, battle of, 755
Austria: rise of, 596–600; attacked by Frederick the Great, 651; enlightened absolutism in, 656; issues Declaration of Pillnitz, 742–743; and First Coalition against Napoleon, 743, 745, 746, 749; in Second Coalition, defeated, 754; in Third Coalition, 755; as Napoleon's ally, 756, 758
Austrian Succession, War of the, 654, 682
Avignon, papal court at (Babylonian Captivity), 407–408
Aztec Empire, 513

Babies, *see* Infants
Babylonian Captivity (papal court in France), 407–408
Bach, Johann Sebastian, 617
Bacon, Francis, 636
Ball, John, 412
Baroque arts, 616–622
Bastille, march on, 738
Bayle, Pierre, 641
Beaumont, Sir Henry, 410
Becket, Thomas, 471
Bede, 427
Belgium, *see* Netherlands
Bernard of Clairvaux, 427, 499
Bernini, 564
Bessarion, John, 426
"Bess of Hardwick," *see* Hardwick, Elizabeth
Bible: Wycliff's reliance on, 409; Luther's translation, 479; Tyndale's 489; King James Version, 549–550
Bill of Rights, American, 724, 732
Bill of Rights, English, 583, 732
Birth control, 697–698
Black Death, *see* Bubonic plague
Blacks: in Renaissance, 441–443. *See also* Slavery
Blenheim, battle of, 571
Bloch, Marc, 666
Blood, Council of, 526–527

Bloodletting, 712–713, 714
Boccaccio, Giovanni, 392, 428–429
Bodin, Jean, 613
Bohemia, 531–532, 533, 597–598
Boleyn, Anne, *see* Anne Boleyn
Bologna, Concordat of, 522
Bonaparte, Napoleon, *see* Napoleon I
Bonhomme, Jacques, 411
Book of Common Order (Knox), 495
Book of Common Prayer (Cranmer), 494
Book of the First Navigation and Discovery of the Indies (Columbus), 511
Books, first printing from movable type, 437–439
Borgia, Cesare, 452
Borgia, Rodrigo, *see* Alexander VI, pope
Borgia family, 471
Borodino, battle of, 758
Bosch, Jerome, 450
Bossuet, Jacques, 560
Boston Tea Party, 729
Botticelli, 430
Bourges, Pragmatic Sanction of, 456, 600
Boyars, 609, 611–613
Brahe, Tycho, 631
Brandenburg, elector of, 600–602
Brassey, Thomas, 774
Breast-feeding, *see* Nursing of babies
Breitenfeld, battle of, 533
Brethren of the Common Life, 471
Britain, *see* England; Great Britain
British College of Surgeons, 718
British Empire, *see* Great Britain
British West Indies, 684
Brunelleschi, Filippo, 431, 433, 441
Bruni, Leonardo, 427
Bubonic plague (Black Death): spread of in 14th century, 388, 389; pathology of, 389–393; consequences of, 393; disappears, 673
Burgundians, 455
Burke, Edmund, 742
Bussy, Sir William, 410

Cabal, 582
Cabinet system, 583–584
Cabot, John, 515
Cabral, Pedro Alvares, 511
Calais, 402
Calvin, John: debt to Luther, 479; life and ideas, 485–487; influence on Knox, 495; quoted, 585; reaction to Copernican theory, 631
Calvinism: tenets of, 485–487; in France, 522, 523–524; in Netherlands, 526; in Germany, 530–531, 534; and Puritanism, 578–579; and the Dutch, 585
Canada, 515; developed by Colbert for French Empire, 566
Cannon, 516–517
Canterbury Cathedral, 471
Canterbury Tales, 404, 468
Capitalism, and cottage industry, 676
Caraffa, Cardinal, 499, 502
Caravels, 517
Caribbean islands, 513, 682
Cartier, Jacques, 515

Inquisition: Spanish, 461–462; Roman, 502–503
Institutes of the Christian Religion, The (Calvin), 485–487
Ireland: and Church of Ireland, 495–496; and potatoes as staple food, 710
Isabella, queen of England, 395
Isabella, queen of Spain, 451, 458, 459–462
Isabella of Este, duchess of Mantua, 443
Islam: in Spain, 459, 460; and Ottoman Turks, 599
Italy: origins of Renaissance in, 422–426; city-states, 452–455; Napoleon's victories in, 751. *See also* Rome
Ivan I, Russian prince, 610
Ivan III, prince of Moscow, 610–611
Ivan IV (the Terrible), tsar of Russia, 611–613

Jacobins, 743, 744
Jacquerie, 411
Jacques de Vitry, 411
Jamaica, 513
James I, king of England, 546, 549–550, 576–577
James II, king of England, 582
James V, king of Scotland, 495
Janissary corps, 599
Jeanne d'Albret, 538
Jefferson, Thomas, 725, 730, 739
Jena, battle of, 756
Jenner, Edward, 718
Jesuits, 501, 502, 533, 616
Jews: attacked in 14th century, 413; in Spain, 460–462; welcomed to England by Cromwell, 581
Jiménez, Francisco, 460, 468, 471
Joan of Arc, 400–402
Joanna of Castile, 462, 480
John, archbishop of Plano Carpini, 609
John II, king of Portugal, 511
John of Salisbury, 427
John of Spoleto, 408
Joliet, Louis, 566
Joseph II, king of Austria, 656
Judeo-Christian tradition, 725
Julius II, pope, 429, 471, 473, 491, 498
Junkers, 605, 651
Justices of the peace, in Tudor England, 458
Justinian Code, 451

Karlsruhe, 619
Kay, John, 678
Kazan, 612
Keynes, John Maynard, 634
Khan, Jenghiz, 609
Khans (rulers of Russia), 609
Kiev, principality of, 607–609
"Killing nurses," 701
King James Bible, 549–550
Kingship, *see* Monarchy
Knighthood, 397–398
Knox, John, 495, 538

Laborers, Statute of, 393, 411–412
Lafayette, marquis de, 733, 739
Lancaster, House of, 457
Languedoc, 388
LaRochelle, 559

La Salle, Robert, 566
Lascaris, Jonus, 426
Las Casas, Bartholomé de, 541, 542
Last Supper, The (da Vinci painting), 431
Lateran Council, 473, 498
Latin language, 428
Laud, William, 579
Law, John, 735
Law: Justinian's codes, 451; Napoleon's civil code of 1800, 752
League of Armed Neutrality, 730
League of Cambrai, 455
Learning, effect of printing on, 438–439
Lefèvre d'Etaples, Jacques, 445
Legislative Assembly (France), 743
Le Havre, founded, 520
Leisure, *see* Recreation
Le Nain, Louis, 567
Le Nôtre, André, 563
Leo X, pope, 429, 455, 457, 471, 474, 498
Leonardo da Vinci, see da Vinci, Leonardo
Leopold II (of Austria), Holy Roman emperor, 617, 656
Lescot, Pierre, 520
Lespinasse, Julie de, 649
Le Tellier, François, 568
Le Vau, Louis, 563
Leviathan (Hobbes), 580
Liberalism: central ideas of, 724–725; roots of, 725–726; attraction of, 726–727
Liberty, concept of, 724–725
"Limeys," English sailors, 708
Lisbon, and Portuguese commerce, 511, 514
Literacy, growth of in 17th, 18th centuries, 705
Literature: development of vernacular, 404–406; writings of Northern Renaissance, 445–450; Montaigne, 544–546; Elizabeth, Jacobean, 546–550; French, encouraged by Richelieu, 559; French classicism, 567–568; of the Enlightenment, 642–647
Lithuania, 612
Locke, John, 583, 642, 726
Lollards, 409, 489
London, Foundling Hospital, 702
Long Parliament, 579
Lords, House of, *see* Parliament, English
Lorenzo the Magnificent, 429
Louis XI, king of France, 451, 457, 480
Louis XII, king of France, 455, 469
Louis XIII, king of France, 558, 560
Louis XIV, king of France, 681; as supreme example of absolutist monarch, 560; early years, personality, 561; building and use of Versailles, 562–565; economics under, 565–567; arts in reign of, 567–568; wars under, 568–572; death of, 572; provides refuge for James II, 582; hatred of Dutch, 584–585; and Peace of Utrecht, 682
Louis XV, king of France, 654–655
Louis XVI, king of France, 655; dominated by nobility, 736; accepts constitutional monarchy, 741; tries to flee, arrested, 742; imprisoned, 743; guillotined, 744–745
Louise of Savoy, 538
Louisiana, 682, 688
Louvre, 520
Low Countries, *see* Netherlands

as factor in scientific revolution, 635–636; instruments developed for, 636

Navigation Acts, 680–681, 684–686

Negroes, *see* Blacks

Nelson, Horatio, 754

Netherlands: ravaged by Louis XI, 480; under Charles V, 525–526; revolt of, 526–528; southern provinces (Belgium) under Habsburgs, northern provinces (Holland) form United Provinces, declare independence, turn to English for help, 528–529; independence of United Provinces recognized at Peace of Westphalia, 534; in 17th century, 584–586; new farming system in, 667–668; and competition for colonial empire, 680–681; declares war on Britain, 730; and First Coalition against France, 743, 745, 746, 749; as part of Napoleon's Grand Empire, 756

Newfoundland, discovery of, 515

New Jersey, 684

New Testament, *see* Bible

Newton, Isaac, 634–635, 640–641, 643

Nicholas V, pope, 427

Nieman River, 756

Nijmegen, Treaty of, 570

Nikon, Patriarch, 613

Ninety-five Theses, Luther, 475–476

Nitrogen-storing crops, 666–667

Nobility: "fur-collar" crime by, 410–411; absolute monarchy's mastery over, 556; Richelieu breaks power of French, 558–559; Louis XIV humbles, 561, 562, 564, 565; in eastern Europe, 592–596; of Hungary thwarts Habsburgs, 600; Prussian, 600, 602; Russian, 609, 611–615; under Catherine the Great, 653; in France under Louis XV, 654; as second estate in France, 735

Nördlingen, battle of, 534

Normandy: in Hundred Years' War, 399–400

North Africa, in World War II, 664

North America: European exploration of, 510–519; French, Spanish, British fight over, 680–684; farming in, high standard of living, 684–686; revolution of British colonies, 727–732. *See also* Canada; United States

Norway, and Reformation, 496

Notre Dame cathedral, 701

Novgorod, 610

Nunneries, *see* Convents

Nursing of babies, 700–701

Nutrition, and European diet, 707–712. *See also* Diet

Old Believers, 613

Oldenbarneveldt, Jan van, 585

Old Testament, *see* Bible

Oleg (Varangian ruler), 607

Olivares, Count, 574

"On Cannibals" (Montaigne), 545

On Christian Liberty (Luther), 477

"On Cruelty" (Montaigne), 545

On Pleasure (Valla), 428

"On Solitude" (Montaigne), 544

"On the Dignity of Man" (Mirandola), 427

On the False Donation of Constantine (Valla), 428

On the Revolutions of the Heavenly Spheres (Copernicus), 630

Open-field agricultural system, 664–666

Orangerie, at Versailles, 564

Oratories of Divine Love, 471

Orléans, 401

Orlov, Gregory, 652

Orthodox Christianity, *see* Eastern Orthodox church

Othello (Shakespeare), 546, 549

Ottoman Turks: as threat to Europe, 510; Habsburgs drive out of Hungary, 598–600; history of, 599

Overseas expansion: 508–519; 541–544; by Vikings, 510; by Turks, 510; by Portugal, 510–511; Columbus, 511–513; Spanish, 513–514; Dutch, 514–515; English-French, 515; colonial administration, 515; economic effects of Spain's, 516; stimuli for, 516–517; motives for, 517–519; slave trade in, 541–544

Oviedo, 518

Paine, Thomas, 730, 742

Painting, *see* Art

Palaces, as symbols of absolutism, 617–618

Palm, Johann Philipp, 756

Panama, isthmus of, 682

Pantagruel (Rabelais), 449

Papacy: and Babylonian Captivity, schism, 407–408; conciliar movement, 408–410; Renaissance popes, 427, 429; French break with, 456; living style of 16th-century popes, 470–471; Luther challenges authority of, 475–476; and reform, 498–499

Papal States, 407, 452, 498

Paper, and printing, 437

Paris: prostitutes in, 697; uprising of poor in, during revolution, 737–739

Paris, Treaty of 1763, 682

Paris, Treaty of 1783, 732

Parlement of Paris, 654, 655, 736

Parliament, English: Hundred Years' War stimulates development of, 403–404; and Tudors, 458; and Stuarts, 577–580; under Cromwell, 580–581; in Restoration, 581–582; triumph of, 583–584; in American Revolution, 729, 730

Paston, John, 414

Paston, Margaret, 414

Paul III, pope, 499, 501, 502

Paul of Tarsus, *see* St. Paul

Pavia, battle of, 498

Peace of Augsburg, 484, 485

Peace of Utrecht, 571–572, 682

Peace of Westphalia, 534, 584

Peasantry: revolts of, 411–413, 477–479; and Lutheran movement, 477; in eastern Europe, 592–596; in east Germany, 600; in Russia, 609, 611–614; as third estate in France, 736

Penn, William, 581

Pennsylvania, 684

Persian Letters, The (Montesquieu), 642

Peru, 514

Peter I (the Great), tsar of Russia: imitates Versailles, 565; his reign, 614–616; builds St. Petersburg, 620–622; abolishes hereditary succession, 651

Peter III, tsar of Russia, 652, 682

Petri, Olaus, 496

Pharmacists, in 18th century, 712–713

Philip IV (the Fair), king of France, 389, 451

Philip VI, king of France, 395

Philip II, king of Spain: Iberian peninsula united by, 462; marriage to Mary I of England, 494; and state finances, 516; inherits Low Countries, Spain, 525, 526; "pacifies" Low Countries, 526–528; as defender of Catholicism, 529; his Armada defeated by England in 1588, 530

Philip III, king of Spain, 530, 574

Philip IV, king of Spain, 574

Philip V, king of Spain, 688

Philip of Burgundy, 462, 480

Philippines, 682

Philosophes: ideas of, 642-646; political thinking of, 650

Philosophical Dictionary (Voltaire), 644

Philosophy: and the Enlightenment, 639-647; the French philosophes, 642-646; liberalism, 725-726

Physicians: Galen, 710-711; in 18th century, 713-714

Physics: Aristotelian, 629-630; Galileo's experimental method, 632-633; Newton's law, 634-635; development of thermodynamics, 865-866

Pillnitz, Declaration of, 742-743

Pinel, Philippe, 716

Pitt, William, 682

Pius II, pope, 427, 470

Pius VII, pope, 752

Pizzaro, Francisco, 514

Plantations, in New World, 684

Poitiers, battle of, 397-399

Poitiers, Diane de, 520

Poland: serfdom in, 594; conflicts with Russia, 612, 613, 614; partitioning of in 18th century, 653-654

Poltava, battle of, 615, 620

Polygamy, 16th-century reformers' attitude toward, 541

Popes, *see* Papacy

Population: decline in 14th century, 388; effect of Black Death on, 392-393; losses in Germany in Thirty Years' War, 534-535; in 17th-century Amsterdam, 668; 18th-century growth, 671-675; in colonial America, 685

Portugal: dominated by Castile, Aragon, 459; united to Spanish crown, 462; and overseas exploration, 510-511

Poussin, Nicolas, 567

Pragmatic Sanction of Bourges, 456, 600

Praise of Folly, The (Erasmus), 439, 448

Premarital sex, 697-699

Presbyterian Church of Scotland, 487, 495, 705

Priestley, Joseph, 742

Primogeniture, among Spanish colonists, 689

Prince, The (Macchiavelli), 436-437, 452

Principia (Newton), 634, 642

Printing, 437-439, 479

Progress: Enlightenment's concept of, 640, 647

Progress of the Human Mind (Condorcet), 647

Prostitution: in 16th century, 538-539; among poor in 17th, 18th centuries, 696-697

Protectorate, English, 580-581

Protestantism: Luther establishes, 474-476; ideas of, 476-477

Protestant Reformation, 473-496; Luther's early years, 473-474; the Ninety-five Theses, 474-476; Protestant thought, 476-477; social impact of, 477-480; effect on political situation in Germany, 480-484; growth of, 484-496; Calvinism, 485-486; Anabaptists, 487-488; in England, 488-495; in Scotland, Ireland, 495-496; in Scandinavia, 496

Protestant Union, 533

Prussia: serfdom in, 593; rise of absolutism in 17th century, 600-606; and Seven Years' War, 682; compulsory education in, 705; issues Declaration of Pillnitz, 742-743; and First Coalition against France, 743, 745, 746, 749 at war with Napoleon, 756, 758

Public health, 674, 706

Puerto Rico, 513, 689

Pugachev, Emelian, 652-653

Purging, medical, 712-713, 714

Puritans: Calvinism as model for, 487; their desire to purify English church, 494-495; urge new translation of Bible, 549; rise to power in England, 578-579; Cromwell and the Protectorate, 580-581

"Putting-out" system, 675-679, 740

Pyrenees, Treaty of, 575

Quackery, medical, 716

Quadruple Alliance, 758

Quebec, 515, 682

Quiberon Bay, 682

Rabelais, François, 449-450

Racine, Jean, 568

Racism, origins of North American, 541-544

Rákóczy, Francis, 600

Rape: Renaissance attitudes toward, 440; of servant girls in 17th, 18th centuries, 696

Rastrelli, Bartolomeo, 622

Rats, and bubonic plague, 673-674

Razin, Stenka, 614

Reconquista, 459, 460

Recreation, in 14th century, 416-417

Reflections on the Revolution in France (Burke), 742

Reformations: Protestant, 473-496; Catholic and Counter, 496-503

Reign of Terror, in French Revolution, 748-749

Religion: Islam driven from Spain, 460; Great Schism ends Christian unity, 473-496; 16th-century practice of, 482-483; as motive for explorations, 517-518; 16th-century wars over, 519-520; English dissension over, 578-583; Dutch toleration of, 585-586; Vikings in Russia convert to Eastern Orthodox Christianity, 607; influence on baroque arts; 616-617; and science, 637-638, 868; and the Enlightenment, 640-641, 644-645, 646

Renaissance: defined, 422; Italian origins of, 422-426; hallmarks of, 426-429; art and artists during, 429-433; social change during, 433-444; in the North, 444-450; politics and the state in, 451-462; contribution to scientific revolution, 635

Reparations, World War I, 1006-1010

Representative government, 724-725

Restoration, English, 581-582

Revolutionary era: ideas of liberty, equality, 724-727; American Revolution, 727-733; French Revolution, 733-750

Richard II, king of England, 409, 413

Richard III, king of England, 458

Richard II (Shakespeare), 546

Richelieu, Cardinal (Armand Jean du Plessis), 533, 534, 558-560

Robespierre, Maximilien, 742, 743, 744-749

Roman Catholic church: 14th-century decline in prestige, 406-410; Babylonian Captivity, 407-408; Great Schism, 408; conciliar movement, 408-410; linchpin of Spanish monarchy, 460-462; church's condition from 1400 to 1517, 468-473; Luther breaks with, 473-476; England breaks with, 488-495; Catholic and Counter Reformations, 496-503; and Council of Trent, 499-501; establishment of Sacred Congregation of Holy Office, Roman Inquisition, 502-503; becomes "national" religion of France, 522; and

519; into Low Countries, 526–528; United Provinces declare independence from, 528; Armada defeated, 530; in Thirty Years' War, 534; 17th-century decline of absolutism, 572–575; in competition for colonial empire, 681–682, 687–689; declares war on Britain, 730; Republican France declares war on, 745; rebels against Napoleon's attempt to make it French satellite, 756

Spanish Armada, 530

Speyer, Diet of, 476

Spice trade, 510, 518

"Spinsters," 679

Stamp Act, 728–729

Standard of living, in North American colonies, 684–686

Star Chamber, 458, 459

State: Machiavelli's theories on, 436–437; in the Renaissance, 451–452; modern, foreshadowed by Louis XIV, 565; emergence of Western absolutist, constitutional, 556, 586–587; rise of absolutist eastern, 592–623

Statute of Laborers, 393, 411–412

Staupitz, 474

Stuart kings, England, 577–580

Suleiman the Magnificent, 599

Sully, Maximilien, 558

Summer Palace (Vienna), 618

Supremacy Act of 1534, 492

Surgeons, see Physicians

Swaddling of infants, 704

Sweden, 613; and Reformation, 496; and Thirty Years' War, 533–534; and war with Russia, 615; in Third Coalition against France, 755

System of Nature (d'Holbach), 646

Tartars, 602, 653

Taxation: under Richelieu, 559; under Ottomans, 599; under Peter the Great, 615; under Louis XV, 654; by Britain of American colonies, 728–729; in France before revolution, 735

Technological developments, as stimuli to exploration, 516–517

Telescope, 636

Television, 438

Tencin, Marquise de, 648

Tetzel, John, 475

Textile industry, as English cottage industry, 678

Theater, see Drama

Theodore, tsar of Russia, 613

Theology: Luther's, 476–477, 478–479; Calvinism, 485–487; of Henrician Reformation, 494

"Thermidorian reaction," 749–750

Thirty-nine Articles, 495

Thirty Years' War, 533–536

Thomas à Kempis, 471

Thought, see Philosophy

Tilsit, treaties of, 756

Tissot, Samuel, 716

Titian, 432

Tobacco, production in 18th century, 684

Townsend, Charles, 668–669

Trade: Neolithic, 7, 9–10; in Mesopotamia, 13; Phoenician, 42, 51; in ancient Israel, 51; Hellenistic, 121–124; in Roman Empire, 197, 202–203; 11th-century revival of, 297–300; in Italy as factor in Renaissance, 423–425; 17th-

century Dutch, 586; 18th-century international growth in, 680–689; 19th-century international growth in, 912–915; recent uncertainty about international, 1082

Trafalgar, battle of, 754

Transportation: railroads, 772–774, 893, 894; public, 839, 844–845; advances in, 913–915

Transylvania, 599

Treatise on the Laws and Customs of England (Henry of Bracton), 364

Treaty of Amiens, 754

Treaty of Chaumont, 758

Treaty of Lunéville, 754

Treaty of Nijmegen, 570

Treaty of Paris of 1763, 682

Treaty of Paris of 1783, 732

Treaty of the Pyrenees, 575

Treaty of Tilsit, 756

Trent, Council of, 499–501

Tridentine decrees, 501

Trinidad, 513

Troeltsch, Ernst, 476

Tudor dynasty, 458–459

Tuileries, built, 520

Tuke, William, 715–716

Tull, Jethro, 669

Tver, prince of, 610

Twelve Articles, 477

Two New Sciences (Galileo), 632–633

Tyndale, William, 489

Ubertinus of Carrara, 433

Ukraine, 606, 614

United Provinces of the Netherlands, 528, 529, 534. See also Holland; Netherlands

United States: British colonies revolt, 727–733; origins of revolution, 727–730; colonies win independence, 730–732; framing the Constitution, 732–733; revolution's impact on Europe, 733

Universities, contribution to scientific revolution, 635

Urban VI, pope, 407–408

Urban VII, pope, 633

Ursuline order, 501

Utopia (More), 445–448

Utrecht, Peace of, 571–572, 682

Valla, Lorenzo, 428

van den Vondel, Joost, 586

van Eyck, Jan, 450

Vasa, Gustavus, 496

Vasco da Gama, see Gama, Vasco da

Vatican, see Papacy

Vatican Library, 427

Venice: prosperity in 14th century, 423; in Renaissance, 426; as city-state, 452, 454, 455; and Index of Prohibited Books, 503; besieged by Ottomans, 599

Vergerio, Peter Paul, 433–435

Vermuyden, Cornelius, 668

Versailles: Louis XIV builds, 562–565; revolutionists march on, 740–741

Vienna: Turks; siege of, 599; palaces in, 617

Vikings, 510, 607–609

Villon, François, 404
Virginia, British colonies in, 684
Visconti, Gian Galeazzo, 424
Vitalism, 714
Vitry, Jacques de, 411
Voltaire (François Marie Arouet), 651, 652; quoted on Louis XIV, 565; life and work of, 643–645; on liberty, 725

Walpole, Robert, 583–584
Walsingham, 403
Warfare: first total effort under French Republic, 749
War of the Austrian Succession, 654, 682
War of the Spanish Succession, 570–571, 586, 600, 682, 688
War of the Three Henrys, 524
Wars of the Roses, 457, 459
Washington, George, 730
Watt, James, 770–771
Wesley, John, 703
Wesley, Susannah, 703
West Indies, 513, 687
Westphalia, Peace of, 534, 584
Wet nursing, see Nursing of babies
What Is the Third Estate? (Sieyès), 751
"White man's burden," 434
White Mountain, battle of, 533, 597
White Russians, 606
William I (the Conqueror), King of England, 440

William III (Prince William of Orange), king of England, 570, 582, 583
William the Silent (first Prince William of Orange), 525, 527, 528
Winter Palace (Vienna), 610
Witches, 401–402, 537
Wittenberg, University of, 473, 474–475, 538
Wolsey, Thomas, 469, 489–491
Women: in 14th century, 413, 414; in Renaissance, 439–440; Luther's views on, 479–480; accused of witchcraft, 536, 537; in 16th, 17th centuries, 537–541; and French salons, 648–650; and sexual emancipation in 18th century, 699; and 18th-century nursing practices, 700–701; march on Versailles in French Revolution, 740–741
Wool industry: after Hundred Years' War, 403; 14th-century Italian, 423, 424; and influence on Elizabeth I, 528; in 18th-century England, 686–687
Worms, Diet of, 476, 481, 484
Writers, see Literature
Würzburg palace, 618
Wycliff, John, 409

York, House of, 457

Zeeland, 584
Zosima, 611
Zwinger, palace, 618
Zwingli, Ulrich, 479